MANAGEMENT CONSULTING

Management Consulting

*Emergence and Dynamics of a
Knowledge Industry*

Edited by

MATTHIAS KIPPING
and
LARS ENGWALL

OXFORD
UNIVERSITY PRESS

OXFORD
UNIVERSITY PRESS

Great Clarendon Street, Oxford OX2 6DP

Oxford University Press is a department of the University of Oxford.
It furthers the University's objective of excellence in research, scholarship,
and education by publishing worldwide in

Oxford New York

Auckland Bangkok Buenos Aires Cape Town Chennai
Dar es Salaam Delhi Hong Kong Istanbul Karachi Kolkata
Kuala Lumpur Madrid Melbourne Mexico City Mumbai Nairobi
São Paulo Shanghai Singapore Taipei Tokyo Toronto

with an associated company in Berlin

Oxford is a registered trade mark of Oxford University Press
in the UK and in certain other countries

Published in the United States
by Oxford University Press Inc., New York

British Library Cataloguing in Publication Data

Data available

Library of Congress Cataloging in Publication Data

Data available

ISBN 0–19–924285–2

1 3 5 7 9 10 8 6 4 2

Typeset by Newgen Imaging Systems (P) Ltd., Chennai, India
Printed in Great Britain
on acid-free paper by
Biddles Ltd., Guildford and King's Lynn

Preface and Acknowledgements

This book is one of the results of a research project on the Creation of European Management Practice (CEMP), which was carried out between 1998 and 2001 with the financial support of the European Commission under the Targeted Socio-Economic Research programme (TSER Contract SOE1-CT97-1072). The CEMP project has looked at the role of different 'carriers', namely multinationals, business education, management publications, and consultancies, in the diffusion and application of new management models across Europe.

Draft versions of most chapters were first presented at a workshop on Management Consultants and Management Knowledge, held at the University of Reading on 15 and 16 October 1999. We would like to thank all the authors for their efforts to respond to our numerous suggestions. We are also very grateful to those who agreed to contribute additional chapters, sometimes at very short notice.

Matthias Kipping and Lars Engwall
Barcelona and Uppsala
July 2001

Contents

Lists of Figures and Tables   ix

List of Abbreviations   x

Notes on Contributors   xii

1. Introduction: Management Consulting as a Knowledge Industry   1
   Lars Engwall and Matthias Kipping

Part I. Historical Perspectives on the Consulting Industry

2. The Acquisition of Symbolic Capital by Consultants: The French Case   19
   Odile Henry

3. The Changing Relationship between Management Consulting and
   Academia: Evidence from Sweden   36
   Lars Engwall, Staffan Furusten, and Eva Wallerstedt

4. Management Consultancies in the Netherlands in the 1950s and 1960s:
   Between Systemic Context and External Influences   52
   Luchien Karsten and Kees van Veen

5. The Rise and Fall of a Local Version of Management
   Consulting in Finland   70
   Antti Ainamo and Janne Tienari

Part II. Organizational Perspectives on the Consultancy Firm

6. The Internal Creation of Consulting Knowledge: A Question
   of Structuring Experience   91
   Andreas Werr

7. Knowledge Management at the Country Level: A Large
   Consulting Firm in Italy   109
   Cristina Crucini

8. Collaborative Relationships in the Creation and Fashioning of
   Management Ideas: Gurus, Editors, and Managers   129
   Timothy Clark and David Greatbatch

9. Consultancies as Actors in Knowledge Arenas: Evidence
   from Germany   146
   Michael Faust

Part III. **Relationship Perspectives on the Consultancy Project**

10. Managers as Marionettes? Using Fashion Theories to Explain
    the Success of Consultancies   167
    Alfred Kieser

11. Promoting Demand, Gaining Legitimacy, and Broadening Expertise:
    The Evolution of Consultancy–Client Relationships in Australia 184
    Christopher Wright

12. The Burden of Otherness: Limits of Consultancy Interventions
    in Historical Case Studies   203
    Matthias Kipping and Thomas Armbrüster

13. Managers and Consultants as Embedded Actors: Evidence
    from Norway   222
    Hallgeir Gammelsæter

References   238
Name Index   262
Subject Index   265

List of Figures

1.1	Consultancies as part of a management knowledge industry	5
3.1	Research orientation and specialization in consulting	38
6.1	A model of knowledge categories and processes of transformation	95
7.1	Training process at GCI	123
9.1	'Cited experts' in *manager magazin*	159
10.1	The arena of a management fashion	169
10.2	A model for the explanation of the extraordinary growth of the consulting market	173

List of Tables

1.1	Three levels of analysis	3
6.1	Summary and comparison of the handling of knowledge at International and Local	106
7.1	A typology of knowledge management systems	113
11.1	Top ten consultancies operating in Australia, 1985 and 1997	197

List of Abbreviations

AFCOS	Association Française des Conseillers en Organisation Scientifique
AFOPE	Association Française des Organisateurs Permanents d'Entreprise
AIC	Associated Industrial Consultants
BCG	The Boston Consulting Group
BDU	Bundesverband Deutscher Unternehmensberater
BHP	Broken Hill Proprietary
BPR	Business Process Re-engineering
CGOST	Commission Générale de l'Organisation Scientifique du Travail (later became: Cégos)
CICF	Chambre des Ingénieurs Conseils de France
CNAM	Conservatoire National des Arts et Métiers
CNOF	Comité National de l'Organisation Française
COP	Contactgroep Opvoering Productiviteit (Liaison Committee for the Improvement of Productivity)
CRM	Customer Relationship Management
DFG	Deutsche Forschungsgemeinschaft
EPA	European Productivity Agency
ERP	Enterprise Resource Planning
FEACO	Fédération Européenne des Associations de Conseils en Organisation (European Federation of Management Consultancies Associations)
GE	General Electric
GITP	Gemeenschappelijk Instituut voor Toegepaste Psychologie (Joint Institute for Applied Psychology)
HSE	Helsinki School of Economics and Business Administration
ICP	Inter-company prices
IMD	International Institute for Management Development
IVA	Ingenjörsvetenskapsakademien (Royal Swedish Academy of Engineering Sciences)
KMS	Knowledge-Management Systems
M-form	Multi-divisional form of organization
MTM	Methods-Time-Measurement
NICB	National Industrial Conference Board
NIPG	Nederlands Instituut voor Preventieve Geneeskunde (Dutch Institute for Preventive Medicine)
NIPL	Nederlands Instituut voor Personeelsleiding (Dutch Institute of Personnel Management)
NIVE	Nederlands Instituut voor Efficiency (Dutch Institute of Industrial Efficiency)

NSP	Nederlandse Stichting voor Psychotechniek (Dutch Foundation for Psychotechnics)
NTL	National Training Laboratory
OOA	Orde van Organisatie-Adviseurs (National Organization of Consultants)
OVA	Overhead Value Analysis
PWC	PriceWaterhouseCoopers
RKW	Rationalisierungskuratorium der Deutschen Wirtschaft (originally: Reichskommissariat für Wirtschaftlichkeit)
SER	Sociaal-Economische Raad (Social and Economic Council)
SG	Schmalenbach-Gesellschaft
SIAR	Swedish Institute (later: Scandinavian Institutes) of Administrative Research
SIOO	Stichting Interacademiale Opleiding Organisatiekunde (Inter-university Centre for Development in Organisation and Change Management)
SSE	Stockholm School of Economics
TNO	Nederlandse Organisatie voor toegepast-natuurwetenschappelijk onderzoek (Dutch Organisation for Applied Scientific Research)
TQM	Total Quality Management
TWI	Training within Industry
USW	Universitätsseminar der Wirtschaft
VDI	Verein Deutscher Ingenieure

Notes on Contributors

Antti Ainamo is Professor at the University of Tampere and Docent at the Helsinki School of Economics and Business Administration. He has also been a visiting researcher at London Business School and Stanford University. His publications include articles in *Organization Science, Business Strategy Review, Supply Chain Management, The Design Journal*, and *Journal of Eastern European Management Studies*, as well as chapters in edited books on international business, product design, and management consulting.

Thomas Armbrüster is a Lecturer in Organizational Theory and Behaviour at the University of Mannheim, Germany. He holds a PhD in sociology from the London School of Economics and previously worked as a Research Officer and Lecturer in Organisational Behaviour at the University of Reading, UK. He is currently working on a book on management consulting and on a critical-liberal approach to organization theory.

Timothy Clark is Reader in Management at the Management Centre, King's College, University of London. He conducted a series of studies on different aspects of the management consultancy industry utilizing the dramaturgical metaphor, published in *Managing Consultants* (Buckingham: Open University Press, 1995). The main focus of his current research is on the nature of speaker–audience interaction in live presentations by management gurus and an examination of the nature and effectiveness of corporate theatre.

Cristina Crucini is completing her PhD in the School of Business at the University of Reading. Her thesis examines the evolution and structure of the consulting market in Italy. She has published several journal articles and contributions to edited volumes based on her research. Before coming to Reading she graduated with a Masters in Economics and Business History from the Istituto per la Cultura e la Storia d'Impresa Franco Momigliano (ICSIM) in Terni, Italy. She is now working with a large international consulting firm in Milan.

Lars Engwall has been Professor of Management at Uppsala University since 1981. He has published a number of books and some hundred articles in the field of management studies. He co-ordinated the EU-sponsored research programme on the Creation of European Management Practice (CEMP). He is a member of several learned societies and is a former Vice-President of the Royal Swedish Academy of Sciences.

Michael Faust is a Senior Researcher at the Sociological Research Institute (SOFI) in Göttingen. He obtained a masters degree in economics and a PhD in sociology from Tübingen University. His research covers the fields of industrial and organizational sociology. He has published on the decentralization of the corporation, the changing roles and work of middle managers, and on the development of the consulting business in Germany.

Staffan Furusten received his doctorate from the Department of Business Studies at Uppsala University and is now Assistant Professor at the Stockholm School of Economics and SCORE (Stockholm Center for Organizational Research). His main research area is the production and diffusion of organizational knowledge. He has published books, book chapters, and journal articles in both Swedish and English, among them, *Popular Management Books: How They are Made and What they Mean for Organizations* (London: Routledge, 1999).

Hallgeir Gammelsæter is Associate Professor at Molde College and Senior Research Fellow at Møre Research Centre in Norway. His main research areas are organizational change, knowledge diffusion, and regional development. He obtained his PhD degree from the University of Bergen, based on a dissertation that examined organizational change across several generations of managers in different firms. His publications include articles on divisionalization, knowledge diffusion, and regional innovation.

David Greatbatch is Visiting Senior Research Fellow at the Management Centre, King's College, University of London. The main focus of his research is on interpersonal communication in organizational settings. His current research projects include studies of management training and development, public speaking, mediation and conflict management, and vocational training. He has written more than forty journal articles and book chapters and is the author of a forthcoming book on mediation entitled *Agreeing to Disagree: The Dynamics of Third Party Intervention in Family Disputes* (Cambridge University Press, 2002).

Odile Henry is a Lecturer at the University of Paris IX (Dauphine) and a research fellow at the Centre de Sociologie Européenne (CSE). She obtained her doctorate from the École des Hautes Études en Sciences Sociales (EHESS) in Paris with a thesis in sociology on the consultancy profession in France. She has published many articles and contributions to edited volumes based on her work and a revised version of her dissertation is forthcoming.

Luchien Karsten is Associate Professor at the University of Groningen, where he teaches the history of management thought as well as organizational development. He obtained degrees in economics and philosophy at the University of Groningen and studied history at the École des Hautes Études en Sciences Sociales in Paris. His PhD was concerned with the history of the eight-hour working day. He recently published, with Kees van Veen, *Management Concepts on the Move* (in Dutch), based on interviews with Dutch CEOs.

Alfred Kieser is Professor of Management and Organizational Behaviour at the University of Mannheim. He has published in such journals as *Administrative Science Quarterly, Organization Science, Organizations Studies,* and *Organization* on the historical development of organizations and on organization theory. He holds an honorary doctoral degree from the University of Munich and is a member of the Heidelberg Academy of Sciences.

Matthias Kipping is currently Associate Professor at the Universitat Pompeu Fabra in Barcelona. He is also associated with the University of Reading in the UK, where he was a Reader in European Management and Director of the Centre for International Business History (CIBH) until 2001. He has written and published extensively on the evolution of different carriers of management knowledge, namely business education and management consultancy. A monograph on the consultancy business is forthcoming with Oxford University Press.

Janne Tienari is acting Professor of Management and Organizations in the Department of Business Administration at Lappeenranta University of Technology, Finland. He publishes in the areas of organizational change, gender and organizing, media discourse, and management, as well as the dissemination and translation of management ideas. His current work is on the social construction of organizational change in financial services and management consulting.

Kees van Veen is Assistant Professor of Organization Sciences at the University of Groningen where he obtained his PhD in sociology. His thesis dealt with flexibility issues within internal labour markets. He recently published, with Luchien Karsten, *Management Concepts on the Move* (in Dutch), and, with Diana Watts, *Management Concepts within Companies: Experiences of Dutch Companies with Process Organization, Teams and ICT*.

Eva Wallerstedt holds a PhD from Uppsala University, Sweden, where she is also Lecturer in the Department of Business Studies. Her research has dealt with the emergence of business education in Sweden and with banking in a historical perspective. She is presently focusing on the professionalization of accountants in Sweden.

Andreas Werr is Assistant Professor at the Stockholm School of Economics and the Fenix Program. He obtained his PhD at the Stockholm School of Economics with a thesis on 'The Language of Change: The Roles of Methods in the Work of Management Consultants'. He has also published a number of articles on this specific topic as well as on management consulting and the basis for its popularity more generally.

Christopher Wright is a Senior Lecturer in the School of Industrial Relations and Organizational Behaviour at the University of New South Wales. His research publications include *The Management of Labour: A History of Australian Employers* (Oxford University Press, 1995) as well as articles on industrial relations strategy, work organization, performance-related pay, and the diffusion of management practice. His current research explores the influence of management consultants on Australian organizations.

1

Introduction: Management Consulting as a Knowledge Industry

LARS ENGWALL AND MATTHIAS KIPPING

1.1. BACKGROUND

Over recent years interest in management consultancy has grown rapidly. Most of the relevant literature has focused on the expansion or, as some say, explosion of the consulting industry during the last decade of the twentieth century, and has tried to identify the reasons behind this development. Authors contributing to this literature come from a variety of backgrounds. They include academics and journalists as well as practitioners and their associations. Their contributions cover a wide range of issues. Some make attempts to quantify the consulting markets, the major service providers, and their growth rates. Others examine consultancy interventions in particular organizations, or try to provide a general overview of how consultants work—or recipes for how they should work (see details in Kipping and Armbrüster (1998), who structure the literature according to the cognitive interests of the authors).

Overall, this literature on the consultancy industry has taken a very critical tone. Thus, some authors have investigated the rhetorical techniques used by management consultants and gurus to leave a good impression on their clients, based on the idea that their performance can only be evaluated in a theatrical sense (Clark 1995; Clark and Salaman 1996). Others have stressed the legitimizing role of consultants in internal conflicts and with respect to external stakeholders (Jackall 1988; Faust 2000; Kipping 2000; cf. also Kieser 1998*a*). A number of popular books have gone even further, highlighting the potential dangers of hiring consultants and identifying the tricks they use to gain and retain clients (O'Shea and Madigan 1997; Ashford 1998; cf. also Argyris 2000). Some have actually characterized the relationship of at least some clients to consultants as a kind of addiction (e.g. Ashford 1998; Ernst and Kieser 2002). This rather negative evaluation of consultants stands in clear contrast to the earlier, much more positive literature (for an overview, cf. Fincham and Clark 2002), which compared consultants to medical doctors (Higdon 1969) or made efforts to understand and categorize their roles in organizational development (e.g. Schein 1988).

It also provides a contrast with studies that have identified consultants as important 'carriers' in the diffusion of scientific knowledge and innovations (e.g. Rogers 1962; Havelock *et al.* 1969; Bessant and Rush 1995). The literature on the diffusion of management knowledge has also highlighted the contribution of individual consultants and consulting firms to the international dissemination of management ideas or 'fashions' during much of the twentieth century (e.g. Barley and Kunda 1992; Huczynski 1993a; Kogut and Parkinson 1993; Fridenson 1994; Guillén 1994). And most recently, in the burgeoning literature on the knowledge economy and society, consultants are given a prominent place and sometimes even seen as a prototype of the new 'knowledge workers' (Starbuck 1992; Drucker 1993; Sarvary 1999).

With a few exceptions (e.g. Hagedorn 1955), there has been little empirical work on the emergence and role of consultants as 'carriers' of management knowledge. A few recent articles have examined the ways in which consulting firms organize their own, internal knowledge systems (e.g. Werr, Stjernberg, and Docherty 1997; Hansen, Nohria, and Tierney 1999). But they remain fairly general and normative, aiming to provide guidance to practitioners. There is also a growing historical literature on the evolution of the consultancy industry during the twentieth century. So far, it has examined mainly the institutional and economic context in which this industry evolved (e.g. McKenna 1995; Kipping 1997, 1999b, 2002). In addition, much of this literature has focused on developments in the United States (McKenna 2000), the expansion of American consultancies abroad (Kipping 1996, 1999a), and developments in other Anglo-Saxon countries, especially the UK (Tisdall 1982; Ferguson 1999) and Australia (Wright 2000). This seems related to the fact that consulting activities have developed and expanded comparatively early in these countries. There are some studies on the developments in other countries, but these are usually not available in English (e.g. Henry 1993; Hellema and Marsman 1997). Thus, much remains to be studied relating to the conditions in which consulting emerged and developed to become such an important component of today's 'management knowledge industry' (Micklethwaite and Wooldridge 1996; cf. also Abrahamson 1996).

Against this background the present volume aims to make a contribution to the examination of the emergence and dynamics of consulting as a knowledge industry. For this purpose the remainder of the introduction will first provide a framework for the analysis of this issue and will then situate the different chapters of the book within this context.

1.2. A FRAMEWORK FOR ANALYSIS

Three Levels of Analysis

In order to acquire a better understanding of the management advice industry it is important to make clear that the literature on consulting deals with a number of issues at different levels of description. At the highest level of description the focus is directed towards the organization of the consulting industry, i.e. the entries and exits of actors, the competition between them, the degree of concentration, and so on. The conditions at this level of description are, of course, crucial to the behaviour of different actors, which can be studied at an intermediate level of description, that of the consulting firm. This level provides the structural conditions for individual or groups of consultants in their work in interaction with clients in the consultancy project, which constitutes the work level of description. The position taken here is that it is significant to systematically combine studies at all three levels of description in order to understand the management advice industry, i.e. (1) the industry, (2) the firm, and (3) the project. On each of these three levels it is relevant to focus on:

(*a*) the system;
(*b*) the basic units of the system;
(*c*) the structure of the system;
(*d*) the interaction between basic units; and
(*e*) the role of knowledge (see Table 1.1).

At the first level discussion is related to the traditional analyses of an industry (e.g. Scherer 1970; Porter 1980), which in recent years in organization studies have been labelled 'populations' (see e.g. Hannan and Carroll 1992) or 'fields' (e.g. Powell and DiMaggio 1991). The basic units are the consultancy firms. Entries and exits by these firms are significant for the structure of the industry, which can be described by different measures of concentration. The interaction is characterized by competition, and the role of knowledge is primarily to provide the basic units a specific 'product' within the industry. In order to illuminate these aspects of consulting we need historical studies in various contexts.

In studies at the second level the system is the firm and its basic units are the employees. In the same way as at the first level entries and exits (recruitment and resignations) play significant roles for the structure of the system, at this level the 'system' means the formal and informal organization of the firm. In consultancies this is often characterized by both cooperation and competition. Employees are cooperating in various projects but they are also competing for status and other rewards in the organization. The role of knowledge at this level is the processing of knowledge, something that includes the extraction, codification, storage, and internal exchange of knowledge. In order to address these issues we need organization studies of consultancies in action.

At the third level research aims at analysing the actual interaction between consultancies and clients, i.e. how consultancies manage to transfer management knowledge to client organizations. Here the system is constituted by individual projects and the basic units are project relationships between consultants and clients. The structure of these relationships can be described as networks, in which the interaction is built on

Table 1.1. *Three levels of analysis*

Level	First	Second	Third
System	Industry	Firm	Project
Basic units	Firms	Employees	Project relationships
Structure	Concentration	Organization	Networks
Interaction	Competition	Cooperation/ competition	Trust
Role of knowledge	Product	Processing	Transfer/transformation

trust. At this level the role of knowledge is to be transferred and transformed into actual organizations. This level is of course the most crucial in terms of the impact of consultancies on management practice. Studies at this level require in-depth studies of consultancy–client relationships.

The Consultancy Industry

The definition of industries is closely linked to the products firms in a particular system offer. In defining the consultancy industry we consider, for the purpose of this volume, management knowledge to be the main 'product' sold or disseminated by management consultancies. This does not mean that consultants do not or cannot have a legitimizing function for the clients, as highlighted in some of the recent literature. But even the legitimacy they might provide with respect to internal or external constituents of the client organization will usually come in the guise of 'knowledge'. In other words, the consultants will only be able to justify certain decisions or support a particular course of action based on the—alleged—superiority of their knowledge. The very nature of this product therefore determines the activities of the consulting industry to a considerable extent (cf. Mitchell 1994; Sauviat 1994; Clark 1995). However, since consulting will only take shape during the interaction of the consultants with the client organization (the third level above), the quality of the consulting service cannot be tested and assessed beforehand.

At the same time, the effect of consultancy work is also impossible to evaluate. First of all, the consultancy intervention is only one—and probably not even the most important—factor determining the performance of companies, making it difficult if not impossible to isolate its impact. Secondly, and more importantly, the intervention itself destroys any base case for comparison, making it impossible to see how the company would have done if it had not called in consultants. Evaluation therefore remains largely subjective, based on the impressions of those involved. Among the latter it is quite obvious that those hiring the consultancy have a clear interest in calling the intervention a success, because otherwise they would be seen to have wasted considerable resources.

Other service industries facing similar problems as the consulting industry have dealt with them by creating and maintaining certain entry barriers, for example in the form of qualifying exams, or through the establishment of widely recognized rules of acceptable behaviour (for examples, see Burrage and Torstendahl 1990; Torstendahl and Burrage 1990). The various associations of consulting firms have made similar attempts—however without much success (e.g. Kyrö 1995). This is mainly due to the fact that the content of consultancy activities, i.e. 'management' in the widest sense, is not easily codifiable, and not even clearly defined. As the above-mentioned research on management ideas and fashions has shown, what is understood to be 'good' or 'modern' management changes over time and also from one country to the next. At least until recently, management as a concept and an activity was not even recognized in certain countries. This is reflected, for example, in the content of advanced management study courses granting access to leading positions in companies (cf. e.g. Engwall and

Zamagni 1998) and in the job titles and definitions of those occupying such positions (cf. Bournois and Livian 1997). All of this makes it difficult for consultancies to establish and maintain their role as 'carriers' of management knowledge (cf. Kipping 2002)—and in certain countries more so than in others.

Members of the consultancy industry have therefore relied heavily on their reputation and on personal relationships to convince clients of the quality of their services (cf. Kipping 1999a). While recommendations from existing clients help to transfer this reputation and to establish new relationships, the process leading to the recognition of the consulting industry as a whole (and individual consulting firms) as 'legitimate' knowledge providers or carriers needs further clarification. In addition to these more general issues, it is also important to highlight that consulting does not operate within a void. As mentioned above, it forms part of the knowledge management industry, i.e. it competes, but also cooperates with academic institutions and media companies in the creation of management practice (see Figure 1.1).

Among these symbiotic relationships, that with academic institutions appears to play a particularly crucial role. Such institutions, primarily business schools, are thus significant providers of future managers in companies as well as of consultants. However, they also play an important role in the development of management knowledge. They developed earlier than the management consulting industry and were actually, as will be demonstrated by the chapters in the first part of the volume, instrumental in the creation of consultancies. In recent years it has been possible to observe an increasing level of cooperation between prestigious business schools and large consultancies in terms of both research and education. Needless to say there is also a competition between the two types of organizations (cf. Kipping and Amorim 1999/2000).

In the same way the relationships between consultancies and media companies have become closer. Formerly it was common for consultants to be very cautious in disseminating information about their methods and basic ideas. However, after the publication of the best-seller *In Search of Excellence* (Peters and Waterman 1982) by two McKinsey consultants it has become more and more common for consultancies to support their business by the publication of monographs dealing with their basic ideas and achievements in consulting. Some of the large international consultancies, such as McKinsey, even publish journals of their own.

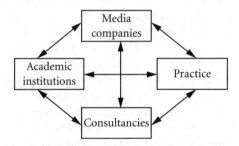

Figure 1.1. *Consultancies as part of a management knowledge industry*

Of all the interactions illustrated in Figure 1.1 that with practice is of greatest importance. Academic institutions have traditionally received feedback through the success of their graduates in the labour market and through unsystematic contacts with employers. However, in recent years it has also become common that companies have an influence on the contents of education through what are called corporate universities (see Crainer and Dearlove 1999). Similarly consultancies and media companies are subject to pressures for adaptation from practice.

It is obvious that the roles of the different actors and the relationships between them vary between different countries. In some countries, such as the Nordic countries, management education has a long history and a large number of management graduates are active in practice, consultancies, and media companies. In other countries, such as France and Germany, other types of elite education play the corresponding role in linking together actors in the different fields of management. It should also be noted that the socio-economic context is crucial for the development of the consulting industry. Highly industrialized countries with large multi-product corporations, particularly with a high degree of internationalization, are thus more likely to exhibit an expansion of consulting than countries with a low degree of industrialization and/or with primarily small companies. Since the United States was an early member of the first group, it has played a significant role in the development of the international consulting industry.

The aim of the first part of this volume is to examine the development of the consulting industry in different contexts. In so doing the chapters in the first part will present historical evidence about the emergence of a consultant industry in four different countries.

The Consultancy Firm

Consultancies obviously belong to a group of firms that in the modern management literature is described as knowledge-based companies (e.g. Halal 1998). They have relatively little financial capital but have instead as their main assets the knowledge and competence of their personnel. For this purpose the selection of competent individuals, often by the employment of novel test procedures (cf. Armbrüster and Schmolze 1999), constitutes an important task in consultancies. Frequent targets of such recruitment are, as mentioned in the previous section, MBA graduates, a large number of whom move on to executive positions in client firms. This circumstance has led some observers (e.g. Mintzberg 1990: 66; Crainer and Dearlove 1999: 163) to see consulting firms as 'the graduate graduate school of business'. This means that large consultancies need a permanent inflow of young personnel in order to match the outflow. In addition it implies that consultancies need to standardize their work in order to train inexperienced people in consultancy work. This also makes it important to save the scarce resources provided by senior consultants for strategic actions in the early and late phases of a consultancy project (Eriksson and Lindvall 1999).

The issues of recruitment and division of labour between junior and senior consultants constitute just one of the organizational problems inside consultancies. Another important issue is constituted by the creation of management structures, i.e. how the knowledge-based consultancy firm should be managed. Consultancies share this problem with other professional organizations—like hospitals, law firms, and research organizations—in terms of selection to and the interplay between professional structures and management structures (cf. Brock, Powell, and Hinings 1999). These lead to features of both cooperation and competition (cf. again Table 1.1). Individual consultants thus need to work together in teams in order to be able to offer sufficient competence and resources to clients. At the same time, these consultants are also professionals in competition for client projects in order to fill their quota of demand for their working time. Obviously this is not just a competition for client orders but also a competition for projects of high prestige.

A further significant problem in consultancies is constituted by the extent to which the organization facilitates the sharing of information. The ability to do this effectively is obviously an important source of competitive advantage. Some aspects of this problem have been explored in the literature, but many of the related questions remain unexplored: for example, regarding the incentives for consultants to share their knowledge with colleagues or knowledge management in smaller, nationally based consultancies. A related and equally important issue concerns the national origin of the past practices, codified and transferred through internal knowledge management systems. In many of the large consultancies, these are likely to come from countries other than the ones in which they are applied (in many instances they probably originate in the United States). The question here is to what extent, if at all, they are adapted to the different national contexts in which these consultancies operate and, if this is indeed the case, how this is done.

Based on knowledge generated in their interaction with other knowledge carriers and/or past practice, consultants will then shape future practice by applying it to their new (or the same) client companies. In terms of Table 1.1 and Figure 1.1 we thus argue that consultancy firms constitute systems for the processing of information on (apparently) successful management practices through their contacts with academic institutions, media companies, and practice. Among these contacts it is particularly important to pay attention to actors such as book editors and journalists who play roles as transmitters of the zeitgeist and as gatekeepers. These latter relationships appear to become deeper over time, since the relationship is mutually dependent and beneficial.

The aim of the second part of this volume is to examine how consultancy firms handle the strategic tasks outlined above. In so doing the chapters in the second part will present four analyses of knowledge information generation, processing, and validation by consultancies.

The Consultancy Project

Our discussion of the consultancy industry has pointed to the fact that it has had to find its place among other players, by primarily competing, and sometimes also cooperating, with them. At the same time, consultants could use their relationships within the knowledge industry to generate new ideas, or market themselves—activities that have yet to be explored in detail in the relevant literature. What distinguishes consulting from the other players is its close interaction with management practice. It could therefore be argued that consultancies actually derive most, if not all, of their knowledge from client firms. Interviews with the CEOs of the ten largest Swedish quoted companies also point in that direction (Engwall and Eriksson 1999). In response to the statement 'Consultants diffuse the ideas of their clients', seven out of ten agreed, while none disagreed.

A number of authors have proposed different models for the consultancy process. But while there have been an increasing number of case studies of consultancy interventions, both in the private and public sectors (e.g. Bloomfield and Danieli 1995; Dyerson and Mueller 1999; Arnoldus 2000; Cailluet 2000; Hilger 2000; Kipping 2000; Saint-Martin 2000), the interaction process between consultants and their clients is still poorly understood. Some of the relevant issues concern:

1. the reasons why managers keep buying consultancy services, even if there seems to be no apparent 'need';
2. the internal and external forces shaping the hiring of consultants and the outcome of their intervention;
3. the barriers, which might lead the client organization to reject the consultancy advice; and
4. the possible strategies used by consultants to overcome such resistance.

Analyses of questions such as these seem to indicate that consultancy firms face quite an uphill struggle when it comes to putting their knowledge into practice. They certainly try to exploit the uncertainty of managers and their need to justify themselves with respect to their peers, and succeed to some extent. At the same time, they have to convince managers and all other stakeholders in companies of the value they might add. The significant concept in this context, which was introduced in Table 1.1, is trust. It is thus of prime importance that the consultants as outsiders are accepted by the relevant insiders. Often, however, they have to overcome considerable reluctance, resistance, and cynicism, particularly from lower levels of management and/ or workers.

For the understanding of questions such as these it appears that there is much to learn from the literature in industrial marketing, service marketing, and technical development (e.g. Håkansson 1987, 1989; von Hippel 1988; Grönroos 1990). It tells us that successive adaptations in the interaction between buyers and sellers constitute a significant force in the innovation and diffusion process. The chapters in the third part of the volume will further demonstrate this.

1.3. THE VOLUME CHAPTERS

Most of the chapters in this volume deal to a certain extent with all of the above issues deriving from the specific characteristics of the consulting industry and its interaction with other parts of the knowledge industry. However, they all have a focus on one of the three levels of analysis.

The chapters in the first part of the volume deal mainly with consulting as an industry. They show that its establishment as a recognized and legitimate knowledge carrier was not simple and straightforward, but a long and often conflictual process, because consultants had to create a space for themselves among other institutions and organizations also involved in the transfer of management knowledge. The chapters in this part suggest that the relationship between consulting and academia is especially interesting, because the two fields have interacted very intensely, sometimes competing with each other, sometimes mutually reinforcing their respective activities. In general, the emergence of the consultancy industry in the different countries seems to have been shaped by the context in which it took place, namely in terms of the national systems of education and selection of company executives. To a greater or lesser extent, it was also influenced by government policy and the geo-political environment and, in all cases, by the expansion of service providers from the United States, which have, sooner or later, become dominant actors or at least 'role models' in all of the countries examined.

For the French case Odile Henry shows how consultants gradually acquired the symbolic capital that made it possible for them to achieve recognition as legitimate advisors. She traces the different steps of the emergence of the consulting profession in France since the nineteenth century, depicting it as a process of emancipation. Thus, during the second industrial revolution, the graduates of the leading engineering schools or Grandes Écoles, destined originally for state service, became increasingly involved in private industry, with many of them acting as 'consulting engineers'. But since the leading actors in the engineering profession advocated an internal role in companies as arbiters based on their 'scientific' credentials, those acting as external advisors remained stigmatized as purely 'commercial'. The growing number of independent consulting engineers were therefore drawn mainly from graduates of the minor engineering schools or those who, for one reason or another, entered but failed to graduate from the Grandes Écoles.

The trend was only reversed after the Second World War following a shift from work organization to issues regarding strategy and, later, information technology. As a result, consulting managed to acquire a symbolic capital independent of the engineering profession—a capital which, in contrast to the earlier period, was vested in the consultancy firms rather than in the individual consultants. While some of the pioneering firms were of French origin, the arrival of the Anglo-American consultancies and accountancy firms certainly reinforced this development. The engineers continued to work as internal organizers, but lost most of their symbolic capital and, from the 1970s onwards, began to call themselves 'internal consultants' in deference to the now dominant group.

In Chapter 3 Lars Engwall, Staffan Furusten, and Eva Wallerstedt develop one of the issues touched upon by Henry, namely the increasing separation between academia and consulting, based on evidence from Sweden. They examine the experience of two leading Swedish management professors, Oskar Sillén and Eric Rhenman, in combining academic work and consulting activities. Their chapter applies a framework which distinguishes two 'ideal types' of consultants: the academic specialist, with high research orientation and high specialization; and the practical generalist with low research orientation and low specialization. Sillén was a practical generalist, an accountant who became an academic specialist. In 1912 he became the first Swedish professor of business administration at the Stockholm School of Economics—a position he held until 1951. Based on his academic reputation, he also advised many Swedish public and private organizations.

By contrast, Rhenman began as an academic specialist but later became more of a practical generalist. Teaching at Lund University from 1965 onwards, he also established a consultancy called SIAR, which initially tried to combine academic and research work with consulting activities, but subsequently moved away from its origins, becoming a 'normal', commercially oriented consulting organization (after a series of mergers, it became part of Cap Gemini Ernst & Young in 2000). The chapter highlights two major reasons for this development. The academic work carried out within SIAR, for example in the form of doctoral dissertations, had the effect of transforming their unique competence into common knowledge. More importantly, Rhenman and SIAR were operating in a completely different environment from that of Sillén. The Swedish consultancy market had developed considerably during the 1960s and 1970s, following the entry of US firms such as McKinsey. This competitive situation exerted strong pressure on Rhenman and his associates to behave in the same way as others did in what had become an 'industry'.

How consulting became such an institutionalized field of management knowledge is the subject of the chapter by Luchien Karsten and Kees van Veen. They suggest that in the Netherlands, this development took place mainly in the first decades after the Second World War, although there had been consultancy activities and consulting firms operating from the beginning of the century. They suggest that one of the main drivers was the Marshall Plan of 1947 and, more specifically, the programme of technical assistance which the United States launched during the 1950s (cf. McGlade 1995; Kipping and Bjarnar 1998). This was taken up enthusiastically by the different actors in the Dutch knowledge community, especially the existing consultancies and the universities, who saw it as an opportunity to expand their activities. The government played an important role in coordinating these efforts through the establishment of a Liaison Committee, which actually survived after the end of the US-sponsored programmes.

But while many of the initial impulses might have come from the United States, the chapter shows that the Dutch 'systemic context' clearly shaped the structure and the activities of the emerging consultancy industry, particularly in terms of the need to maintain a balance between the different (confessional) groups in Dutch society, known as 'pillarization', and the influence of Christian values in transforming American management ideas. At the same time, the process was also marked by the competition between engineers and social scientists which had marked consulting activities in the Netherlands almost from the outset. While highlighting US influence, this chapter also suggests that it should not be overestimated. Thus, Dutch consultancies also had close connections with Britain, especially in the field of human relations (e.g. the Tavistock Institute), and to a certain extent initiated a reverse flow of ideas by opening offices in the USA. The direct American influence increased only from the mid-1960s onwards, with the arrival of consultancies such as McKinsey, which expanded rapidly, largely to the detriment of the engineering-based consulting firms. By contrast, many of the social science research centres established in the post-war period, which also offered consulting services, retained their specific role for much longer.

In the Finnish case, a local version of consulting seems to have survived even longer than in the Netherlands. As Chapter 5 by Antti Ainamo and Janne Tienari shows, American service providers only established a strong and increasingly dominant position in Finland during the 1990s. While this might have been partially driven by the peripheral location and economic 'backwardness' of the country, the authors highlight the role of the historical and geo-political context, which favoured the development of a local version of management consulting in the post-war period. In their view, it was the shared experience of the war against Nazi Germany and the Soviet Union which prompted a 'few great men' to develop a specifically Finnish rhetoric of management based on heroic leadership. This also enabled them to reject any outside influences and ideas, namely the 'Swedish model' which appeared closer and more appropriate than the American one. However, since Sweden had remained neutral during the war, it was easy to brand its experience as irrelevant to the Finnish context. In the post-war period, these 'great men' developed a close-knit and somewhat hermetic social network, which included those working as managers and others active as consultants.

The local version of consulting crystallized in 1950 with the formation of Rastor, which was not a commercially oriented firm but rather an association, since it was owned by a multitude of Finnish companies. Under the leadership of Leo Suurla, it became the major Finnish consultancy and aimed at promoting consulting as an activity, attempted to find solutions adapted to Finland's needs, and also tried to control the flow of ideas from abroad, sometimes in competition with universities. In this respect, Rastor's activities included the direction of a US-sponsored management development programme in the 1950s and a joint venture with the US consultancy H.B. Maynard, known for its Methods–Time–Measurement system, in 1968. Despite all these efforts, Rastor and the Finnish version of management consulting gradually lost their predominance, mainly following the changes in Finland's geo-political and economic context, including the demise of the Soviet Union, deregulation, and EU membership.

While the chapters in the first part of the volume trace the development and legitimization of consultancies as knowledge carriers in different national contexts, the contributions in the second part examine how the consulting firms generate, store, and transfer their knowledge internally, and to what extent external actors are involved in the generation and validation of consulting knowledge. In general, these contributions show that consultancies have developed a range of tools and techniques to manage their knowledge-base. But they also point once again to the importance of the context in which they operate.

Based on what could be called a 'laboratory study', simulating the writing of a new proposal, Andreas Werr compares the systems of knowledge management in a large international and a small internal consultancy, both operating in Sweden. His detailed analysis highlights similarities and differences in their respective approaches. Thus, both consultancies rely on previous experiences, which are codified and transferred internally in the form of (standardized) methods and tools, as well as summaries of old cases. Regarding the differences, his study reveals a scale effect in knowledge management (cf. also Kipping and Scheybani 1994). The international consultancy clearly benefited from its size in Sweden and its network of offices around the world, which enabled it to draw on a large number of previous projects and to benefit from a hierarchical division of labour in the organization of knowledge management activities. More importantly, he also highlights the fact that the crucial process for both consultancies, regardless of their size, is not the storage and exchange of previous experience into methods and cases, but its application ('translation') to new, specific situations.

  In the following, closely related chapter, Cristina Crucini reports on her experience of working for several months in a large international consultancy in Italy, based on an approach which could be characterized as 'self-ethnography'. She not only examines the consultancy's knowledge management in the narrow sense, but also its human resources practices more generally, namely the selection of new consultants. Her work shows that recruitment is an integral and very important part of knowledge management, since it provides the consultancy with the 'raw material' on which all the subsequent efforts have to be based. While the selection process obviously tries to identify those with the 'right profile' in terms of their knowledge-base and the consultancy's organizational culture (cf. also Armbrüster and Schmolze 1999), the choice is to a certain extent constrained by the education system in the given country, in this case Italy. However, she also shows that this international consultancy not only reacts passively to the national context in which it operates, but also proactively adapts the 'templates', which are disseminated within the international consultancy organization, to the specific Italian situation.

  While both chapters draw on the previous literature on knowledge management in general and in consultancy firms in particular, they also transcend these. For example, regarding the distinction between personalization and codification strategies proposed by Hansen, Nohria, and Tierney (1999), both Werr and Crucini suggest that these strategies complement each other rather than being alternatives. Thus, even the small, internal consultancy in Sweden went beyond face-to-face exchanges of knowledge and relied on explicit methods to capture and transfer some of their experiences. At the same time, personal contacts continued to play an important role in the internal transfer of knowledge in both the Italian and Swedish offices of the large international consultancies despite their sophisticated IT-based systems. In addition, both already hinted at the role of external influences on knowledge management in consulting—an aspect which has so far received little attention in the existing literature. Werr's study highlights the importance of existing management practice, captured by the consultants mainly in the form of 'old cases'. Crucini's experience suggests an even more direct influence, through the local recruitment of new consultants and the adaptation of international templates to the national context. The two subsequent chapters in this part of the volume examine the role of external actors in the generation and validation of consulting knowledge even more explicitly.

Thus, Timothy Clark and David Greatbatch go beyond the stereotype of 'lonely creative geniuses' in their study of how certain individuals create fashionable management ideas. Based on interviews with five contemporary management gurus, they stress that collaborative relationships make an important contribution to the creation and popularization of these ideas. Book editors play a particularly important role in 'discovering' these gurus, usually at one of their public performances, in encouraging them to summarize their ideas in a book, and helping them to shape the book in terms of content and form. Their contribution to the discovery and promotion of new talents therefore closely resembles the practice in the world of the arts, especially in popular music. But editors are not the only external influences on successful management gurus, even if their contribution appears to be the most direct and explicit. Gurus also rely quite extensively on managers for the development of their ideas. Quite often they generated their ideas when working as consultants or researchers with companies or individual managers—an experience they will subsequently refer to in their publications or live performances. Managers attending these performances will also provide feedback, helping the gurus to modify or refine their ideas.

Since Clark and Greatbatch look at individuals rather than organizations, their findings are not automatically transferable to consulting activities. As other authors (e.g. Micklethwaite and Wooldridge 1996) have shown, however, many consultancy firms also use publications and presentations to popularize their approaches. Further research on knowledge management in consulting will therefore have to go beyond the consultancy organization itself and try to identify the collaborative relationships involved in the fashioning and dissemination of consultancy ideas.

With respect to publications, the research carried out by Michael Faust in Germany, summarized in the Chapter 9, constitutes a first step in this direction. His study shows that consultants are using a variety of media and arenas to establish their reputation as experts and trendsetters and to validate their knowledge. This includes, for example, articles in the business press and presentations to various associations of German senior and middle managers. An analysis of articles published between 1980 and 1996 in *manager magazin*, one of Germany's leading monthlies for business practitioners, confirms that consultants play an important role as 'cited experts', second in most years only to actual managers (whose share has been decreasing in the long run) and usually ahead of academics.

From a contemporary perspective these findings, confirmed by face-to-face interviews with managers and consultants, therefore lend considerable support to the historical processes examined in the first part of this volume. At the same time, the interviews carried out for this research revealed the crucial role of business journalists as 'gatekeepers', following the growing commodification of management knowledge. While journalists rely to a certain extent on consultants and managers as 'heroes' for their stories, they also exercise some control over access to these media and therefore over the 'popular' validation of consultancy knowledge.

The chapters in the first two parts of this volume suggest that consultants have managed to establish themselves as 'legitimate' knowledge carriers in addition to, and in competition with, academia, and that they have developed quite elaborate systems to capture, store, develop, and transfer knowledge. The contributions to the third part of this volume show, however, that they still face quite an uphill struggle when it comes to putting this knowledge into practice. The first two chapters in this part examine the relationship between consultants and managers at a general level, whereas the next two contain detailed case-studies of consultancy interventions. Together they show that convincing managers and all other stakeholders in the client organization of the 'value' of consulting knowledge remains a constant challenge for the consultancies.

In Chapter 10, Alfred Kieser uses general theories of fashion to explain the recent expansion of consultancy activities. He suggests that consultants exploit managers' need to achieve control, or at least a semblance of control, over their organizations in order to promote their services. By constantly launching new management fashions, consulting firms increase the fundamental uncertainty of managers, their fear of being out-of-date or being left behind their competitors. By hiring consultants, managers alleviate these fears and take a relatively low-risk strategy, because they are following what is widely perceived as 'best practice'. They cannot be wrong and, even in the case of failure, which is as difficult to measure as success, it is difficult to blame them personally, since they only did what the consultants suggested and what everybody else in the industry was doing. However, their relief remains temporary, since somebody will soon launch a new management fashion, often only a slightly modified version of the previous one, and the whole cycle will begin again. In this way, consultants have been able to make all but a few exceptional managers dependent on their services or, as he puts it provocatively, 'marionettes on the strings of their fashions'.

In his interview-based overview of the consultancy–client relationship in Australia, Christopher Wright comes to somewhat different conclusions. His chapter traces the evolution of this relationship in three major stages or waves: scientific management, strategy, and IT-based consulting (cf. also Kipping 2002). It shows that consultants did indeed use similar approaches during each of these waves, trying to create 'uncertainty' among managers in order to promote their services. At the same time, however, managers were more than simple victims of the fashion-setting consultants. Especially during the first stage, when consulting was a 'new' activity, the pioneering consulting firms encountered considerable scepticism, reluctance, and sometimes resistance from management in general and from the different levels in the client organizations. This meant that they had to make great efforts to build credibility and acceptance. In the Australian case, they did this by highlighting their experience and credentials with foreign companies and countries, such as Britain and the United States, which were widely perceived as being more advanced. Similar to the large international consultancies elsewhere (cf. Kipping 1999a), they also invested in building personal relationships with the captains of Australian industry and enhanced their general reputation by intervening in public debates on major issues, such as the flexibility of labour markets. At the same time, this chapter also confirms that in the long run consultants were, in a way, victims of the changes in management fashions, because their services could become outdated (cf. Kipping 2002). Wright suggests that the consultancies from the scientific management wave managed to overcome these difficulties by broadening their expertise, whereas many of those in the strategy wave encountered difficulties and some of them subsequently withdrew from the Australian market.

The final two chapters of this part and the whole volume rely on detailed case-studies to examine consultancy knowledge in action. Contrary to a widely held belief in the existing literature, Matthias Kipping and Thomas Armbrüster stress that the 'otherness' of consultants can prove to be a considerable burden when it comes to the interaction of consultants and the client organizations. Managers hire consultants to benefit from this otherness in terms of consultants' (public) reputation, their ability to transfer and transform different types of knowledge and to promote the change of the existing routines in the client organization. However, as the five detailed historical case-studies presented in the chapter show, these potential benefits are not automatic. In a number of cases, the otherness of consultants prompted resistance from within the client organization, because of reactions from middle managers and/or workers who:

1. saw the consultants as 'emissaries' of top management;
2. felt they had done (too) little to understand the specifics of the organization; and
3. were reluctant, in general, to modify the established practices following the consultants' recommendations.

The cases examined in this chapter also show the ways in which the management of the client organization tried—successfully or unsuccessfully—to overcome these problems derived from the otherness of the consultants. These included:

1. removing some of the most contested features of the consultancy recommendations;
2. negotiating the solution with those directly concerned; or even
3. 'deception', in this case pretending that the consultants were employees of the company in question rather than outsiders.

More generally, the available evidence from these cases suggests that in order to embed the suggestions of the consulting firms in their own organizations, managers needed to enlist the active support of those concerned, during and beyond the consultancy project.

In Chapter 13, Hallgeir Gammelsæter examines the role of consultancies in the implementation of organizational changes in two Norwegian companies. He argues that the change process and its outcome can best be understood as combining the insights from the 'new' and the 'old' institutionalism. While the former has focused on the relationship of managers with their external environment, the latter has seen them as actors embedded in an inner context. Within this framework, consultants are part of the external environment, but their advice is likely to have profound consequences for the inner context, i.e. if it modifies the existing power structure of the organization and thus challenges those in powerful positions.

In the two cases analysed in this chapter, managers in both companies were faced with serious external challenges, albeit from different directions. While one of the companies had been growing and diversifying its activities, the other was faced with a serious performance crisis, including the loss of market share in its home market. Nevertheless, the consultants involved in the organizational change projects found it difficult to translate their advice into action due to the constraints imposed by the inner context. Despite their difference in performance, both companies were actually marked by long-term stability in their internal structure and in top management.

Since the consultants' recommendations challenged established norms and power-holders, they either had to make small, step-by-step changes (in the case of the successful company) or wait until the top management team was disbanded (in the case of the unsuccessful company). In both cases, their internal support tended to come from those in the inner context who were set to gain from changes in the power structure, i.e. the young, ambitious managers.

Overall, the chapters in this volume will provide the growing literature on management consulting with some much-needed empirical evidence, especially with regard to:

- the development of the consulting industry in different countries, especially the efforts of consultants to become recognized as 'legitimate' knowledge carriers by their clients in competition (and sometimes cooperation) with other suppliers of management knowledge, notably academia;
- the ways in which consultancy firms (and management gurus) generate, manage, and validate their knowledge, which is influenced partially by their own characteristics in terms of activities and size, partially by the (national) context in which they are operating, and partially by the influence of 'gatekeepers';
- the 'success' of consultancy projects, in terms of convincing managers of the need to hire outside advisors, in terms of the reaction of those concerned in the client organization towards the consultants' recommendations, and ways of overcoming their possible reluctance and resistance.

From a more theoretical point of view, these chapters show that research on the management consulting industry has to take into account the different levels of analysis: industry, firm, and project. Each of these is characterized by its own dynamics for which the framework presented in this Introduction has tried to provide a first approximation.

PART I

HISTORICAL PERSPECTIVES ON THE CONSULTING INDUSTRY

2

The Acquisition of Symbolic Capital by Consultants: The French Case

ODILE HENRY

2.1. INTRODUCTION

The consultant claims to be an expert and to be vested with a symbolic power (Bourdieu 1987), that is a power to produce, by making a diagnosis, an opinion acknowledged as official and transcending individual interests. The power of the expert and, to a lesser extent, the power of the consultant, is a power that creates social reality, by consecrating or revealing that which already exists. When company executives treat the work of the consultant as a farce, claiming that the consultant is only using their opinions, they underline the symbolic (or magical) aspect of that power which enables a consultant to transform a commonly held and hitherto ignored opinion into an official vision of the company and its failures. The ability to exercise this symbolic power results from having acquired a certain kind of capital, symbolic capital, which is built on reputation, credit, esteem, trust (etc.) and which cannot be reduced to other kinds of capital (economic or cultural).

Therefore, contemporary consultants are very careful to avoid being included in the objectification studies conducted in sociology, both because in that world the quality of a consultant depends much more on his relationship with others than on his academic degree or position, and because any explanation of what consultants objectively are or do tends to shatter the group's charisma and challenge the collective belief from which this symbolic capital originates. However, unlike other categories of experts (Memmi 1996), whose symbolic capital has been 'bureaucratized', that is to say legally guaranteed or instituted and whose legitimacy is rarely questioned, the consultant has a symbolic capital that is more vulnerable and open to suspicion (as there are no official qualifications for admittance into this profession). Following the example of the nobility of medieval times, the consultant must constantly believe in his specific qualities, both within and outside the group. This analysis seeks to describe the main historical stages of accumulation by consultants and experts of a symbolic capital.[1]

---

[1] This chapter is based on a detailed study of consultants in France, using a wide variety of sources and research methods. The reconstitution of the positions held by consulting engineers in the nineteenth and

2.2. THE INDEPENDENT CONSULTING ENGINEER:
A STIGMATIZED PROFESSIONAL IDENTITY

The profession of expert and consultant appeared during the nineteenth century. It was exercised by engineers or technicians and formed part of the global movement which sought to redefine the profession of the engineer. In his study of the successive definitions of the term 'engineer' proposed by the encyclopedias, Terry Shinn showed that until the French Troisième République, an engineer was a 'civil servant with a leading part to play both in areas of State defence and all other areas concerning the State'. At the end of the century, an engineer was defined as having an equal share in the responsibility for state matters and in matters relating to industrial production, whereas before the outbreak of the First World War, the title of engineer applied primarily to engineers in the industrial sector (Shinn 1978, 1980).

As the profession of engineer shifted away from the public sector, specifically into that of the army, and into the private sector, a new population of consulting engineers emerged, seeking to legitimize a new definition of the engineering profession which, due to its adaptability to industrial needs, played a key part in economic and social progress. This new definition opposed the old one, which considered an engineer either as a senior civil servant or as a company director. There are two distinct categories of engineer that contributed to the emergence of this profession in the nineteenth century: the civil engineers from the École Centrale, a private institution created in 1829; and the engineers from the highest section of the French administration and more particularly from the Corps des Mines.[2]

The Consulting Engineer of the Nineteenth Century

Based on the Anglo-Saxon model, the civil engineering profession, defended by some of the alumni of the École Centrale who founded the French association of civil engineers (Société des ingénieurs civils de France) in 1848, sought to serve the interests of the private sector by developing the technical know-how to solve problems encountered on large-scale projects such as road, canal, or railway building. These engineers, who fought for the recognition of the status of the industrial engineer, and who acted

early twentieth centuries was the subject of a prosopographic survey conducted using various sources (private and public archives and printed sources), whereas the work on the contemporary period combined the collection of quantitative data (questionnaires and the annuals of the French Grandes Écoles) and qualitative data (more than 100 interviews conducted at the beginning of the 1990s with consultants, clients, journalists, and company executives). This corpus was completed with a number of ethnographic observations carried out in consulting firms of different sizes. For other findings of the research as well as more details about the methodology and sources used, see the author's doctoral thesis (Henry 1993: esp. 119–25), which is currently being revised for publication; an unpublished research report (Henry and Sauviat 1993), as well as several journal articles (Henry 1992, 1994, 1997, 2000).

[2] Simultaneously with the creation of the *manufactures royales*, which had a monopoly on the manufacture of a number of products considered as strategic by the state, the first engineering corps were created in the 17th century (military engineering, artillery, civil engineering, and geological engineering). Far from contesting them, the École Polytechnique, created in 1793, was in charge of recruitment to the different state corps.

as a link between applied science and industrial progress, seem to have come from classes with less economic capital, as compared with the École Centrale recruits, and formed the breeding ground for the consulting engineering profession. As they did not belong to the business bourgeoisie and seemed unlikely to occupy a leading position in a family-owned business or an engineering position in a firm, these civil engineers often only had the opportunity of occupying the position of independent consulting engineer, acting as a kind of general practitioner for a number of industries (Grelon 1986; Ribeill 1985). This was because of the small number of opportunities available in industry until the 1880s. Many tasks were performed by the technicians of the École des Arts et Métiers and the engineers from the Corps des Ponts, who had the monopoly on all engineering positions available in the railway industry.

Until the second industrial revolution, the term 'civil engineer' and 'consulting engineer' were used equivalently. In France, where the state still controls the engineering profession, these civil engineers had to conquer their own market and strive for recognition of this new 'obscure' function, exercised by 'new' men who were often looked down upon by the graduates of the École Polytechnique. They considered that a career in industry was degrading and tarnished their profession. Indeed, the knowledge of the civil engineer and of the consulting engineer differed from the knowledge of the Polytechniciens. The occupation of civil engineer was not measured against an art defined as being unexploitable; on the contrary, the civil engineer was subject to the condition of profitability and had to fight for recognition and profit (Auclair 1999).

The 'industrial science' defended by these engineers combined experimental research (in the fields of metallurgy and the study of the subsoil), manufacturing processes, and industrial economy. The civil engineers' struggle to defend their diploma and their profession paralleled the struggle to impose a more open market economy against the state's grip on the French economy, by defending private enterprise and a market economy based on profit. In order to exist as civil engineers in competition with state engineers, they had to cast discredit on the supervisory duties of the state engineers, and thereby on the control of the state over industry, and make the French state one of the most powerful obstacles to the development of capitalism and industrialization.

The history of the profession of consulting engineer is closely linked to the history of the relationship between the Polytechniciens—and, more particularly, the engineers of the Corps des Mines—and the industrial world. Although the role of consultant was indeed considered as part of the duties of the engineers of the Corps des Mines, the change in that profession at the end of the century may be considered in terms of the passage from the role of consultant to one of collaborator, and then actual manager in industry (Thépot 1979, 1998). The French administration encouraged the activities of consultants and experts and, more generally, participation in business matters which enabled French industry to benefit from recent developments in science.

The first act passed in 1810 provided for different types of cooperation between the engineers of the Corps des Mines and industry. To achieve this collaboration the engineers were entitled to leave of absence, that is they could occupy a position in industry for a given period of time where the use of their specialized know-how could serve the public interest. They could also act as experts to industry or other administrations. Although before 1840 the percentage of engineers per year on leave of absence varied considerably and seemed to be influenced by the political context, industrial development due to the railways seems to account for the sudden increase in the number of engineers on leave of absence between 1840 and 1860. However, the careers examined by A. Thépot, though not claiming to be exhaustive, showed that those engineers on leave of absence mostly held technical management positions in the big mining and rail firms, the term consulting engineer first appearing in the middle of the 1850s. It was the civil service engineers who were authorized to take leave of absence, and who held the position of expert, arbitrator, and consultant until the second industrial revolution.

As these positions were mainly taken up by high-ranking civil servants, simultaneously with their main supervision and control duties, the positions of expert and consultant were progressively developed by the numerous paradoxes they exposed in the Corps des Mines and by the attempts to solve its internal conflicts. Indeed, in view of the development of free-market theories and the increasing objection to state control, these occupations were considered as a benign form of control and they supplied the state with an efficient substitute for its own control. They were therefore encouraged by the administration. However, as evidenced by the number of circulars seeking to regulate these practices, the belief that the agents of the state represented the general interest was called into question by the fact that these occupations that were initially unpaid rapidly became highly lucrative. To prevent the occupation of expert from becoming a regular fixture, a circular of 1886 prohibited the engineers of the Corps des Mines from registering with the courts as experts, and required their absolute discretion, no form of advertising of their occupation being allowed.[3] The administration was very keen to condemn those who tarnished the image of a disinterested body because they requested leave of absence or considered this secondary occupation as a means of personal enrichment. Indeed, the administration endeavoured to impose the belief that the duty of the expert was to serve the development of industry by bringing the light of science to the entrepreneur.

Finally, the administration, wishing that its reputation of excellence should remain intact, defined the duties of the consultant and the expert in such a way that they excluded any form of intervention in corporate management. The purpose of the administration's warnings was to encourage and control these civil servants, who were in a delicate position halfway between public service and economic interests, from serving their own private interests, and more particularly, their economic interests. The constant reference to 'the values of neutrality and disinterested devotion to the public interest' was used to impose the 'official vision of the State as a place of universality and serving the general interest' (Bourdieu 1996). These engineers could then use the symbolic capital that they contributed to create and impose a belief in what they did, and in suggesting that the profession of expert or consultant has a magical quality that transcends personal opinions on a given question and can provide a neutral,

---

[3] The administration's hesitation when faced with the engineers' requests for leave of absence reflected the challenge of the role of the state in the economy throughout the 19th century: to intervene or to adopt a *laissez-faire* policy (Charle 1987a).

disinterested, absolute, and official point of view. In other words, their point of view can be considered as universal. In fact, these duties, entrusted to the mining engineers, who were recruited among the professors or the academics of the Corps des Mines, that is those who displayed the greatest resources both technically (in terms of scientific competence) and symbolically (their high moral principles being a guarantee of their neutrality), represented for them an ultimate form of social consecration.

In the 1880s, in a context of industrial development, mergers, and an increase in the number of specialized schools of engineering, the profession of engineer progressively appeared as a career option in industry and as a step towards a managerial position in the economic field. In this way, these careers gradually became more attractive than the engineering careers proposed by the state.

The changes in the economy had various impacts on the activity of consulting engineers. Following the second industrialization, the graduates of the École Centrale seemed to be less specialized than the engineers from the newly founded schools and too technical when compared with the state engineers, who were competent in the administrative and legal fields, this being essential to obtain the dominant posts in the economic field. Consequently, company directors had less recourse to independent civil engineers, who were the victims of their more general training. Of the positions filled by the Centraux upon leaving their École, the civil engineering profession represented 19.2 per cent of the 1832–40 cohort in 1864, 22.2 per cent of the 1850–5 cohort in 1873, as compared with 7 per cent of the 1890–2 cohort in 1910. As the scope of positions filled by the Centraux extended, the name 'consulting engineer' came to mean, in a more restricted or specialized sense, an independent engineer in the service of a company, which seemed to replace definitively the civil engineer in the nomenclature of the positions filled by the Centraux (Ribeill 1985).

Furthermore, between 1880 and 1909, the proportion of engineers from the Corps des Mines who sought a career in industry increased: before 1880 less than one quarter pursued that type of career as compared with more than half during the period from 1900 to 1909. As a result, the duties of the expert and the consultant were no longer considered as exceptional duties carried out by outside high-ranking civil servants and became a profession integrated into the corporate hierarchy with the same status as that of a manager, an assistant manager, or a deputy director.[4] It was the company directors—who needed engineers capable of providing them with solutions to technical and strategic issues on a permanent and regular basis—who more or less imported into the private sector an occupation traditionally reserved for high-ranking civil servants. The position of consulting engineer integrated into the corporate hierarchy provided the engineers of the Corps des Mines, until the beginning of the twentieth century, with a stepping-stone to the corporate board of directors.

After 1906 the engineers from the Corps des Mines were called upon to hold the highest corporate positions. Consequently, the internal positions of consulting engineers

---

[4] As the number of requests for leave of absence increased, the requests filed by the engineers of the Corps des Mines who had remained in the administration tended to diminish, thereby confirming the assumption that this occupation had been internalized (Charle 1987*a*).

seemed to lose their appeal and were filled by other categories of engineers from the École Centrale. However, as the position of consultant to the management of a big company had historically represented a sort of antechamber leading to economic power usually held by the representatives of the state, it was considered, until the Second World War, as an attractive model in contrast to the position of 'independent' consulting engineer, which appeared to be a negative or a temporary occupation. As evidence, when the wage gap between engineers increased in 1920 and 1930, the position of 'internal' consulting engineer remained among the highest paid, even though the academic and social characteristics of the engineers were changing and their chances of finding a leading position in the economic sector was declining (Thépot 1986).

The Consulting Engineers of the Consultancy Firms

The definition of the consulting engineer was actually indirectly clarified during the course of the debate on time-and-motion studies, which started in the inter-war years. With the spread of these ideas, the first American-style scientific management departments appeared in France and the first applications of these ideas were tested before the war at Renault, Berliet, and Michelin (Moutet 1975, 1985, 1997).[5] Louis Loucheur, who succeeded Albert Thomas at the Ministry of Armaments, invited a group of American consulting engineers to assist in the implementation of these new working methods in the arms factories at the end of the war. Among this group, C. B. Thompson—an engineer, a disciple of Taylor, and a lecturer at Harvard—started his own firm in France and trained French technicians who, in turn, started their own firms at the end of the 1920s. In 1927 Wallace Clarke started his own firm and Charles Bedaux, a Frenchman who had fled to the United States in 1906 and founded a consultancy firm on the principles of scientific management, opened a subsidiary in France. In 1929 Paul Planus, formerly with the firm founded by C. B. Thompson, started his own firm. In 1931, Ernst Hijmans, a Dutchman, entered into a partnership with Jean Coutrot and started BICRA, a French subsidiary of the Dutch firm RBO. Finally, in 1932, Sabine Garcin-Guynet, who had also trained with C. B. Thompson, started her own firm.

The staff of these firms quickly increased: Planus's firm, which had 12 employees in 1934, employed 40 in 1939, and Bedaux France, which totalled 6 employees in 1929, employed 80 engineers before the outbreak of the war (Kipping 1997, 1997/98). The increase in the number of consulting engineers specialized in work organization formed part of a general increase in the number of experts and technicians working on a self-employed basis. In 1896 they totalled 27,600 but by 1936 they amounted to 126,415 (Toutain 1963). The numerical increase was paralleled by a diversification of the social characteristics of these engineers. The results of a survey to reconstitute the careers of some 20 agents who were consulting engineers during the inter-war years show that the agents born between 1850 and 1875 were usually graduates of the major

---

[5] The first firm of consulting engineers in work organization in France was created in 1914 by Morinni, a disciple of the American Harrington Emerson (Moutet 1975; Kipping 1999a).

engineering schools, held the position of consulting engineer at the age of 45 to 50, that is, halfway through their career, and usually held these positions in addition to a career in research or teaching. The agents born at the beginning of the twentieth century were usually self-educated or graduates from second-rank schools or low-ranking graduates of the major schools, who held the position of consulting engineer at the age of 30 and had made it their career, after founding their own consultancy firm.

Whether founded on social or scientific capital, the symbolic capital of the experts of the first generation (once they had achieved distinction), which was necessary to acquire the authority to impose on the employers or the state one's own views on the question of organization and to obtain unequivocal recognition, free from any personal and subjective point of view (Bourdieu 1987), was infinitely more significant than the symbolic capital of the experts of the second generation. For example, Sabine Garcin-Guynet was employed in an ironworks, with no proper qualifications, learned from her own experience whilst in C. B. Thomson's firm, and then founded her own firm in 1932.

This new group, which made the application of new methods of work organization its business, was heavily criticized by the older consulting engineers. Henry Le Chatelier (1850–1936), who had been the top-ranked graduate of his cohort at the École Polytechnique, was an engineer from the Corps des Mines, a chemist, a professor at the École des Mines, the École Polytechnique, the Collège de France, and then the Sorbonne, and became a member of the Académie des Sciences in 1907. He had translated and published the works of F. W. Taylor, and criticized those 'foreign' consulting engineers who, lacking any real scientific culture, used empirical methods that depreciated Taylor's pure doctrine. Le Chatelier's obsession with Taylorism can only be understood in the context of the discredit into which the careers of certain engineers of the Grandes Écoles had fallen and the erosion of the technical and scientific bases on which their power was established in the economy.

First, the fact that the engineers from the Corps des Mines resigned from their positions during the final years of the century to follow brilliant careers in industry revealed a global movement of capital reconversion, more organizational, social, or economic than strictly technical or scientific, which legitimized the power they exercised over the economy. This was difficult for engineers who considered the challenge to their technical power as a loss.[6] Moreover, although the highest-ranking graduates of the École Polytechnique were able to benefit from this movement, there were, as a result, massive resignations of the Polytechniciens who, due to their rank, would have followed a career in the army, as well as a significant increase in the number of requests for leave of absence filed by those who had pursued their career in the army. At the same time the number of engineering schools was growing, and this contributed to the fact that between 1880 and 1914 a large number of Polytechniciens had difficulty in

---

[6] The first signs of the technician's loss of his specific power appeared in the middle of the 19th century: engineers, who wielded authority over the economy in the name of a technical and scientific capital, were subject to the economic and organizational requirements of the business world (Beaune 1985). Antoine Picon notes, in his study of the Ponts et Chaussées engineers (1992), that many of them risked losing their identity as the administrative and managerial aspects had taken over from the technical aspect.

finding positions in industry, which was hitherto unheard of at the École Poly-technique (Shinn 1980).[7]

Le Chatelier considered Taylorism to be a science that would give the engineers work-ing in industry the authority and managerial positions they wanted: the engineer acted as a kind of arbiter between management and the workforce, rendering his decision in the case of conflict in the name of science. Le Chatelier's definition of the consulting engineer provided a remedy to the crisis in certain categories of engineers: considered as a high-ranking engineer whose duty it was to introduce 'science' to management methods and who would form a dual partnership with the company director, the con-sulting engineer was primarily a scientific engineer defined both as a fully integrated member of the senior management of the company and as an established 'disinter-ested' scientist or expert. Having acted as consulting engineer for J. A. Pavin de la Farge (later Lafarge-Coppée) from 1895 to 1932, Henry Le Chatelier looked down on the practice of 'knowledge marketing', typical of outside consulting engineers, and pre-ferred to refer to an 'expert consulting engineer' advising a limited number of company directors. This was more in keeping with his idea of serving the general interest and the ethics of public service, and within the framework of the engineers of the Corps des Mines of the last century, which his own father, Louis Le Chatelier, had defined.

Le Chatelier considered that the consulting engineer in a consultancy firm, who sold his services and was therefore subject to the needs of his clients, was part of a het-eronomous group faced with the risk of having to sacrifice the cause of science and thereby the cause of the engineer. Indeed, he is in the position of having to respond strictly to the needs of the company directors, that is, only applying the basic prin-ciples of Taylor to enable the company to increase its production without fundament-ally changing the methods of management or even its vision of the world. This is why Henry Le Chatelier refused to become involved in the activities of the Comité National de l'Organisation Française (CNOF), which was created in 1926 and was the first institution in Europe to bring together technicians specialized in organization (Le Chatelier 1969).

The model of the consulting engineer defined by Le Chatelier was based on past experience, but increasingly challenged by the growing rift between the scientific and the economic fields. While Le Chatelier reaffirmed that it was in the name of science that engineers could legitimately wield their power over the economy, the engineers who intended to follow a scientific career found it more and more difficult to compete with the graduates of the École Normale Supérieure for prestigious positions (Charle 1987b), and administrative competence was better paid than technical or scientific competence. Indeed, the agents responsible for introducing Taylor's principles to French industry in the 1930s were a far cry from the model of the scientific engineer defined by Le Chatelier (Lette 1998).

There are two partly independent explanations for the growth in consultancy firms and the social characteristics of the population of consulting engineers in those firms.

---

[7] More engineering schools were created between 1900 and 1940 than during the 18th and 19th centuries put together. The number of graduates increased from 1,000 in 1900 to 4,000 in 1920 (Boltanski 1987).

The first is attested by the failure of Léon Guillet (1873–1946) in the 1920s to teach the graduates of the major French engineering schools the scientific methods of organization defined by Taylor. A Centralien, Guillet was first head of the applied research laboratory at Dion Bouton, then professor of metallurgy at the Conservatoire Nationale des Arts et Métiers (CNAM), and from 1923 head of the École Centrale. These ideas seem to have been rejected both by the industrialists, whose concern was more focused on commercial and administrative issues than on technical problems relating to production (Moutet 1997), and by the engineers of the Grandes Écoles, who sought employment in industry and were very wary of such methods which seemed unworthy of them and could not easily be negotiated in the employment market. These methods sought to ensure that the workmen and the foremen accepted Taylor's principles.

In this context, Léon Guillet finally decided to introduce day classes and evening classes at the CNAM, with the aim of teaching these new methods to a mixed class of junior executives, heads of small businesses, corporate engineers, and, most importantly, candidates who had failed the entrance exam to the major schools. The latter, who were on the same social level as the engineers who would later become the future captains of industry, were, however, in a different professional circle due to their academic failure. For Léon Guillet they constituted the ideal candidates to transform industry by introducing the new methods of scientific management. Far from being 'irregular', the high number of engineers who had failed academically speaking was anything but difficult to explain, and appeared on the contrary to be the result of a highly efficient recruiting strategy, even if it was not Léon Guillet's intention. These technicians, who had encountered an academic setback, were ready for revenge and, unlike their more academically successful counterparts, prepared to take risks by trying to promote new ideas in industrial circles.

These technicians were mostly born at the end of the nineteenth century, became familiar with the principles of Taylor by the end of the First World War or during the 1920s, and had had their university education interrupted by the war. They entered the employment market at the end of the 1920s, just as the supply of engineers was beginning to exceed the demand from the industrialists. This is the second reason for the growth in consultancy firms. Indeed, the lower-ranking graduates who were promoted to replace the high-ranking engineers who had been called up no longer succeeded in finding positions as corporate engineers and this had a significant influence on their decision to become consulting engineers.

This was the case with Charles Émile Hugoniot, who was self-educated and became an engineer following his experience in the United States. He was appointed as consultant to Albert Thomas at the Ministry of Armaments and then became a consulting engineer in 1919, having failed to obtain a position as an engineer in a major company. Following the economic crisis of 1929, the main issue concerned production outlets, pushing production issues into the background, and thereby increasing competition within companies, between the engineers themselves, and between the engineers and their commercial counterparts. During that period, the wage gap increased; engineers bereft of any kind of capital held positions as foremen, whereas the engineers from the major schools held the position of company managers in the economic field.

After 1930 unemployment spread to all categories of engineers, the entire profession being one of the hardest hit by the economic crisis (Grelon 1986). At this time, engineers familiar with Taylorism took over the consultancy sector which, despite the American consultancy firms and the agencies for the promotion of Taylorism, was still virgin territory. Among them were Paul Planus, who was admitted to the preparatory class of the major engineering schools but had no official title; Jean Coutrot, who was accepted at Polytechnique but was called up; or Jean Milhaud, who was accepted at Polytechnique but left and then resigned. To these engineers, who did not have all the required academic assets, the new, as yet undefined consultancy firms appeared preferable to the industrial or commercial firms, which only had over-qualified posts to offer.

2.3. THE STIGMA REVERSED

From a Commercial to an Independent Profession

Although a historical review of the major structural changes that affected the group of engineers highlights the connection between periods of shortage of factory engineers and periods of development of the profession of independent consulting engineer, it remains to be seen how these 'temporary' engineers overcame the stigma attached to their profession. How did the independent consulting engineers finally convince themselves and their clients that they were experts, in spite of the numerous difficulties they encountered, notably not being able to claim that they held a store of knowledge and morality certified by the state, unlike their predecessors of the nineteenth century? The implication is that they collectively sought to hide the commercial aspect of their occupation both from themselves and from their circles, this aspect being one of the characteristics of their profession, and that the economic leaders progressively accepted these work organization 'specialists', at the risk of losing partial control over the firm's 'secrets'.

The profession progressively acquired a moral system based on those of various professional organizations and more particularly that of the Chambre des ingénieurs-conseils et experts de France. Created in 1912, it became the Chambre des ingénieurs-conseils de France (CICF), and after the war it was in charge of promoting the profession of consulting engineer and drawing up its rules and code of conduct. From its inception, the CICF was more concerned with the moral qualities of the consulting engineer (professional conscience, honesty, financial independence, impartiality, integrity, sense of honour) than with technical qualities (the know-how). It advised those who were not 'certain of being able to make a decent living out of this profession without losing their freedom' to refrain from exercising it. The rules specified that a consulting engineer who assisted a client on a permanent basis and received a fixed remuneration should give up that remuneration if this prevented him or her from giving impartial advice to one of the client's competitors. This prohibited consulting engineers from occupying a managerial or administrative position in a firm and condemned the commercial strategy of client research, which transformed colleagues into competitors and hindered the emergence of an esprit de corps. This reflected the instructions issued by the Corps des Mines in the nineteenth century to high-ranking civil servants on leave of absence.

These regulations, which defined a certain number of moral obligations, sought to transform a commercial profession into an independent profession with a title, thereby granting the profession the authority and the trust it needed to exist.[8] This undertaking to moralize and organize the profession resulted in the creation in 1937 of the French association of consulting engineers, chaired by Paul Planus and based on the Belgian association of consulting engineers. This association seems to have disappeared at the end of the Second World War. In 1914 the CICF numbered 30 consulting engineers and experts specializing in economic matters such as public works, metallurgy, mechanics, transport, etc. During the inter-war years, the number of members of the CICF slowly increased and totalled some 1,000 by 1951, when it merged with the Syndicat général des ingénieurs-conseils (created in 1947). During the 1940s the consulting engineers specializing in work organization left the CICF to start their own professional association—the Association des conseillers en organisation scientifique (AFCOS)—which became the Association française des firmes de conseillers de direction (AFFCOD) at the beginning of the 1950s, and which represented firms rather than individuals.

The consequence of this development was that the profession was reorganized: consulting engineers who occupied the position of personal adviser to a small number of company heads, and who were vested with the utmost legitimacy during the first half of the century, were swept aside. At the same time, the Commission générale de l'organisation scientifique du travail (renamed Cégos), which was one of the main bodies of the French employers association (Confédération Générale du Patronat Français), became, during the 1950s, the heart of the profession (Weexsteen 1999).[9] After the war, Cégos was the first consultancy firm to import American management methods, which it transformed into short training sessions, adapted to the needs of industrialists and the state. This stimulated its development, as it grew from 40 assistants in the 1950s to 600 in the 1960s (Boltanski 1987).

The reason for this development and the development of the profession of consulting engineer is linked both to the growth of the middle classes at the end of the 1930s and to the change in the attitude of employers towards this new bourgeoisie, whose growth stemmed from the need of the economic sectors for executives during the inter-war years. The shock caused by the strikes of 1936 paradoxically served to 'reveal' to the economic leaders the social role played by the consulting engineers, thus constituting their collective identity. Faced with the risk that the engineers and technicians would join the unions affiliated to the communist CGT, the employers actively supported the engineers' trade-union associations and adopted and even reinforced the elitist and corporatist tendency of the profession. Paying close attention to their collaborators, the employers implemented recruitment and training strategies for their managers. These strategies were developed by Cégos (Kolboom 1986), using the theories of Henri Fayol, who had classified the different categories of executive according to their capabilities,

---

[8] See esp. Couturaud (1913/14).
[9] Cégos started to change its by-laws in 1941 and became an association governed by the 1901 Act in 1948.

and whose administrative doctrine, together with Taylor's had formed the basis of the organizers' activity over the previous twenty years. By providing consulting engineers with a new market, that of management training, and also a new status as experts in management issues, the employers not only contributed to differentiating them from 'mere' engineers but also to their evolution into a separate group.

Following the increase in the number of staff in the consultancy firms, the profession was officially created as an independent profession: whereas before the war, the independent engineer's role was contested and had little prestige, after the war, the consultancy firms, financially 'independent' economic entities, became the holders of the symbolic capital. It seems that the charisma hitherto conferred on individuals (the personal adviser or the expert) had been conferred on firms or even on a new profession, whose agents were competitors but nevertheless interdependent. To refer to Weber's cherished opposition, during the two decades following the Second World War, 'careers' in consultancy firms became progressively governed by a set of codes, thereby standardizing a profession that, in differentiating itself by adopting a specific culture, was paradoxically to become considered as exceptional.

The Emergence of a Competitive Field and the Invention of a Consultancy Culture

New consultancy firms were created during the German occupation: in 1942 G. Bardet, a Polytechnicien close to J. Coutrot, founded Cofror, and A. Vidal, another Polytechnicien who had started with Planus, founded his own firm. In 1943 a group of engineers founded the Compagnie d'organisation rationnelle du travail, which became CORT Consultants. From the middle of the 1940s until the end of the 1950s, with the creation of the Association française pour l'accroissement de la productivité (AFAP), which was in charge of organizing productivity missions to the United States, a number of new firms, mostly founded by Polytechniciens, were created, and they developed rapidly (Henry 1994). The profession acquired a certain prestige and began attracting better-educated agents than those of the pre-war generation. The arrival of Jacques Lesourne, Polytechnicien and top of his cohort, as the head of the Société de mathématiques appliquées (SMA) set a precedent: 'we all thought he had come to restore the profession's reputation', said Sylvère Seurat, the head of Euréquip (interview with Sylvère Seurat conducted by C. Sauviat, 1990; cf. Henry and Sauviat, 1993). Until the beginning of the 1960s, most French firms continued to apply the traditional methods of productivity increase inspired by Taylor, even if Cégos and the Organisation Yves Bossard (created in 1956; it later became Bossard Consultants) tried to diversify their areas of practice into account management and economic policy matters.

The arrival in France in the 1960s of new competitors radically changed the division of labour between consultancy firms. The first American firms of corporate strategy, the Anglo-Saxon firms of auditors and accountants providing management system consultancy services, and the information technology firms arrived in France at the end of the 1960s and the beginning of the 1970s. On the one hand, the American firms that had become leaders in corporate strategy and management pushed the French firms out of these sectors and, on the other hand, the information technology firms took over most of the industrial and administrative production control duties that had been carried out by the organizers. Robert Mallet, a Polytechnicien and founder of the Compagnie Générale d'Organisation, which became the Compagnie Générale d'Informatique in 1968, was one of the most virulent critics of the organizers:

[Organization] is now a thing of the past, it is IT which controls production. You know, reorganizing procedures by using computer techniques is a far cry from filling in forms, it is quite a change, it is a revolution of the mind. And we were convinced that this was the shape of things to come (interview with Robert Mallet conducted by O. Henry, 1990).

In this new context, where the firms became the dominant factor, the French consultancy firms seemed to be relegated to the technical or the social field, specializing in human resources. For example, the only choice left to a firm like Bossard Consultants was to maintain its activity in the human resources sector, a sector it had ignored until then:

We have been kicked out of the management consultancy field by the Big Eight and we have gone into the human resources field. We are now leaders in this field. The funny thing is that it was not in keeping with the Bossard philosophy, as we had consultants who were engineers and very strict and who loathed psychological and sociological nonsense (interview with J. P. Auzimour, who became CEO of Bossard Consultants in 1993, carried out by O. Henry in 1989).

A new field seemed to be emerging (Henry 1992): the psychological or social dimension of management and the technical dimension of organization appeared to be interdependent. Without the new industrial and administrative production-control methods 'the social technologies of manipulation would never have produced all their effects' (Boltanski 1987: 197–9).

In this new space, the oldest consultancy firms, whose history is linked to the struggle of the engineers of the first half of the century to impose the belief that Taylorism could provide a solution to social conflict, seemed incapable of specializing in one or other of the new management techniques. Their members had engineering degrees from second-rank schools, remained faithful to the 'science of organization', claimed to be disciples of Taylor and his disciples of the first half of the century, and—at a time when their knowledge, treated as 'authoritarian technicism', seemed more than ever unadapted to the new methods of control—seemed to be completely unreceptive to new methods that incorporated a psychological or social dimension. Did this mean that the profession of organizer was condemned to disappear? On the contrary, the creation of internal organizer positions encouraged by the consulting engineers showed that the question of organization as part of the management brief had far from disappeared. In 1958 the internal consultants created their own professional association, the AFOPE (Association Française des Organiseurs Permanents d'Entreprise) to defend and promote the profession of internal organizer, as opposed to the consultant. This was a clear reference to the followers of Taylor of the inter-war years. Louis Danty-Lafrance (1894–1956, a graduate of the École Centrale des Arts et Manufactures de Paris), under whose moral authority the AFOPE was placed, had held the chair of scientific management at the CNAM since it had been created in 1930.

Henry

However, although scientific management methods tended to grow within companies, consultancy firms specializing in scientific management encountered serious difficulties. Thus, the firm founded by Paul Planus in 1929 was bought in the 1960s by André Vidal, who in turn met with financial difficulties and disappeared in 1980. A significant number of André Vidal's consultants, who had become internal organizers, joined Renault and founded the internal scientific management department there. As the profession of organizer had become internalized with the result that the knowledge specific to the profession of consultant was being acquired by company executives, these consultants seemed more and more incapable of proving their distinct role, and thereby weakened the symbolic capital attached to the entire group. The heads of Cégos tended to consider the internal organizers as drudges and criticized their unwillingness to depart from their operational methods and offer new services to companies, their lack of social ease, their rigidity, and their inability to adopt a broader outlook to economic issues, that is, to be one step ahead of the executives.[10] In fact, the consultants, by unwittingly contributing to the development of the internal organizer, hastened the disappearance of the firms that employed them.

The creation of a field in which consultancy firms are competitors but nevertheless interdependent, means that the agents are players in games such as passing the buck, playing tricks, provoking debates, opposing one another, and thereby mutually reinforcing one another. Each agent brings its competitors to life in order to exist, acknowledging their existence because they depend on them for their own existence. In this way, the social energy created contributes to reinforcing the social authority of the consultants (Henry 1992). For example, since internal consultants are sometimes in competition with consultancy firms, their strategy is to try to destroy the charisma that consultancy firms inspire by arguing that the so-called independent relationship between consultants and company management is actually false. They point to their highly developed sense of commerce, and by doing so use the arguments developed by Henry Le Chatelier. By placing themselves on the side of technology and engineering science, considered as 'neutral' and therefore apolitical, the internal organizers assimilate the external consultants as actors of the political world and try to show that their lack of resolution, which results from their habit of compromising, means that they are apt to change their opinion and adapt themselves to comply with the requests of corporate management.

In this warlike context, which marked the relationship between internal and outside consultants in the 1960s and 1970s, the AFOPE tried to implement the internal assessment procedures of the consultancy firms within companies and attempted to persuade

---

[10] 'One of the rules dated from the time when the scientific organisation of work was a science. We studied movements and gestures and determined which were rational and efficient. And the organisers had to refrain from giving any advice or intervening with the policy or the strategy of the firm. Cégos did that a little . . . And in the eyes of the profession that was bad. It's funny, it was wrong to talk about anything else. It was the factory or the office but those were the methods, the paper circuits and the organiser was to refrain from enquiring about the new products.' (Interview with Octave Gélinier, ingénieur des Mines de Paris and one of the main heads of Cégos from 1947 onwards, conducted by O. Henry in 1993.)

the Association Française de Normalisation (AFNOR) that the relationship between companies and consultancy firms should be governed by a set of regulations. By lobbying for the profession to be recognized as a group of specialists capable of imposing the values of its members and their products, the AFOPE contributed to giving the profession a serious image. It took part in the discussions reported in the press, notably the business press, on issues such as relations with consultants, valuation of fees, etc., thereby unwittingly generating a form of belief in the value of a particular firm and therefore the value of the profession as a whole. When the members of AFOPE were obliged in the 1970s to extend the scope of the definition of 'organization' and modify their by-laws, in order to take into consideration the development of information technology, the progressive substitution of the term 'organizer' by the term 'internal consultant' may, in this context, be considered as paying tribute to the dominant group.

The emergence of this field, where the question of defining its limits and membership criteria was addressed in terms of competition between firms, was simultaneous with the collective definition of a professional and social identity, resulting in the definition of a real 'consultancy culture' entirely reserved for an elite (Henry 1997). In fact, contrary to what happened during the first half of the century, consultancy firms attracted young graduates from the major business or engineering schools. Even if this policy of selective recruitment could be viewed within the framework of the acquisition of symbolic capital, that which is sacred being defined as that which is separate, it was in the interest of the consultants' group to maintain the belief that it constituted a separate profession, distinct from executives due to the high number of graduates from the elite schools. It is nonetheless necessary to examine the reasons for the strong attraction this profession holds, beyond the fact that the levels of remuneration exceed by 20 to 30 per cent those of the other economic sectors, which has resulted in the reversal of the stigma hitherto attached to it.

An analysis of this professional ethos reveals the social logic of regulating the characteristics inherent to the profession and the self-perception of the consultants who join these firms (Henry 1993). The vision of the consultancy firm, and of the profession in general, as a world apart, is based not only on extremely selective recruitment policies, but also on a socialization process that results in the reinforcement of the belief in the elitist values celebrated by these firms. On the one hand, the harshness of the internal selection procedure, and the creation of a self-contained competitive field, contribute to progressively transforming the perception that young consultants have of themselves, and lead them to adhere to an official vision of a profession that seeks to gather together the elite of competence, in other words, to consider themselves as part of that elite. On the other hand, the ambivalence of the principles that define the methods of assessment and the internal hierarchy (qualities that are rewarded are often contradictory and client satisfaction is rarely considered as a sufficient criterion for promotion) leads the consultant to exert a sort of self-control over his ambitions. This enables the firm to maintain a balance between those who leave to join a company and those who remain, and to avoid clearly defining the question of the hierarchy of these two careers (leaving the firm is often considered as a sign that there is no future and those who have left the firm often remember it as paradise lost).

As this socialization process tends to reinforce the misreading of the profession's specificity, it could only be a total failure if it did not correspond to the social expectations of the agents who, for objectively different reasons that all stem from the relation between academic achievement and social origin, are ready to receive the elitist message and to achieve social consecration. The construction of a professional identity, through a process of socialization, binding, and exclusion, tends to define each firm as a 'separate' body and to produce an esprit de corps, with the result that all the consultants employed by the same firm form a relatively integrated group, this being the prerequisite to forming and maintaining a collective social capital. The 'old consultants' associations, founded by the big firms, seek to rekindle the feeling of attachment of the consultants to their old firm by reminding them that they owe their present situation to it.

2.4. CONCLUSIONS

Following the example of the civil engineering firms of the nineteenth century that were founded by the graduates of the École Centrale waiting for a position in industry, the consultancy firms of today seem to act as outplacement agencies for high-ranking executives. However, unlike their predecessors, the consultants of today have benefited more from this profession: although part of the appeal of the profession lies in the fact that it offers legitimate positions in companies, it nevertheless constitutes a sort of rite of passage for certain social categories. This means that it can act as a place of training for executives, as opposed to school and academic hierarchies and the methods of socialization used by companies. It can be the place where the real excellence criterion of the economic field is defined.

This chapter has described the social and historic processes through which this profession, which was stigmatized for so long, was able to reverse the trend and acquire the symbolic capital necessary to achieve recognition. An analysis of the historic struggles between the 'independent' consulting engineers of the nineteenth and early twentieth centuries and the engineer 'experts' of the Corps des Mines for the monopoly of the legitimate definition of the profession, clarifies the structural traits that the profession owes to its history, that is the strategies to reverse the trends that were imposed by the very conditions under which competition came into play.

Although the independent consulting engineers of the nineteenth century represented a professional model, as compared with the experts of the highest sections of the administration who advocated open market theories, the struggles between these categories obliged the consulting engineers to regulate their profession. The model they chose was collegiate, based on the German brotherhoods and a Puritan system of ethics, defending elitist ideals, voluntary membership, equality between members, self-government, and independence from the state (Dubar and Tripier 1998). It is in this light that we may consider the sectarian nature of the profession, which inspired the rhetoric used by the members of the profession and presented them as virtuosos who surpassed themselves, as one of its structural features inherited from past struggles. Focusing on analysing how the belief came to be formed, the second part of this chapter has demonstrated how the emergence of the field of consultancy (including both consultants and specialists, and journalists or scientists who have also played a part in defining the value of consultants and their products) and the creation of a specific professional culture based on the cult of difference and the celebration of elitist values both contributed to imposing this rhetoric on the public. This public, made up of high-ranking civil servants, economic leaders, graduates, and professors, became convinced by the idea that consultants form a special group or, to use Durkheim's phrase, a sacred group.

3

The Changing Relationship between Management Consulting and Academia: Evidence from Sweden

LARS ENGWALL, STAFFAN FURUSTEN, AND EVA WALLERSTEDT

3.1. INTRODUCTION

It is not uncommon for management scholars to question the work of consultants (e.g. Kieser (2002) and Chapter 10 in this volume). Consultants and practitioners also tend to adopt a similar attitude towards management researchers. Needless to say, these attitudes create problems for the development and diffusion of management research and its findings, since the ultimate justification of management studies lies in their usefulness in helping us to understand and interpret reality.

A number of management scholars do indeed try to build such links by combining academic research and consulting. In this way they play a 'liaison role' (Galbraith 1973, 1977) and act as 'linking pins' (Likert 1961) between academia and the world of practical business. They promote the diffusion of management research results and direct many management graduates into the practical field, as well as bringing practical management problems to the attention of management researchers. From their base in the academic world, they communicate with their counterparts in the academic field through seminars and academic journals. At the same time they also interact with the non-academic world by direct contact and popular writings.

Those who work in this way frequently argue that the ideal situation is a combination of consultancy and research. Gummesson (1991), for instance, maintains that the consultant role helps to bring greater depth to the analyses of business studies. He even suggests that if more researchers also acted as consultants, the research produced would be of a higher quality (Gummesson 1991: 7–8). In the same vein, Lind and Rhenman (1989: 167) argue that a 'real theoretical breakthrough [seems] to come out of in-depth consultative work with a few organizations, or often best of all with one'.

However, as already indicated, it is not always easy for academic scholars to be involved in consultancy. It can even be argued that it has become more difficult over time as a result of the specialization of academic research. Adding to these difficulties and even more important has been the expansion of the consulting industry.

Management consulting has become an industry with a number of large multinational, often Anglo-American, players, such as McKinsey or Accenture (formerly Andersen Consulting). These are likely to attract a reputation just through their visibility and their advice to prominent firms. Against this background the present chapter aims to analyse the changing conditions for the combination of academic work and consultancy. For this purpose in the following section we will present a framework of four ideal types. In two subsequent sections two Swedish case studies will be presented, one from the early part of the twentieth century, and one from the later part. A final section compares the two cases and provides conclusions.

3.2. A FRAMEWORK FOR ANALYSIS

An important claim to emerge from post-war organization studies is that the core technology or major tasks of an organization should be a matter of major concern when it comes to organizational design (see e.g. Woodward 1965 and the Aston studies). Whitley (2000) has also drawn attention to this point in analysing the characteristics of different scientific fields. The earlier perception of a unitary science, which can even be seen in a work such as Kuhn (1962), has thus been challenged. Whitley identifies two major variables that are important in differentiating between disciplines:

1. the degree of mutual dependence among scientists; and
2. the uncertainty that characterizes the task.

These two dimensions, which have been successfully used by Whitley to analyse differences between scientific fields, also promise to be useful in the present context. However, they need adapting, since this chapter is not dealing with systems of scientific fields but with individuals who are linking academic work and practice. The chapter will therefore assess the first variable (dependence among scientists) in terms of the extent to which a player relates to scientists in his work. This variable is called research orientation. The second variable (the uncertainty in the task) can be seen as another way of expressing the range of activities embraced by a player. That is, the lower the task uncertainty, the greater the likelihood that the range of activities is limited to certain special tasks, and vice versa. This second variable is called specialization. A significant feature of the latter variable is the closure mechanisms discussed in the literature on professionalization (e.g. Abbott 1988; Burrage and Torstendahl 1990; Collins 1979; Larson 1977; and Torstendahl and Burrage 1990). The higher the specialization, the more likely it is that a player can provide exclusive expertise, and in this way exclude competition from others.

Combining the two dimensions and making a distinction between low and high values, leads to the matrix shown in Figure 3.1, which thus provides four ideal types of consultant: (1) the Practical Generalist, (2) the Academic Generalist, (3) the Practical Specialist, and (4) the Academic Specialist.

Historically, the Academic Specialist is a product of the post-war period and the increasing specialization in academia. At the same time the Academic Generalist has

	Research Orientation	
Specialization	Low	High
Low	Practical Generalist	Academic Generalist
High	Practical Specialist	Academic Specialist

Figure 3.1. *Research orientation and specialization in consulting*

faced competition from consultancies with a broad supply of services. It can therefore be argued that Generalists had a good chance of combining academic work and consulting before the Second World War, but that today there is a need to be an Academic Specialist to successfully be able to create a closure mechanism and thereby make the combination.

In order to investigate the expectations just outlined, this chapter presents case-studies of two Swedish professors who combined academic work and consulting before and after the Second World War. They will demonstrate moves in opposite directions illustrated in Figure 3.1. The first case presents a Practical Generalist who became an Academic Specialist, while the second deals with an Academic Specialist who became a Practical Generalist.

The fact that the cases represent two different periods implies that different methods of data collection had to be used. To some extent the studies are based on the published work of the consultants in question. In the first case, however, the study also relied on archival studies reported in Wallerstedt (1988). In the second case, about twenty people were interviewed, but advantage was also taken of relevant literature (e.g. Carlsson 2000; Stymne 1995). In view of the nature of the cases, there was no attempt to capture the behaviour of the two players in quantitative terms. Instead, the analysis relied on extensive accounts of their development.

3.3. COMBINATION OF ACADEMIC WORK AND CONSULTING BEFORE THE SECOND WORLD WAR

The first case is that of Oskar Sillén (1883–1965), professor of business administration at the Stockholm School of Economics (SSE) for almost 40 years (1912–1951), who served simultaneously as an adviser to a large number of Swedish corporations and public authorities. Sillén's first appointment at SSE was initially combined with part-time work in a consulting organization; later he became the founding father of the Swedish auditing profession.

The First Swedish Professor of Business Administration

Oskar Sillén is without doubt one of the founding fathers of modern Swedish business administration. He was the first Swedish professor at the Stockholm School of Economics (SSE), founded in 1909, and was preceded by only two years by a German, Ernst Walb. Sillén may also be regarded as a model in terms of linking academic research and consulting. He did not accept the appointment at SSE until he had also received an offer to lead a consulting organization (the recently established Industrial Office of the Federation of Swedish Industries). The main reason for this action was not to link academic work and practice, but simply to provide Sillén with adequate remuneration. For about five years after his graduation in 1905 from the Städtische Handelshochschule in Cologne, Sillén had worked in executive positions, mainly for a Swedish company in Germany. His academic experience at the time of his appointment was therefore not impressive; it was limited to two and a half years of study in Cologne (Wallerstedt 1988: ch. 3).

The need for organizational consulting in Sweden around the turn of the century was met in part by the Industrial Office where Sillén worked half time as a consultant, parallel with his professorship. This arrangement obviously offered Sillén excellent opportunities to encounter all kinds of problems in Swedish industry. Private and public clients turned to the Office for advice on bookkeeping, organization, auditing, and valuation principles. The Office immediately acquired a large number of clients. Consequently Sillén was unable to manage the Industrial Office on his own, and more staff were taken on. In response to the problems of the times, a number of new departments were created: the Technical Department was founded in 1914, the Department of Transportation in 1918, and the Department of Factory Organization in 1921 (Wallerstedt 1988: ch. 7).

As the only associate professor of business administration at SSE, Sillén lectured in many fields that might be considered part of the subject. He was clearly influenced by the German approach in deciding which fields these should be. Sillén's publications were on topics closely related to his consulting work at the Industrial Office and to his teaching at SSE. The key idea that he stressed at the beginning of his career, both as consultant and professor, was the importance of cost calculations. According to Sillén, Swedish manufacturers disregarded these calculations because they believed that price decisions were outside their control. He was also very eager to emphasize the advantages of the new technical innovations of the time: mechanical calculating machines, card systems, loose-leaf notebooks to be used in bookkeeping, and various methods of duplication. His ideas were published in several different publications (Sillén 1912, 1913a, 1913b, 1915). They made a valuable contribution to the Swedish literature in the field, which was rather meagre at the time. These publications gave him the formal competence for the professorship in 1915 (Wallerstedt 1988: ch. 4).

One common feature in Sillén's publications was his concentration on practical matters. These not only dealt with problems that were highly relevant at a time when the Swedish industrialization process had just started, but they were also clearly normative.

Since Sillén had acquired his scientific and practical training in Germany, it is not surprising that the inspiration for his publications came mainly from that country. Obviously Sillén's work cannot be judged by the scientific standards of today. It clearly met the standards of the time, however. An analysis of the curriculum of one of the most important German business schools at the time, the Städtische Handelshochschule in Cologne, shows that hardly any theoretical discussions in economics or business administration were included (Wallerstedt 1988: ch. 2). Instead, the purpose of the literature was to inform industry of relevant knowledge within the field. It was also clear that industrialists expected a professor of business administration to help industry by providing practical knowledge. This is exactly what Sillén did.

Some reorientation in Sillén's interests occurred in the early 1920s, when he made a study trip to the United States. He visited universities, business schools, banks, and companies all over America. What he saw impressed him, and his later work both inside and outside SSE testified to the inspiration he gained from this trip. In terms of his research orientation, his involvement in starting a research institute modelled on those at Harvard University and Northwestern University was particularly important. After his trip to the United States he also tended to put more emphasis on the need for teaching in the behavioural sciences at SSE (Wallerstedt 1988: 166–73).

The Professionalization of Auditing

In 1912—the year Sillén became head of the Industrial Office—the Stockholm Chamber of Commerce authorized him and five other people to act as public accountants. They were the first six accountants to be authorized, and can therefore be called the pioneers of the Swedish auditing profession. As a result, Sillén worked in auditing on a professional basis from the time the Industrial Office was set up. In later years these operations gradually expanded and he became increasingly engaged in auditing and related activities. For instance, he was the auditor at AB Sveriges Litografiska Tryckerier, a dominant firm in the Swedish graphical industry, from the inception of the company in 1913. He was thus able to follow the company's development over time. Since he regularly visited the company's subsidiaries all over Sweden, he kept in close contact with its various managers. As time passed, quite an impressive number of other large Swedish companies also sought his services, and Sillén thus became a highly respected and well-known representative of the auditing profession in Sweden, and in other Nordic countries. In 1923 he founded the Authorized Public Accountants' Association (FAR), of which he was chairman until 1941. And in confirmation of the gradually increasing importance of auditing activities, the Industrial Office changed its name to the Department of Auditing in 1930. Most of Sillén's auditing assignments after that seem to have been an extension of consultations on various organizational matters in the companies during the 1920s (Wallerstedt 1988: 238–54).

At the beginning of the 1930s Sillén's most important client outside SSE was one of the Swedish commercial banks, Svenska Handelsbanken. Like many Swedish banks, this one encountered considerable difficulty during the period 1918–23 as a result of its inability to evaluate the future prospects of Swedish companies. Credits granted by

Svenska Handelsbanken to Swedish industry against collateral in shares had expanded very rapidly during the war. Between 1919 and 1923 Sillén thus wrote several reports on the companies in which the bank had an economic interest. He examined the relevance of the content of their balance-sheets and estimated the value of the companies' assets. The aim of his investigations was to estimate the profitability and liquidity of the companies (Wallerstedt 1988: 258–70).

Further Specialization

Investigations that were made after the Kreuger crash in 1932 included some critical comments about one of Swedish Match's auditors. This prompted Sillén and three of his younger colleagues to start an auditing bureau of their own (STEO). They soon took on five more auditors, but Sillén continued his earlier practice of working alone. It was not until 1941 that he employed his first assistant, who was followed by two others after the Second World War.

The demand for STEO's services gradually increased. When Sillén left the Industrial Office, he was auditor for eight quoted companies. Less than ten years later, in 1940–1, he audited a total of 27 companies of different sizes in many industries. His bureau also obtained a great deal of work as a result of various investigations connected with the Kreuger crash. On several occasions Sillén was personally selected as an expert for government commissions on matters primarily concerning accounting, auditing, and legal issues (Wallerstedt 1988: 324–6). Sillén was thus highly influential in Sweden in this area, eventually becoming the grand old man of the Swedish auditing profession. It is particularly worth noting in this connection that at a very early stage he adopted new principles in his work, paying attention not only to accounting figures but also to selling, purchasing, and production aspects. In other words, he paved the way for management auditing (Wallerstedt 1988: 248).

In his academic role at SSE Sillén continued to occupy the only chair in business administration until 1934, i.e. for more than twenty years. For the whole of that time he was supposed to cover the entire field, but after 1934 he was able to concentrate on his own main interests—accounting and auditing. In his later writings Sillén continued the work of his former teacher at the Städtische Handelshochschule in Cologne, Eugen Schmalenbach, who was also the founder of the school of the dynamic balance-sheet. In this way Oskar Sillén was responsible for introducing Schmalenbach's ideas on accounting and the balance-sheet into Sweden. In particular, Sillén's book on new principles for evaluating balance-sheets (Sillén 1931) was read by business administration students throughout Scandinavia for several decades. The book was published in its tenth edition as late as 1970 (Wallerstedt 1988: 208–12, 220–1).

Sillén's books and articles also had an audience beyond the walls of the business schools. This was also his intention, as he always dealt with matters of great practical relevance and his close connections with work in the field naturally provided him with the necessary practical knowledge. It is also worth noting that Sillén endeavoured to tailor his publications to a variety of audiences. Sillén stayed on as professor at SSE until 1951, when he retired from his chair at the age of 68. However, he continued to work as an auditor at STEO until 1955, and then at his own auditing bureau until his death in 1965. After his retirement he was active primarily in the practical sphere, although he did publish a paper on the valuation of inventories in 1954 and another on retirement pensions in 1956.

Characteristic Features of the Case

There are at least five features that are important to note from this first case-study regarding Oskar Sillén. First, he was a practical man who gradually turned into an academic man. Secondly, Sillén maintained a link between practice and academia right from the start with the support of his own school. Thirdly, with the passage of time he became more and more specialized in the accounting and auditing field. Fourthly, he was an early player in this field, who managed to influence its standards, thereby generating a closure mechanism and a competitive edge. Fifthly, he worked on a relatively small scale.

3.4. A COMBINATION OF ACADEMIC WORK AND CONSULTING AFTER THE SECOND WORLD WAR

The second case concerns Eric Rhenman (1932–93), who held various positions in business administration at Lund University from 1965 onwards. In the mid-1960s he set up a consulting organization known as the Swedish Institute (later Scandinavian Institutes) of Administrative Research (SIAR). In the late 1970s this was described by Argyris and Schön (1978: 225) as 'one of Europe's leading research-consulting organizations with a world-wide multinational organization [and] one of the few that is highly sophisticated in conducting organizational diagnosis to assess, and in designing intervention activities to enhance learning, especially of the double-loop variety'.

Clinical Research and Consulting

Eric Rhenman's route to consulting was characterized by rapidly growing parallel careers in the academic world and in industry (*Vem är det* 1993; *Dagens Nyheter*, 6 Aug. 1964; *Expressen*, 28 May 1961). He graduated from the Stockholm School of Economics (SSE) and from the Royal Institute of Technology at the age of 23. He was employed by Swedish Esso (1955–6), and then by the Swedish Nuclear Energy Company. He remained there until 1964, and was administrative manager for his last three years. At the same time he was working with the Swedish Air Force (1957–8) and teaching at SSE (1960–5). He received a licentiate degree at SSE in 1961 with a thesis on management games (Rhenman 1961).

In 1964 Rhenman took up a position at the SSE Research Institute as head of a research group concerned with administration (GAU). At that time he and two colleagues had just published a book on conflict and cooperation in business organizations (Rhenman, Strömberg, and Westerlund 1963, 1970), which was based on a project initiated by the top management of one of the Swedish banks, Svenska Handelsbanken (R5 = Respondent 5; cf. the list of interviewees at the end).

The creation of GAU was an attempt to transfer the American idea of the contract research institute to Sweden. Rhenman had recognized the potential for such an arrangement during a study tour of the United States in 1959, after which he tried unsuccessfully to convince the Royal Swedish Academy of Engineering Sciences (Ingenjörsvetenskapakademien, IVA) to become involved in the project. He eventually succeeded in obtaining support from the Swedish Council for Personnel Administration (PA-Rådet) and the Stockholm School of Economics (R5). The main purpose of the organization was explained by Rhenman in a newspaper interview (*Svenska Dagbladet*, 5 Aug. 1964; translation by the authors) as follows: 'We need a better understanding of the way companies behave, so that we can evaluate the effects of different operations; we also need to develop better instruments for managers to work with. The aim of this research group is to develop useful tools for managers involved in long-term planning, and if necessary to train them.'

In another interview, Rhenman emphasized that clients should be given the opportunity to influence the direction of research, thereby generating relevant and important work. He also thought it was likely to be the most successful kind of research. However, Rhenman's approach proved to be controversial at SSE, since the policy of the school at that time was to maintain the boundaries *vis-à-vis* consulting by requiring that the results of all research projects be published (Söderlund 1989: 50; R3). The group and its activities thus left SSE, and created the Swedish Institute for Administrative Research (SIAR) in 1966. A year earlier Rhenman had also obtained a new academic platform through his appointment as associate professor at Lund University.

Rhenman's academic platform was more firmly established in 1967 when he was appointed to a chair in business administration at Lund University. SIAR consequently opened a second office in Lund. Projects in the SIAR portfolio at the time specialized in hospital administration and organizations in the building industry. A significant theoretical concept underlying the work within these projects was the coalition model proposed by March, Simon, and others (March and Simon 1958; Cyert and March 1963). Eric Rhenman became the main proponent of this framework in Sweden (e.g. Rhenman 1968*a*), where it was often referred to as 'Rhenman's stakeholder model' (e.g. Therborn 1966, 1971; Rhenman and Skärvad 1977; Lundahl and Skärvad 1982). However, Rhenman and SIAR found their most important theoretical inspiration in Selznick (1957; R5).

The SIAR group adopted the clinical research methodology at an early stage. There were probably several reasons for this. First, it is not unlikely that the hospital project provided inspiration for such a choice. Secondly, both Eric Rhenman and his collaborator Bengt Stymne had a number of friends in the medical profession, with whom they discussed their research. Thirdly, during the late 1960s there was a tendency to regard organizations as living systems (e.g. von Bertalanffy 1955), and analogies were often drawn between medical and organizational research. Fourthly, it is worth noting that an action-research-oriented Norwegian, Eric Thorsrud, was a member of the

SIAR board. All in all, these factors produced an approach that Mintzberg (1990: 168) characterized as consisting of a culturally oriented conceptual framework, an open-ended style of theorizing, and a methodology based on a few intensive case-studies (see also Lind and Rhenman 1989).

Early SIAR activities were financed by private scholarships, industrial organizations, grants from research councils, and income from teaching at SSE and the universities of Lund and Stockholm. The principle was that SIAR staff members should have a fixed salary, i.e. external remuneration reduced their pay from the organization (R4).

Throughout the late 1960s, SIAR maintained its practice of publishing the results of its consulting activities. In 1968 Rhenman published a study of organizational consultants (1968*b*). The following year, he reported on the project at a Swedish central hospital (1969*a*, 1973*a*), and published a synthesis of long-range planning projects (1969*b*, 1973*b*). The latter was based to a large extent on restructuring projects, particularly those involving divisionalization (see Edgren *et al.* 1983).

Other team members reported project results as licentiate and doctoral theses (Wallroth 1968; Normann 1969; Olofsson 1969; Sandkull 1970; Stymne 1970). These theses also provided inspiration for Rhenman's work. In the preface to a work from this time (Rhenman 1973*b*: v), for instance, one can read that Richard Normann's and Bengt Stymne's dissertations 'have probably been my greatest single source of inspiration'. Thus a research orientation permeated the organization. According to one member (R12), writing a thesis 'was not directly an order but it was that kind of environment. Everybody had scientific ambitions, research was more important than economic considerations.... We were very research-oriented [and] learning was our linchpin'.

These varied academic activities established a knowledge-base at SIAR. They also communicated the SIAR ideas to the scientific world as well as to practitioners. This helped the organization to link up with the international scientific community, as the number of foreign scholars who visited SIAR can testify. Guests in the period around 1970 included Walter Buckley (see Buckley and Sandkull 1969), Alvin Zander from Ann Arbor, and Larry Bennigson, Larry Greiner, and Jay Lorsch from Harvard, each of whom stayed for at least a year. Chris Argyris also visited SIAR for several shorter periods. Some of the guests (Buckley, Bennigson, and Greiner) participated in consulting activities (R12).

SIAR's financing through consulting gradually became more firmly established and a special company—SIAR Planning—was founded in 1970 with the explicit ambition of making SIAR's consulting activities more efficient and professional (R6). Not all of its associates appreciated SIAR's growing consultancy orientation. One of these was Bengt Stymne, who had played a very important part in the development of SIAR's scientific profile. After defending his thesis in 1970, Stymne left SIAR for SSE and a more research-oriented career (R2). Christer Olofsson had also resigned a few weeks earlier, apparently due to the diminishing research orientation (R4). Other resignations followed around this time. In 1969 and 1970 a total of 13 members left SIAR, after having worked there on average for three years. This amounted to almost two-thirds of the organization's staff at the time (SIAR Alumni Register). This was obviously a very marked defection, which some of those interviewed referred to as the 'cultural revolution' (R10–11).

Drifting from the Original Idea

An important reason for the 'cultural revolution' seems to have been an increasing tendency to look at what was going on in competing consulting organizations. Of these, McKinsey appears to have served as the model of a top-quality consulting firm (R12). As a result, a reorganization was undertaken at SIAR in 1971 (Läckgren, Westerling, and Öberg 1989: 15). This development was probably due as much to SIAR's own evolution as to pressure from clients that the organization should exhibit more 'normal' consultative behaviour. Those who stayed tended to be more oriented towards consulting than those who had left. Moreover, several people of a more practical orientation were recruited in the early 1970s, particularly in connection with several industry studies. The research connection was also maintained, however, by recruiting young PhDs or PhD students. In this way the cultural heterogeneity within the organization was enhanced (Läckgren, Westerling, and Öberg 1989: 15–16).

Although Eric Rhenman remained the undisputed leader, Richard Normann became increasingly important to SIAR's development. Previously one of Rhenman's assistants, he now became a partner and CEO of SIAR's consulting operation. Normann also became responsible for passing on the tradition of synthesizing consulting experiences in written form. His doctoral thesis (Normann 1975, 1977), a kind of follow-up to Rhenman's earlier work (1969b), provides the main evidence of this. Interestingly enough this work was not originally intended as a thesis, but was well regarded by the academic community and was successfully defended as such (R6). It has also enjoyed considerable success outside the research context: in the early 1990s it was the management book in most frequent use at Swedish universities (Furusten and Kinch 1993; Furusten 1999: ch. 4). It certainly also helped to promote a more precise SIAR identity. Another contribution along the same lines was a book in which Rhenman discussed organizational problems in society (Rhenman 1975).

At the time, both Rhenman and Normann were associated with the Department of Business Administration at Lund University, Rhenman as professor and Normann as associate professor (R6). This arrangement also meant that there was still an implicit ambition that junior employees should write theses based on their SIAR experience (e.g. Danborg *et al.* 1975). In this connection it was quite important that Normann was involved in the doctoral programme as research advisor and was very active in discussions on methodological issues (e.g. Normann 1970).

Despite this lasting association with Lund University, the early 1970s can be said to have represented the start of a new era for SIAR, with a concerted effort to make consulting more efficient and to stabilize the organization's income. This in turn was linked to the ambition to expand (R11). In order to improve efficiency, SIAR standardized its operations with a regular set of analytical techniques (Lind and Rhenman 1989: 171). Even newer employees could thus be entrusted with diagnostic work. The techniques included the analysis of company history, a product–market matrix, and the consideration of cash flow (R12, R16). The results of the diagnoses, at least in large projects, were usually discussed at internal, clinical SIAR seminars. Many consulting projects in the early 1970s also tended to be larger. Several were concerned with the restructuring of Swedish industries. One of the more prestigious projects of this period was a study of the organization of UNICEF (SIAR 1975), which was, in fact, considered a major breakthrough for SIAR (Argyris and Schön 1978).

Becoming an Ordinary Consultancy

Normann's defence of his thesis in 1975 seems to have marked the end of yet another era in SIAR's history. The research orientation was now further reduced, as can be seen, for example, in the gradual disappearance of clinical seminars. In the words of one respondent (R11), 'the intensive coaching in the ideology of SIAR lasted until Normann's dissertation in 1975, and then diminished'. An important reason for this development was probably Rhenman's decision, at the age of 44, to leave his chair at Lund in 1976, and remain associated with the Department as adjunct professor. He had been a visiting professor at the Harvard Business School for two years (1974–6) and had even been offered a chair there. However, he decided to concentrate on consulting, and declined the offer. As a result, SIAR became even more oriented towards consulting, a trend that was reinforced by the further internationalization of the organization. Although this had begun as far back as the early 1970s, with the establishment of offices in Helsinki (1970), London (1972), Copenhagen (1972), and Boston (1974), this process now accelerated. The earlier establishments were thus followed by offices in Manila (1975), Paris (1978), Milan (1979), and Singapore (1981). Once again, client demands appear to have been the driving-force. A number of SIAR's clients expanded into other countries, and the SIAR management considered it necessary to go with them. Links with specific industries also prompted SIAR to build up its competence regarding conditions and developments in a number of industries world-wide: the forestry industry, steel, shipyards, and health care. This became part of a new approach, i.e. to examine strategic conditions in different industries (Lind and Rhenman 1989: 171–3).

Despite tendencies towards diversification and internationalization in SIAR after 1975, research and scholarly writing were not neglected. For this purpose Rhenman gathered some PhDs and a few senior consultants together to form the SIAR Think Tank Division, a part of the organization described as a place 'where you don't earn money, but you do become famous' (R11). Another part of the organization with a similar purpose was SIAR II, or the SIAR Societal Organization, in which two long-time employees were active.

Rhenman himself appears not to have been very involved in the think-tank. Instead he was working mainly on his own on a book with the preliminary title 'Corporate Growth Mechanisms', which was intended as a follow-up to his 1969 book on long-range planning. However, it was never published, probably because he was afraid of revealing too many of SIAR's business ideas to competitors (R11). It is also likely that the work of developing SIAR into an internationally respected consulting firm had a negative influence on Rhenman's writing at this stage of his career.

Thus scientific production noticeably diminished in the late 1970s. At the same time, it seems clear that the organization was more competent than it had been in the

1960s. But the amount of time and interest devoted by SIAR consultants to academic literature seems to have declined drastically. Two factors probably lay behind this development: first, tougher competition for projects, and secondly, rising standards in the academic world (R12). It therefore seems fair to say that none of SIAR's publications after 1975 were at the research frontier in the way that they had been around 1970.

One effect of the changes during the third SIAR period was that some very senior people resigned, among them Richard Normann, a SIAR associate since 1967. In 1979 he had started the International Management Group for Services (IMS), which he took with him when he left SIAR in April 1980 to create his own consulting bureau, the Service Management Group (R6). His work there eventually led to the publication of a book on service management (Normann 1984).

In the early 1980s another group of long-time associates with a decade or more at SIAR behind them also left the organization. The consulting culture now seems to have won out at SIAR, which had developed into an ordinary consulting organization. Eric Rhenman made this clear in an interview in 1988, when he stated frankly: 'We have finished training professors!' (Bengtsson and Skärvad 1988). Very few publications now appeared from SIAR. In the last one (Andersson *et al.* 1982), six authors discussed the possibilities of using reorganizations for strategic purposes. This clearly adheres to the ideas developed at SIAR both before and after Rhenman's work in the late 1960s (1969*b*), but Rhenman himself was not altogether happy about this publication. Again there was the question of whether or not SIAR's business secrets should be revealed (R10–11).

As part of its increasing 'normalization', SIAR acquired a logistics company and a computer consulting company (Läckgren, Westerling, and Öberg 1989: 16). SIAR's internationalization also continued. Rhenman, who had lived in Boston since 1981, even came to the conclusion that SIAR could not survive on its own due to global competition. He therefore arranged a merger between SIAR and the French consulting firm Bossard. In 1991 this new constellation was among the thirty largest consulting firms in the world. It was the fourth largest management consulting firm in Sweden with a turnover of SEK 76.5 million. In terms of competence and geographical representation, the two partners complemented each other (*Affärsvärldens konsultguide* 1992: 8–11). This was the situation in early 1993 when Eric Rhenman suddenly died at the age of 60. At the time he was still active as Vice Chairman of the Board in the recently created SIAR–Bossard. In 1998 the consultancy became part of Cap Gemini which, after acquiring the consulting arm of Ernst & Young in 2000, is one of the world's largest professional services firms.

Characteristic Features of the Case

If one compares Rhenman with Sillén, one finds that they differ in terms of the five features discussed above. First, Rhenman, although he had remarkable practical experience for a modern Swedish university professor, was initially basically an academic man. Secondly, Rhenman did not have support from his school for the link between practice and academia: on the contrary, his efforts were questioned. Thirdly, with the passage of time, he moved into broader and broader management problems, thereby moving away from specialization and the possibility of creating a closure mechanism. Fourthly, he was acting at a time when competition from other players had become fiercer. Fifthly, over the years his consulting business developed into a large-scale organization.

3.5. DISCUSSION AND CONCLUSIONS

The cases represent two patterns that are, in essence, diametrically opposed responses to the dilemma of combining academic work and consultancy. Oskar Sillén, who ranked low in research orientation and specialization at the beginning of his career, but proceeded gradually towards a stronger research orientation and greater specialization, was able to maintain this link. Eric Rhenman, on the other hand, reduced both his research orientation and his degree of specialization, and appeared to have problems in doing this. In explaining the differences between the two cases it appears important to point out changes that had occurred in the two fields of management before and after the Second World War, i.e. in management research and management consulting.

Changes in Management Research

In terms of changes in management research it is important to note that Oskar Sillén took over the chair at SSE as the first Swedish professor in 1912 and remained in that position until 1951, while Eric Rhenman started his academic career in 1964 and was appointed to a chair in business administration at Lund University in 1967. The time-span between the two players is about 50 years and it is obvious that management research had changed, both in its research orientation and in its specialization, during these years.

At the beginning of the century there were no academic scholars in the field of business administration in Sweden. When the SSE was founded in 1909 the uncertainty about how to arrange these studies was accordingly very high. To reduce this uncertainty, the school was largely patterned on the German business schools of a decade before. Besides arranging studies within the discipline, the object of the first professors in business administration was the development of what Whitley (2000) has called a 'reputational work organization', that is, developing a form of intellectual and social organization distinct from those of other sciences. In order to develop these rites of passage there needs to be a substantial number of producers of knowledge in a specific field. Since until the 1940s there were just three professors of business administration in Sweden, it seems quite natural that this process took time.

It is obvious that those who supported the launch of an academic education in business administration (businessmen and industrialists) at SSE had specific expectations of the new business school. They expected it to help them to solve their practical problems. The students must not appear too theoretical to their prospective employers. A professor in business administration accordingly had to be a man with practical experience in the field of business. This conclusion is supported by the fact that, in the reports from the evaluation committees to the chairs in business administration, practical experience was considered an important qualification for a professorship. It even outweighed scientific output, since the first professor, Sillén's predecessor Ernst Walb, was appointed although he had not produced any scientific works. This feature was noticeable until the beginning of the 1950s, even though the candidates from the beginning of the 1930s were able to present more extensive academic records than they had been able to do in the first centuries of this decade (Engwall 1992: 76–9).

The situation in 1967 was quite different. There were sixteen chairs, and the number of institutions had grown from one in 1909 to five in 1967. This meant that business administration had now started to penetrate the academic world in Sweden. The reports from the evaluation committees to the chairs in business administration no longer pointed to the importance of practical qualifications. After 1960, in fact, all qualifications other than the scientific had disappeared from the evaluation reports (Engwall 1992: 81–3).

Still further evidence of the differences in the academic world between the two cases is the attitude of SSE towards consultancy. At the time of Sillén the school did not regard the combination of an academic career and consulting as problematic. This in turn seems to have been due to SSE's weak bargaining position at a time when the supply of candidates for chairs in business administration was rather small, combined with the fact that this solution harmonized with expectations drawn from industrial life. In this way Sillén came to be the first management consultant in Sweden. At the time of Rhenman, on the other hand, the combination was rejected because of the necessity of publishing all research results.

In terms of the model in Figure 3.1, it is evident that in the first decades of business administration most professors or professorial candidates were closest to the north-west corner of the matrix, while by the 1960s they were to be found in the north-east or south-east corner. According to the development within the subject, the majority of the professors had increased their research orientation in keeping with the standards that had gradually developed in their field.

Changes in Consulting

A second very significant difference between the two cases is that consulting developed considerably in Sweden in the post-war period. At the time of Sillén his consulting operations at the Industrial Office did not have much competition, while Rhenman faced a totally different kind of environment. In 1948 an association for Swedish management consultants was formed. One of the prominent members was Ekonomisk företagsled-ning, founded in 1943. Another sign of the increasing demand for consultants was the establishment in the 1950s of foreign consultants in Sweden. Of these the American Maynard MEC, established in Stockholm in 1956, was particularly successful. Other foreign consultancies started operations in Sweden from their offices in other countries. In the 1980s they became more active in Sweden through the establishment of local offices. Among them was McKinsey, which opened an office in Stockholm in 1981. At that time there were, in addition to Eric Rhenman's SIAR, also a number of Swedish players in the Swedish consultancy market. Bohlin & Strömberg, founded in 1961, was the most prominent of these (Furusten and Bäcklund 2000: 65; see also Kipping 1999a).

In the 1980s the competition became fiercer. Many international consultancies tried to establish themselves in Sweden: the German Roland Berger, the British LEK, the American Alexander Proudfoot, etc. However, the late 1980s and the early 1990s were turbulent periods and several of the newly established consultancies withdrew from Sweden. In the wake of this turbulence all the big American and semi-American consultancies established themselves in Sweden: the Boston Consulting Group (1989), Andersen Consulting, now Accenture (1990), A. T. Kearney (1990), Arthur D. Little (1993), Price Waterhouse (1993), Gemini Consulting (1993), and IBM Consultants (1993). As a result thirteen consultancies with an American origin accounted for 81 per cent of the sales of the twenty largest consultancies in Sweden in 1997. This constituted a remarkable change from the late 1980s, when only two consultancies with an American origin belonged to the list of the twenty largest consultancies, representing only 14 per cent of the sales (Furusten and Bäcklund 2000: 65–7).

In view of these changes in the market it is not surprising that Eric Rhenman found a pressure to adapt to the new environment. As time passed the shift towards a less academic approach therefore became more marked, and gradually it seems that research (already completed) was a way to do business. The idea held earlier—that consulting was a means of both obtaining data and acquiring funds for research—was thus replaced by the belief that the money should be spent on the organizational expansion of the consulting business and development of its market position. One can thus discern a phenomenon that has also been observed in other organizations (e.g. Engwall 1985, 1986), namely the conflict between ideology and business that Lodahl and Mitchell (1980) call 'organizational drift'. This drift into a more market-oriented consulting business appears to have been largely a result of pressures from clients and competitors in the organizational field (see DiMaggio and Powell 1983; Meyer and Scott 1992).

The differences in the market implied that Sillén managed to develop a competence that could to a large extent be protected from competitors. In fact he was such an expert that he could set the standards in his field, as well as transforming his expertise into professional status by creating the Authorized Public Accountants' Association. This situation provided Sillén with the opportunity to create a closure mechanism and a position of power, which also had positive repercussions on his academic status. This, of course, was also reinforced by the fact that the number of professors in the field at that time was very small.

Rhenman was not able to develop a closure mechanism, although he tried to develop a niche by building up a special kind of client confidence in his consulting business due to its connection with scientific work. In order to cultivate this image, however, he and his associates had to communicate their research results continuously to the research community. This meant that Rhenman feared that their unique competence would become common knowledge, and that competitors could easily adopt SIAR's ideas. Consequently, with the passage of time, the enthusiasm for publishing withered. However, in view of later developments in the wake of the publication of Peters and Waterman (1982), with consultancies supporting their business by publications, it appears as if Rhenman was just a bit before his time.

Implications

The evidence presented in the present chapter suggests that the linking of academic research and consulting has become more difficult over time. This is as a result of developments in both the academic field and in consulting. Over the passage of time both fields have become more professionalized. In academia the selection criteria have become more and more strict. Practical experience, which was appreciated at the beginning of the century, has gradually been downgraded as a criterion for academic promotion. Simultaneously, professors, who like to work as consultants, have faced strong competition from large transnational consultancies with considerable resources to offer expertise in a wide range of areas. By sheer size these players can be expected to provide role models for others, a circumstance which in turn will make it difficult to be different.

Despite these changes in the academic and consulting environments one can still observe a number of management professors who have been successful in consulting: Robert Kaplan, Henry Mintzberg, and Michael Porter to mention just a few. For all of them it appears that popular publication of their research ideas has played an important role in their success. This in turn points to another feature of the relationship between management research and management consulting, i.e. management publications. As mentioned above it appears as if Eric Rhenman was on the right track with his publishing ambitions. However, at the time the symbiosis between academia, consulting, and the media had not developed to the extent it now has. Nowadays media exposure constitutes an important feature for the positioning of both transnational consultancies and professors involved in consulting.

INTERVIEWS

The following is a list of all those interviewed for this research in alphabetical order. They were selected on the basis of their relationship to SIAR. Interviews lasted between one and two hours and were documented in protocols, which were fed back to the interviewees for comments and corrections. The reference numbers in the text [R1, R2, R3, etc.] refer to these protocols.

Olof Arwidi, telephone interview on 18 February 1993 by Lars Engwall.
Malcolm Borg , interview on 28 January 1993 by Staffan Furusten.
Bengt Brodin, interview on 18 February 1993 by Staffan Furusten.
Lars Bruzelius, interview on 9 February 1993 by Lars Engwall and Staffan Furusten.
Rune Castenäs, telephone interview on 15 February 1993 by Lars Engwall.
Jan Edgren, interview on 12 February 1993 by Lars Engwall and Staffan Furusten.
Henrik Fock, interview on 26 January 1993 by Staffan Furusten.
Christer Kedström, telephone interview on 16 February 1993 by Lars Engwall.
Curt Kihlstedt, telephone interview on 9 February 1993 by Lars Engwall.
Bertil Näslund, telephone interview on 11 February 1993 by Lars Engwall.
Richard Normann, telephone interview on 16 January 1993 by Staffan Furusten.
Christer Olofsson, telephone interview on 21 December 1992 by Lars Engwall.
Eric Rhenman, interview on 15 January 1993 by Lars Engwall.
Per-Hugo Skärvad, interview on 9 February 1993 by Lars Engwall and Staffan Furusten.
Sten Söderman, interview on 19 February 1993 by Lars Engwall and Staffan Furusten.
Bengt Stymne, interview on 12 November 1992 by Lars Engwall.
Christer Wallroth, interview on 4 February 1993 by Lars Engwall.

4

Management Consultancies in the Netherlands in the 1950s and 1960s: Between Systemic Context and External Influences

LUCHIEN KARSTEN AND KEES VAN VEEN

4.1. INTRODUCTION

During the twentieth century an institutionalized field of management knowledge slowly emerged. This field rapidly grew in size in the 1980s and 1990s. The number of people involved in all kinds of management activities increased quickly, as did the number of consultancy offices; business schools multiplied within and outside universities; periodicals increased in number; and finally gurus began to populate the spectrum. In this field, managers, consultants, government officials, and scientists are the four main categories of agents who together form a kind of community which carries the knowledge on management issues. This contribution will focus on some earlier stages of development in this field: the activities and interrelation of consultancies and social scientists in the 1950s and 1960s.

Before entering into detailed analysis, the chapter will first briefly discuss some theoretical background. The reason for this is that the four categories of agents in the knowledge community are mutually dependent. These subgroups of agents were involved in an ongoing structural process that resulted in the institutionalized field of management issues as we know it today.[1] This institutionalized field has a varied and ever-changing character through time and space as agents interact with each other and

The authors would like to thank Rolv-Petter Amdam, Lars Engwall, Matthias Kipping, and Robert Locke for comments on an earlier version of this chapter. They are grateful to Henny Poelman, who assisted at many stages of the process, and are also indebted to Jan Verschoor (Berenschot), F. Haselhoff (Berenschot), A. Ribourdouille (Dutch MTM Association), R. A. J. van der Moolen, and C. A. M. Mul (both Liaison Committee), for providing much useful information. The usual disclaimer applies.

[1] Galaskiewicz (1991: 293) describes such a process as follows: 'Our focus ... is on how, within organizational fields, programs or rule systems come about which are neither imposed by external authorities nor absorbed from the larger culture, but rather are built or created by system participants and lead actors to pursue collective goals'. DiMaggio (1991: 267) makes a similar statement which is closely related to the approach

create a configuration of relations (Bourdieu 1993a). Institutionalized fields can take different forms which can be clearly observed in terms of management issues.

This chapter will explore the role and position of consultants in the constitution of the Dutch field of management knowledge and how the development of this category was closely connected to the way the Dutch government intervened in the field. We will therefore take into consideration the 'systemic context' (Lundvall 1992; Kipping 1996). The development of the field shows specific patterns of interaction over time in which ideas are adopted, modified, and adapted (Benders and Van Veen 2001). This is especially apparent when management knowledge stems from other systemic contexts such as another country—for example the United States—and is being transferred into other countries—such as the Netherlands. As Alvarez (1998: 42) underlined: 'there is no adoption of ideas by social groups without adaptation of these ideas to the local cultural assumptions, ideological views and interests of social groups'. The nature of the recipient culture and general societal environment affects the way new practices are received and applied in the new context. This chapter will concentrate on the consultants with an 'engineering' and 'social science' background as distinctive agents and describe how they defined themselves in transferring and translating management know-how. It will underline how the two subgroups of consultants developed after the Second World War in the local Dutch situation and how they translated and transformed management ideas.

Part of the institutional field was already in place when, after the Second World War, the constitution of a new field of management knowledge took shape in the Netherlands. As will become clear, the Dutch government played a remarkable and sometimes decisive role, similar to that of the government in France (Djelic 1998: 205–7), in the construction of the new field.[2] Within the circle of consultants, those with an engineering background took the lead, the social scientist as consultant increasingly manifested himself only after the mid-1950s. However, before presenting these details, we should sketch in the background of the Dutch knowledge field by describing its pre-war development.

4.2. THE PREMISES FOR DUTCH MANAGEMENT CONSULTING IN THE POST-WAR PERIOD

The first signs of the emergence of a Dutch knowledge community on management issues was probably the establishment of the first bookkeeping firm in 1883 (De Man

adopted in this chapter: 'to understand the institutionalization of organizational forms, we must first understand the institutionalization and structuring of organizational fields. Where institutional process has the greatest impact on organizational change, such fields are not simply investigators' aggregative constructs, but are meaningful to participants and include specialized organizations that constrain, regulate, organize, and represent at the level of the field itself'.

[2] This chapter will, to a large extent, leave the Dutch universities aside because they played a highly ambivalent role and initially played an indirect role as the field developed. For further details see Baalen and Karsten (2000).

and Karsten 1994). Accountancy started to develop slowly in the following decades. After the First World War, the field of management began to proliferate more significantly in the Netherlands. Most interesting in this period was the role of engineers. Civil engineers were trained at the Polytechnic School of Delft in subjects like bookkeeping, economics, business administration, and social hygiene. These educational efforts culminated in the foundation of the first management consultancy firm in the Netherlands by two alumni of Delft, Ernst Hijmans and Vincent W. van Gogh, a nephew of the famous painter.

Dutch Consulting before 1945

In 1922 Berend Willem Berenschot joined Hijmans and Van Gogh. Berenschot became one of the prominent actors in the shaping of the field. He strived for a different reputation for consultants who were, up till then, mainly seen as speed-up drivers and reorganizers. He therefore actively supported the establishment in 1925 of the Dutch Institute for Efficiency (Nederlands Instituut voor Efficiëncy, NIVE), which could enhance public relations about the new role of consultants and spread the available management knowledge within the Dutch business community. In the 1930s the consulting branch was mainly coloured by the activities of these engineers. However, some initial signs that social scientists were becoming active could be observed in the field, such as the foundation of the Dutch Institute of Preventive Medicine (Nederlands Instituut voor Preventieve Geneeskunde, NIPG) and the Dutch Foundation for Psychotechnics (Nederlandse Stichting voor Psychotechniek, NSP). With the establishment of these two institutes and the emergence of consultancy firms outside the engineering tradition, the first institutionalized structures of management know-how in the Dutch knowledge field were put into place.

Contextual Developments in the Late 1940s

The Dutch economy had been severely damaged during the Second World War. 'Everybody important in the Dutch policy-making elite agreed that unemployment could only be avoided if the country embarked upon a program of rapid industrialisation' (Visser and Hemerijck 1997: 92). The Dutch government embarked on a major publicity campaign to restore a productive work attitude (De Vries 1997). It decided to establish the Initiating Committee on Labour Productivity in 1946 (Gosselink 1988). This general increase in concern for productivity was remarkable in a society characterized by a high level of social and political compartmentalization—or pillarization— among the four main social groups of the population—Protestants, Catholics, Social Democrats, and Liberals. Dutch society was structured along the lines of these four different and independently organized groups. Contacts between the group members were rare in daily life, except at the political and governmental level, where mutual relations were arranged (Van Iterson and Olie 1992), and which subsequently enhanced its peculiar synthesizing position.

A policy of sobriety and hard work was accompanied by a centralized low-wage policy. Stimulating production was the main goal in order to solve all kinds of important production shortages. In this context, the announcement of Marshall Aid was enthusiastically welcomed. Industrial production increased by 40 per cent from 1947 to 1952, by which time it had returned to the pre-war level (De Haan 1992). In this period the government installed a Technical Assistance Working Group in November 1948 to implement the Technical Assistance Programme; it replaced the former Initiating Committee on Labour Productivity. The Working Group was transformed into the Liaison Committee for the Improvement of Productivity (Contactgroep Opvoering Productiviteit, COP) in 1950. The Liaison Committee consisted of 13 regional productivity centres and organized 29 business meeting days over a period of nine years. During the meetings, people from the business community met and discussed issues such as productivity, cost price calculation, human relations, and work instructions, based on guidelines prepared by NIVE.[3] These business meeting days were specifically for different agents to discuss their strategic behaviour and frame it *vis-à-vis* others. They therefore became a concrete example of the framework of the knowledge field (cf. Fligstein 1997: 35).

The Liaison Committee brought knowledge about productivity very explicitly to the attention of specific companies and industries (Roholl 1992: 112). To enhance the diffusion of knowledge the Liaison Committee initiated research, propagated training programmes, and installed working groups to cover several aspects of productivity (Inklaar 1997: 60). Consultants played an important role in the distribution of ideas and the realization of planned activities. Soon, the Liaison Committee broadened its scope and decided that productivity increases should be studied from a wider societal perspective: education, management theories, and consumption patterns should be included in the analyses. It monitored the Technical Assistance activities and drew up different projects for consultants as well as for social-scientific research centres.

Put in general terms, the Liaison Committee reflected mainly a diffusionistic approach in which the knowledge transfer from the United States was itself based on mimetic considerations, but created in its institutional setting a coercive pressure on other parties to follow its lead (cf. DiMaggio and Powell 1983: 150–1). The Committee was highly involved in the organizational and technical aspects of the promotion of productivity by dealing directly with consultants. However, it left activities concerning research topics to a special committee: the Working Group on Social-Scientific Research within Industry on Human Relations. Before long translational issues emerged, but they were left to the people who were involved with the application of new practices: consultants and social scientists.

4.3. DUTCH CONSULTING 1945–1960

In order to promote industrial development and safeguard the policy of low wages the Dutch government was convinced that it had to train all kinds of personnel.

---

[3] See *Negen jaar COP 1950–1959* (The Hague, 1960).

This initiative, which was supported by unions and employers, legitimized the idea that the skills that were produced would be regarded as useful by firms (cf. Whitley 1997). But it lacked regular training centres to cope with this urgent demand. Consultancy firms responded to this need and started to offer industrial training programmes for industry. Even before Marshall Aid had been received, the consultant B. W. Berenschot and the psychologist J. Herold, who was working for the State Mines, had become familiar with Training within Industry (TWI) in the United States, and had developed this new method in the Netherlands. At about the same time some other Dutch companies tried to introduce TWI following visits to Britain. Visits became so frequent that the British government became concerned and even complained about it to the Dutch government. Impressed by the sudden interest and the remarks from the British government, the Dutch government abandoned these mimetic attempts and decided to embark on a local approach (Karsten and Van Veen 2000).

The Development and Activities of Dutch Consultancies

With Dutch industry growing rapidly after the War, and the demand for trained personnel exceeding supply, the Berenschot consultancy firm started to expand its work on the introduction of a system of accelerated training. These training schemes were meant to train unskilled workers within weeks and months to a skilled level. The concept they used was actually developed during World War II with the support of Plesman, the founding father of Royal Dutch Airlines KLM. He worked with Berenschot to create internally a department of business psychology to offer another consultancy product to their clients: the selection of personnel (Metze 1994). The training programme was directly linked to a selection programme, although initially no trained psychologists were involved in the selection process. In order to improve on this, Berenschot very soon established links with Géza Révész, professor in psychology and director of the Psychological Laboratory of the University of Amsterdam. Later on psychologists and sociologists were employed to improve the testing and selection methods.

This training programme was quite successful and Berenschot's firm—also called Berenschot—grew quickly during 1949 from 20 to 100 employees. The Liaison Committee supported the extension of this training programme. In the years to come, accelerated training turned out not only to be a national success, but also became a highly valued export product. In 1951 Berenschot carried out their first training assignment in the United States and opened an office in White Plains, New York. Very soon these assignments were called 'Truman's point 4 in reverse', because they sold their consultancy practices to the USA instead of the other way around (Karsten 2000). In the 1960s this office offered Berenschot consultants the possibility of building up practical experience in America and discussing their work with consultants like Igor Ansoff, Chris Argyris, and Joseph Juran to improve their theoretical insights. Juran even became a coach for the Berenschot consultants in the USA. Until the 1970s the office in the United States was very profitable with start-ups and accelerated training, but the economic crisis of the 1970s blocked the further development of Berenschot in the USA.

Another area where consultants were very active was the measurement of productivity. Although this is a classic theme in the consultancy field, it had a very specific flavour in the Dutch setting. In the 1950s the government had a tight control over prices and wages. Wage increases would only be allowed by the government if they were accompanied by higher productivity. This centralized policy created problems within companies because they were not free to increase wages as they pleased. One important way to make higher productivity visible and, as a result, have higher wages approved, was to hire consultants. Consultancy firms with strong engineering backgrounds— such as Berenschot, Bosboom & Hegener (REB), and Ydo—employed industrial engineers to execute these auditing and monitoring assignments.[4] These consultants analysed labour output and matched it with corresponding measured tariffs. In this way, consultants obtained an important position in the institutions which were regulating the labour market. Sometimes they found themselves in a unique position. Consultants were every now and then invited by companies to be present within their offices when necessary, but were not allowed to interfere in the way the firm was organized. Their mere presence was enough to convince government officials that serious study was being done to set up a tariff system and that therefore the salaries of employees could be increased. Meanwhile, the consultants were paid to go fishing behind the factories (Hellema and Marsman 1997: 216).

The strict centralized wage policy promoted the work of consultants not just in this area but in others as well. Consultants also became active in work classification, another area of national interest. Work classification depended on the identification of the main characteristics and content of a job, to ensure that employees received the same salary for the same job. Several consultancy firms developed different systems for classifying jobs (Hellema and Marsman 1997: 220).

Companies' labour studies also measured labour intensity by timing the work with a stopwatch. Consultants were invited to execute time studies, an area in which American practices were well known. Berenschot, Bosboom & Hegener (REB), Ydo, Van der Bunt (who, since 1933, had run a consultancy firm made up of consulting engineers and accountants), Kerkhoven (who had founded his firm after successful publications about time-measurement techniques), and Bureau Univers (which had been established as a spin-off from the Foundation of Labour-Time-Measurements in the late 1940s), sent some staff members to a Methods–Time–Measurement (MTM) training programme, which had been developed by Maynard.[5] In 1952 these six Dutch consultancy firms created—with the support of Philips, Unilever, and the fibre producer AKU—a Dutch MTM society. However, MTM did not become widely popular in the Netherlands. Philips actually withdrew after a few years, preferring another time-measurement method offered by the Work Factor Company.[6]

---

[4] The engineer P. H. Bosboom took Hijner's position when he died in 1943.

[5] By the late 1960s Maynard had become one of the largest American consultancy firms in Europe with about 330 consultants in eight European countries (Kipping 1999a: 205; cf. Volz *et al.* 1955).

[6] This information is due to Dr. I. Blanken, the Philips company historian, who provided the relevant sources, including 'Verslagen Groepsleidersbesprekingen, Philips Nederland, 1951–1954'.

In general, it can be said that in the 1950s the activities of consulting firms were strongly connected to specific institutional arrangements which were defined by the Dutch government. In particular, their strong position in the realization of labour-market policies greatly increased the diffusion of many of the techniques related to productivity and job design that originated in the United States. The same consultants from the Berenschot firm who brought one Dutch technique to the USA were under strong normative influences and diffused these new ideas within the knowledge field. Those returning from the American subsidiary instructed the consultants still working in Holland to make them familiar with American practices. The spread of practices was also strongly stimulated by institutional incentives, such as the wage policies of the government. In this way the Dutch government implicitly used coercive mechanisms in order to spread management practices within the knowledge field.

In the community of consultants, however, not everyone welcomed the straight-forward application of these American practices. Some engineer-consultants rejected the narrow-minded Taylorist measuring policies which consultants used to analyse productivity increases and tariffs. In particular, the engineer Ydo resented the lack of any moral element in the studies of consultants and resisted plain Taylorism as it had been propagated in the United States, where measuring productivity with a stop-watch was all that seemed to matter. Instead he preferred to develop calculated tariffs, which meant that he had lengthy discussions with the employees involved and based his calculations on analyses of the prevailing working habits and methods. He did not accept a straight diffusionistic application of time-measurement techniques but insisted on translating them into the specific Dutch situation.

Ydo's criticism, however, was somewhat limited because he carried out his analyses in companies with small batch production. Berenschot and other consultancy firms, on the other hand, audited large-scale companies with standardized production processes. In the first case, improvement of organizational structures and workflow preparation were more important than the application of accurately measured production norms (Kijne 1986, 1990). However, the issue itself was given serious consideration within the business community and it was left to social scientists to pursue the matter. Ydo's attempts show that management practices have not always been seen as neutral, efficiency-raising tools which serve the main goals of a company. These practices intervened directly in the existing employer–employee relations, which had been strongly influenced by the national and historical context, making questions about the direct translation of management practices more urgent.

The discussion around these translational issues did not stop the consultancy branch from proliferating further. Some of their junior consultants were trained at a newly founded institution: the Foundation for Interacademic Training in Business Administration (Stichting Interacademiale Opleiding Organisatiekunde, SIOO) that was established on 24 October 1958. Academics with a background in engineering or economics who wanted to become professional consultants were trained at this insti-tute. They were offered courses on leadership, based on American textbooks. It is inter-esting in this context that this institute was founded by a collaborative effort between eight different Dutch universities and agents from the consultancy branch. Thus a close connection between science and consultancy was institutionalized and the Foundation is, even today, an agent with a good reputation within the consultancy field.

Social Scientists as Consultants

The Technical Assistance Programme described above made Dutch industry familiar with the concept of Training within Industry and similar American training techniques. There was general concern to apply these techniques efficiently, although the pressure to adapt them to the local Dutch situation was strong. Consultants helped to improve organizational structures in which production, planning, and training were properly matched to each other. Training within Industry or Business Executive Training (Bedrijfskadertraining, BKT) became quite popular in a number of large industrial enterprises, including Philips, the State Mines, the steel producer Hoogovens, the retailer Honig, textile companies such as Van Heek & Co, Unilever, and in several banks.[7] But some distrust was observed about the rigidity of this American approach, and its lack of attention to the human side of work was apparent.

In particular, the quality of the Human Relations element within these training programmes was questioned and Dutch reports based on company visits to the United States financed under the Marshall Plan—the so-called productivity teams—recommended a cautious approach to adopting American management practices. A proper translation of American practices into the Dutch situation was requested. This kind of criticism once more reflected a broadly expressed consensus in the post-war years that a new Dutch society should be based upon harmony, sharing Christian humanistic principles and norms. Important members of the Dutch business and governmental elites were sensitive to this criticism because of the influence of the European Moral Rearmament Movement, and they feared social disintegration if a purely American approach was pursued.[8] The Dutch government was sensitive to this Movement too and decided to give its Dutch branch—the Truly Serving Foundation (Fundatie Werkelijk Dienen)—the task of organizing appropriate training for foremen, bosses, managers, and directors in the spirit of Christian humanistic and spiritual values.

In 1946 the Truly Serving Foundation had organized a conference with representatives from trade and industry, trade unions, and governmental departments to discuss the future training of bosses and businessmen. The conference paid a lot of attention to Training within Industry (TWI) and the works of the Swiss psychologist Alfred Carrard—a fervent defender of the Moral Rearmament Movement. The conference led to the creation of the Dutch Institute of Personnel Management (Nederlands Instituut voor Personeelsleiding, NIPL) and was granted a national monopoly on instructing the trainers for TWI by the Dutch government. The NIPL offered a training programme

---

[7] Some people were not pleased with this particular translation; cf. Penders 1962: 99. Penders had been head of the department of the State Mines.

[8] The Moral Rearmament Movement was created in 1938 by the American Protestant Reverend F. Buchman and became influential among leading elites in Europe.

for trainers who then applied programmes such as Training within Industry to junior staff members of consultancy firms.

The NIPL had a co-creator, the previously mentioned Dutch Institute of Preventive Medicine (NIPG). After the Second World War the director of the mental health department of the NIPG, Koekebakker, was convinced that only multidisciplinary teams were capable of research in accordance with the new guidelines on mental well-being within firms.[9] He pursued a policy of cooperation between medical doctors and social scientists at the University of Leiden and established strong links with the Liaison Committee for research projects financed by the Marshall Plan. He even became chairman of the Liaison Committee's Working Group for Social Scientific Research on Human Relations (COP werkgroep sociaal wetenschappelijk onderzoek binnen de industrie) and had direct contact with government authorities.

To reinforce its research capacities in the area of mental well-being, the NIPG began to establish linkages with the Tavistock Institute of Human Relations in London, which had been created in 1946 with a grant from the Rockefeller Foundation, and the Research Centre for Group Dynamics and the Survey Research Centre, both at the University of Michigan in Ann Arbor. From the Tavistock, they imported sociatry, originally coined by Moreno as sociometry (Guillén 1994: 63), as a psycho-social intervention practice based on applied social research to improve the 'health' of the relations between company members (Hutte 1966). NIPG accepted the moral over-tones of the Moral Rearmament Movement and the pressure to translate the Training within Industry techniques to the Dutch context and train the trainers accordingly. But for its scientific research it was clearly inspired by the scientific developments at the Tavistock and the research centres of Ann Arbor. The NIPG obtained a central position in the knowledge field and promoted applied scientific research based on methods coming from Anglo-Saxon countries. However, the translation of many practices was discussed in terms of their applicability in the Dutch context. Besides the diffusionistic overtones, the translational problems became strongly underlined amongst this group in the knowledge field, and attention was paid to the moral aspects of the application of new management practices.

Pillarization and the Consulting Market

Both the NIPG and the NIPL became highly influential in the Dutch economy through their involvement with the Liaison Committee. However, other research-based consult-ancy firms were also active and became equally important. To understand why, we have to refer once more to the pillarized nature of Dutch society. According to Van Elteren (1992: 157), 'this pillarized system … offered ample opportunities for the psy-chosocial sciences and associated practices. At that time within industry too, the rule that people of one's own side should be favoured applied to a great extent. This con-tributed much to the deep penetration of these sciences into Dutch society'. This had

---

[9] J. Koekebakker subsequently became professor of social psychology at the University of Amsterdam.

specific implications for the proliferation of the field. In particular, the Catholics and Protestants wanted to have their own consultancy firms based on their own religious denomination.

Before 1940 some scientists were already active in practical work in psychotechnics. This had led to the creation of several institutes, such as the Dutch Foundation for Psychotechnics in 1928, but they were only focusing on selection procedures for individuals and occupational choices and were not yet addressing organization problems. After the war this situation changed completely. One illustration of this effort to create a more dense, but fragmented field of institutions is the Catholic University of Nijmegen, created in 1923, which decided in 1946 to establish a para-university institute to offer paid consultancy activities. The new institute sought to support the restoration of Dutch society through applied psychology, to reinforce the position of the catholic religion in Dutch society, and to promote scientific research (Van Ginneken 1994). The Catholic University knew that in the pillarized Dutch society the Protestant Free University of Amsterdam already had its own laboratory for applied psychology and that the Catholics could not lag behind. In 1947 it created, together with the Catholic Polytechnic of Tilburg, the Joint Institute for Applied Psychology (Gemeenschappelijk Instituut voor Toegepaste Psychologie, GITP). At the opening ceremony, not only representatives of the Catholic Church were present, but also officials of the Ministries of Economic Affairs, Social Affairs, and Education. Their presence illustrated the importance the government attached to this kind of initiative.

The first clients of the GITP were companies such as the Dutch Railway Company, retailer Vroom & Dreesmann, Philips, and a professional textile school. GITP reviewed and selected applicants for companies. Once big companies began to install personnel departments themselves, the demand for this activity declined; GITP shifted its portfolio and started to focus on the selection of managers at all levels, as well as offering a programme for individuals to select their ideal profession and developing a full range of training programmes.

GITP was eager to become involved in Training within Industry projects because it was afraid that non-Catholics would not train Catholic bosses, foremen, and supervisors properly. In order to pursue this target effectively, GITP, together with other Catholic research institutes, developed some research proposals concerning the selection, training, and tasks of bosses and foremen, as well as a project on the problems of adjustment to industry (labour neurosis) in close cooperation with the Liaison Committee. The Committee approved the proposals and assigned the budgets, but it forced the Catholic institutes to cooperate with institutes of other denominations.

In this way, a dense network of consultancy firms and research centres emerged, which proliferated partly along the lines of the pillars. The Liaison Committee propagated contacts across the boundaries of the pillars in order to stimulate research. However, the organizations themselves usually found their clients within the pillars they were connected to and diffused American practices only when they could be related to their own moral convictions. As a result of this particular Dutch situation in the 1950s, many activities within the field were implicitly or explicitly coordinated by the government or government-related institutions and all kinds of links between organizations involved in diffusing and translating knowledge were deliberately stimulated.

Like most people within the Protestant and Catholic pillars, the social scientists in these groups worried about the ways in which Christian-humanistic and spiritual values could be safeguarded after the outbreak of the Cold War. Although fear of communism was felt in large parts of society, many intellectuals also maintained a critical distance from what they considered to be the materialism and pragmatism of the US way of life and the shallowness of American culture. At that time Dutch sociologists were to a large extent still embedded in the German *Geisteswissenschaften*. Only a few took a growing interest in the work of modern sociologists like Talcott Parsons, Robert Merton, Daniel Bell, and Gunnar Myrdal (Goddijn *et al.* 1977), who were quite critically opposed to Human Relations. Bell even called the manipulative aspect of human relations 'cow-sociology' (Guillén 1994: 72). Academic psychology mainly focused on psychological testing and qualitative diagnostics operated during the processes of selection and occupational guidance. Increasing contacts with the Anglo-Saxon world fostered analysis and prediction based on statistics. Although in general sociology and psychology kept some distance from the 'American way of life', this was not the case with social psychology and the psychology of work (Haas 1995).

In these areas an interesting link with American practice took place. In 1960 about a hundred psychologists worked in companies (Veldkamp and Van Drumen 1988). Many of these Dutch social and industrial psychologists were trained and socialized within the framework of mainstream American social psychology and industrial psychology. However, the application of modern methods such as sociatry assumed typical Dutch moral overtones that sprang from the Moral Rearmament Movement. Dutch social psychologists, financed by the Liaison Committee, became involved in different kinds of research projects. But in the mid-1950s, the general interest in Training within Industry waned (Gosselink 1988: 54–5). Standard American practices did not meet the specific training needs amongst the Dutch bosses, foremen, and managers and did not fit in with prevailing Dutch practice.

At the end of the 1950s the Liaison Office began to initiate social-scientific research activities which analysed Dutch human relations within companies from a broader perspective, taking into consideration the pillarized character of the Dutch society. Koekebakker of the NIPG became the chairman of the Working Group to promote research.[10] He was much inspired by the Tavistock vision that perceived labour organizations as sociotechnical systems for which management needed to balance the requirements stemming from new technologies and the social structure of occupational roles in order to achieve optimal results (cf. Guillén 1994: 239). The Tavistock approach helped Koekebakker to develop large-scale survey research financed by the Liaison Committee. He started to employ social scientists in this kind of research, a policy initially not much appreciated by the medical doctors of the NIPG (Boer 1990: 35). In this way, part of the Dutch knowledge field started to shift its attention and began to

---

[10]   See the website of GITP at www.gitp.nl.

ask and answer its own research questions about human relations in companies. As well as these new initiatives, research centres willingly introduced consultants to new research methods: some staff members of the REB firm, for example, were trained by NIPG to apply research methods based on Kurt Lewin's sensitivity training as it was practised at the National Training Laboratory (NTL) in Bethel (USA) (Hellema and Marsman 1997: 104).

NIPG, GITP, NIVE, and TNO—among others—became highly involved in the research projects being financed by the Liaison Committee. The NIPG managed projects which examined methods to improve cooperation within industries and which studied the improvement of communication lines between top and middle-level managers using sociotechnics as their approach (Boer 1990: 29–30). The report 'What do you think of your work? (Hoe denkt u over uw werk?)', published in 1958 and based on a standard survey of 11,000 employees, had some impact, as several consultancies embraced this issue and set up methods to improve communication within firms. GITP managed projects concerning the proper adjustment of individual employees to industry and gauging selection methods and the training of foremen. The research results were again applied by all kinds of consultants. Another remarkable project was an investigation into shift work. The Liaison Committee presupposed that shift work would promote productivity increases, but there was some prejudice against this kind of work. Scientific research supervised by a university professor undermined these unfounded misconceptions. Several projects resulted in dissertations by researchers who had been actively involved in the analysis of the material that was obtained.[11]

Although the Liaison Committee had used only 1 per cent of the total Netherlands fund of Marshall Aid to improve productivity (Van der Eng 1987), its effects on technical progress and the modernization of management techniques were quite important. The Committee had a key function in the further development of the knowledge field on management issues in the 1950s. Its original focus on the diffusion of American techniques was gradually replaced by the stimulation of indigenous research. The growing emphasis on translating concepts to the local context—as pursued in the social research projects—had a powerful impact. When the American professors Argyris and Cumming reviewed the projects financed by Marshall Aid while visiting the Netherlands for the European Productivity Agency (EPA), they concluded that the Human Relations concept had taken on a life of its own in Holland and that the assigned meanings of the concept were quite heterogeneous. Although the EPA had certainly been a necessary institutional force for transferring information on training techniques and the improvement of management, that in itself had not been sufficient to implement the Human Relations concept as it had been developed in the United States. Argyris and Cumming noticed that in the Netherlands, Human Relations had undergone a peculiar translation and they even spoke of a particular Dutch Human Relations 'hype' (Inklaar 1997: 221). However, things started to change in the 1960s, and although economic growth continued, a slightly different systemic context began to emerge.

---

[11] Examples are Daniels, Mulder, and IJzerman.

4.4. DUTCH CONSULTING IN THE 1960s

In the 1960s, the field in which consultants, social scientists, and governmental bodies had developed particular positions *vis-à-vis* each other, came under pressure due to some contextual developments. Although the economy blossomed in the early 1960s, a tighter labour market made it impossible for the government to safeguard centrally regulated industrial relations. In a short period of time the Netherlands developed into a high-wage economy. From the mid-1960s onwards, Dutch companies were active in mergers and acquisitions, which led to a significant increase in the level of concentration in Dutch industry. At the same time, it became saddled with a series of structural crises within its mainly labour-intensive manufacturing industries. 'In the second half of the 1960s coal mining was shut down, textile, clothing, footwear and leather manufacturing all but disappeared, and shipbuilding began its long-term decline. Tens of thousands of workers lost their jobs' (Visser and Hemerijck 1997: 121).

In this period, state involvement was primarily focused on creating a favourable climate and addressed itself to the Liaison Committee for active participation. Due to the fact that Marshall Aid had dried up, in 1962 the Liaison Committee obtained a new mandate as a consultative body under the Social-Economic Council (Sociaal-Economische Raad, SER) and added to its activities dealing with management and research issues concerning the structural readjustment of several industries and branches of industry.[12] Matters became even more complicated because this period coincided with the breakdown of social pillarization. The Liaison Committee once again sought support from consultants and social scientists.

The Development and Activities of Consultancies in the Netherlands

At the beginning of the 1960s consultants, who as industrial engineers had primarily focused on production, personnel, and other services, began to broaden their scope. The establishment of the European Economic Community in 1957 opened new industrial markets for growing Dutch companies, but the entry of large French and German companies also threatened Dutch markets. An increased emphasis on internationalization changed the focus of Dutch firms from industrial production. They needed more advice in areas such as marketing and corporate strategy. Several industries became increasingly aware of the fact that all types of marketing and strategic management practices were needed. Igor Ansoff, author of *Corporate Strategy* (1965), became a regular visitor to the Netherlands to explain to the business community what strategy was all about. Shell, Philips, Unilever, and Hoogovens soon developed strategic planning departments and asked their internal company consultants to promote the development of new company structures.

Some indigenous Dutch consultancy firms responded quickly to the new interest in marketing and strategy. Berenschot set up a marketing group, which received many

---

[12]　The SER was founded in 1950 as the top of a three-tiered nationwide, sectoral, and firm-level system of consultation. The SER functioned mainly as an advisory council to the government.

assignments in the 1960s that helped Dutch firms to learn about and operate in the European Economic Community. But it went further than that. In 1960 the Berenschot firm entered into a joint venture with John Diebold in the electronic data-processing field. In 1964 the non-profit market, for example health care and the councils of cities and provinces, began to attract its attention. By 1972 Berenschot had a separate health-care division. The firm started to serve financial institutions in 1967, and by 1972 it had captured a large segment of the consulting market for Dutch banks, brokerage houses, and insurance companies (Monroy 1970; Loudal 1973). The firm grew to a size of 300 consultants and was for years the largest indigenous Dutch consulting organization. Around 1964, however, it faced an internal management crisis and partners, such as Twijnstra, left and created their own firms.

Besides these internal developments, there were other international economic processes which forced Dutch consultants to review the products they were offering. With the industrial growth of the European market, some American consulting companies started to set up subsidiaries in Europe (cf. Kipping 1999*a*). These companies followed their clients, which prevented European competitors from dealing with them. Other consulting companies expanded into Europe to promote their own strategy concepts and disseminate corporate organizational concepts. Following a study for Shell, McKinsey had opened an office in London in 1959. 'With its top level organisational studies, McKinsey proved to have the most important and long lasting influence on the consultancy market in Europe' (Kipping 1996: 118). Dutch consultancy firms were well aware of the new threat coming from the American as well as British firms such as Associated Industrial Consultants (AIC), PA Management Consultants, and Urwick International, which had opened Dutch branches in the 1960s. However, Dutch consulting companies had barely developed their own approaches in these areas. Instead they followed a more diffusionistic approach and implemented as craftsmen what was developed by consultancy firms coming from abroad. Economic arguments prevailed while new management concepts in these areas were imposed.

McKinsey, in particular, attracted a great deal of attention. It had established its name amongst the business elite after acting as consultant for the Dutch airline KLM on its strategy and for KZO (Koninklijke Zout Organon—a forerunner of AKZO) on its introduction of a divisional company structure. Mergers and acquisitions amongst Dutch enterprises striving for economies of scale constituted another area in which McKinsey became an important player (cf. Arnoldus 2000). There was, however, one domain where McKinsey and Dutch consultancy companies and accountancy firms frequently met and collaborated. Due to rapidly rising wages, labour-intensive industries lost important market positions. The Liaison Committee promoted sector-specific studies to bring forward proposals for the survival strategies of those labour-intensive industries. Several consultancies—those who for several years had been involved in finding solutions to the problems of the leading firms in dealing with rationalization and efficiency, training, and improvements of company administration—were suddenly asked to conduct sectoral analyses in close cooperation with civil servants from the Ministry of Economic Affairs. They evaluated the survival potential of those industries on the basis of technological, economic, financial, and social criteria. McKinsey was often regarded as the company that set the strategy agenda for the sectors involved. Shipyards were the first area where such research was carried out. Accountancy firms were invited to study the financial consequences of industrial restructuring, to determine the fair value of the companies concerned, and to audit the final results. Consultancy firms specializing in organizational change and personnel issues were asked to deal with the social topics once a plan for restructuring had been approved.

Due to conflicting interests, companies within the threatened sectors did not always accept the blueprints for sectoral restructuring and organizational renewal. This generated new activities for the consulting firms that were hired to offer second opinions. As a result the consultancy market itself expanded quickly. In 1947 there were only 15 consultancy firms registered as members of the National Organization of Consultants (Orde van Organisatie-adviseurs, OOA). This had doubled by 1963; and by 1971 there were about 200 independent firms (Karsten and Van Veen 1998: 99). A Dutch management journal reviewing the development of the consultancy business in Holland nevertheless talked about the Dutch consultants being weighed down by a McKinsey-complex. Apparently the 'outsiders' were spreading an American approach to management with which many Dutch consultants were not yet familiar, although it became quite popular amongst their clients.

The Continued Involvement of Social Scientists in Consulting

Whereas Dutch consultants faced competition from American and British consultancy firms, the social research centres continued to propagate their own version of Human Relations by extending the approach which they had developed in the late 1950s. The Liaison Committee, with its 27 members, continued to play a key role in this extension and commissioned further research in several areas such as management, social integration within the firm, motivation and salary systems, automation, quality control, planning, and labour-market issues. In general many young, recently graduated researchers and consultants were able to be involved in these research topics.

A few of these topics dealing with social-psychological issues drew a great deal of public attention. Social integration within the firm was one of them. Research centres were asked to make comparative analyses of Yugoslavia and the Scandinavian countries to improve Dutch labour relations within firms. Research in this area eventually led to an international conference on Industrial Democracy in the Netherlands in 1969, which was attended by eleven European delegations. Presentations covered issues such as the role of works councils, the integration of white-and blue-collar workers, and responsibility on the job. The results reported were based on field research and company visits in Europe.[13]

Another area of interest that drew similar attention dealt with topics like work classification, merit rating, job satisfaction and pay schemes, job motivation, and job

---

[13] See *Industrial Democracy in the Netherlands* (Meppel, 1969).

enrichment to promote productivity increases, thereby respecting the particular Dutch circumstances surrounding the implementation of these techniques. To share the results with the general public a conference was organized in 1971 entitled The Management of Applied Social Science Research by Productivity Centres. Both conferences had been organized under the auspices of the European Association of National Productivity Centres (EANPC), which promoted comparative studies within Europe and had replaced the former European Productivity Agency.[14]

There was one other area in which some social scientists and consultants began to manifest themselves during the second half of the 1960s. In those years the business community became sensitive to social changes that were actually taking place in society at large (Bergsma 1965). With the growing interest in industrial democracy, trade unions put the government under pressure to commission extensive research on co-determination. Their enthusiasm about the Yugoslavian system of self-management was one of the important issues put forward for further research (Broekmeijer 1968). The issue of co-determination had initially been settled in 1950, when an act on works councils had been adopted, but this act was strongly resisted and the implementation had not been very successful; few employers felt the urge to install works councils. The act had not been designed to encourage the independent expression of workers interests but was meant to contribute, with due recognition of the autonomous function of the employer, to the general interest of the enterprise. The elected council members were to have no representative role on behalf of their constituency since it would betray the view of the firm as a community (Visser 1993). During the 1960s trade unions asked for further research to explore new perspectives on co-determination.

A younger generation of scholars in the social sciences and critics from the left began to raise their voice against the professionals who were working for the social research centres, characterizing them simply as 'servants of power'.[15] They were not convinced that those professionals seriously executed consultation that was agreed not only by the management group but by representatives of the workers as well, as Jacques (1951) from the Tavistock Institute had clearly issued as a principle. A political anti-Americanism arose and subjects like corporate responsibility, co-determination, worker participation, alienation, and emancipation gained popularity. Approaches such as sociatry and sociological studies of shift-work fell into disfavour because they either did not emphasize the technical and organizational aspects of firms at the same time or did not analyse power and conflicts within organizations.

This academic and societal critique put strong pressure on the authorities and a network of radical social scientists that had established connections within the Ministry of Social Affairs enforced the experiments the trade unions had been striving for (De Man 1988). In 1973 a new left-of-centre government announced action plans with respect to co-determination and works councils. The government wished to stimulate

[14] *De COP is een tijd tussen twee tijden 1962–1972* (The Hague, 1972).
[15] The phrase 'servants of power' was coined by Baritz (1960). He argued that social psychology and anthropological studies, and especially the Hawthorne experiments, are paradigmatic of the relationship of intellectuals to American society.

scientifically guided experiments in close cooperation with the social partners to promote industrial democracy. Social scientists from several different universities defending the interest of emancipation became involved in the experiments. This new development diminished the American influence and forced the traditional social research centres and consultants to readjust their earlier approaches. Their perspective on planned change in companies based on order, stable structures, and adaptation had to switch to one of fundamental change. New approaches were discussed, but the oil crises of the 1970s dampened this new challenge.

Comparing the 1950s and 1960s

When we compare the 1960s with the 1950s some similarities and differences come to mind. In both periods the Liaison Committee played a dominant role in promoting and structuring the field of management know-how. Although the systemic context changed, the role of social scientific research centres did not alter dramatically: in both periods they asked consulting firms to execute research projects which offered a sound basis for their own practices.

The role of some of the consulting firms changed from one period to the other. Under the banner of productivity, consultancies focusing on matters of production were invited directly or indirectly by governmental bodies to be involved in disseminating management concepts that were linked to the productivity drive. It was left to them to translate these concepts into local practices respecting governmental policies. In the 1960s many consultants continued their involvement in similar activities. However, some of the consultancy firms—such as Berenschot—broadened their scope and became involved in areas of marketing and strategy too. But they applied new management concepts in these areas in a more mimetic way following the American pattern.

4.5. CONCLUSIONS

Before the Second World War, the first signs of a developing Dutch consultancy branch can be observed. Consultants with both an engineering and a social science background established their first firms. After the war, the field developed quickly and extended in a number of directions, such as the stimulation of productivity, training within industry, occupational choice, and personnel selection. The systemic context in which these developments occurred was strongly determined by the initiatives of the Dutch government and the pillarization of society.

The government established the agenda in the field of management knowledge and organized, with help from the Marshall funds, a central player in the field: the Liaison Committee. Once the Liaison Committee was in position, it started to direct efforts in the field by defining issues, distributing money, and assigning responsibilities to other agents. The Liaison Committee became a spider in the web of relationships and networks within which the activities of consultants and research centres were coordinated. This Liaison Committee acted as a national centre for the execution of the

Marshall Plan and for the diffusion of foreign management practices. It nevertheless demanded that the norms, rules, and regulations imposed by the Dutch government should be respected. As the network between the different agents in this field of knowledge became more strongly aligned, the diffusion and translation of best practice became more successful. Consultancy firms played an important role in these activities. The alignment itself was the result of a properly functioning set of typically Dutch codifying regulations which had not been created within the network itself but were— as the case of the Moral Rearmament showed—imposed externally. Although the Liaison Committee was on the brink of disappearance because of its dependence on Marshall Aid, it was kept alive under the umbrella of the Social Economic Council and continued its activities.

Another important factor in the proliferation of consultants as a separate group was their necessary role in the realization of government policies such as wage developments in the labour market. The pillarization of Dutch society stimulated a further fragmentation of the field as a result of the need to establish similar institutions within different pillars. As a result, the development of the consultancy branch was strongly determined by the directive activities of the government and some peculiar characteristics of Dutch society.

This situation changed in the 1960s. Certain government policies changed and became less directive due to economic developments (such as a new labour-market policy as a result of a tight labour market) and political developments (such as the next phase in the development of the European Union). Subsequent economic restructuring created new demands for managers and added new issues to the portfolio of consulting firms. Issues such as strategy, leadership, the coordination of large organizations, and marketing were increasing in importance. American consulting firms started to enter the Dutch market and Dutch consultants started to diffuse new American practices. The government focused mainly on issues related to the restructuring of the economy, which generated a new kind of demand for consultants. The field became more and more fragmented due to these developments. At the same time, new issues gained in importance. In particular, social scientists were involved in large-scale research involving experiments with co-determination within companies. In the 1960s the government's direct role declined. This was, however, only the first step in this direction. In the years to come, consultancy was to grow rapidly and would increasingly constitute an independent force in the structure of this institutionalized field of management knowledge in the Netherlands.

5

The Rise and Fall of a Local Version of Management Consulting in Finland

ANTTI AINAMO AND JANNE TIENARI

5.1. INTRODUCTION

Modern management consulting is an institution carrying independent advice across time and place directly into the managerial boardroom. The evidence is clear that this kind of modern consulting was first institutionalized in the United States in the 1930s. It diffused into such European core countries as Britain, France, and Germany in the 1960s as an afterwave of post-war American Marshall Aid (McKenna 1995, 1997; Kipping 1996, 1999*a*, 2002; Engwall 1999). Developments in more peripheral countries, where consulting began to diffuse only in the 1980s and 1990s, are less well understood. The studies about the process of diffusion in the latter (Kostera 1995; Amorim 1999; Amorim and Kipping 1999; Furman and Soylu 1999) have usually been largely descriptive and have not enabled generalization about the institutionalization of management consulting beyond the countries studied.

To address this gap in the literature, this chapter presents a historical account of the emergence of management consulting in Finland from the Second World War until the late 1990s. The historical account of the creation of the local version of management consulting in Finland is generally informative about how management consulting becomes institutionalized in countries where American-style consultants lack access to the boardrooms of corporations, where cultural norms resist learning about working with consultants, or where there exist other obstacles to consultants becoming a link for knowledge transfer across managers in different locations.

Most research has focused on management ideas and practices of American origin. This research has emphasized a gradual, linear evolution towards global convergence on the American model of management, at least across countries of roughly equal levels of development (Chandler 1962, 1977, 1990). Within such a perspective, 'firms that produce most cheaply will dominate' (Fligstein 1990: 301). Advances in information technology and other modern analytical and coordination techniques reduce the costs of centralized problem-solving (Levinthal and March 1993: 97–8). In contrast, studies less biased by an American perspective have pointed to the caveat that foreign ideologies and mentalities that ignore the peculiarity of 'economic backwardness' (Gerschenkron 1962) are not always likely to be successful. The 'international environment is a concrete political and geopolitical arena, characterized by multiple, multilateral, and context dependent cross-national interactions' (Djelic 1998: 8–9). The 'dominant patterns of politics and public policy and administration set limits on the repertoire of organizational approaches that is either possible or necessary' (Guillén 1994: xi).

Key individuals and local elites mitigate the transfer of foreign ideas, practices, and consultancies into the national 'systemic context' (Kipping 1996). Local 'great men' (Swedberg and Granovetter 1992: 18–19) and close-knit social networks carry valuable local norms and network linkages forward, synthesize them with foreign ideas and practices, and attract the critical number of followers necessary to institutionalize the integrated system of norms, networks, ideas, and practices. The individuals and networks can, even for an extended period of time, effectively function in place of a model of management originating from another country (Djelic and Ainamo 1999: 635).

This chapter finds that local 'great men' and close-knit social networks are indeed agents of change which adapt the local system to fit shifts in geopolitics, jolts in patterns of international trade, or other such critical changes. They can act as a bridge between extant legacy and tradition and changing convention. They are a local 'pull' mechanism which can mobilize local support for a global model. The chapter makes an important contribution to research on management consulting and, more generally, comparative research on economic and sociological models of management. The argument is that before a peripheral economy can efficiently adopt a global model, it benefits from the personal fiat of local key individuals and a temporary local version of that model.

The historical account of the rise and fall of the Finnish version of management consulting draws from multiple sources of text: economic and business history, the newspaper and business press, archival material from consultancies and various industrial associations, as well as the unpublished memoirs of the single most significant consulting pioneer in Finland (a full source list is provided at the end of the chapter). These items of text were cross-checked through interviews with several of the early pioneers in the Finnish consultancy market, as well as with contemporary actors.

The chapter is divided into an introduction and three main parts: the creation of the local version of management consulting, the maturation of the localized version, and the demise and replacement of that version with one closer to the American original. The chapter concludes with a summary and interpretation of the history. The conclusion also presents implications for further research.

5.2. THE CREATION OF MANAGEMENT CONSULTING IN FINLAND

After the Second World War, Finland was in an economically and geo-politically peripheral position due to its location in north-eastern Europe. The country was to a large extent left outside the post-war wave of Americanization, 'struggling to maintain balance in the Cold War no man's land between East and West' (Kuisma 1998b: 138). Finland struggled on its own to catch up with what represented the core of the global economy—the United States, Continental Europe, and Sweden, the rich next-door neighbour—and only made it in the latter half of the 1990s. However, from the start, a handful of men refused to take any of the obstacles for granted. These entrepreneurial and pioneering management consultants built on the existing institutions, legacies, and norms of the national historical context, used every possible new opportunity that came their way, and crafted a local management consultancy market. This market began to emerge as these men retired in the late 1970s.

Much of the recognition that these men received in the 1970s was forgotten after the invasion of American and American-style consultancies in the mid-1990s. Yet, the passage of time and the lack of modern recognition of their achievement ought not to lessen the importance of these men, but rather underline it. Access to the Finnish system or integration of new and foreign ideas and practices that clashed with the established and complex system of local tradition, legacy, or norms would have been virtually impossible for outsiders. The only option would have been to destroy the established system, or at least to completely ignore it. As it turned out, the process of creating the Finnish version of management consulting did not take place in a vacuum, but was embedded historically, culturally, and socially.

Background

The story can be said to begin in the 1860s, when Finland was a Grand Duchy of Imperial Russia. In the 1860s new railway links to the rest of Russia brought foreign entrepreneurs to Finland to create new industries. For example, they converted the country's abundant forests into timber and paper products for the large home market of the Empire. The early pattern of Finnish industrialization was characterized by scattered mill communities in remote forest areas (Lilja *et al.* 1992; Lilja and Tainio 1996). This contributed to a tradition of paternalism towards labour; management was personalized but authoritative (Fellman 2000). German influences were adopted in, for example, corporatism, a bank-centred financial system, and a German-style educational system.

The model was transformed soon after Finland declared its independence from Soviet Russia in 1917. The newly independent country then experienced a short but bloody civil war. In an effort to bridge the gap between the right-wing and socialist coalitions of the war, the first governments allowed private corporations to grow, but also adopted interventionist policies and established large state-owned industrial corporations.

In the Finnish model, the large-scale forestry industry remained the dynamic driving force across the private and public sectors. The Finnish business elite leading the forestry industry took part in a national search for identity that 'produced strong structures of state-owned industry and entrepreneurship' (Kuisma 1998a: 433). In international correspondence, they identified with European civilizations such as Germany, 'from where they adopted and transferred innovations at an increasing pace and adapted these to Finnish conditions' (Kuisma 1998a: 414). This meant that they talked about their rivalry in the domestic market, but worked together to close the market off from foreign influence. They also cooperated to form export and sales cartels in order to enter Western markets.

With the nexus of Finnish industry in forestry and its process technology, the local search for appropriate management innovations was dominated by engineering issues. Some Finnish engineer-managers experimented with the ideas and practices of Taylorism in their factories. Many found that Taylorism was too American for them (Hernberg 1938; Fellman 2000). By contrast the German version of scientific management—industrial rationalization (Rationalisierung)—had been designed to be responsive to latent labour unrest (cf. Guillén 1994), an important phenomenon in Finland. Hence, it was industrial rationalization, not Taylorism, which gained popularity among Finnish engineers and managers (Kettunen 1994; Interview Kallio 2000; Interview Mannio 2000).

In the Second World War, Finland ended up as the only country to fight both the Soviet Union and Germany. When the war ended in 1945, young Finnish men typically lacked business education or training of the standard of countries that had been spared the destruction of war, such as Sweden. The war had been their leadership school. In the immediate post-war period in Finland, the managerial elite was a tight cadre of men united by wartime experiences. The Finnish economy was in dire need of reconstruction. The Soviet Union demanded extensive war reparations from her small neighbour. The war reparations to the Soviet Union were to be delivered as products of metal industries that demanded large-scale investment. This also strengthened the role of engineering in Finnish industry and business (Fellman 2000). In turn, this led to a revival of the pre-war rationalization movement.

Under Soviet pressure, Finland refused Marshall Aid. Thus, Finland ended up in a peripheral position of little importance to the West. 'Finland's social and economic system, her political traditions and her main export industry (wood-processing) linked her to Western Europe, but the Soviet Union's political influence in the wake of the Second World War was pulling her ever closer to the Eastern bloc' (Kuisma 1998b: 136). Established in 1948, the Treaty of Cooperation, Friendship and Mutual Assistance, though basically a military treaty, became the foundation for economic relations between Finland and the Soviet Union (e.g. Hentilä 1998). Americans also had a language barrier in Finland—German influences and language had predominated for decades in Finnish schools and business—and American investments were few.

Despite the great challenges confronting them, Finnish managers were confident of their ability to cope without direct access to American management knowledge. Evidence of Finland's war success was clear to local men (as in most countries, women were at that time for the most part excluded from positions in top management). Finland had stayed independent, fighting off Russian (and German) forces that were superior in numbers. In their guerrilla warfare, Finnish officers had shown great skills in mobilizing the energy of their subordinates with a mix of authoritarian leadership and a sense of mutual trust and camaraderie. War imagery also prevailed at the macro level. Centralized national negotiations about wages and working conditions between the employers' confederations and labour unions continued. This was a system first agreed in January 1940 in the midst of the Winter War against the Soviet Union (Tainio *et al.* 1999).

The Foundation of Rastor

In 1948 the Finnish Association for Industrial Work Efficiency (Teollisuuden Työteholiitto) adopted a new identity. The Finnish government had organized the Association during the war to ensure the smooth and efficient procurement and delivery of production in support of the war economy. The new name was the Association for Work Efficiency in Industry Rastor (Teollisuuden Työtehoseuraliitto ry. Rastor); Rastor was an acronym for RAtionalization, STandardization, and ORganization. In 1950 the association's administrative board dissolved the association, formalized the short name, and transferred its assets and liabilities to Oy Rastor Ab, a limited liability company. Leo Suurla became Rastor's managing director at the age of 28. He was a graduate of industrial rationalization from the University of Technology in Helsinki (Suurla 1987: ch. 7; Tienari 1999; Interview Kallio 2000).

Rastor was Finland's first management consultancy. It was legally independent. At least in principle, Rastor was supposed to earn a profit. Its shareholders were large Finnish companies, each with a very small share. The managers of these companies did not have the time, expertise, and/or interest to govern Rastor. The small size of the individual investments by the shareholders justified only the most nominal kind of corporate governance. In this respect, Rastor deviated from the partnership model prevalent in management consultancies in the West. In the words of Leo Suurla (1987: ch. 8), 'Rastor was not a profit-seeking business. It was a bunch of people who believed they could create something new, fit especially for Finland's needs'. Rastor and its business were minuscule compared with the needs of the immediate post-war reconstruction period in Finland. Yet few could ignore the nationalistic tone and the way Suurla and his 'management consultants'—as they called themselves—talked about their role in the post-war years. They considered themselves heralds of the 'free' market economy. Rastor's mission was to prepare for a life after war reparations and the war economy (Suurla 1987; Interviews Kallio 1999, 2000).

Considering Rastor's aim of 'creating something new, fit especially for Finland's needs', Sweden would have been a natural model for the reconstruction of a Finnish model of management. Sweden's institutions and social infrastructure were fully intact after the war. There were many links between Finland and Sweden. Swedish was (and still is) the second official language in Finland and there is a 6 per cent Swedish-speaking minority. A significant economic power bloc centred on 'Swedish-speaking money' (Tainio *et al.* 1999). However, the same factors that made Sweden an obvious model made the country unpopular in Finland. Prior to being a part of the Russian Empire (1809–1917), Finland had been a part of Sweden. Yet in the Second World War Sweden had been a non-belligerent, and now Sweden's institutions and social infrastructure were fully intact, while Finland's were not.

Sune Carlson, a distinguished Swedish professor, gave a lecture to Finnish managers in 1950. Most of them discounted Carlson's talk as 'academic humbug'. Perhaps the most positive remark came from the chairman of the event, who thanked Carlson for an interesting 'tam tam message from the tribes of the south seas', referring to Carlson's description of how important it is for managers to pay attention to the 'war dances and rituals of the organization' (Mannio 1979: 2). Finnish top managers assessed Sune Carlson's seminal book *Executive Behavior* in 1951, and were 'struck by how little time Swedish managers dedicate to visiting the shop floor'. They promptly made it explicit that Swedes could not provide the Finns with any kind of model because they lacked 'hands-on experience about leadership at the front' (Mannio 1979: 3).

Post-war Finnish managers were a tight cadre of men who represented a strange mix of wartime camaraderie, local management wisdom, and geopolitical awareness of Finland's position in the no man's land between East and West. Within this context, Rastor and diverse non-profit organizations jockeyed for position in creating new knowledge about management and the organization of work, fitting in with both the era of post-war reconstruction and the pre-war legacy of the old Finnish model. In the tradition of the rationalization movement, most concentrated on shop-floor rationalization and work organization. Contemporary Finnish managers were reluctant to accept advice apart from shop-floor rationalization. But, in contrast to Rastor's rivals, Leo Suurla was determined to convince Finnish managers of the value of the idea of top management counsel. In 1952 he set up Rastor's building and construction department to act as a Trojan horse for this kind of consulting. He employed Antero Kallio, a building and construction engineer, to head the department (Suurla 1987: ch. 7).

Although bilateral trade with the Soviet Union continued to underpin central planning and control, Finland was now pulling out of the wartime economy. The last war reparations were delivered to the Soviet Union in 1952. In the same year the summer Olympics in Helsinki internationalized the social and cultural climate of Finland. The economy and the society as a whole began a reorientation towards the West. The interest of American and Western European companies such as Coca-Cola awoke from a deep slumber. Leo Suurla invited Professor Palle Hansen of the Copenhagen Business School to lecture for the Rastor network. This individual event exemplified a new atmosphere in Finnish business. New Western management knowledge had traditionally entered Finland via Germany or Sweden. The signal sent by inviting Hansen was that Rastor had independent access to management knowledge beyond Sweden and Germany, in the direction of the United States.

An Initial Translation of American Management Knowledge

In 1955 a $200,000 donation from Finnish immigrants in the United States made it possible to invite American management experts to Finland. A coordinating body (TTT American Associates) was established between the American organizers of this funding and the Finnish recipients, including representatives of the Helsinki School of Economics and Business Administration (HSE). Professor Henrik Virkkunen was initially the most active representative of HSE in this endeavour.

In 1958 the Ford Foundation approved a grant of $75,000 to support an exchange of professors in management between Finland and the USA (Amdam 1998). The funding contributed to the establishment of the first 'long' management training programme in Finland. This was organized through HSE. Managers of the previous generation recruited before, during, and immediately after the Second World War still formed the majority of the managerial ranks in Finnish companies. The new business graduates, educated in part with the help of American funding, differed from the older cadre by being more educated, less nationalistic, and on average more capable of taking an international perspective. These differences would become particularly apparent in later decades (Fellman 2000; McKenna, Djelic, and Ainamo 2000), but the first signs were already present in the late 1950s (Michelsen 2001).

By the time of the local allocation of the American funding described above, Leo Suurla had already established a firm position in the social business network. Within the context of the professionalization of management in Finland, Rastor's name and corporate form were discursive advantages in comparison with its rivals. Rastor's identity freed it from the legacy of an association and permitted many degrees of freedom in comparison to more industry-based, education-based, or research-related associations or foundations. Many of these had been created from scratch. With its Finnish experience of at least some version of scientific management, industrial rationalization, and work research, Rastor was a management consultancy with a secure legacy in contrast to many of its rivals. In an example of Finnish understatement, Suurla (1987: ch. 8) describes in his memoirs how he was 'forced to become the Finnish director' of the coordinating body between the American funding donated in 1955 and the Finnish players. The directorship in TTT-AA was critical in providing Leo Suurla and, through him, Rastor with a unique window on new American ideas and practices. It was here that members of the coordinating body conceptualized 'modern' management in the Finnish context. This was taking place simultaneously with the creation of the Finnish version of management consulting.

Faculty members in universities that might have created early alternatives in management consulting in Finland were busy first applying for and then allocating American grants with which to update the contents of their libraries, which still reflected German scientific superiority, a legacy of the pre-war era. It is worth noting that teachers in HSE still had to use books on 'management and organization' that had been translated from Danish in the immediate post-war period. This was, at least in part, due to the tight financial situation of the school (Michelsen 2001). Providers of business education—individual teachers at HSE, but also the Helsinki University of Technology and the Swedish School of Economics in Helsinki—became influenced by American ideas, while at the same time American funding created constraints on their time and efforts.

Leo Suurla and Henrik Virkkunen remained friends, but cooperation between their subordinates soon turned into competition for positions and resources. The new cadre of the American-minded HSE faculty sought to differentiate themselves from those providing management consulting and training services 'without proper scientific grounding' (Suurla 1987: ch. 9; Interview Kallio 1999; cf. Honko 1998). Suurla provided a link between the American top-floor orientation and the need for sensitivity about what takes place on the shop floor. L. Edward Scriven, an American consultant, first came to Finland in the 1956 group of TTT-AA management experts (Tienari 1999). Scriven did not present himself as a management consultant, but as someone who had practical managerial experience (Interviews Kallio 2000; Scriven 2000; Mannio 2000). His personal charisma and hands-on (military) sense of authority provided access to Finnish top managers, who revered charismatic front-line leadership: 'senior managers did not award such access to "young officers" with little experience of the front' (Interview Kallio 1999).

Scriven was a dedicated follower of Peter F. Drucker. He taught Leo Suurla the contents of Drucker's seminal book *The Practice of Management*. Drucker's philosophy became the basis for Suurla's—and Rastor's—consultancy work. Relatedly, Scriven elevated the concept of management consulting in Finland from the level of work organization to also encompass planning and control at the managerial level (Suurla 1987: ch. 9; Interview Kallio 1999). *The Practice of Management* was translated into Finnish in 1959. Drucker's book had symbolic value in the application of American theories to Finnish management and consultancy work. Professor Henrik Virkkunen wrote as follows in the preface to the Finnish translation (Drucker 1959: 13–14):

We are making, if we have not already made, a transition from [isolated] 'tools' of work research, rationalization and standardization to modern management methods and principles as a whole. . . . *It is difficult to translate a book into a language that doesn't exist!* The management vocabulary in Finnish is insufficient—nonexistent in part—and its concepts as yet unestablished. (Emphasis added)

Scriven himself was perhaps too much of a missionary, lecturing rather than listening. Despite the great respect they still held for him, Finnish top managers helped Scriven realize what they had concluded among themselves: a foreign expert's concepts and theories could not be applied directly to the Finnish economy where legacies of the war and the subsequent 'reconstruction' still prevailed. Paradoxically, many top managers who appreciated Scriven's concrete advice on clearly defined issues also considered him too theoretical in making strategic choices. Scriven's habit of producing thick memos and manuals was a source of irritation (Suurla 1987: ch. 9).

Leo Suurla and Antero Kallio wanted Rastor to focus on management consulting in addition to providing management training, while the academic faculty would become predominantly preoccupied with the latter. Scriven began to direct his efforts towards business school education. Since this was a direction remote from Rastor's experience, Leo Suurla and Antero Kallio set out to extract what was practically valuable in Scriven's work, given the Finnish way of working (Interview Kallio 1999). Before leaving in 1958, Scriven did the Finns one last favour. He helped organize Ford Foundation funding for management education in Finland 'according to the Harvard model' (Suurla 1987: ch. 8; Interview Mannio 2000). The Ford Foundation and Scriven designed the funding to assist Finland in developing good management practice and hence to improve the competitiveness of her firms. There was also a geo-political element: 'A strong Finnish economy was . . . necessary "for the maintenance of national independence in the face of Soviet encroachment". The grant . . . "would also have important pro-Western political effects by strengthening links between important Finnish leaders and the United States" ' (Amdam 1998: 378–9).

At about the same time, Leo Suurla learned that the funding for American experts channelled through TTT-AA, including Scriven, did not really originate from 'Finnish immigrants in the United States' as he had thought. The funds could be traced back to a number of American corporations seeking to increase their market penetration in Finland (Suurla 1987: ch. 9). In 1958, with Scriven's contacts and access to sources of funding, Leo Suurla made a study trip to the United States which included a number of visits to major consultancy firms. He learned that an international transition was 'taking place from scientific management to professional management' (Suurla 1987: ch. 9). Suurla wrote a series of articles (1959–61) about management 'direct from the United States, as opposed to being filtered by the Swedes' in *Tehostaja*, a journal published by Rastor and targeted at practising managers.

In 1959–60 Leo Suurla and Antero Kallio heard of an international initiative whereby national associations were setting up the European Federation of Management Consultancies Associations (Fédération Européenne des Associations de Conseils en Organisation, FEACO). Suurla quickly set up a management consultants' association in Finland (Liikkeenjohdon Konsultit LJK), which then joined FEACO immediately. The LJK consisted almost exclusively of Rastor consultants.

5.3. MATURATION OF THE LOCAL VERSION

Leo Suurla and Antero Kallio developed a loose philosophy whereby Rastor would best succeed if all its key individuals were 'competent consultants'. They considered Rastor an alliance of senior experts. Rastor's ownership structure perhaps did not support entrepreneurial commitment in consultancy work, but it was developing a unique profile for running its business (Suurla 1987: ch. 10). Rastor soon gained its first major assignment for consultancy work when Huhtamäki, a Finnish consumer convenience goods corporation, began to diversify and decentralize its organizational structure. Rastor's consultants trained the management of Huhtamäki in the fundamentals of profit centres. Antero Kallio, who was more business-oriented than Leo Suurla, counted on similar larger assignments becoming Rastor's staple fare. In turn, Suurla remained mostly motivated by innovative day-to-day work at individual client sites, based on a portfolio of personal contacts and social networks (Interview Kallio 1999).

An increasing number of major Finnish companies sought to diversify and divisionalize their organizations (Fellman 2000). The general division between a forestry industry oriented towards internationalization and the West and other industries dependent on domestic and Soviet demand persisted in the Finnish economy. By 1966 it was estimated that Finnish companies used as many as 20–30 foreign management consultants, at a time when Finnish management consultants numbered at most 70 (Ritvala 1966). Foreign management consultancies, such as the Stanford Research Institute and H.B. Maynard of the United States, EK Konsulterna of Sweden, and Habberstad of Norway gradually set up operations in Finland. Leo Suurla and Antero Kallio were also aware that, for example, the Finnish forestry industry used British management consultants when it operated in the UK, its main export market (Interview Kallio 1999).

On the surface, many Finnish management consultants complained about how Finnish managers jealously guarded their trade secrets and lacked trust in external experts. Finnish managers considered Finland a small country where everyone knew everyone, and one had to be careful in terms of business secrets (Rothberg 1968; *Kauppalehti* 1968). The apparent appeal of foreign advice triggered bitter comments from Finnish management consultants: 'The breakthrough of foreigners is due to the traditionally great respect for foreign expertise that we Finns have, and to the active offering [by foreign management consultants] of services, which is an alien idea to our domestic consultants, on top of being suspect by international norms, too' (Ritvala 1966: 347).

There was a division of management consultancy assignments in Finland into those carried out by Rastor and those carried out by small independent Finnish management consultants, and a division between domestic assignments and those carried out by foreign management consultancies for Finnish companies outside Finland's borders. The 'infiltration' of Finnish companies outside Finland's borders by foreign management consultancies undermined the integrity of Rastor's Finnish version of management consulting. Some commentators claimed that some of the blame for the breakthrough of foreign consultancies belonged to Rastor and its domination of the Finnish domestic market: 'It is evident that the absence of competition is conducive to slowing down the evolution and utilization of management consulting' (*Tehostaja* 1966: 6).

Rastor needed to break away from management training, to extend its business beyond the particular Finnish version of small-scale process consulting, and to move on into more systematic consulting practice that would enable growth in volume. Leo Suurla and Antero Kallio began a search for an international partner that would help Rastor escape the trap of being a purely Finnish management consultancy. Kallio in particular recognized that there was a need for routines that would be systematic and techniques that would be generally applicable across individual assignments (Suurla 1987: ch. 10; Interview Kallio 1999).

The Establishment of Mec–Rastor

In 1968 Rastor established a joint venture with Mec, the Finnish subsidiary of the Swedish subsidiary of H.B. Maynard. The new firm was named Mec–Rastor. H.B. Maynard and Rastor each owned a 40 per cent share of Mec–Rastor. Antero Kallio was appointed managing director with 10 per cent of the shares, while Eric Bill-Nielsen, the head of H.B. Maynard's European operations, held the remaining 10 per cent. Rastor now concentrated almost exclusively on management training and education. Based on Rastor's legacy, Mec–Rastor was built up to become the market leader in Finland. At first, Finnish business managers were suspicious of a joint venture with foreigners. H.B. Maynard, as an American shareholder, soon raised interest in Mec–Rastor. Maynard brought standardized procedures and techniques to the marriage. These procedures worked to convince engineering-minded Finnish managers of the cost savings and increases in efficiency provided by outside experts. The quantity, size, and profitability of Mec–Rastor's assignments increased almost immediately (Interview Kallio 1999).

Recruitment became easier for Mec–Rastor. Potential recruits had earlier had low regard for management consulting which had an ambiguous profile, and was thus an uninteresting career path. Now Mec–Rastor swarmed with 'good men'. Antero Kallio was mainly interested in recruiting candidates with practical business experience. He encouraged experienced managers to use Rastor as a springboard from an existing managerial position to managerial or expert positions elsewhere. 'Youth was not appreciated as much' by clients as was experience, and there was a need for a springboard, through which to access experience in a new industry (Interviews Kallio 1999, 2000).

Rastor was still owned by a large number of Finnish companies, each with a relatively small share. The case of Marimekko illustrates the constraints this ownership
structure posed for Mec–Rastor. Mec–Rastor was not allowed to rationalize and
restructure Marimekko, an internationalized Finnish fashion firm that had fallen into
serious financial trouble in the late 1960s under managers from the family that owned
the firm. The boards of Mec–Rastor and Marimekko overlapped. The chairman of
both boards was not confident that Mec–Rastor could keep Marimekko's serious problems a secret in a small country like Finland. EK Konsulterna, a Swedish management
consultancy, was given the assignment of bringing in new knowledge about accounting and finance, 'terminating' unprofitable products, and paving the way for the
recruitment of salaried professional managers (Ainamo 1996: 177–9).

To spur growth in Mec–Rastor, Leo Suurla and Antero Kallio 'let a thousand flowers
bloom' (Interview Kallio 1999). If they managed to find a good applicant, they would
let him create a work profile for himself, according to what he considered to be the best
use of his skills (Interview Kallio 1999). Suurla and Kallio worked hard on defending
Mec–Rastor's dominant position in the domestic Finnish consultancy market, and
concentrated on differentiating themselves from other, smaller Finnish management
consultants.

The Marginalization of the Local Version

Finnish–Soviet trade relations grew and intensified, especially in the 1970s and 1980s.
The first oil crisis in 1973 rendered Finland increasingly dependent on Soviet crude oil.
Industrial products were typically used to pay for oil purchases. Trade with the Soviet
Union came to account for over 20 per cent of Finland's total foreign trade. Almost all
of the exports from the metal-working and engineering industries went to the Soviet
Union (Kuisma 1998b). In the 1970s US administrations used Finlandization—or
Finlandisierung, a term first coined by a German journalist—as a negative label for a
country trying to straddle the 'abyss' between American-style global free trade and
Soviet-style totalitarianism (Hobsbawm 1994: 251). Regardless of whether the goal
of the US administrations was to somehow reverse this trend, or whether there was
simply no explicit policy for a relatively peripheral country like Finland, the gap
between the Finnish model of management and its American (and other Western)
counterparts began to widen rather than narrow.

In terms of popular culture, Finland was experiencing a process of Americanization
in the 1970s (Hentilä 1998). In terms of investments, however, Finland was a country
of relatively high political risk. American export regulations prevented American companies from bringing most high technology products into Finland, which further
lowered the status of Finland as a market. Americans were careful not to sell to Finns
anything that they considered to have strategic value. They were often suspicious of
this peripheral and backward market.

Within this context, Mec–Rastor did not develop sufficient international experience. The managers of internationalizing Finnish companies sought out other sources
of American management knowledge. In 1972 the top managers of two construction

materials companies, Partek and Lohja, completed executive education programmes at MIT and Harvard, respectively. When they returned to Finland, they began to internationalize the management thinking of their two companies. The envisaged process of internationalization produced a need for management consultants. Partek and Lohja used the services of Arthur D. Little as well as Mec–Rastor. Arthur D. Little in particular advocated an aggressive diversification of business. The Swedish-based SIAR—Scandinavian Institute for Administrative Research—established an office in Helsinki in 1972 (see Chapter 2, above). In the Finnish market, SIAR's influence grew especially in strategy consulting. Throughout the 1970s and early 1980s, SIAR would present the most significant single threat to Mec–Rastor's dominance in the Finnish domestic market (Tienari 1999).

In the early 1970s the Finnish government adopted an industrial policy whereby it sought to promote regional development of small and medium-sized businesses. A state fund (Kera) and a foundation (PKT-Säätiö) began to carry out this mission, for example by organizing management consultants for its target group (businesses in less developed regions) and subsidizing the costs of these consultants. Mec–Rastor diversified into the new state-funded assignments in small and medium-sized firms, but the overall volume of this business proved a disappointment (Interview Kallio 1999).

There was a recession in Finland from 1975 to 1977, and Mec–Rastor's growth in domestic sales lagged behind target. Fortunately, rationalization and downsizing assignments increased in volume, offsetting the falling value of individual consulting assignments. Finnish companies increasingly competed in the Soviet market on the basis of volume and low cost, which produced a need for efficiency-seeking assignments for management consultancies such as Mec–Rastor. Mec–Rastor began working on management consulting related to bilateral trade between Finland and the Soviet Union, which was still growing in volume. Leading Finnish companies, such as the forestry industry firms and Huhtamäki, Partek, and Lohja continued to expand their business in the West. They hired international management consultancies for assignments that were large, expensive, and/or based abroad. Mec–Rastor dominated its home base. Throughout most of the 1970s, it controlled a domestic market share of 60–70 per cent in Finland (Interview Kallio 1999).

The local Finnish version of management consulting was now clearly established. As Leo Suurla and Antero Kallio reached retirement, they were also elevated to the top cadre of Finnish society. In 1976 the President of the Republic of Finland conferred an honorary professorship on Leo Suurla for furthering Finnish management education. Suurla retired two years later from the position of managing director of Rastor. In 1976 Rastor bought the shares of Antero Kallio and his colleague at H.B. Maynard. In 1978 the President also conferred an honorary professorship on Antero Kallio, who retired from the position of managing director of Mec–Rastor in 1980. With Leo Suurla, Antero Kallio, and the entrepreneurial leadership of Rastor out of Mec–Rastor, the consultancy was a 'giant with clay feet' (anonymous source).

By the late 1970s H.B. Maynard's stake in Mec–Rastor had become a promotional asset but otherwise a burden for Mec–Rastor. H.B. Maynard's royalties were based on the volume of the (growing) Finnish business. H.B. Maynard was floundering internationally (cf. Kipping 1999*a*). Rastor bought out H.B. Maynard from Mec–Rastor in 1980. Rastor was still owned by a large number of Finnish companies, each with a small stake, and little incentive for governance.

5.4. THE DEMISE OF THE LOCAL VERSION

For Mec–Rastor, the retirement of Leo Suurla and Antero Kallio signalled the end of an era. Mec–Rastor subsequently experienced a swansong of growth in the early 1980s, after which its position deteriorated. Antti Sääskilahti, the new managing director, re-established negotiations for cooperation with the Boston Consulting Group (BCG) that had recently begun but were eventually aborted in the 1970s. Negotiations initially materialized in joint consulting projects in Finland. Mec–Rastor helped BCG to enter the domestic Finnish market. However, BCG merely used Mec–Rastor as a spring-board; after becoming acquainted with Finnish companies, it dropped its local companion, and ran subsequent projects with clients in accordance with their own procedures (Malin 1989; Interview Kilpeläinen).

Other American-based global consultancies continued to 'infiltrate' Finnish com-panies outside the boundaries of Finland. In the 1970s the number of Finnish companies international and large enough to interest the global consultancies had grown somewhat. In the 1980s it was the small, local, or regional (e.g. the Swedish SIAR) management con-sultancies that first rivalled Mec–Rastor's dominant position in specific segments of the domestic Finnish market. Nevertheless, it seems to have been internal strategy decisions combined with external events that began to undo Mec–Rastor's Finnish version of man-agement consulting, rather than a direct threat from competitors.

Mec–Rastor in a Competence Trap

Winds of 'liberalization' began to blow in Finnish business and the wider economy in the early 1980s. This was most apparent in the Finnish financial system, which was forcefully deregulated from 1983 onwards. Although the process of deregulation continued until 1991—and there was subsequently further harmonization with EU regulations—the most important decisions were taken in 1986 and 1987, when regulation of the average lending rates of deposit banks and the ceiling on credit interest were abolished. Deregulation of the financial markets contributed to a boom in the Finnish economy in the latter part of the 1980s. The competitive practices of the banks changed and money was 'pumped' into the flourishing economy (Tainio *et al.* 1997; Tienari and Tainio 1999).

Cap Gemini set up an office in Helsinki in 1987. Accenture (back then Arthur Andersen and later Andersen Consulting) as well as McKinsey & Co set up their respec-tive offices in 1988. Nevertheless, the domestic Finnish market was still largely insu-lated from the large-scale invasion by the global consultancies, which took a similarly patient stance to establishing their operations in Finland as Rastor had in its time.

In the early 1980s Mec–Rastor continued to diversify its domestic business aggress-ively, often through acquisitions of smaller Finnish management consultancies

(Interview Sääskilahti). Many of these acquisitions proved less than satisfactory. Mec–Rastor attempted to establish a position in the Swedish market, but failed (Interview Kilpeläinen). Meanwhile, Mec–Rastor, feeling secure about its domestic market leadership, continued to bet on benefiting internationally from Finland's pioneering position in Soviet trade. It even established a subsidiary in the Soviet Union during the *perestroika* years (Interview Sääskilahti). The value of the developed contacts depreciated surprisingly quickly as the Soviet Union began to collapse. By the late 1980s many commentators in the Finnish business press seemed to be of the opinion that Mec–Rastor was in a serious profitability crisis (e.g. Vihma 1990). It is likely that the policy of 'letting a thousand flowers bloom' contributed to a heavy cost structure for the company as a whole when the domestic Finnish demand for consultancy projects began to diminish dramatically. The transformation of Mec–Rastor started in 1990, when the board appointed a new managing director, Asa-Matti Lyytinen, who set out to rationalize the company's organization and business. Lyytinen and Jaakko Kilpeläinen, his closest colleague, acquired ownership of the consultancy in a management buy-out in 1992 (see Tienari 1999 for more details).

During 1991–2 the economic boom in the Finnish economy suddenly turned into bust. The Soviet Union collapsed and Finland was plunged into the deepest peacetime recession in its history as an independent nation. Finnish–Soviet bilateral trade disappeared, and the recession was accompanied by a banking crisis (Tainio *et al.* 2000). Legislative changes continued in Finland in the midst of the recession. Limits on foreign ownership in Finnish corporations were abolished at the beginning of 1993. Foreign ownership in major Finnish firms increased when international financial investments produced a wave of changes in ownership and governance. With international financial investments, the severe recession began to wane in the mid-1990s. Finland joined the European Union at the beginning of 1995.

During the boom-and-bust cycle, several forces had their full effect and began to cause a convergence in management consulting in Finland towards global American-based standards (McKenna, Djelic, and Ainamo 2000). A management consulting market of industrial standard, rather than dominated by a single player, emerged when global consultancies began to acquire Rastor's small Finnish rivals (Tienari 1999). Americanized business and engineering schools continued to produce internationally minded graduates, some of whom began to join the global consultancies as junior consultants. Finnish companies continued to internationalize. Decades of learning had taught Finnish companies the benefits of contact with global consultancies. The fact that many of them were busy pulling out of the recession produced a sudden need to exploit the coordination and cost advantages of recent advances in information technology and mobile telephony.

The American Invasion

The Finnish version of management consulting was the foundation on which convergence with the American model was built. Markku Silén, the Finnish partner and managing director of Andersen Consulting (renamed Accenture in 2001), emerged as the outstanding promoter of the need for management consulting in Finland. When Silén took over as managing director in 1994, Andersen Consulting Finland concentrated almost exclusively on computer programme development and implementation (as was the case with Cap Gemini, Silén's previous employer). Following Andersen Consulting's worldwide policy change towards a more general management consulting approach, Silén took advantage of its global knowledge-base and the emerging market opportunities in Finland. Business process re-engineering (BPR) was in great demand (Interview Silén, 12 Aug. 1999).

Markku Silén dominated media coverage of management consultants, chaired LJK, and frequently provided benchmarks by which other consultancies have positioned themselves (see Tienari 1999). Andersen Consulting emerged as the largest consultancy company in Finland. The domestic turnover of Andersen Consulting Finland increased from FIM 75 million in 1995 to FIM 280 million in 1998 (approximately US \$12m. and US \$46m., respectively). While Finnish business managers had typically postponed large-scale investments in both technological infrastructure and organization development activities during the recession and its immediate aftermath, the demand for external advice on these issues was now recovering. The atmosphere among Finnish managers was pro-rationalization and pro-technology.

Silén was in a position to react and to shape the Finnish market for management consulting further. His consultancy began selling projects based on the globally fashionable BPR-concept, using both Finnish consultants and visitors from Andersen Consulting's offices in other countries in his endeavours. Silén and Andersen Consulting were also at the forefront of the next step. The overall market for management consulting was still growing rapidly in Finland. When the consequences of BPR became evident, Andersen Consulting were ready to offer 'comprehensive, integrated transformation programmes' to their Finnish clientele (Interview Silén, 12 Aug. 1999). Local consultancies were slow to develop rhetorics and procedures that could compete with those of Andersen Consulting.

Silén targeted large, technology-driven projects to a growing number of customers. In the Finnish media, he successfully constructed Andersen Consulting as one of the few capable providers of 'all four areas of modern transformation programmes: business diagnosis and corporate strategy, operative strategy and process development, IT-architecture and systems solution definition, and IT-implementation' (Andersen Consulting, company presentation). Other consultancies with similar agendas—such as Gemini Consulting and A.T. Kearney—followed suit, but could not immediately match Andersen Consulting's advantage as the first global consultancy to penetrate the Finnish domestic market. Andersen consulting created a 'home base' of well-proven consulting services for the local market similar to that previously enjoyed only by Mec–Rastor (Interview Silén, 22 Mar. 1999).

Mec–Rastor ended up as a part of Coopers & Lybrand in 1996 and, when the latter merged with Price Waterhouse in 1998, PricewaterhouseCoopers (PWC). Mec–Rastor's disappearance as an independent Finnish consultancy was soon followed by a number of its local rivals moving under the umbrella of global consultancies (Tienari 1999). At the same time, the remaining local consultancies adopted a less local and more international outlook. The Finnish version of management consulting designed by Leo Suurla and Antero Kallio for the domestic Finnish market had for all practical purposes ceased to exist.

5.5. CONCLUSIONS

This chapter has presented a historical account of the emergence of the management consulting institution in Finland in the period after the Second World War. The conclusion that can be drawn from the account is consistent with historical and comparative studies specifically in the domain of management consulting (Kipping 1996, 1999a), as well as with the general idea of punctuated equilibrium (Gersick 1991) that cuts across disciplines.

A few 'great men' created a local version of management consulting in Finland to bridge the gap between a more modern outlook and local tradition, legacy, and norms. The local version of management consulting provided them and other consultants with access to local managers. For decades this amounted to a local market for management consulting. Eventually, both the local version and the local market matured and met its demise, making room for an American invasion.

The initial success of the local version in the immediate post-war period was based on personal links to the dominant cadres of managers developed by key individuals, and rhetorics based on war imagery that had penetrated the economy and business in Finland. The pioneer consultants knew how to pick and choose from the foreign alternatives those ideas and practices that could first take hold with self-assertive Finnish managers in a context where the professionalization of management itself was only just taking root. The pioneers exploited their networks to position themselves in structural niches in the local market for management knowledge. They had the patience to wait out the period when Finland was straddled between two institutional systems. They used every opportunity to learn while there was little demand for a return to the owners of their consultancy, a large number of Finnish companies each involved with a small stake and little interest in corporate governance. The localized learning about American management knowledge would benefit both the local consultants and those local managers who financed their process of learning.

The pioneering individuals made themselves and their consultancies known and eventually developed their trade into a legitimate institution in Finnish industry (McKenna, Djelic, and Ainamo 2000; cf. Wright 2000). Little by little, local managers who had observed the process of learning by the local management consultants became convinced that the consultants had now learned enough to give important 'modern' advice. The reciprocal giving and taking of advice triggered a self-reinforcing cycle of management consultant use in Finland (see Sturdy 1997). As the clients learned what the local consultants knew, and vice versa, the success of the local version of management consulting became self-defeating. In other words, the local version of management consulting was only a tool that became expendable rather than one infused with permanent value that would have kept it from de-institutionalization. The rise and fall of the local version of management consulting was a temporary constellation in service of a

86 *Ainamo and Tienari*

higher purpose. The development ensured that foreign ideas and practices overcame the obstacles presented by the local cultural, industrial, economic, and geo-political system to enable Finnish managers and the economy as a whole to catch up with the West.

The international environment is a concrete political and geo-political arena with structural niches for management knowledge and its carriers (Djelic 1998). The proposition that the personal fiat of local key individuals and a temporary local version of management consulting are needed before peripheral countries can efficiently adopt global models suggests at least two avenues for future research.

First, in elaborating the theoretical proposition of the research, historical and cross-national comparative data come most readily to mind. For example, a comparison between data from several cultural, political, economic, or geo-political peripheries ought to capture several localized versions of management consulting; increase understanding of the commonalities, differences, and evolution of diverse forms of management consulting; and provide a foundation for meaningful criticism of the apparent contemporary dominance of the American-style management consultancies (Kipping 1999a; cf. Fligstein 1990; Guillén 1994).

Secondly, it is clear that any understanding of a historical phenomenon remains subject to the discursive strategies of both the actors and the researchers involved. The dominant cadre of consultants and clients in Finland were all men, bound together by common experiences. The creation of the Finnish version of management consulting (and the subsequent American invasion) links with a distinctly masculine rhetoric, with war imagery and male bonding surfacing constantly. A feminist re-reading of this chapter would enable a deconstruction of the gendered foundations of management consulting. We encourage feminist and other critical re-readings of management consulting histories. Some discursive strategies in creating versions of management consulting may well be constant across temporal and spatial domains.

PRIMARY SOURCES

Printed Sources

Hernberg, R. (1938), 'Industriell företagsorganisation: jämförande iakttagelser under en studieresa i Europa och Amerika', in *Tekniska Föreningens i Finland Förhandlingar*, Vol. 58, 30–7.
Honko, J. (1998), 'Taloustieteen virtausten tulo Suomeen sodan jälkeen', in *Studia Economica: talous ja itsenäisyys* (Helsinki: HeSE print).
Kauppalehti (1968), 'T.K. Ritvala suomalaisesta liikemiehestä: sydämellä ajatteleva nurkkapatriootti', 20 Aug.
Malin, R. (1989), 'Maailma haastaa kansalliskonsultin', *Talouselämä*, 3: 44–6.
Mannio, P. (1979), *Liikkeenjohdollisen tutkimusryhmän alkutaival* (Helsinki: Liikkeenjohdollinen tutkimusryhmä LJT).
Mec–Rastor (1978, 1989), *Vuosikirjat 1977/78–1988/89* (Helsinki).
Michelsen, K.-E. (2001), *Vuosisadan tilinpäätös: Helsingin kauppakorkeakoulu 1911–2001* (Helsinki: Edita).
Ritvala, T. (1966), Onko konsultti pop: eli liikkeenjohdon konsulttitoiminnasta Suomessa', *Talouselämä*, 15, Apr.
Rothberg, L. (1968), 'Ennakkoluulot esteenä konsulttien käytössä', *Kauppalehti*, 6 Mar.

Suurla, L. (1987), *Unpublished Memoirs* (in Finnish), chs. 7–13. Quoted with the permission of the author's estate.

Tehostaja (1966), 'Miksi teollisuutemme ei käytä enemmän konsultteja', No. 9.

Vihma, P. (1990). 'Konsultit joutuvat eurokierteeseen', *Talouselämä*, 28: 24–6.

Interviews

Antero Kallio (Manager at Rastor 1952–68 and Managing Director of Mec–Rastor 1968–80; Chairman of the Board of the Finnish Association of Management Consultants 1979–80). Interviewed by Janne Tienari on 17 August 1999 and by Antti Ainamo on 22 March 2000.

Jaakko Kilpeläinen (Partner of Mec–Rastor PricewaterhouseCoopers). Interviewed by Janne Tienari on 13 August 1999.

Pekka Mannio (Member of the Board of the Finnish Association of Management Consultants 1976–79; Chairman 1978–79). Interviewed by Antti Ainamo on 12 November 2000.

Antti J. Sääskilahti (Managing Director of Mec–Rastor 1980–90). Interviewed by Janne Tienari on 9 August 1999.

Markku Silén (Managing Director and Partner of Accenture Finland). Interviewed by Antti Ainamo on 22 March 1999 and by Janne Tienari on 12 August 1999.

L. Edward Scriven, II (son of L. E. Scriven, American TTT-A representative in Finland, 1956–58). Interviewed by Antti Ainamo by e-mail on 1 June 2000.

PART II

ORGANIZATIONAL PERSPECTIVES
ON THE CONSULTANCY FIRM

6

The Internal Creation of Consulting Knowledge: A Question of Structuring Experience

ANDREAS WERR

6.1. INTRODUCTION

As a growing phenomenon in business practice, management consulting is receiving increasing interest from researchers. However, the emerging image of the consulting service varies to a large extent according to the research tradition followed. Two main opposing perspectives have emerged—the functional and the critical. From the functional perspective, management consulting is depicted as a knowledge-based service aimed at improving the performance of its client businesses. Management consultants are seen as possessing unique knowledge of management techniques, and consulting organizations are treated as knowledge-intensive firms with an ability to generate and explore management knowledge through knowledge management activities. The knowledge content of the consulting service is questioned from a critical perspective, and alternative rationales for the consulting service are presented. Examples of such rationales are uncertainty reduction and consultants' ability to convince managers of their need for consulting services by creating impressions of value.

This chapter focuses on the knowledge base of the consulting service. Against the background of the juxtaposed functional and critical perspectives on consulting, an empirical investigation of the knowledge content in management consulting aims at increasing the understanding of the origin, nature, and handling of knowledge in management consulting. After a review of the critical and functional perspectives' respective views on consulting knowledge, a theoretical framework distinguishing different kinds of knowledge and knowledge processes will be sketched out as a background for discussing the character and handling of knowledge in two consultancies—International and Local.[1] The cases will be presented in two sections. The first section focuses on the sources of knowledge in the consulting organization and the second on the utilization of this knowledge through different kinds of codification and the application of this codified organizational knowledge in the individual consulting project.

---

[1] To protect the anonymity of the companies studied the company names are fictitious.

6.2. CONSULTING KNOWLEDGE

Functional and Critical Perspectives

From a functional perspective, management consulting is described as a knowledge industry. It is about selling knowledge and experience of bringing about organizational change towards a more effective and efficient operation within a client organization (Greiner and Metzger 1983; Schein 1988; Golembiewski 1993). Bessant and Rush (1995) identify four ways in which consultants can create value for their clients with their expertise. First, they can transfer specialized expert knowledge. Secondly, they can share their experiences from other organizations and assignments 'cross-pollinating between firms' (cf. also Hargadon 1998). Thirdly, they can act as marriage brokers, providing access to specialized services delivered either by the consultant or by other organizations. Finally, consultants can take a diagnostic role, helping the client to articulate and define his or her needs for knowledge and expertise. In all these roles, the consultant is assumed to possess some kind of expert knowledge.

Against this background, the continuing growth of consulting is explained by managers' increasing need for expertise. In an increasingly global and complex business environment, managers require the support of experts to stay on top of developments in their organizations, industries, and the business world at large (Huczynski 1993a; Kipping and Scheybani 1994). Recent downsizing trends have also eliminated experts and thereby the knowledge reserves within the client companies, further increasing the need for external experts (Kieser 1998a). Management consultants are thus depicted as important sources of knowledge to their client organizations. They are expected to provide state-of-the-art business knowledge continuously. Some interest has therefore been directed towards consulting organizations as knowledge-intensive firms (Starbuck 1992; Robertson and Swan 1998). A central aspect of such organizations is their internal handling of knowledge—their 'knowledge management' (e.g. Chard 1997; Martiny 1998; Hansen, Nohria, and Tierney 1999).

It is argued that the process of knowledge management has a central position in management consulting companies, as most knowledge in this industry is generated in ongoing client assignments. Collecting and making knowledge available from individual projects to the rest of the organization is a core process, which is closely linked to the value of the service a consultancy can deliver (cf. Hansen, Nohria, and Tierney 1999; Sarvary 1999). The functional perspective thus highlights the knowledge content in consulting, and has in recent years also directed some attention to the origins and handling of this knowledge in the consulting organization. Studies, such as those by Hansen, Nohria, and Tierney (1999), Sarvary (1999), and Bartlett (1997) give some insights into the origins and the influence of such knowledge in consulting organizations. However, these studies are generally at a rather abstract level, giving few insights into the detailed processes through which knowledge is created, spread, and applied in management consulting.

Mainly as a reaction to the functional perspective and its assumed and naive view of knowledge, a critical perspective on consulting has emerged (Kipping and Armbrüster 1998; Fincham 1999). This critical perspective questions the prevailing view of management consulting as a service based on functionalist knowledge of management practices and aimed at improving the performance of its client organizations. The value of management consulting services is regarded as highly uncertain, and the existence of any functional knowledge in the consulting process is largely denied. The management consulting service is no longer viewed as being driven by the clients' needs for functional, managerial knowledge but rather by the anguish they experience in the managerial role. Successful consulting in this perspective has little to do with a functional knowledge-base but rather focuses on the consultants' ability to reduce their clients' angst and manage their perception of the value of the consulting service (as opposed to creating real business value). A recurring picture of the consulting client in the critical literature is that of an insecure and anguished manager facing a nearly impossible task:

The nature of organisational life places responsibility on managers to perform and achieve in a context where often they neither understand how their actions produce results, nor are able to influence the most volatile element in the organization—other people. Second, partly as a result of this uncertainty, their assessment of themselves is also under downward pressure. A similar low assessment tends to be made of them as individuals and of management as a profession (Huczynski 1993a: 171).

This position of managers creates two basic managerial needs—one for predictability and control, another for increased social and personal esteem. Both these needs can be fulfilled by management consultants, without the application of any functional management knowledge. A sense of predictability and control is supported by the consultants' use of and referral to management concepts that are built up around simple cause-and-effect relations (Huczynski 1993a; Watson 1994; Clark and Salaman 1998). Through management concepts such as Business Process Reengineering (BPR) or Total Quality Management (TQM), the client organization's problem is framed and categorized, and a remedy is outlined. In this process, the consultant generally establishes him or herself as the actor able to lead the client to the desired situation outlined by the management concept (Bloomfield and Best 1992; Sturdy 1997; Berglund and Werr 2000). By adhering to a technical rationality, the consultant further reduces the uncertainty felt by the client: presenting a step-by-step method with simple cause-and-effect relations gives the impression of a controllable change process and of the consultant being in control (Sturdy 1997; Werr 1999; Rogberg and Werr 2000).

In addition, the need for social and personal esteem is fulfilled by management consultants, as the theories and images presented during the consulting process contribute to the reproduction of the managerial role as an important one. Guru theory, which is what consultants often present, is described by Clark and Salaman (1998) 'not as a body of expert knowledge that gurus make available to their grateful clients, but as a means, as a language for representing negotiated and mutually acceptable ways of knowing, defining and talking about management, organization and managers' (Clark and Salaman 1998: 146). In their interactions with clients, consultants thus support the creation of an acceptable role for their client managers—'They tell managers why they are important, why they matter, why their skills are critical' (Clark and Salaman 1998: 153).

The critical perspective thus depicts the management consulting service as unlikely to improve client businesses through contributing specific managerial knowledge. Rather, the consultant is described as someone providing the client with simple management concepts that depict the organization as a controllable entity and confirm the importance of the role of the manager. Management concepts here become an important knowledge base for consultants. These management concepts, however, are better understood as fads and fashions rather than functional knowledge (Abrahamson 1991; Furusten 1995; Kieser 1998a).

From a critical perspective, the knowledge content in the consulting service is further questioned on the basis of the character of the service. The intangibility of the service, its interactional character—implying that its value is derived from the interaction between consultant and client—its heterogeneity—making the service hard to standardize—and its perishability, make an objective judgement of the value (and the knowledge content) of the service impossible. Rather, Clark and Salaman (1996a) argue that value creation in management consulting is about creating the client's impression of value. This makes impression management a central aspect of management consulting: 'The impact of consultants is dependent upon beliefs about them being able to offer something of value to clients. These beliefs are formulated not by an objectivistic and functionalist knowledge-base but by the manipulation of myths and symbols through language' (Clark and Salaman 1996a: 176).

The perception of knowledge in management consulting is thus seen as the result of the successful management of the client's impression of the consultants and their services. This is irrespective of the existence or absence of any functional knowledge possessed by the consultant in the form, for example, of extensive experiences and methods. The critical perspective on management consulting thus denies the importance of any knowledge related to the management task in the delivery of the management consulting service. Rather it points to the consultants' ability to reduce the client's uncertainty and angst by presenting simple management concepts, framing the client's situation in an oversimplified way, and creating a desirable identity for managers, as well as manipulating myths and symbols in order to create an impression of value.

But is this really an accurate view of the consulting service? What about all the clients who claim to hire consultants for their knowledge and expertise (see, for example, Poulfelt and Payne 1994; Engwall and Eriksson 1999)? Are they just the victims of self-deception or of the consultants' skilful impression management? The contrasting perspectives of the nature and knowledge content of management consulting presented above can both be criticized for their incompleteness. To a large extent the functional perspective takes the existence of knowledge in management consulting for granted. However, it has little to say when it comes to the question of the origins and character of this knowledge, and how this knowledge is applied in consulting organizations. The critical perspective, in contrast, completely denies the existence of knowledge in management consulting. Against this background, two empirical questions arise.

The first question concerns the potential knowledge content in management consulting. What is the character of knowledge applied by consultants in a consulting assignment? Is this knowledge mainly about fads, fashions, and impression management or do consultants rely on a more functional and managerial knowledge base? The second question concerns the origins and handling of this knowledge within consulting organizations. Where does the consultants' knowledge come from? How is it used in the consulting organization and how is it applied? These questions will be addressed through an empirical study of the creation, dissemination, and application of knowledge in two quite different management consulting organizations.

A Typology of Knowledge

As background to the empirical descriptions of consulting knowledge in consulting organizations, two dimensions recurring in the literature on knowledge and knowledge management will be described below. The first dimension is the epistemological, distinguishing between explicit and tacit knowledge. The second is the ontological dimension, distinguishing between individual and organizational knowledge (see Figure 6.1) (cf. Hedlund 1994; Nonaka and Takeuchi 1995; Lam 2000).

Explicit knowledge is codified or easily codifiable. It can be abstracted from a specific situation and stored, for example, in a database or report detached from the individual who produced the knowledge. Examples of explicit knowledge in consulting organizations are different kinds of checklists, manuals, and designs of previous cases. Explicit knowledge is easily transferred between individuals. A manual or an old project design can be made available to an entire organization by placing it in an organizational database. However, making the knowledge available is not the same as ensuring its successful use by others. Explicit knowledge has to be adapted to each specific situation through a process of translation (Czarniawska and Sevón 1996). In this process,

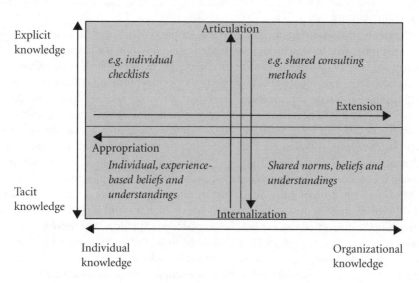

Figure 6.1. *A model of knowledge categories and processes of transformation (based on Hedlund 1994)*

choices are made regarding the suitability of the knowledge and the need for its adaptation in the specific situation. Translation can also involve the redefinition of the situation in the light of the available knowledge.

As opposed to explicit knowledge, tacit knowledge is described as non-verbalized, often even non-verbalizable, intuitive, personal, and situated (Polanyi 1967). It is gained through practical experience in relevant contexts and therefore bound to a specific person and situation. Tacit knowledge is central to human action, as it, as opposed to abstract, explicit knowledge, handles the complexity, inconsistency, and unpredictability of everyday life (Brown and Duguid 1994). However, the personal character of this knowledge makes it difficult to communicate. Transferring tacit knowledge requires face-to-face interaction generating shared experience (Nonaka and Takeuchi 1995). An example of tacit knowledge in management consulting is the consultant's understanding of the client's organizational culture. Consultants often have quite a clear understanding of what this is about and the related dos and don'ts, but they can seldom articulate the procedures and clues through which they arrive at this understanding.

Explicit and tacit knowledge have a partly complementary relation in that some tacit knowledge is always necessary for the understanding and translation of explicit knowledge. Knowledge can never be entirely articulated, as there always remains a need for expertise concerning the translation of knowledge to the idiosyncrasies of the specific situation. This expertise is generally acquired through extended experience and represents tacit knowledge. The experience-based tacit knowledge thus makes appropriate action and use of explicit knowledge possible (Göranzon 1988; Josefson 1988; Kim 1993; Lillrank 1995). Knowledge can also travel on the explicit–tacit dimension through processes of articulation, in which tacit knowledge is made explicit, or internalization, in which explicit knowledge is internalized, making it more readily available for action (Hedlund 1994).

The second dimension important for the description of different kinds of knowledge concerns the extent to which the knowledge is shared within the organization. In the present study of knowledge in consulting companies, examples such as checklists were found both at the individual level (developed by a specific consultant and used exclusively by him or her) and at the organizational level (part of the company's overall methodology and widely used by all consultants). Knowledge at the organizational level can be stored in a number of different ways. Starbuck (1992) identifies three such 'containers' of organizational knowledge—capital, routines and culture in the organization, and professional cultures. Hansen, Nohria, and Tierney (1999) are broader in their categorization of knowledge containers, distinguishing between databases and peoples' minds.

The transformation of individual to organizational knowledge is a central aspect of knowledge management. In this process, which Nonaka and Takeuchi (1995) call extension, the individual shares his or her knowledge with the rest of the organization. When this sharing concerns explicit knowledge it will often take place by means of written or spoken language. If it concerns tacit knowledge it will require face-to-face interaction in real-life situations—such as the senior consultant coaching the junior consultant in a project. In the reverse process of appropriation, the organizational knowledge is individualized by a specific actor.

6.3. KNOWLEDGE IN CONSULTING ORGANIZATIONS

Against the background of the ambiguous picture of consulting knowledge in the literature and the knowledge framework sketched out above, this section turns to the empirical investigation of knowledge in management consulting. The empirical investigation is carried out in two steps. The first step explores the nature and origin of consulting knowledge and concludes that it is mainly based on experience. The second step focuses on the organizational implementation of this knowledge, involving its articulation into methods and documented cases, as well as the use of this explicit knowledge in consulting projects.

Research Design

Two consulting organizations form the empirical basis of this chapter. In choosing the two organizations a logic of contrast was applied and differences rather than similarities were sought. This led to the choice of one large, multinational consultancy (referred to as 'International') and one small, internal consultancy (referred to as 'Local'). However in order to facilitate comparison, both consultancies provide consulting in the area of process improvement.

International is a large, international consultancy based in the USA and involved in many different types of consulting projects ranging from strategy projects to IT projects. Process improvement projects were a large part of International's business. International has about 40,000 consultants worldwide. The Swedish subsidiary, which is the focus of this study, employs a couple of hundred consultants. The structure of the company is hierarchical, and recruitment is focused on young MBAs direct from university.

Local is a considerably smaller consulting organization than International. Local mainly acts as an internal consultancy to a large Swedish concern. The group within Local examined in this study works with process improvement projects and comprises about ten consultants all located in the same office space. The organization is flat, with no formal distinction between junior and senior consultants. Recruitment is focused on people with a university degree in business or engineering and a couple of years of business experience. Local also differs from International in terms of its primary market, which mainly consists of the subsidiaries of the group it belongs to. Local is an autonomous company and its relationship to the rest of the group is of a consultant–client character rather than a staff-line character.

Methodology

The data about the knowledge system at International and Local has primarily been collected through interviews conducted in connection with a simulation of consultants' proposal writing. Based on information accessible from a computer on the consultants' demand, three consultants with varying lengths of experience from each company were asked to sketch a project proposal for a process improvement project. Before as well as after the simulation, a semi-structured, in-depth interview was carried out regarding the sources of information for writing the proposal and the discrepancies between the laboratory situation and a 'real-life' situation. The interviews, which took up between one and two hours of the four-hour simulation, were taped and transcribed. A content analysis was then carried out to determine which sources of knowledge were mentioned in the interviews. The design of the data collection using a simulation of proposal writing as a trigger for discussing the use of different kinds of knowledge in the proposal-writing process made it possible to be very specific in regard to the knowledge applied during this process. However, it also imposes a risk that the descriptions of the knowledge system reveal information only about the knowledge available and used in the early phases of the project. In order to reduce this risk, the above-mentioned data was complemented with three additional interviews with a junior consultant, a senior consultant, and a consultant with an intermediate level of experience in each organization. These interviews, lasting between 60 and 90 minutes, were captured by note-taking and concerned the use of structured methods and other formal sources of knowledge in the consulting process. The experiments were carried out during the spring of 1997, the interviews during 1996.

Experience as the Main Source of Consulting Knowledge

Designing a project proposal for a client is an iterative process involving more than one consultant. Even if one person does the bulk of the work, this is continuously discussed with the manager responsible for the project and the partner owning the client relation. At least four people have seen and commented on a proposal before it is submitted. This involvement of experienced consultants is imperative for the quality of the proposal. (International Consultant)

We use our experience from earlier projects when we estimate project time and apply our approach to an organization with these characteristics. We have a standard approach, but this is used differently in different cases. We add some activities and eliminate others from the standard approach based on our knowledge of the client organization and our experience from earlier cases. (Local Consultant)

Common to both these descriptions of the proposal process is a focus on experience—lessons learned from earlier consulting projects—as a basis for the consultants' actions. Experience helped the consultants to determine the activities needed in the change process, staffing, timing, etc. The main concern for the consultants in the proposal phase was how to design the project in order to ensure that a lasting value would be created for the client organization. The experience, laying the basis for the design of the consulting project, could be described in the cases of both International and Local as organizational knowledge rather than individual knowledge. Even if experiences were generated by individuals in specific projects, making this knowledge primarily tacit and individual, mechanisms existed in both organizations, through which the individual consultants' experiences were made available to the other consultants in the organization. However the mechanism for this differed between the two organizations.

In International, the individual consultant's experience was regarded as a central organizational asset. Given the personnel structure of International, with a large number of junior consultants and a considerably smaller number of senior consultants, experience was a scarce resource, making the utilization as well as the extension of experience in the organization imperative. In order to maximize the use of the experienced consultants' knowledge, the organizational hierarchy in International was based on the level of experience, ranging from junior consultant to partner. This hierarchy was the basis for a division of labour aimed at the efficient use of experience. Taking the proposal process as an example, this involved consultants representing the entire organizational hierarchy. A client relation was always owned by a senior consultant. He or she had the initial contact with a client. But this senior consultant was only involved to a limited degree in the actual work of writing a proposal. The responsibility for this was transferred to a consultant with intermediate experience, who worked together with junior consultants. Junior consultants did most of the work, following the company's standard procedure, as well as the documentation from earlier projects (such as old proposals) found in International's knowledge database. The junior consultants continually discussed what they were doing with consultants at an intermediate level. Finally, before the proposal was sent to the client, it was approved and commented on by the partner owning the client relation. The main job of the more senior consultants was the adaptation of the standard approach and the old proposals to the specific situation, a task that was described as 'mainly a question of experience'.

The hierarchical division of labour observed in International not only took advantage of the senior consultants' experience, but also had a role in extending this experience to the more junior consultants. In order to transfer experience, which to a large extent must be regarded as a tacit kind of knowledge, interaction leading to shared experience is imperative. Without this, people would not be able to share each other's thinking processes (Brown and Duguid 1994; Nonaka and Takeuchi 1995). The hierarchical organizational model observed in International and described above had this kind of interaction built in through the mentor system, as well as in the conscious composition of project teams mixing both competences and levels of experience. Working together with more experienced consultants in these teams was described by the junior consultants as their most valuable learning experience.

However, all the consultants' experience could never be directly included within a single project team. Therefore, the involvement of senior consultants in the projects was complemented by the more indirect means of making available individual consultants' experience at an organizational level. One such mechanism was the creation of a clear, knowledge-based structure. In order to make it easy to find the right person to answer a specific question, a number of expert networks (centres of excellence) responsible for the accumulation and dissemination of expertise in different areas existed. Within all these specified areas, there was always someone able to answer the consultants' questions. In order to increase the accessibility of these 'experts', voice and e-mail systems were used.[2]

A second, indirect way of making the individual consultants' experience available to the rest of the organization was through its articulation. International put considerable

---

[2] For a description of the implementation and working of such a system of experts in another consulting organization—McKinsey—see Peters (1992), and Bartlett (1997).

effort into the development of impersonal forms of storing and transferring experience from other projects. Two types of articulate experience were found in International—methods and tools and documentation from previous cases. Both of these served as ways of making available the experience applied and generated in the different consulting assignments carried out in the company. The articulation of knowledge at an organizational level was formalized, with expert groups responsible for the extraction and documentation of important individual experiences in different knowledge areas. The articulate representations of the experiences made in projects (methods) or the artefacts of the application of experience (the documentation of cases) were stored in a world-wide database.

Turning to Local, both similarities with and differences from the previous description of International can be found. As at International, Local consultants relied on their own as well as their colleagues' experience in designing a project, but the handling of these experiences was less systematic than at International. Experience exchange at Local mainly took place on an individual and ad hoc basis through both informal and formal face-to-face contacts between consultants. The consultants knew who the experts on different issues were and often made informal contacts in order to obtain feedback on ideas or receive new ideas for solving a specific problem. A number of more formal arenas for the exchange of experiences also existed in the form of monthly project review meetings, competence development days, etc. Consultants also identified working together with colleagues on a shared project as their main source of learning. They only regretted that this happened too rarely, as budget constraints often did not allow for more than one consultant on a specific project.

The efforts at Local to articulate the consultants' experiences into methods and tools and cases were much more limited than at International. Local also had a methodology and saved copies of documentation from old cases. However, the use of these methods and cases to identify and diffuse experiences made in the organization was limited. Due to time and money constraints, the existing method, which was licensed from an outside supplier, was not updated to reflect the consultants' experiences. Instead these were communicated in different face-to-face interactions between the consultants. The consultants had also developed personal approaches to different aspects of the consulting task—such as proposal writing—which made it harder to reuse other people's material. Others people's cases were only occasionally used as sources of knowledge at Local.

Knowledge exchange at Local thus mainly took place on an individual-to-individual basis. The knowledge was seldom articulated at an organizational level. This exchange of experience was not seen as unproblematic: sharing knowledge with colleagues was said by the consultants not to be a natural trait of theirs. Starbuck (1992) indicates the generality of this pattern. Local therefore had actively tried to establish a culture fostering a 'giver mentality'.

The above descriptions of the knowledge sources in two consulting companies indicate that in planning and carrying out the consulting task, the consultants applied substantial knowledge concerning how to diagnose an organization and design and carry out a process of change in order to improve the client organization's performance. This knowledge was firmly based in the consulting companies' collective experiences of what worked in practice and what did not. Experiences were continuously updated in the consultancies' ongoing projects, which indicates the existence of knowledge in management consulting that goes beyond the mastery of impression management or knowledge of the latest management fads and fashions.

The Codification and Utilization of Experience

Given the importance of experience as a basis for consulting, a major challenge for consulting organizations becomes the utilization of this experience. The importance of this process for consulting organizations has been acknowledged, for example, by Sarvary (1999) and Martiny (1998). The detailed mechanisms underlying this application, however, remain largely unstudied, with some rare exceptions, such as work by Hansen, Nohria, and Tierney (1999), who identify two distinct strategies through which knowledge in organizations is exchanged and transferred and thus extended. The first strategy is called codification and relies heavily on databases, in which knowledge is codified and stored. A second strategy, called personalization, instead focuses on the individual as a carrier of knowledge and aims at facilitating connections between individuals. Knowledge exchange in this latter case relies to a large extent on person-to-person contacts. According to Hansen, Nohria, and Tierney (1999) these two strategies are alternatives rather than complements. It is argued that successful companies focus on one of the strategies using the other in a supporting role.

As indicated by the examination of knowledge sources in International and Local, methods and tools and old cases played important roles in the processes by which experience was exchanged between consultants, although, as we shall see, in slightly different ways. In the following section, the role of these explicit forms of experience in the consulting companies' generation of knowledge will be further discussed.

Methods and Tools. Formalized and documented, company-wide methods and tools existed at both International and Local. However their use and origin differed. At International, methods and tools existed for a large number of areas and problems and at many different levels of detail. They were stored in the overall knowledge database and continuously developed in order to reflect the experiences gained in the ongoing projects. The different methods were owned by so-called 'centres of excellence', consisting of consultants at several levels. These groups periodically gathered consultants active in their area of expertise in order to identify successful cases—as well as failures—and to learn from these. The centres of excellence also reviewed projects carried out with 'their' methods in order to find innovations made within the method or to detect problems requiring further developments of the method.

Methods were seen as providing a basic structure to the activities in International's consulting projects. This basic structure was important primarily to inexperienced consultants, as it gave them a language and activity structure to depart from and discuss with the more senior consultants in the project teams. This made the methods an important enabler of the hierarchical organization of projects through which the senior consultants' experience was exploited. The more senior consultants also saw methods as a way of communicating what was new in the company's way of working. Consultants working with a specific method were expected to stay updated on its developments, reflecting International's learning in consulting projects. Methods in International were thus viewed as an organizational repository of the company's state-of-the-art consulting practices.

Local also had a common method for its projects. However, unlike at International, this method was not developed and maintained internally, but rather licensed from a US consultancy. This main method was complemented by other externally acquired methods and tools learned in different courses and seminars. Local only developed its own methods to a very limited degree, due to a claimed lack of resources and the high visibility of the cost of such activities in a small organization such as Local (cf. Starbuck 1992). Instead, some effort was put into the adaptation of the external methods to Local's and its clients' needs. However, these adaptations seldom led to an updating of the method documentation (except for the methods developed in-house). Experiences were, rather, transferred verbally from consultant to consultant. In this context, methods acted as triggers and structures for knowledge exchange between consultants. Several consultants at Local explicitly mentioned the method's structure and concepts as an important common language for the exchange of experience.

The method at Local was also seen as a valuable source of knowledge about what actions to take in the consulting projects: 'Methods are a perfect way of quickly entering a new field of knowledge without a lot of experimentation and reinventing the wheel. They work like recipes. The first time you follow them, then you improvise' (Local consultant). This role of methods was especially important for newcomers, but more experienced consultants claimed that once in a while they too went back to the method for ideas about what to do next. The method refreshed their memory about the educational activities connected to them and provided a checklist, which ensured that no important activities were forgotten.

A central contribution of methods at both International and Local was thus the commonly available structure and language of different activities in the consulting process. At International this common structure and language was important for enabling the hierarchical organization to tap the senior consultants' experience as well as an organizational memory (cf. Orlikowski 1988). At Local the common structure and language were important for the communication between the consultants, in which they made available and shared their personal experiences.

Old Cases. In attacking the task of designing a project proposal, both International and Local consultants based their proposals on similar, previous cases, which were used as models for the design of the new proposal. Searching for old proposals was the first measure taken by the consultants. In the old proposals, consultants looked for the logical design of the process, possible suggestions of solutions to the client's problem, and estimates of the time needed for different steps in the process. In later phases of the project, consultants described the documentation from these old cases as a valuable source of ideas for solutions of various kinds.

At International the search for documentation from similar projects was facilitated by the organization's world-wide knowledge database and the standardized methods and tools of the company that prescribed a common structure and terminology for the cases and their documentation. Cases were also a way of establishing personal contacts for experience utilization and exchange between consultants. The level of specificity and detail in the stored proposals and documents produced in and describing old projects was seldom sufficient. Therefore, the study of old cases was usually complemented by personal conversations with people involved in the project.

At Local efforts were also made to document old cases as a source of knowledge for future projects. Generally all proposals—as well as documentation such as process charts from the projects—were saved in a company-wide database. However, the use of the database was limited. It was mainly used as a vehicle for finding the right people. In connection with the first contact with a potential client, the consultant checked whether the company had run any projects there before. This check was mainly carried out through personal contacts. In some cases, the project database was consulted.

As in the case of International, previous proposals were an important source of knowledge in the proposal-writing phase, especially concerning planned timescales and adaptations of the method to specific situations. However, the consultants rarely used others' proposals as such templates, as different consultants had developed their own templates. One Local consultant also identified a general problem with using previous cases as models, in that they became 'old' very fast. The reuse of ideas was said to be limited due to the products' limited lifespan.

At both International and Local, documentation from old cases was thus an important source of knowledge when it came to designing the approach in specific cases. However, the degree to which these cases were utilized organizationally differed between the two consultancies. At Local they were mainly individual, as the result of a lack of standardization, whereas at International they were organizational. In their application as blueprints for the design of specific projects, cases are an important complement to the general methods and tools. With their basis in specific projects, they reflect the important experience-based tacit knowledge of how to adapt the general method to a specific case. They illustrate the translation of the general method to the specific situation.

The strategies for making use of the experiences at International and Local described above are similar to Hansen, Nohria, and Tierney's (1999) codification and personalization strategies. However, the above examples also point to some limitations in the conceptualization of these strategies. International mainly reflects what Hansen, Nohria, and Tierney (1999) describe as a codification strategy involving great efforts to articulate knowledge into methods and cases that could be stored in databases. However, the case of International also shows that this strategy has its limitations in transferring the knowledge essential to become a successful consultant. Different kinds of face-to-face interaction transferring individuals' experience are a central complement to the transfer of the explicit kinds of knowledge stored in databases.

Local's strategy for utilizing its experience is similar to Hansen, Nohria, and Tierney's (1999) personalization strategy, which relies heavily on personal contacts for knowledge transfer. While such contacts were important at Local, the case-study also points to the importance of the existence of a common, explicit method as a trigger to and facilitator of the personal contacts through which knowledge was extended. This thus indicates that the two strategies for managing knowledge sketched out by Hansen, Nohria, and Tierney (1999) are complementary rather than alternative strategies. The codification strategy requires a personal exchange of expertise related to the adaptation of the method to the specific case, whereas the personalization strategy is facilitated by the existence of an explicit, formalized method providing a common framework within which the face-to-face transfer of experience can take place.

The Translation of Experience. A largely blind spot in the knowledge management literature is the application of knowledge. The focus is mostly on the gaining and formation of organizational knowledge, whereas the application of this knowledge is not generally discussed (e.g. March 1997; Hansen, Nohria, and Tierney 1999; Sarvary 1999). This study, however, indicates that the application of knowledge from a general method or an old case to a new specific situation is crucial for the success of a consulting assignment. In spite of the efforts to codify knowledge that were observed, especially at International, neither cases nor methods were copied exactly for new projects. Rather, the adaptation of the existing knowledge to the specific case was highlighted by the consultants as a central success factor: 'You may not become a slave under the method, but you have to understand the client's situation. The method is in fact only a way to collect experience and guarantee quality' (International consultant).

Consultants at neither Local nor International saw methods and tools or cases as direct guides for action. Their generality is characteristic of methods and tools: they do not suggest solutions for specific situations (as the cases do) but try to generalize knowledge. This is both the method's strength and its weakness. On the one hand, their generality makes them applicable to many different cases and thus of general interest, on the other hand, the general methods cannot be directly applied to a specific situation but have to go through a process of translation in which they are made applicable to the specific situation. Such a process of translation is also required for cases, as no two cases are ever exactly the same.

The main challenge for the consultants is thus the design of a unique approach for the specific situation. This process of translation, in which the methods and cases are adapted to the individual client's needs, is described by the consultants as crucial for success. In the simulation studied in this chapter, the translation of the methods and cases to the new specific case was a central issue. It meant both eliminating certain activities that were regarded as irrelevant for the specific case, as well as adding other activities that were not included in the method or an earlier case, but regarded as important for solving the client's problem. In this context consultants went outside their main methodologies to other toolboxes, or, when they could not find a suitable tool, they would create a new approach or tool for the specific case (Werr 1999). Putting together an approach that fitted the specific case was described by the consultants as being a question of experience, which to a large extent was regarded as a tacit kind of knowledge:

I have difficulty explaining how I choose tools. It doesn't feel like a technique. It is something happening in here [the head]. A connection between experience and knowledge about how to use different tools. It is difficult to articulate how I think. I think it is this ability to choose tools and the depth of analysis to fit the situation that is the consultant's core competence (Local consultant).

General rules for how to use the method in a specific situation with all its idiosyncrasies were very hard to specify and something that was described as learnt through experience.[3] The constant adaptations of earlier approaches as manifested in methods and tools and old cases were what fuelled the continuous development of the method at International, and the direct updating of the collective experiences at Local. However, methods not only facilitated the development of new knowledge, but also to some extent limited it (Robertson and Swan 1998). Methods and tools influenced the aim, purpose, and, of course, the design of the change process. Consequently, the use of a given method limited the range of actions taken and thereby experiences gained. The range of experiences was further limited by the concepts and notions, i.e. the language provided by the method, which influenced the perception and interpretation of these experiences (Alvesson 1992; Kim 1993). Given the experiential basis of the methods this limiting mechanism thus also entailed method development.

The above thus indicates that the accumulated experience of individual consultants was closely interlinked with the methods and tools and cases of the consulting organization. Methods and tools and cases were all a product of the common stock of experiences, as well as an artefact reproducing this stock of experience, not the least through the language they provided (cf. Orlikowski 1988). However, as the examples of International and Local showed, this was by no means a closed loop of reproduction. Rather, the room for innovation was considerable.

6.4. CONCLUSIONS

The focus of this chapter has been the knowledge base of the management consultant. Based on the ambiguous treatment of knowledge in consulting in the literature on management consulting, two questions were identified. A first question concerned the knowledge content of management consulting, and a second concerned the sources, utilization, and application of this knowledge. These two questions were studied in two quite different management consulting organizations—one large, multinational US-based consultancy and one small, Swedish, internal consulting organization. The knowledge sources, knowledge levers, and application of knowledge in the two consultancies are summarized in Table 6.1.

In much of the critical literature on management consulting, functional knowledge on managerial issues is largely denied as a basis for management consulting. Instead, simplified, abstract management fads and fashions as well as the consultants' (rhetorical) skills in manipulating symbols and myths in order to create an impression of knowledge and value are emphasized. However, this study of consultants' work at International and Local, respectively, shows that the consultants' actions were to a large extent based on

---

[3] See also Stolterman (1991), Fristedt (1995), and Fitzgerald (1998), who show a similar pattern for IT consultants.

Table 6.1. *Summary and comparison of the handling of knowledge at International and Local*

	International (Large, international, hierarchical organization)	Local (Small, Swedish, flat organization)
Knowledge sources	—Experiences in a hierarchical project team —Experiences in expert networks —Articulate experiences in methods, tools, and cases	—Individual experiences —Colleagues' experiences gained in informal contacts —Articulate experiences in methods, tools, and cases
Knowledge levers	Methods as: —Enabler of hierarchical division of labour —Organizational memory —Communication of new knowledge Cases as: —Organizational examples of method application —Organizational blueprints for design —Trigger for personal contacts	Methods as: —Knowledge source for newcomers —Facilitator of face-to-face exchange of experience (common language) —Uncertainty reduction for consultants Cases as: —Individual examples of method application —Individual blueprints for design
Knowledge application	—Translation of methods and cases to the specific client situation as an experience-based process	—Translation of methods and cases to the specific client situation as an experience-based process

detailed functional knowledge aimed at improving the operations of the client organization (rather than creating an impression of such improvements). Based on their own and colleagues' earlier experiences, the consultants put considerable effort into the design of solutions and approaches that fitted the specific client situation. The design of a consulting project was an experience-based activity in which methods and old cases were adapted to the specific situation. Methods and cases were handled pragmatically and changes, additions, and omissions to what was prescribed by the method were common (see also Benders, van den Berg, and van Bijsterveld 1998).

The mechanisms through which the individual consultants' experiences were applied were the subject of the second question addressed in this paper. Here, methods and cases were found to be important levers, although in slightly different ways in the different organizations (see Table 6.1). At International the articulation of experience into methods and cases was an important aspect of its exploitation. Through this articulation, individual consultants' experience was made easily communicable through the company's knowledge database. Methods had a role as organizational memory and as a way of communicating new insights within the consulting company. However, the method was not viewed as a directly applicable blueprint for a specific consulting project. Rather, its main role was to provide a common structure and language, which made possible a hierarchical division of labour based on the senior consultants' experience. The method provided the basic structure and language which enabled an efficient interaction between consultants with different levels of experience in the project teams. The experienced consultants continuously managed the translation of the method to the specific case. Old cases were another important vehicle for transferring experience between consultants at International. The documentation from old cases, as artefacts of consultants' experience, was regularly used as a blueprint for the design of both approaches and solutions. However, as was the case with the methods, the cases had to be translated to the specific situation. This required the involvement of experienced senior consultants and often led to personal contacts with the consultants directly involved in the old cases.

At Local, the sharing of experience involved the articulation of this experience to a lesser degree. Rather, it took place in more or less formalized face-to-face meetings between consultants. However, methods were also especially important in this case. They provided a knowledge source for newcomers and, more importantly, a common language facilitating the face-to-face exchange of experience. The translation of the standard approach provided by the method to the specific situation was also described in this case as a main success factor involving the consultants' experience. However, the sharing of experience at Local was much less systematic than in the case of International. A comparison of the two cases indicates that smaller organizations might actually have a disadvantage compared with large organizations, linked to their ability to build and maintain their knowledge base. This disadvantage is related to knowledge sources as well as the ability to extract and apply the knowledge generated.

Given that the main source of knowledge in consulting is experience from projects, a larger number of projects proportionally broadens the knowledge base of the consultancy. The larger number of projects at International compared to Local supports the generation of a more comprehensive as well as more contemporary knowledge base, which is made available to the organization as documented cases and constantly updated methods and tools. At Local one of the reasons given for the low degree of interest in old cases was that they were regarded as outdated when the next similar project came up. The volume of knowledge available on a specific issue was also limited. At International, on the other hand, it was usually possible to find a number of recent projects relevant to the current topic. Another problem named by Local consultants in relation to the accumulation of knowledge within the consultancy was the difficulty in motivating the costs of engaging in activities connected with a formalization and condensation of consultants' individual experiences. This was not an issue at International, where a considerably larger volume of business could carry the continuous involvement of a large number of people in the creation and formalization of knowledge.

The larger consultancies' advantages in relation to the smaller ones are further related to the ability to make use of previous experience. An important enabler of this utilization was the hierarchical division of labour in projects. As shown above, the hierarchy at International greatly facilitated the efficient utilization of the organization's key asset—experience. The spreading of this knowledge within the organization was supported by the collaboration of consultants in large project teams as well as the vertical division of labour—again, functions linked to company size.

In conclusion, the case-studies point to the existence of economies of scale related to knowledge in management consulting (cf. also Kipping and Scheybani 1994). Realizing these economies of scale is a question of both managing the knowledge generation process, i.e. supporting the articulation of knowledge in a way that makes it possible to spread it to the organization's members, as well as providing these members with the key—the experience—needed to decode and successfully deploy this explicit knowledge. With either of these functions missing, the potential advantages of size will not be realized. Without a mechanism for identifying knowledge in the ongoing projects and for extending this knowledge to the organization, the knowledge generated in the different projects will remain individual, and of no value to the organization at large. The same is true when a shared set of experiences enabling the translation of explicit knowledge to the specific case is missing. Without this, consultants will be unable to put the explicit knowledge into productive use. Only when both these functions exist simultaneously can the economies of scale identified above be realized.

7

Knowledge Management at the Country Level: A Large Consulting Firm in Italy

CRISTINA CRUCINI

7.1. INTRODUCTION

The issue of knowledge management in consulting organizations has been at the core of a recent stream of research (e.g. Morris and Empson 1998; Morris 2001; Sarvary 1999; Hansen, Nohria, and Tierney 1999). For 'knowledge-intensive firms' (Starbuck 1992; Maister 1993) such as management consultancies, knowledge represents a key resource and a competitive advantage. Most of these studies are derived from large American consultancies implying, in one way, that they represent a sort of 'best model' to be replicated in similar companies, without regard to the context in which they operate. This is not surprising given that the largest and most visible management consultancies—like McKinsey or Andersen Consulting (Accenture from 2001)—are of American origin and are often seen as representing consulting as a whole (Kipping 1996, 2002). As a consequence, the existing literature tends to treat professional service firms as one entity, that is to say as global organizations adopting the same strategies and approaches worldwide, almost unaffected by the external context in which they operate. This assumption seems to imply a certain degree of standardization, both in terms of content (e.g. the products available to clients) and structure (e.g. the internal organization of consultancies).

It has been suggested that management knowledge, in the form of tools and methodologies, can easily be transferred within professional services firms (Werr 1998; Hansen, Nohria, and Tierney 1999; Sarvary 1999). At the same time, the intrinsic nature of management consulting as an intangible service rather than as a concrete product, implies that every step of the process through which the service is provided involves a direct interaction between various institutional actors embedded in their specific context. Moreover, the tacit dimension of knowledge deployed by consulting firms, largely 'embedded' in consultants, can be 'sticky' and does not flow easily inside organizations (Morris 2001). These assumptions raise questions about the viability of those analyses that present large consulting firms as 'one global firm' and disregard the contingent environment in which they operate.

Therefore, a number of studies (Kipping 1996; Kipping, Furusten, and Gammelsæter 1998/1999; Crucini and Kipping 2001) have highlighted how cultural and structural differences among countries often require an adaptation of general management knowledge and ideas. In fact when there is a process of transfer involving organizational practices or knowledge, as in the case of consulting, the success of the transfer is determined to a great extent by the transferability of meanings, values, and knowledge. Indeed, such processes of transfer do not occur in a social vacuum but, rather, are 'contextually embedded' (Kostova 1999: 4). Hence it might happen that the country-specific contexts in which management consultancies operate lead to the development of different strategies for managing knowledge. This phenomenon manifests itself not only among different kinds of consultancies (in terms of size or nationality) but also within the same company operating simultaneously in different countries. In fact, 'it is difficult to ensure a unique interpretation of best practices residing in information repositories since knowledge is created by the individuals in the process of using the data' (Malhorta 2000: 54).

However, most of the literature on knowledge management has only partially analysed how the knowledge of consultancies is adapted to specific circumstances. Thus, Werr (in Chapter 6, above) concludes that, when faced with new cases, consultants need to adapt their existing knowledge to fit the specific client situation. And Morris (2001) has highlighted how local adaptations of consulting activities continually arise within any centralized product, as consultants interpret problems and make adjustments to contextual demands. Hence, the issue of how management consultancies adapt management knowledge to a specific context has so far been examined only as an external phenomenon, as a necessity linked to the need to provide personalized and innovative solutions to context-driven demand. What has not been taken into account is that the need for 'adapting' and 'translating' knowledge and experiences is also an internal phenomenon taking place within these organizations and affecting their knowledge management strategy as well as other practices.

This seems to be particularly the case for HR management, given that consultants represent a primary source of knowledge for their companies. In order to maximize this resource, consultants' embedded or 'pre-installed' knowledge has to be integrated into the collective knowledge existing within the firm. In other words, because tacit knowledge can be considered as context-specific, the process through which consultants' knowledge background on one side and the consultancy's own corporate knowledge on the other, integrate and adapt to each other has to be taken into account. As suggested by Sarvary (1999: 100), 'a good knowledge management system incorporates the organization's culture' and, at the same time, is accepted by its employees who 'use it, but also ... feed into it'. Any adaptation and translation process should therefore not only address clients (and the external context) but also consultants within the firm, and consultancies themselves, in order to minimize eventual ambiguities resulting from different interpretations of information, procedures and behaviours.

Against this background, this chapter focuses on knowledge management in professional service firms and attempts to examine how and to what extent management consultancies are affected by the external environment in which they operate when managing their knowledge asset. It is based on the case of a large professional service firm (called 'Global Consulting Italia' to preserve anonymity) operating between two different institutional and cultural dimensions: its international and corporate identity and the local specificity of the Italian environment. Information and data are derived from an internship held by the author within the company, from January to April 2000. The detailed description is based on the observations of the author, on internal company documents and Intranet sources, as well as on interviews with ten consultants at different levels within the firm.

The interviews presented in this chapter were carried out between the middle of February and the middle of March 2000. All the interviews lasted between 45 minutes and one hour. The names of the consultants to be interviewed were chosen by the head of HR at Global Consulting Italia according to the following criteria:

- Profesional level—we wanted to include consultants at different stages of their career so the following interviewees were chosen: two consultants, two senior consultants, one manager, one specialist, one senior manager, one senior specialist, and one partner.
- Date of employment—we wanted to include consultants with at least two years' experience within the company so that they had already taken part in other Performance Appraisal processes.

The interviews included both open-ended questions and questions where responses had to be given according to fixed scales of 1 to 5.

The initial theoretical section of this chapter will introduce the main concepts and categories on knowledge management systems, and on the different kinds of knowledge deployed within consulting firms. The second section will present the empirical case, including some background to the international consulting firm studied and a detailed description of the knowledge management systems and of the HR policies adopted within its Italian office. Conclusions on knowledge management and on its 'degree of adaptability', internally, as well as externally, will follow.

7.2. KNOWLEDGE MANAGEMENT IN CONSULTING: A FRAMEWORK

Knowledge generation, management, and diffusion has been addressed in an increasing number of studies ever since management gurus, such as Porter or Drucker, pointed out that firms' most recent strategic assets are represented by knowledge. Management consulting is not only 'knowledge-bearing and knowledge-disseminating' (Stehr 1994: 171), but also a people-intensive business, largely dependent on 'knowledge workers' (Drucker 1993: 5). This definition seems based on two main assumptions. The first is that knowledge is an asset whose value (also in terms of money) is directly dependent on its innovative impact and on the velocity of its obsolescence (Martignago 1998). The second assumption is that the knowledge deployed by these organizations comes from two different sources: from their employees (individual dimension) and from the company's accumulated experience (collective dimension).

Recent developments in IT (like the Internet or Intranet) have offered powerful and fast tools to collect and codify the scattered knowledge within organizations into knowledge repositories or knowledge banks. The main reason behind this process is that 'IT can enable the sharing of information between various employees, thus preventing duplication of information while offering the advantage of immediate access to information ... at any time, at any place and in whatever form' (Malhorta 2000: 39). At the same time, though, such devices can demonstrate limitations due to the fast-changing environment in which consultancies operate, and to the diverse interpretations that the different users might attribute to the available knowledge.

This dichotomy between 'technology' and 'people' also emerges from the existing studies on knowledge management and knowledge management systems (KMS from now onwards). Hansen, Nohria, and Tierney (1999) distinguish between two main strategies: 'codification', largely based on IT and focusing on the systematization and storing of knowledge, and 'personalization', which focuses on people and stresses the importance of the communication of knowledge. The choice between the two depends on the company's competitive strategy; companies preferring a codification strategy count on the 'economics of reuse', while those relying on a personalization strategy focus on the logic of 'expert economics' (Hansen, Nohria, and Tierney 1999: 100). Even though he uses a different terminology, Sarvary (1999: 96) suggests a similar approach to distinguishing KMS. In his analysis, 'decentralized' KMS place more emphasis on people (as a source of knowledge) rather than information technology (as the infrastructure for its distribution). At the other extreme, 'centralized' KMS are built on advanced IT systems connecting and distributing the firm's knowledge (Sarvary 1999: 102–3).

Codified/centralized KMS aim at institutionalizing 'best practices' (e.g. processes, procedures, reference works, etc.) by embedding them in IT in order to facilitate the efficient handling of routines, 'linear', and 'predictable' situations (Malhorta 2000: 43). In doing so, organizations' efforts are focused around the archiving of best practices for at least two main reasons. First, for later reference by other employees; it is believed that the observance of these practices would facilitate efficient problem-solving and prevent unnecessary search processes. Secondly, to ensure compliance with fixed regulations and procedures, in other words they minimize the variance between the pre-specified rules and the actual executions (Malhorta 2000: 48). Codified/centralized KMS seem to treat knowledge as an 'object' that can be identified and handled in information systems supported by IT (Sveiby 1996: 1).

On the other hand, personalized/decentralized KMS aim at incorporating the human dimension of organizational knowledge creation (Manville and Foote 1996). The main assumption behind these systems is that successful knowledge transfers do not involve computers or documents but rather interaction between people. Personalized/decentralized KMS reject the idea that knowledge can be unproblematic, pre-defined, and pre-packaged (Boland 1987). On the contrary, they emphasize that, because 'knowledge originates in the minds of the knowers' (Davenport and Prusak 1998: 5), KMS should be 'open-ended to allow diversity of multiple personal perspectives' (Malhorta 2000: 51). Personalized/decentralized KMS seem to emphasize that 'knowledge is a process', a complex set of dynamic skills, know-how, etc., that is constantly changing (Sveiby 1996: 1). Table 7.1 presents a summary of these differences.

Table 7.1. *A typology of knowledge management systems*

Type of strategy	Form of management	KMS based on	Type of firm	Degree of standardization
Codification	Centrally from the top	IT	Operational consulting	High
Personalization	Decentralized; limited central coordination	People	Strategy consulting	Low

It seems, therefore, that codification/centralization strategies follow an 'IT-track' approach (Sveiby 1996). They are usually built and managed from the top and establish connections through large central organizations (e.g. 'knowledge banks', 'knowledge repositories', etc.). In collecting and codifying knowledge they aim at institutionalizing best practice that will be redistributed within the organization with high levels of speed and conformity. This in turn means that the contents diffused appear highly standardized and therefore do not need to be adapted before being used. As for personalization/decentralization strategies, they seem based on a 'people-track' approach (Sveiby 1996). The process of interaction only is centrally coordinated to a limited extent and is left more open-ended in order to leave people the central role. IT is used to connect people more efficiently rather than for other purposes. Such systems are based on the belief that IT does not allow the transfer of 'associated emotions and specific "contexts" in which the information is embedded' (Imai, Nonaka, and Takeuchi 1985: 63). These assumptions imply that the contents diffused through these systems display a low degree of standardization and rather depend on the users.

On the basis of the previous reasoning, the choice of one strategy or the other should impact on the organizational strategies of consulting firms, especially on large consultancies operating in different countries at the same time. In fact, some assumptions can also be drawn from the table above with respect to context dependency. As mentioned earlier, KMS seem to show different degrees of standardization. The choice of codification strategies seems to imply that knowledge management is highly standardized and centrally managed. Technical or product-based knowledge is easier to codify, store, and transfer, especially through IT support (Hansen, Nohria, and Tierney 1999; Sarvary 1999), therefore codification strategies seem to be more appropriate for those consultancies whose advantage lies in this area of expertise (operational consulting). Besides, the codification of knowledge management seems to require a limited degree of adaptation, mainly to update old and codified knowledge to face the changes in demand. These assumptions allow the advancement of the hypothesis that codification strategies in knowledge management display a low degree of context dependency.

On the other hand, personalization strategies are built on people and require decentralization. They emphasize the value of the 'human factor' in terms of knowledge and expertise, implying that knowledge management cannot be reduced to the pure codification of technical knowledge (Morris 2001). Personalized KMS are usually adopted by those consultancies whose strength lies in their unique problem-solving expertise (strategy consulting). Such strategies seem to require adaptability rather than standardization of knowledge management, especially as they seem to display a high context dependency. Such a distinction, though, should not be interpreted as a mutually exclusive polarization (the authors do not seem to imply it either). On the contrary, it seems possible to suggest that the two strategies can co-exist, maybe with one prevailing over the other according to the chosen approach and activities of consulting firms. International consultancies in particular, given the scale and scope of their operations, might need to use both strategies at the same time. They have to pay attention to people issues in terms of motivation, culture, reward, trust, etc., and to focus on IT for the packaging, storing, and distribution of knowledge.

In order to examine to what extent these assumptions are reflected in the knowledge management strategies of the case-study presented in the following section, this chapter looks mainly at three different issues:

- The organization and structure of the company, with respect to its Italian development and activities. The aim of this overview is to place the firm in its country-specific environment. An attempt will be made to describe what the two types of knowledge management strategies mean for the organizational structure of the company presented in the case-study; it will show how the coexistence of the two strategies outlined above implies a high level of centralization in some organizational aspects (the IT-track) and a more flexible and adaptive approach in others (the people-track).

- The development, strategy, and main operations of its KMS. This analysis will examine two main aspects. First, how and why the shift of focus from one knowledge management strategy to the other takes place within the company. The background assumption here is that the KMS should reflect this duality integrating the IT-processing aspects and the human creative processes. Secondly, if and to what extent knowledge management has been adapted at the country level. The background assumption this time is that knowledge management strategies and systems vary not only among different firms but also within the same firm operating simultaneously in different countries.

- The human resources (HR) management within the firm, especially with respect to selection and evaluation procedures. If the knowledge management strategies of the company include personalization, this should also emerge from the organization's HR strategy, reward system, and resource allocation system, which should stress the link between individual knowledge creation and the company's general performance. This analysis should enhance the understanding of the inter-dependence between HR management and knowledge management within consulting firms. The background assumption is that, if 'knowledge resides in the users' (Churchman 1971: 10), HR management is an integral part of wider knowledge management strategies. This fact in turn implies that, because the users (in this case consultants) are endowed with a 'pre-installed' knowledge, mainly constituted by their educational and professional background, the KMS integrating their contributions can be standardized to a very limited extent.

Disregarding the various labels given to this practice ('knowledge sharing', 'intellectual capital management', etc.), the literature has so far dealt with knowledge management either by stressing 'what' is to be shared (contents) or 'how' to do it (mechanisms). The understanding of knowledge management in the consulting field has to include the analysis of the process through which general strategies and systems are adapted to fit specific companies in specific contexts. A starting-point might be to include 'who' (consultants) are sharing 'where' (context) in this analysis.

7.3. BACKGROUND ON THE CONSULTANCY STUDIED

Global is a large professional service firm of Anglo-American origin. It has more than 700 offices located in 134 different countries. Management consulting is among Global's main activities, and its consulting group is ranked among the top five consultancies worldwide. In 1998 Global Consulting had a turnover of between $10 bn. and $12 bn. and a growth rate of 20 per cent with respect to the previous year. This introductory overview of the company aims at explaining how a large foreign professional services firm has developed its Italian activities. More importantly, it takes into account the degree of centralization or decentralization (or 'adaptability') displayed in the company's organizational choices and structures that might allow us to understand what kind of knowledge management strategies have been adopted and why.

The Activities in Italy

In 1990 Global started its activity in Italy by acquiring an Italian firm in a sector related to consulting. A few years later it also officially launched its management consulting activities in Italy under the name of Global Consulting Italia, incorporating four Italian consultancies. In the following years the range of activities performed in Italy increased greatly and today the group in Italy is composed of fourteen companies, each specializing in a specific activity including: management consulting and IT, mergers and acquisitions, accounting, financial consulting, internet consulting, computer security, etc. Since 1993, the whole Global group in Italy has registered constant growth in its activities, both in terms of profits and in terms of consultants.

Given the focus of this study, attention has been directed specifically at the consulting arm of the group: Global Consulting Italia (hereafter GCI). GCI has five main offices (four in the North and one in the Centre of Italy), but the total number of branches, including all minor branches, rises to about twenty. In 1999 it employed around 900 consultants. Within the company, employees are subdivided into five levels: consultants represent 45 per cent of all employees, senior consultants 24 per cent, managers/specialists 16 per cent, senior managers/senior specialists 10 per cent, partners/principals 5 per cent; staff members (i.e. support staff not involved in consulting activities) represent around 10 per cent (data for 1999/2000). The average age within GCI is 31 years. Apart from the managing partner and two other partners, the number of foreign consultants is quite low (much less than 10 per cent of the total). GCI has clients in all main industry and service sectors, both in the private and in the public sector.

The Internal Organization of GCI

GCI is organized by internal competences and not by client industries, so that people can move among sectors and work on different projects where their specialization is required. In theory this organization should allow the allocation of 'the best resources' to where they are needed at any one time, suggesting that a strong emphasis is put on human capital as a source of knowledge. The firm's internal organizational structure is based on three main areas called 'dimensions', each of which is composed of a number of sub-dimensions.

The first dimension, called 'Approach to the Market', is comprised of three units: Products (Chemical, Manufacturing, Electronics, etc.), Services (Banking, Media, Government, etc), and Middle Market.[1] The second dimension is called 'Solution Set' and it represents Global Consulting's offer-set for the Italian market. The units included in this dimension are Shared Services, Strategic Advisory Services, Knowledge-Based Management, Supply Chain, Customer Connections, and New Product Development. The third dimension is that of Competence Centres, and its main units are Business Transformation ERP (Enterprise Resource Planning: SAP, BaaN, JDEdwards, etc.), and Business Transformation Management (BCI/Change Management, CRM (Customer Relationship Management) Technologies, etc.).

One or more partners are responsible for each dimension, but there is also an ulterior subdivision according to the various units of industries or products. As a result some partners have direct responsibility for more units at the same time; consequently the three main dimensions are very closely connected, while maintaining a degree of independence. Each unit has its own targets and time schedule, and all the units contribute to the total revenue and objectives according to centrally established percentages. In addition, there is a direct and vertical relationship between the managing partner and the other partners, to whom all the units report regularly, thus allowing a high level of coordination and control. This closer insight into the internal organization of GCI confirms that the company, despite some centrally decided coordination mechanisms, displays a propensity towards maintaining a flexibility in the setting of goals and strategies and in the use of resources.

Apart from these main dimensions that are directly involved in the consulting process, as they deal directly with clients, there are at least four other independent units to be considered: Culture, Education and Training, Knowledge Management, and Human Resources. They are specifically dedicated to internal functions and could be defined 'transversal' as they are involved with the work done by all the other units, especially with respect to the management of knowledge within the firm.

---

[1] According to GCI classification, the middle market is composed of companies with a turnover of up to 200 bn. Lira (approx. 103 million Euro), with no industry distinction.

Under the Culture unit are grouped all those activities and initiatives that promote Global Consulting's corporate identity and its chosen 'one firm' approach both at the international and the national level. At the same time, the unit is in charge of promoting those professional values in which the company believes (e.g. integrity, trust, positivity, etc.) and that should be reflected in the working experience. It follows that it supervises quite a large part of the work performed by Education and Training (e.g. checking the training activities), by Knowledge Management (e.g. stressing the importance of knowledge-sharing procedures), and by Human Resources (e.g. in the performance appraisal process). Behind their declared mission, it seems possible to suggest that the other function played by these transversal units is the matching of the internal and external cultural diversity (embedded in the consultants and in the context) with the 'one' corporate culture of GCI.

The 'Home' Structure

GCI has a particular system of internal mentors called 'Home'. Every new employee gets his own Home within the first month. Consultants within GCI become Homes for other colleagues only from the level of manager onwards. Every Home has some major roles: defining, together with the new employees, their career path and their professional development process, managing the performance evaluation process, and acting as 'counsellor' for concerns and advice. The Home and the project leader may not be the same person; in this way the Home can act as an external and neutral 'judge' in a disputed case on a professional matter of any kind, and during the performance appraisal.

The emphasis put by GCI on its 'human assets' seems confirmed by the hierarchical structure within the company, which is arranged in such a way that junior consultants are constantly supervised by more senior ones. This mechanism seems to enhance the learning programme as well as the transfer of competences, given that in consulting 'expertise increases with seniority' (Morris and Empson 1998: 615). These observations suggest that knowledge management implies a kind of 'rediscovery of the human factor: every competitive advantage connected to a new product or technique is fragile because rapidly reproducible; what cannot be reproduced, instead, is the human knowledge asset of each firm' (Chinnici 1999: 1).

7.4. THE KNOWLEDGE MANAGEMENT SYSTEM OF GCI

On the basis of the information collected by the author it seems possible to say that the Global Consulting KMS has been set up mainly following a codification/centralization strategy. With the support of a strong and pervasive IT infrastructure, knowledge is codified and stored in databases where it can be accessed easily and quickly by anyone in the company worldwide. At the same time, though, the company relies heavily on the specialist knowledge of its consultants and therefore generates its competitive advantage by combining intellectual capital and information technology. The following section will attempt to show how these two strategies are combined within GCI.

Developments in the KMS in Italy

The GCI Knowledge Management Group was set up in 1997, in a way confirming the fact that knowledge management is quite a young practice whose affirmation only started at the beginning of the 1990s. At that time, no search engine was available in Italy and consultants had to individually search the central knowledge-bases replicated locally from the global repositories of Global Consulting worldwide.

The mechanisms through which the KMS within Global Consulting have evolved seem to represent an example of what Sarvary (1999: 103) defines as 'relatively centralized systems that are built and managed from the top'. In fact, the KM Group in Italy works according to the Company Knowledge Sharing Agreement, which regulates submissions to the consulting service's worldwide document repository. Following the indications coming from the USA, where the whole process was most advanced, the Italians started working on the submission process and on the submission database. They began preparing a Word questionnaire to collect information, to create a submission form, and to collect deliverables from consultants. As a result, the way knowledge is collected and implemented in the KMS within GCI is quite a precise 'replication' of the central system existing in the USA. As suggested by Hansen, Nohria, and Tierney (1999: 108) the 'people-to-document' approach allows many people to search and retrieve codified knowledge at the same time, thus opening the 'possibility of achieving scale in knowledge reuse'.

E-mail submission was presented to Italian consultants (650 at the time) in August 1998 and in November they started piloting the system. According to the Italian KM Group data, in 1999 Italy provided the largest number of submissions to Global Consulting's global repositories (relative to the number of projects carried out in Italy). Starting from 1997, the KM Group defined incentives for submissions, from giving a prize to the best contributor and the best team every month to evaluating the quality of deliverables in terms of career advancement. This fact shows that consultancies have to take into account that 'professionals might be reluctant to share their knowledge with their colleagues who are also competitors in the internal market for promotion' (Morris and Empson 1998: 617) and find solutions to overcome this impediment. GCI has also addressed this issue by incorporating 'knowledge sharing' evaluation in its performance measures both for monetary and career rewards (see below).

The Aims and Activities of the KMS

Knowledge within Global Consulting worldwide, and consequently in Italy, is collected centrally and then re-distributed mainly through deliverables and documents from old projects, through information and data on industries and markets, and through 'operational' tools. Everything that is produced during a project—such as business check-ups, presentations, etc—is stored in a global thematic database (running on the Global Consulting server) accessible by all consultants. The database is organized according to country, industry or sector, type of intervention, and consulting practice. Consultants use such information to look for ideas and procedures that have already been tested in other engagements. The advantage is that, being a codified and centralized worldwide database of almost everything done within the company, it becomes possible to access rapidly projects conducted by teams with the strongest expertise in one specific sector or practice. This fact seems to confirm the observation that 'much higher efficiency gains and, more importantly, qualitative improvement in knowledge creation can be gained if the synthesis, the integration of the firm's experience is done centrally' (Sarvary 1999: 99). At the same time, as pointed out in the theory section, codified or centralized strategies speed up the search process and ensure compliance with the company's pre-established formats (Malhorta 2000).

According to Global Consulting's 'one firm' approach, in fact, every type of document has to be written according to the company 'format'. In this way all the stored information and documents become a sort of 'tool', a formalized guide to what has to be produced next. For example they show the average length or structure of a presentation, what kind of project proposal is more suitable for a certain type of client, and so on. The 'accessibility' of such materials everywhere and at all times can also be seen as a kind of continuous training to which consultants regularly submit themselves. Besides benefiting from this KMS, they understand practically the importance of shared and re-usable knowledge. Global Consulting's knowledge databases also include specific external data and information on market trends, industries, etc. at an international level. Some of them are collected and elaborated internally, some are commissioned from specialists (e.g. the Gartner Group), and some are taken from the web or other sources.

To these centrally codified knowledge sources another, less formalized, source has to be added. That is the consultants' accumulated experience and expertise. In fact, consultants moving among countries with their accumulated competences and qualifications enrich the knowledge stored in Global Consulting's knowledge database. This seems to suggest that Global Consulting is trying to integrate the advantages derived from a codification strategy with those coming from person-to-person knowledge exchanges in order to benefit from the tacit knowledge embedded in every consultant. As a matter of fact, the simplification of contextual information necessary for storage in IT-enabled repositories does not allow the retention of internal diversity and multiple viewpoints associated with human involvement in knowledge creation (Malhorta 2000). Therefore, even if a codification KMS appears predominant in GCI, the company also seems to have invested in a personalization strategy, which tries to counterbalance the limits of the former.

To facilitate this process, the main services offered by the KM Group within GCI range from the simple collection of sources and information for all practitioners to the management and diffusion of competence databases at an international level. More precisely, the activities performed by the KM Group might be classified as those treating knowledge as an 'object' and those treating knowledge as a 'process' (Sveiby 1996), implying a different degree of standardization. To the first group belong standardized services, such as the internal library and the acquisition of new sources through which GCI consultants can obtain various types of data. Navigation support (Help-Desk assistance) for the submission procedure to the knowledge bank and the coordination of submissions also belong to this group. On the other side, to the group of services that are less standardized, belong specific training activities organized and performed in cooperation with the Education and Training unit. More significantly, this group includes all activities related to the so-called competence databases and CV management, which Global Consulting considers to be one of its main assets. These databases collect the CVs of all employees in a standard format (those in the specific case of Italy are both in Italian and in English); all the CVs are updated at the end of every project and training course. In this way they are always available for the other Global Consulting branches, which, in case of need, can ask for the help of one or more consultants. This mechanism helps to create what the company calls 'mobility of resources'; consultants with 'unique' skills and competencies can join other teams, even in other countries, and bring their expertise to bear.

All these procedures seem to confirm what has been pointed out by Werr (in Chapter 6, above) with respect to the use of old cases and formalized methods and tools. Also in the case presented here, they seem to constitute a sort of 'company format', a common base (language, style, approach, etc.) for employees to develop new knowledge and solutions according to the company's general vision. On more theoretical grounds, it could be argued that these mechanisms characterize the codification knowledge management strategy within GCI and resemble what Malhorta (2000: 45) calls 'consensus building models'. According to Malhorta, such models use knowledge repositories to store 'best practices' that tend to institutionalize the organization's chosen status quo. In doing so, the stored knowledge in the form of objects requires a limited adaptation level (mainly external adaptation to fit the demand) and the company's corporate culture seems to prevail over the national culture in which it operates, thus displaying very low context dependence.

On the other hand, it has been pointed out that the use of codification strategies for knowledge management within GCI does not exclude a quite evident focus on people. As suggested by the existing literature, especially by Morris (2001) and Werr (see Chapter 6, above), different strategies in knowledge management might be complementary rather than alternative. Person-to-person knowledge exchanges are promoted and highly evaluated within GCI; knowledge moves around with people and contributes to the success of best practices within the company at an international level. Taking an opposite approach to the 'static' view of knowledge as objects, the importance attached to people's contribution seems rather to derive from a perception of knowledge as 'a fluid mix of framed experience, values, contextual information and expert insight' (Davenport and Prusak 1998: 5). Instead of promoting an unquestionable adherence to pre-specified routines and procedures, this 'participative model' enables a certain level of internal diversity that matches the complexity of the changing environment 'facilitating organizations' self-designing' (Malhorta 2000: 48). The adoption of personalization strategies therefore implies a significant level of adaptation, sometimes even translation, more than the standardization of knowledge; adaptation to the human capital employed within a consulting firm in a specific environment is especially vital. In this respect, personalization strategies can be defined as context dependent.

The extent to which consultants are willing to share their individual accumulated knowledge constitutes a complication in the implementation of personalization strategies. Evidence from this case seems to confirm that consultants need incentives to share their personal knowledge and experiences with other colleagues within the company. Morris and Empson (1998: 617), for example, mention the gain of 'high personal prestige' as a vehicle to overcome consultants' reluctance. GCI addresses this issue in two different ways: at a macro level by putting a strong emphasis on the collective sharing of knowledge and creating mechanisms in which consultants at different levels interact with one another; at a micro level through a system of rewards and 'game-like' internal competition. A similar strategy seems to have been adopted by McKinsey through their 'Practice Olympics' (Bartlett 1997: 13), in which teams of consultants worldwide were encouraged to develop ideas and present them in regional competitions.

7.5. HUMAN RESOURCE PRACTICES

Consultants, as illustrated in the previous section, seem to play a significant role in the knowledge management strategy within GCI. This section will therefore focus on human resource management within the company. In doing so, it aims to point out the link between HR and knowledge management within consulting firms, as well as adding more detail on how and why personalization strategies can only be standardized to a limited extent. The HR unit within GCI is centralized in the main Italian office. Its activities are subdivided into two main areas, one dealing with administrative issues (retribution, social security, etc.) and the other taking care of all the other processes such as research and selection of personnel, hiring, career advancement systems, and performance appraisal. Education and Training is a partially independent unit operating under the joint supervision of the HR and Culture units.

From Selection to Hiring

Before a consultant at any level (apart from senior managers and partners) receives a formal job offer from GCI he or she has to go through quite an articulated selection process. The first phase of screening is based on the selection of curricula. There are three main ways in which the company obtains CVs from candidates: some arrive spontaneously, some arrive following specific adverts in the national press, and the others from head-hunters, who cooperate with the company on a regular basis. In special circumstances, for example when the company is seeking competences that are very much in demand, GCI organizes so-called 'career days' within different Italian universities. In this way the company creates a direct link with the students (who usually hand in their CVs on these occasions) and the universities, which become a sort of 'reservoir' of potential candidates. All CVs are then sorted according to the candidates' qualifications. The rest of the hiring process has a first phase consisting of a written test session, followed by at least three individual interviews.

This process exemplifies the interrelation between HR policies and the wider strategies through which consulting firms acquire new knowledge through people. When hiring new consultants they decide a priori what kind of competences they are looking for, but they also know that such competences and knowledge are highly context-specific, especially in terms of educational background. Morris and Empson (1998: 612) have pointed out that the way in which knowledge is 'created, deployed and updated has implications for recruitment and training' within professional service firms. In this respect it seems that the contrary is also true, as the selection and training of consultants has implications for the knowledge management of these firms, as they come with a pre-installed knowledge base. With respect to the initial theoretical assumptions, these facts confirm that personalization strategies are people-dependent but also context-dependent and might therefore display a certain level of variation from one country to another.

The HR unit in the main Italian office manages the whole selection and hiring process unless there are special circumstances (e.g. when the number of candidates to be selected is really high), in which case the first screening and selection is outsourced to external companies specialized in this field. When this happens GCI gives the external company exact descriptions of the professional profiles they are looking for, but then the other company is responsible for the whole screening and selection process except for the last 'technical' interview. This in turn means that, despite being a large and foreign company, GCI finds its standards compatible with those of smaller and national companies operating in the HR field in Italy. The reasons behind this could be either that the company has somehow adapted its HR practices to the local market, or that the methodologies relative to this specific practice are homogenized to quite a wide extent within the Italian context.

This in turn might also be taken as another indication of how the context in which companies operate exerts an influence on their strategies. The information provided on HR management within GCI seems to represent an example of how, in response to external contextual influences, professional service firms adapt internally. One issue that draws attention to this influence is that the company is to some extent dependent on the specific Italian context for the selection of its consultants, who carry with them an Italian educational and cultural background. This issue has to be taken into account given that consultants' cultural identity will have to match the company's own corporate identity.

Education and Training

The same assumptions about the context's influence on HR practices seem validated by the Education and Training procedures. The training programme at GCI has been based on the Global Competency Model that tries to meet global and country-specific needs. This approach can be interpreted as an attempt to generate added value if, as Morris (2001) suggests, adding value derives from the conjunction of consultants' generic content expertise and familiarity with the context in which they operate. This implies quite high levels of homogenization of the training procedures, in terms of tools and topics, among the countries where Global Consulting operates. For example, one of the mandatory courses, called Value Management, is said to be the same across the various national training centres, and in fact the experts holding the course in Italy are also among the teaching staff in the UK and other European countries. At the same time, the fact that a major part of the training is done 'on the job', implies that a significant proportion of expertise generated in projects is also context-specific.

The training programme, composed of common compulsory courses and different specializations, is established according to the professional level and the role performed by each consultant; he or she has a personal training card on which the mandatory courses for the year, as well as the progress of attendance, are recorded. Learning is based on a combination of classroom training and on-the-job training, coupled with specific engagements with clients and business experience. The annual training programme developed within GCI is a process that takes place according to the phases outlined below.

The process starts with a self-assessment through which the newly hired employees evaluate their skills and competences relative to the competency model established within Global Consulting. A training programme for the six months of activity is fixed with the assistance of the mentor (the 'Home'), establishing which training activities will be put on the consultant's training card. The evaluations marked on the training card, together with the evaluation of the engagement experiences conducted over the same period (including the application of the tools and techniques taught in class), are then assessed during the performance appraisal. This is the moment when the performances of all consultants are tracked and evaluated; the results of this process are then utilized to update and refine the training programme for the following six months. The knowledge-base of consulting firms is constantly evolving through every assignment they carry out; therefore these firms aim to protect and improve their intellectual capital by checking and adding new intelligence to the existing knowledge-base. In this respect, the training of consultants seems to represent a process in which the two knowledge management strategies (codification and personalization) converge in order to enhance the creation and enlargement of the knowledge-base, both individual and collective, that constitutes GCI's competitive advantage.

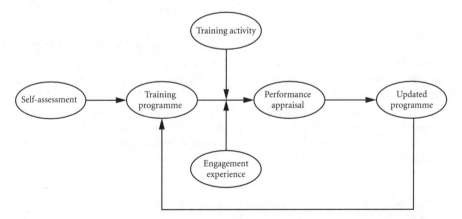

Figure 7.1. *Training process at GCI*

Performance Appraisal

Performance appraisal within Global Consulting can be seen as an 'evaluation tool' within the wider framework of business control systems usually defined as Performance Management.[2] From a range of definitions on this subject, the following appears appropriate to describe the system adopted within GCI. It defines performance management as 'a system allowing the measurement of business results by putting them in line with the company strategy and by identifying the best performance measures to support both the decisional process and the improvement strategies to reach the planned strategic objectives' (Agostini 1999: 1). It could be said that such systems aim at introducing both a culture of management by objective and also an objective measurement of results through the evaluation of individual performances.

In the specific case of GCI the performance appraisal is an internal process that takes place twice a year; it allows the company to track periodically every professional performance within the company, to update and redefine the training programme on a personal basis from year to year, but also to decide about promotions and bonuses (monetary incentives). Performance appraisal takes place every six months alternating the Project Appraisal and the Home Appraisal. The process of appraisal within GCI is developed through three main phases. Every professional is first evaluated at the 'Home-tree' level, then at a local level (within every office), and finally at a national level, where a definitive evaluation is established. This procedure appears to consume time and money (especially considering that time not spent with clients means a loss of money in the consulting business), but it is believed 'to result in a more objective evaluation of resources'.[3] At the same time, this kind of procedure might also be seen as one of the implications related to the adoption of personalization strategies in knowledge management. In fact, 'the human infrastructure requires investment, just as the IT infrastructure does. Human infrastructure investment means money spent on people meeting each other in person, spending time on proper dialogue, creating environments conducive to the sharing of knowledge' (Sveiby 1996: 2).

Performance Standards

In order to 'measure' the individual performances of its consultants, a sort of 'evaluation grid' has been set up and has been in use worldwide within all Global Consulting branches since 1996. The original grid was elaborated in the USA (similar to what happened for KM)—possibly because that is where the company has its headquarters and the central brain of its organization—and then diffused to the other offices. It should be mentioned that the main differences in this grid across countries concern some quantitative data, which can be considered as 'market specific'.

---

[2] The Balanced Scorecard, perhaps better known, is another of the tools used within the performance management systems.
[3] Quote from a conversation between the head of the HR unit in Italy and the author in January 2000.

The parameters composing this grid are called Performance Standards and they are divided into five main dimensions: people, knowledge, sales, service, and culture. For each dimension consultants and staff get a 'score', ranging from 1 (the lowest) to 5 (the highest), according to the level of their performance. Performance standards 'define what Global Consulting expects from every professional level, they bind individual performances to global business objectives and performance improvement, they try to fix a common rule to recognize top performers, and try to balance the company, clients, and professional's requests'.[4] Using the same parameters Global Consulting aims at reinforcing its consulting group identity (everyone is evaluated according to the same criteria regardless of the country in which they work), but also at creating 'inter-changeable resources' because, as mentioned before, consultants can move across countries. It therefore seems that as for knowledge management, where 'old cases' and 'formalized methods' constitute a 'basic structure within the firm' (see Werr in Chapter 6, above), the setting up of common and relatively fixed performance standards is intended to create a 'basic structure' for the evaluation of resources. The extent to which this process can be standardized, though, seems questionable given the difficulties encountered within GCI following the adoption of this procedure.

In fact, despite the previously described advantages of having the same performance standards within the group worldwide, a number of problems that emerged within GCI seem to suggest that some of the procedures involving human capital can be standardized only to a limited extent. Since the adoption of performance standards (in Italy it was in April 1997) the company has realized that the process was encountering some difficulties, especially with respect to its understanding and application. The main problems were linked to the fact that, apart from the quantitative ones, the other indicators did not always allow the impartial evaluation of resources, so that both the consultancy's and the consultants' expectations were not satisfied. This fact seems to confirm that there are limits to the standardization of practices and procedures, especially when they include value- or culture-related aspects that are context-specific, and supports the assumption that management consultancies need to adapt internally to the specificity of their human resources.

As an attempt to solve these problems, an internal process of revision of the performance standards grid was started in Italy at the end of 1999. Within this process, the author was in charge of identifying the main difficulties linked to the understanding of the grid and was required to prepare a report for the HR unit. The results of this action will now be briefly described, as they can help to explain some of the problems that large consulting firms have to face when operating in foreign markets. The analysis of the existing documentation on performance appraisal and on performance standards within GCI revealed two main types of difficulties linked to the understanding of the performance standards grid:

- Linguistic and content difficulties: the grid is in American English and some of the concepts expressed do not have an exactly corresponding Italian term; in addition they appear at times too abstract to be applied to the common working experience.

---

[4] From internal GCI publications.

- Structural difficulties: the grid is based on the assumption that totally objective performance evaluation will be provided, but does not take into account the complexity of transforming qualitative indicators into quantitative values, namely as 'scores'.

In order to overcome these difficulties, the second step in the revision process was to identify the key points, in each of the five dimensions, that could constitute a 'standard performance', corresponding to a score of '3', given to those employees performing at 100 per cent of their capacity.[5] On the basis of this study a standard professional profile for each dimension (people, knowledge, sales, service, and culture) and each of the five professional levels has been elaborated and has been used as a basis for interviewing various consultants. They have been asked to confront their real professional experiences with those described in the pre-elaborated profile and to identify which elements can distinguish a performance below or above the standard, as the company defines it.

The final result of this process of 'performance benchmarking' has been the setting up of a complementary explanatory grid for each professional level. This grid is in Italian; it summarizes and translates the original grid of performance standards, giving precise examples and indicators (including quantitative ones) of what constitutes a standard performance and what is below or above it. Starting from the performance appraisal held in April 2000, this accompanying grid has been distributed to all consultants, representing a first step in the revision (and maybe adaptation) of the performance appraisal process within GCI.

Discussion

The analysis of the HR practices within GCI has highlighted the value attributed by the company to the search for and selection of new knowledge and the implications it has with respect to its knowledge management strategies. At the same time, what has been described with respect to the performance appraisal process suggests that there is a continuous check on the quality and quantity of available knowledge within the company as well as on employees' involvement and performance. In fact, 'if the knowledge base is not updated, the firm runs the risk of offering yesterday's solutions to new problems' (Morris and Empson 1998: 614).

A specific example showing the need for internal adaptation processes can be derived from the case of performance management. The grid of performance standards elaborated centrally in the USA and then distributed to all branches worldwide exemplifies how the standardization of knowledge in terms of content and value is viable only to a limited extent. It offers empirical evidence of adaptation and translation phenomena taking place within management consultancies because of internal rather than external needs. More precisely with respect to translation, it seems possible to suggest that it represents a very significant phenomenon within the consulting field

---

[5] It should be clarified that according to Global Consulting a score of '4' indicates a 120 per cent performance and a score of '5' indicates a 150 per cent performance, which makes them 'top performers' who, besides a bonus, might also expect a promotion.

and supports the idea that knowledge management strategies can be affected by the context in which they are applied.

Translation is not only done externally for clients, when 'labels are translated into more understandable terminology and concrete products' (Crucini and Kipping 2001); translation is also done internally for consultants, as the empirical evidence here seems to suggest. The described 'linguistic and content difficulties' related to performance standards show how even the previously identified 'basic structure' (see Werr in Chapter 6, above) might generate difficulties and misunderstanding, when it implies values and behaviour that are culture-specific. This in turn relates closely to Sarvary's observations that good KMS incorporate the organization's culture but at the same time are accepted by consultants using them and constituting them.

The fact that GCI, part of one of the largest and most well-known management consultancies in the world, and belonging to the group of those consultancies that establish 'best practices', has recognized the need to adapt internally to meet the understanding of its consultants seems very relevant. It suggests that sometimes it is more important for organizations 'to understand what might fit the situation they are in' (Kanter 1984: 305) rather than how things should ideally be done.

7.6. CONCLUSIONS

The case of GCI has been examined as an example of the dynamics and mechanisms that are behind the knowledge management and human resources activities of a large consulting firm operating in a specific context different from its original one. An attempt has been made to show how both these practices are at the core of the generation, accumulation, and diffusion of knowledge within the company. At the same time, given the strong interrelation between 'personal' and context-specific knowledge and 'codified' and collective knowledge within consulting firms, an attempt has been made to show how knowledge management and HR management are also strongly interrelated.

Some of the facts examined in this chapter, such as the knowledge management and performance appraisal processes within GCI, seem to suggest that large international consulting firms tend to conform to quite a precise model, clearly of American origin, which they try to replicate worldwide. This fact might reinforce the assumption that 'management consulting as such, independent of the contents, must be viewed as an American form of knowledge-transfer' (Kipping and Ambrüster 1999: 132). US consultancies have in fact represented a model of success 'exported' to other markets since the 1950s. In addition, the fact that they have powerful IT-based instruments seems to allow them to maintain very high levels of centralization among their international branches, which results in a strong common knowledge- and identity-base.

In spite of this, the evidence derived from the case-study presented in the chapter seems rather to indicate that even the largest and most visible consulting firms cannot be treated as 'global firms', as they are affected, both internally and externally, by the country-specific context in which they operate. Because countries differ in their institutional characteristics, organizations have to cope and adapt to the specific environment

of the country in which they have been developed or established. Management consultancies as institutions are no exception in this respect and have to adapt their practices
at a country level, given that they constantly interact with at least two actors: their
employees and their clients, who are both embedded in their context. Last but not least,
the local context seems to exert an influence, as large foreign consultancies are increasingly using local, smaller consulting firms for specific services (as described in the
case of HR). Out-sourcing and other forms of cooperation of this kind might end up
creating a kind of bilateral exchange and adaptation of know-how and expertise.

As opposed to other studies on knowledge management, the case presented in this
chapter shows to what extent the process of adaptation in knowledge management is
also an internal phenomenon, having an impact on consulting firms' structures and
strategies through their employees. In these organizations consultants are the first producers and consumers of knowledge, but this process of generation and diffusion is not
'neutral', given that they also act also according to their pre-installed knowledge- and
cultural base. It therefore seems necessary to consider the impact of human resources
management on the choice and development of knowledge management strategies
and systems within consulting firms. The international and accumulated knowledge of
large consultancies has to confront and include the tacit knowledge and experience of
consultants that are highly context-specific. Therefore the way in which management
consultancies look for, select, evaluate, and improve the knowledge embedded in their
employees is an integral part of their strategic knowledge management. Knowledge is,
after all, both the input and the output of the consulting black-box.

These facts seem to have at least two main implications affecting the way in which
management consultancies deal with their knowledge management. The first is that in
order to maximize their knowledge asset, management consultancies appear to require
the adoption of different KMS at the same time. It therefore seems possible to say
that the previously described 'codification' and 'personalization' strategies to manage
knowledge are complementary rather than mutually exclusive. The second implication is that even codification strategies, which appear to be more standardized and
relatively easily replicable, require a certain degree of adaptation, both externally (in
order to make their services saleable) and internally (in order to fit their human capital).
These facts in turn strongly challenge the assumption that even codification strategies
for managing knowledge can be considered as low context-dependent.

8

Collaborative Relationships in the Creation and Fashioning of Management Ideas: Gurus, Editors, and Managers

TIMOTHY CLARK AND DAVID GREATBATCH

8.1. INTRODUCTION

The management advice industry is an interrelated community of knowledge entrepreneurs and organizations which include management consultants, management gurus, business schools, and mass media organizations. Each of these groups is concerned with the creation, production, and dissemination of ideas and techniques to managers. These groups compete with each other and thrive or falter on their ability to convince the management audience why it is imperative that they should pursue certain organizational goals and why their particular technique offers the best means to achieve these goals. The findings of a number of studies suggest that management consultants and gurus currently dominate contemporary notions of the organizational ideal and the nature of the management role (Barley, Meyer, and Gash 1988; Gerlach, 1996; Spell 2000). Hence, those ideas with popular appeal and being disseminated by media organizations are primarily the ones created by these two groups. In contrast, the academic literature tends to lag behind the popular management press, so that the research agenda is not being set by academics. Management academics increasingly research the outcomes of management actions that are influenced by the ideas of a small number of consultants and gurus.

The focus of this chapter is on one of the groups of advice-givers who are currently pre-eminent—management gurus. Many gurus are, or were at one time, successful management consultants. However, they do not generally conduct organizational analyses or present reports with their recommendations which they subsequently implement. Rather, they offer advice to managers through their best-selling books and live presentations on the international management lecture circuit. It is through these

The research reported in this chapter would not have been possible without a grant from the Economic and Social Research Council (Grant No. R000222860) for the project titled Talk in Training: The Live and Video Recorded Performances of Management Gurus.

activities that they create a receptive climate amongst managers for particular sorts of ideas which consultants then incorporate into marketable packages.

This chapter argues that their portrayal within the existing literature on management gurus as extraordinary individuals who have extraordinary ideas and extraordinary powers of self-promotion does not stand up to empirical scrutiny. It shows that they collaborate with a range of professional groups during the course of developing, disseminating, and revising their ideas. These groups include book editors and publishers, fellow consultants, academics, and managers (in their capacity as clients or research subjects). The full extent of the role of these 'support' groups is often hidden from view or acknowledged only briefly in the gurus' books, lectures, and videos. Whilst they are critical to the success and popularity of the gurus' ideas their role has been completely overlooked. Yet, without a detailed understanding of the contribution of these support personnel the factors accounting for the mass popularity of gurus' ideas cannot be fully understood.

In order to overcome this deficiency in the current literature this chapter examines gurus' relationships with two of their support personnel—book editors and managers. It reveals that these two groups often play a critical role in the creation, development, and dissemination of gurus' ideas. In concluding, the chapter argues that management scholars should abandon their essentially individualistic conceptions of the development and dissemination of 'fashionable' ideas in the corporate marketplace. Instead, they should focus on the ways in which such ideas emerge as the result of a series of collaborative relationships with a number of usually unseen heads and hands, whose roles have previously been overlooked and so are presently little understood.

The chapter is structured into three main sections. It begins by reviewing the literature on management gurus, noting a number of critical deficiencies. In the following two sections it reports the results of an empirical study of the role of managers and book editors in the production and dissemination of gurus' ideas. These collaborative relationships are examined from two perspectives. In the first they are viewed as objective descriptions of a set of relationships that are necessary to the successful production of their ideas utilizing Becker's (1974) notion of an 'art world'. In the second they are portrayed as characterizations which gurus deploy in order to construct a particular image of themselves and their ideas. The first perspective is applied to the gurus' relationships with their book editors, whereas the second is applied to their relationship with managers.

8.2. MANAGEMENT GURUS AND THE PRODUCTION OF THEIR IDEAS

To date the small, but growing, literature on management gurus has been guided by an overarching concern to understand the reasons for the apparently powerful impact of their ideas on managers. In a comprehensive review of this literature Clark and Salaman (1998) identified three conventional explanations for the appeal of guru theory for managers. The first draws implicitly upon a psychoanalytical approach to leader–follower relations in that it argues that guru theory satiates managers' psychological needs. The guru–manager tie is seen as an outgrowth of a psychological exchange arising from tensions in the follower's personality. These tensions arise from the manager's incapacity to control a world that appears chaotic, unstable, and increasingly uncertain. According to this explanation it is their search to resolve their internal psychic tension, and in the process obtain greater certainty, control, and predictability, which renders managers vulnerable to the blandishments of different gurus. Versions of this argument are most prevalent in the work of journalists (e.g. Crainer 1997), but are also found in the writings of a number of academic commentators (e.g. Furusten 1999; Huczynski 1993a; Watson 1994).

A second type of explanation argues that the popularity and impact of a particular guru's ideas is related to their ability to (re)frame their analyses of contemporary management problems and solutions in such a way that they resonate with and are in harmony with the expectations of their target audience. As Abrahamson (1996: 267) argues, in his model of the management-fashion-setting process, if a management technique is to become widely adopted it must 'create the belief that the technique allows managers to pursue an important managerial goal in the most efficient fashion'. In this sense this explanation is linked to the first in that the popularity and impact of particular guru ideas is related to their ability to elaborate rhetorics that suggest that their ideas enable managers to overcome their most pressing difficulties, thereby gaining greater control; but it goes further in that these rhetorics must also convince managers that the guru's ideas are the best means for achieving this. If they fail to convince their target audience of the plausibility and appropriateness of their ideas then they are very likely to be ignored. As Grint (1994: 193) notes 'for this "plausibility" to occur the ideas most likely to prevail are those that are apprehended as capturing the zeitgeist or "spirit of the times" '. In addition, a number of commentators have noted the affinity between guru theory and the values of the politico-ethical project of developing an enterprise culture (du Gay 1996). Other writers have highlighted the correspondence between guru packages and core national values (Grint 1994; Guest 1990; Jackson 1999).

A third type of explanation argues that the success and impact of gurus' ideas is due to the form in which they are presented—their powerful public performances. Following Huczynski's (1993a) study of management gurus, a number of commentators have argued that management gurus' public performances are exercises in persuasive communication (Clark 1995; Clark and Salaman 1996a). Using the work of Lewin (1951) and Sargant (1997), the main purpose of these events has been understood in terms of the conversion of the audience to the guru's way of thinking by re-structuring managers' ways of thinking and in so doing transforming their consciousness. As Huczynski (1993a: 245) writes, a 'realistic aim of the guru's persuasive communication is not that his ideas should necessarily and immediately modify the actions of his audience, but that they should alter their beliefs, attitudes and feelings towards his suggestions'. Using Tom Peters as the prototypical management guru it is claimed that gurus achieve this transformation in the audience's consciousness by adopting a powerful presentational style which is characterized by high levels of energy, passion, and commitment that generates an emotional intensity in the audience. Therefore, their performances are not about dry exposition, but are concerned with drama and show business. Indeed, Furnham (1996: 80) describes gurus as 'academics gone Hollywood'.

These types of explanations of guru impact and appeal are open to several criticisms. The first, and perhaps most significant, failing of the extant literature on management gurus is the complete lack of empirical research on the gurus themselves. Despite the research agenda being dominated by a concern to understand the impact of gurus and their ideas on managers, the gurus themselves have only been studied in terms of the artefacts they produce. Previous research has either been entirely theoretical (e.g. Abrahamson 1996; Kieser 1997; Clark and Salaman 1996*b*, 1998; Huczynski 1993*a*); largely focused on textual analyses of the gurus' books (e.g. Furusten 1999; Gerlach 1996; Grint 1994; Jackson 1996, 1999); or comprised of evaluations of the effectiveness of the change programmes they inspire (e.g. Watson 1994; Fincham 1999*a*). Hence, although these studies purport to examine the work of management gurus they have nevertheless completely ignored the central character—the management guru. There is therefore a pressing need for the guru to be instated at the centre of an inquiry into their activities.

A second criticism is that the literature assumes a simplistic and unidirectional process of communication between the gurus and their managerial audiences. Gurus are portrayed as the dominant, initiating partners who exploit the naiveté and vulnerability of their audiences of managers by selling them glib promises, and converting them to their way of thinking through their persuasive rhetoric and dazzling performances. Managers, on the other hand, are conceived largely as passive, docile consumers of gurus' ideas and recommendations, inherently vulnerable to gurus' blandishments, anxiously searching for reassurance and support, and looking desperately for new ideas.

A third criticism of the existing literature is that management gurus are portrayed as solely responsible for their success. They are depicted as lone creative geniuses who gain unique insights into modern organizational life. Their initial popularity and success is founded on a best-selling book, written by the guru, which contains unique ideas, created and developed by the guru, which are depicted as being fundamental to current organizational success. They then further popularize their ideas by presenting them to audiences of managers in compelling performances on the international management lecture circuit. In other words, the individual management guru is credited with being wholly responsible for the creation and dissemination of the ideas for which he or she is known. Management gurus are, therefore, self-sufficient.

The present chapter seeks to overcome these three deficiencies by first reporting the initial findings of a research project which is developing an empirically based understanding of gurus and their work. This chapter draws on data emanating from a study of five leading management gurus, which has involved interviews with each individual, in addition to analysis of their books and videos in order to develop an explanation of their particular impact and success. The five gurus in our study represent a range of popular ideas that have had a major impact on organizational life in the last 20 years with their popularity peaking in the early 1970s for one guru, in the late 1980s for two gurus, and the early 1990s for another guru. One guru has maintained his popularity for 20 years. These five individuals are also representative of the range of gurus in terms of the source of their ideas (three are 'academic' gurus and two are 'consultant' gurus), their gender (one woman and four men), and their nationality (one European and four Americans). This is essentially an American and masculine phenomenon.

The interviews with Gurus A, B and C were conducted face-to-face; the interviews with Guru D and E were conducted via the telephone. The interview schedule comprised a series of general topic headings concerning the ideas for which each guru is well known, their explanations for their own success and failure, how they disseminate their ideas, and their plans for the future. The interviews, each of which lasted about an hour, were transcribed and were then subjected to qualitative analysis using the constant comparative method (Glaser and Strauss 1967). This method enabled similarities and differences between the gurus' perceptions of their role and impact to be identified.

With respect to the other two deficiencies in the current literature on management gurus, the next section draws on the interview data to show that gurus' ideas, like other cultural products, 'do not spring forth full blown but are made somewhere by someone' (Peterson 1979: 152). This approach contrasts with that taken in the current management guru literature, which is concerned solely with understanding the reasons for the reception accorded to ideas subsequent to their publication. Instead of focusing on the front-stage activities of management gurus the focus in this chapter is on the backstage processes by which their ideas are deliberately created and fashioned for the intended audience. These processes determine which ideas are 'discovered' and then sponsored and turned into products which are likely to be successful with the intended audience. The milieux within which they are produced therefore influences the form and content of the ideas (Peterson 1976, 1979). Although gurus are often portrayed as lone individuals, there are a number of individuals and organizations whose decisions and actions either block or facilitate the successful linking of gurus to their potential audience. Gurus' ideas, from this perspective, just like other cultural goods, can be viewed as the outcome of a form of collective action (Becker 1974).

8.3. COLLABORATIVE RELATIONSHIPS WITH BOOK EDITORS

In the interviews with the five management gurus they often portrayed the development process of the ideas for which they are each well-known as one of collaboration with others. One way of viewing the gurus' portrayal of their collaborative relationships is as objective descriptions of a set of relationships that are necessary to the successful production of their ideas. This characterization is similar to Becker's (1974) observation that any cultural product requires the coordination of a series of activities before it can appear in its final, public form. He argues that although the list of necessary activities varies from one cultural product to another, for example making a film is different to producing a music CD or gurus' ideas, they are nevertheless all produced as a result of collaborative relationships between a number of different people. Becker's point is that no one person can create and make everything, then perform it and experience the result without some kind of assistance or cooperation from someone else. As he writes 'Whatever the artist, so defined, does not do himself must be done by someone else . . . Wherever he depends on others, a co-operative link exists' (Becker 1974: 769).

Typically, many people participate in the creation of a work without which it could not have been produced. Usually, their identity is hidden or acknowledged only in passing. Becker (1982: 34) has termed this network of support personnel an 'art world' which he defines specifically as 'all people whose activities are necessary to the production of the characteristic works which that world, and perhaps others as well, define as art'. In this section the notion of an art world is used as an organizing framework within which to analyse the gurus' relationship with their book editors. Two aspects of their work with gurus is examined: their role in 'discovering' a number of the gurus, and their role in assisting with the framing and presentation of the gurus' ideas prior to publication of the book.

Discovering the Guru

In the interviews the gurus highlighted a set of collaborative relationships that were particularly crucial during the process of writing a book.[1] The first point to emerge from the interviews was the importance the gurus placed on forming links with large multinational publishing organizations that had experience of marketing books to a mass audience, rather than specialist, niche academic publishers. As one guru stated, 'I judge my success not in terms of book sales but impact on practice. I wanted my ideas in —— to influence as wide a group of people as possible. I was delighted when the publisher actively promoted the book not only in the US but Europe and Asia. This was very important to the success of the book' (Guru B). Making the same point another guru stated:

To do well you need to get a lot of attention. Today even if you have something that is really really good, unless it is promoted like crazy it is hard to get attention for it out of all the clutter. So people have to feel that they have to have it and that it is available everywhere to buy it. Like any other retail product you need the shelf-space and only a few publishers can get you this (Guru E).

However, of greater importance was their relationship with a book editor at the publisher. The interviews indicate that the book editors had two important roles. First, in four cases they 'discovered' the guru. As one guru said, 'I owe a great deal to ——. She found me, nurtured my ideas, and kept me going. Without her there I wouldn't have written that book' (Guru D). As the following quotations indicate one way in which they came across the gurus was by attending their live presentations:

I was giving talks and telling stories about different companies that we were working with, and there was ——, an editor at one of these presentations, who wrote to me and said 'this is great

---

[1] Crainer (1998) has argued that several recent best-selling management books have been ghost-written. He points out that a company run by the 'queen of ghost-writers', Donna Sammons Carpenter, and several other individuals are behind many of the recent management best-sellers.

stuff and you should write a book'. I wrote back saying that I really appreciated her interest but was not interested in writing books. We exchanged correspondence on and off for a couple of years and then it suddenly hit me and I felt the time was right for the book and I got back to her and said well let's talk, maybe this is the right time and it would be useful to write something (Guru C).

I got a rather excited call from someone to say that they had attended a recent seminar I had given. They were very flattering about me and the day and suggested that the ideas would make a good book (Guru E).

These quotations suggest that the gurus believed that the editors were enthused, just like other members of the audience, by their live performance. Using their own reactions, and that of the rest of the audience, they made a judgement that the ideas they had just heard could be successfully translated into a book and reach a mass audience. As the following quotations show, the second way in which the editors initially identified the gurus was by reading articles they had published in the popular business press:

I published an article in Harvard Business Review which got a tremendous response. I was invited to talk to a couple of corporations and was interviewed by the press and on television. One of the people who contacted me was——explaining that she thought the ideas in the article would make a great book. I hadn't planned on writing a book at that time and was a little reluctant to do so. But we met and she explained what she thought would make a really great book and I told her what I was planning . . . eighteen months later the book was published (Guru B).

It started when we wrote an article for——. Suddenly we were news and everyone wanted a piece of us. We got a letter from——who said she really liked the ideas in the article and were we interested in writing a book? We thought that it would be a lot of work but a great way of expanding on the ideas (Guru D).

The interviews indicate that the role of book editors in 'discovering' a number of the gurus is similar to that of 'contact people' in other cultural industries. Publishing, film, and music companies all employ people to locate new book manuscripts, new film scripts, and new singers. These people essentially go out into the field and act as scouts attempting to identify potential stars from the existing pool of talent which can then be signed up by their organizations. In this sense, book editors are key gatekeepers whose decisions can either facilitate or block the career of a would-be guru. The critical nature of their role can be gauged by the number of gurus who mentioned that they owed a considerable debt of gratitude to their book editor for 'discovering' them. The gurus' depiction of the editor's role indicates that one key function is to select the guru from other would-be gurus. The interviews suggest that it was the gurus' success in presenting their ideas orally or in high-circulation and prestigious popular business magazines that led to their initial contact with an editor.

The Writing Process

The Shaping and Framing of the Gurus' Ideas. Having signed a book contract the second function of the book editor identified by the gurus was as a creative collaborator during the writing process. The interviews indicate that for a number of the gurus their book editors had an important and in some cases very influential role on the process by which the ideas were shaped and framed for the managerial audience prior to the publication of their first book. Three gurus described the process of writing their first book in the following terms:

I wasn't used to the discipline of sitting down and writing so many words. What I had done in the past was short articles of 1000 words or so. I think my first draft was all over the place. It was probably double the length of the final manuscript. I probably produced about five or six complete drafts. Each one would go to —— and they would write back with loads of comments and suggestions. I tell you, if you saw that first draft you wouldn't recognize the published book . . . Looking back on it I feel that they were almost a co-author (Guru B).

The hardest thing when writing the book was that I had written all these darn academic papers all my life. I had never written a book. I was very fortunate in that I had a wonderful editor who was a great consultant. He really helped to deconstruct my writing style. He would write samples of what he thought would work for the audience, which I never liked and so re-wrote them. He also told me to bring my personal speaking voice into my writing which was hard. It was a real learning process which did produce a different kind of book. But I was pleased with that (Guru C).

I had written other things before but not a book so as I wrote a draft I would send it to ——. They would send me pages of comments and we would talk on the telephone. This happened many times. Over the months we formed a very close team and I feel that the book is better for their input (Guru D).

What is very evident from reading each of these quotations is that the gurus portray themselves as being initially inexperienced authors. Indeed, these three gurus indicate that they had not written a book before; they were all first-time authors. Because of their inexperience they therefore relied on the editors to convey to them the conventional understandings which dictate the form of a potential management best-seller.

Becker (1974) notes that conventions cover all the decisions with respect to the production of a given work. They dictate the materials to be used, the form in which it will be presented, the appropriate dimensions, size, and shape of a work, as well as the ideas or experiences it will convey, and how all these will be combined in the final work. Critically, these 'Conventions regulate the relations between artists and audience, specifying the rights and obligations of both' (Becker 1974: 771). Thus, as in the production of any cultural good, the relationship between the gurus and their editors is partly governed by the former's familiarity with conventional understandings of the ingredients of a management best-seller. In the interviews the three gurus above characterized the relationship as one in which, as first-time authors, they were very dependent on the advice and knowledge of the editor. This had both positive and negative consequences for these gurus. With respect to the former it enabled the gurus and book editors to collaborate easily because decisions could be made quickly with reference to the conventional way of doing things. They thus made it possible for the easy and efficient coordination of the fashioning of the gurus' ideas into a potential best-seller.

But they also placed strong constraints on the gurus, since they had to present their ideas in a particular format whether they liked it or not. They had very little room for manœuvre. Becker (1982: 34) argues that if breaking conventions 'increases the artists' trouble and decreases the circulation of their work... we can understand any work as the product of a choice between conventional ease and success and unconventional trouble and lack of recognition'. Thus, according to Becker, adhering to the conventions for a particular work increases its likelihood of success with the intended audience.

Conventions for the Presentation of the Gurus' Ideas. It is likely that editors worked very closely with some gurus in shaping their ideas prior to publication because they may see their role as identifying raw material which they bring into the organization. This then needs to be reshaped in various ways in order to produce a book that at least meets the expectations of the managerial audience, and hopefully exceeds them so that it becomes a best-seller. But as Hirsch (1972: 644) has noted, there is widespread uncertainty over the best-seller formula. Given the difficulty in predicting shifts in consumer tastes, it is not possible to determine with any degree of certainty what is likely to be a best-seller. Editors therefore minimize this uncertainty by producing books according to rules that have been successful in the past. It is these conventions, based on their understandings of past successes and failures, which they seek to convey to the gurus during the writing process. The main way in which the editors communicated these conventions was by reading and commenting on drafts of the book as they were produced. As Becker (1974: 770) writes, 'People who co-operate to produce a work of art usually do not decide things afresh. Instead, they rely on earlier agreements now become customary, agreements that have become part of the conventional way of doing things in that art'.

In the interviews the gurus identified a number of the conventions which underpinned the fashioning of their books for the managerial audience. Each of these is now considered in turn. First, the gurus were encouraged to present their ideas in a readily accessible form by reducing the main elements to a pithy list, acronym, mnemonic, story, etc. that is immediately graspable, understood, and remembered. As one guru stated:

Writing the book in this way [with the editor] was a wonderfully reflective process and it led to a way of organizing the ideas that I had not planned at the outset. The grouping of the ideas into a number of general principles came with the book writing. So the book writing tied together a number of loose ends in my thinking and in the process made them more accessible. I owe a lot of this to the input of —— (Guru C).

Another guru was encouraged to put greater stress on story-telling with the advice that 'many people tell stories. You will only have impact if the stories are closely tied to a really key point, are plausible, and are backed-up by plausible evidence' (Guru E). In a similar vein another guru stated, 'I remember being told that what works best is stories, and some stories can be quite telling for readers... I can remember having some good-natured discussions with the editor at —— over the relevance of the stories and how they illustrated the point' (Guru A).

Several gurus also highlighted the importance of focusing on the visual nature of ideas. As one guru stated: 'I said you know I don't think we will ever get a better label for it but I don't think it will ever sell in the world of practice. But both of us said that was not the issue. What was critical was that the label describe visually the concept we were trying to develop' (Guru A). Similarly, another guru stated: 'I have interpreted existing ideas, into a language and metaphors you can understand... in the management world, these sort of ideas aren't original, but the metaphors are original... I'm putting the memorable and visual together. It's very important that they are visual metaphors and images' (Guru B). Visual metaphors were so important to this guru that he identified the source of the failure of a particular idea as the failure of the metaphor to have an impact when he stated, 'No one remembers that [idea] because it was not visual enough. That was one of the things that did not click. It's terribly important actually. I did not get the right kind of metaphor for it... I tried to' (Guru B).

The gurus were also encouraged to present their ideas in a form that was consonant with the constraints many managers work under. In particular, the interviews indicate that editors conceived of managers as being extremely busy with a focus on the tangible and immediate and a tendency towards superficiality and short attention spans. The gurus were therefore encouraged to present their ideas so that they were easy to read and could be assimilated immediately. As one guru was reminded:

The publisher [editor] emphasized that I was writing for managers who are relatively intelligent and can take ideas to work with them, and who are very busy. And a key market for my books was people who take four or five hour flights. When I think of my readers now, I think that on the whole managers read on aeroplanes, or they take my books on holiday which I find a compliment (Guru B).

In a similar vein another guru was advised to 'write clearly and have your readers in mind. It's got to be easily digestible and memorable. Managers are busy people and do not want to wade through lots of waffle' (Guru D).

Building on the previous point, editors also sought to encourage the gurus when writing their books to emphasize and demonstrate that their ideas were relevant to practitioners and that they had been successfully implemented in many organizations. In this way they sought to emphasize the practical relevance of the gurus' ideas. Thus, the gurus were exhorted to include examples of their principles being put into practice in order to persuade readers that their analysis and solutions were not only relevant but also the most appropriate.[2] As one guru was told 'you've got to got to show them that it really works. Who's going to buy into something that's never been tried' (Guru A). Another was given the advice that 'in telling stories you have to show that the idea behind the story is backed up by rigorous research but also company practice. So, you have to tell stories about real managers facing real problems in real organizations. Doing this makes the idea more real to the reader' (Guru E). This last quotation indicates that for some editors the examples are there to show the readers that the gurus' ideas work in practice.

The assumption is that if readers can see that organizations have implemented the changes advocated by the guru then it is also possible for the reader's organization to

---

[2] Fincham (1995) has termed these illustrative case studies 'naïve exemplars' in that they are very simplistic, highly formulaic, and emphasize how the idea has led to a dramatic improvement in performance.

achieve the same benefits by adopting the guru's ideas. However, comments from another guru indicate that these examples can also serve another function in that they may help to legitimize their vision. This is achieved, in part, by carefully selecting organizations that are household names and so well known to the readers of these books; possibly even admired by them. As one guru stated: 'the companies chosen had to be recognizable to large numbers of people otherwise they will think: so what? But if X, Y or Z did this then it must really be important' (Guru D). As another guru said:

I had been working with a number of well-known organizations for many years. I knew the ideas worked. The point of the book was to share their experiences and success with a wider audience so that we could form a critical mass as more organizations became aware of and sought to implement the ideas. One area where —— was really helpful was in getting me to illustrate the ideas with some well-chosen examples (Guru C).

Again what was important was to present the ideas in such a way that the readers felt that they too could implement what the guru was advocating. Thus, with respect to the nature of the conventions that relate to the production of a management best-seller, in the interviews the gurus identified the following factors as important to the successful presentation of their ideas:

• their immediate accessibility;
• their visual nature;
• their universal applicability;
• their relevance to practitioners; and
• proven practicality.

These factors are very similar to those identified by Davis (1986) in his analysis of the common elements underpinning 'classic' social theories. It could therefore be argued that similar to 'classic' theorists such as Durkheim, Marx, Simmel, and Weber, the gurus' success is partly founded on 'following a specific rhetorical programme that spoke to their audience's common concerns' (Davis 1986: 298). As indicated earlier this is achieved by following the conventions imparted by their book editors.

8.4. COLLABORATIVE RELATIONSHIPS WITH MANAGERS

In the interviews the five management gurus identified managers as the second key element of their network of collaborative relationships. Managers were credited with having an important influence on their ideas at different points in their development. As the following quotations show, the gurus indicated that their ideas arose not from working in isolation but as a result of working with and observing managers either within a consulting or a research setting.

Our ideas evolved and developed from a series of assignments over several years in which we were actively engaged in helping corporations develop new techniques that would allow them to survive in an increasingly harsh competitive environment. The point of the assignments was not for us to feed back results to them but create an environment in which they could make fundamental insights into what they were doing. The point was to create learning relevant to these corporations. And so when I came to write the book I drew on their experiences and how they had sought to deal with these issues. It was really about my learning through their learning (Guru C).

The ideas in —— derived from a project we had been working on for several years . . . They were the findings of a large-scale project for a number of clients. Several people worked on the project and we used to get together and brainstorm ideas before reporting to the clients. It was the cumulative process of these sessions and the feedback from clients and other colleagues that led to the development of the framework (Guru D).

However, as the following guru stated, managers played a continuing role in the development of their ideas—they were not just the source for their initial creation. In the following quotation, as in the two instances above, they characterized the development of their own ideas as a process which began with the observation of managers at work. Following this they organized their reflections and analysis into an oral presentation which they then used as a critical sounding-board for their ideas. Indeed, in some instances depending on the response to the initial presentation of their ideas in a live performance they either dropped or amended them.

Of course I have been influenced by other people's research. But I find that if I want to know what's going on, what's happening out there, I need to speak to managers. And this is what I do. I speak to thousands of managers every year. What they tell me helps to structure my ideas. Trying ideas out on them and seeing their response, hearing their views helps me to choose those ideas that seem most relevant and are more likely to work. I do not claim to have original ideas. Rather I am a translator and popularizer of ideas (Guru B).

With respect to the nature of their relationship with audiences of managers, all the gurus stated that an important function of their live performances was that they provided them with an opportunity to test new ideas on their audience, and to gauge their reactions. As one guru stated 'if it goes down well verbally I know its going to work on the written page' (Guru A). Another guru made the same point when describing a live presentation several years before which had not been well received: 'I persuaded the course director to allow me to do a new concept which was about learning as far as I can remember. It went down like a dead duck. It didn't work. I was never invited back. This gave me the idea that the idea didn't work—or not in the way I presented it' (Guru B). Similarly, another guru described how he used his lectures to test new ideas: 'I use the talks as a test-bed really. I stand up in front of managers and say this is how I see the world. And if it goes down well I say OK. So they are a test-bed really for what goes in the books' (Guru E). In using their presentations in this way these gurus were treating their live audiences as surrogates for other consumers of their ideas. They therefore portrayed the live audience as crucial, since for several of the gurus it acted as a forum within which they could receive immediate and unmediated feedback.

Similarly, several of the gurus used an article in a leading popular management journal, such as the *Harvard Business Review*, as an opportunity to test their emerging ideas on the potential audience for their forthcoming book. As one guru explained, feedback from these articles was an important part of the development process:

Publishers like you to write an article for these publications because it creates some pre-publicity for the book. For my part it enables me to present a condensed version of the ideas and then gauge the reaction of the readers. I find that you often get letters responding to the points you are making, or people call you up. Often times these can be very useful comments. Perhaps something is not clear, or an example has not worked. Whatever they are about, comments are always useful (Guru D).

Another guru described how the reactions of readers and journalists to an article he had written led him to re-write a number of different sections of the book:

I thought that the ideas were novel and relevant. But clearly from the negative comments in my mailbag and the bad reviews others didn't see it that way. So I had another look at the [book] manuscript and changed bits here and there. I showed it to a few colleagues and they all seemed to like it, but I was still nervous about the reaction to it. When it was published the response was very positive. I think that seeing the whole argument helped (Guru C).

In summary, the gurus characterized managers as having a critical role in the initial creation and development of their ideas. Managers provided them with the practice and discussions from which they derived their ideas about the nature of modern management and organizational life. In addition, the responses of managers at their live presentations and to their articles in popular business magazines provided the gurus with a key source of direct feedback on their ideas, thus alerting them to any limitations or potential difficulties.

Whilst this depiction of the gurus' relationships with managers can be seen as an objective description of a further set of collaborative processes within their support networks, this chapter argues that they may also have been deployed by the gurus to accomplish certain tasks *in situ*. Specifically, the gurus may be employing these characterizations of the creation and fashioning of their ideas with managers in order to portray a particular image of themselves. As Clark and Salaman (1998) have argued, impression management is central to guru work. Persuading audiences of their value is necessary, since guru status is insecure and ephemeral. As Carson *et al.* (2000) have demonstrated, the average length of a fashionable idea, the life blood of the guru, has shrunk from just under fifteen years in the 1970s to under three years in the 1990s.

Indeed, management gurus, like those working in entertainment, sports, and the arts, operate in what Frank and Cook (1995) have termed a 'winner-take-all market'. The single most important characteristic of these markets is that the pay-offs for participants are determined by relative rather than absolute performance. How much a guru earns depends much less on his absolute performance than on how well he performs relative to other gurus. Thus, a guru's status and earnings are dependent not upon the sales figures of his books, for instance, but on how the book performs relative to other books. A second feature of winner-take-all markets is that the rewards tend to be concentrated among a small group of individuals who comprise the top tier. Small differences in the perceived quality or utility of ideas therefore leads to enormous differences in recognition and rewards within the guru community.[3] In these circumstances successful gurus

---

[3] For top management gurus the rewards could run into many millions of dollars or pounds and would include royalties from book sales, fees for public lectures, consultancy fees, royalties from video sales, earnings from syndicated newspaper columns, fees for public lectures, and so forth. This has been termed the 'guru gravy-train' (Furnham 1996).

are those individuals who convince the managerial audience both of the indispensability of their ideas and of their star status. The discussion in the following sections shows how the depiction of their relationships with managers supports this activity.

Demonstrating the Authority of the Gurus' Knowledge

First, in seeking to persuade managers of the superiority and necessity of their ideas gurus are confronted with a difficulty. On the one hand they want to convince managers that they have identified the key problems within modern organizations and that their ideas represent the best solution. Yet, when extolling the virtues of their ideas they cannot simply rely solely on their own endorsement. Whilst some people may be convinced by the gurus' arguments and evidence, many more will want proof that the ideas work in practice and that they have been adopted by other managers and organizations. The fact that management gurus lack a formal and authoritative body of knowledge leaves their statements and ideas vulnerable to active questioning and criticism by other established gurus, would-be-gurus, journalists, and academics (Clark 1995; Clark and Salaman 1998). Disclosing the nature of the collaborative network that supported the creation and development of their ideas is one way in which the gurus can demonstrate the authoritativeness of their knowledge and ideas. In particular, by portraying the creation of their ideas as the result of a collaborative process with managers the gurus can indicate to their audiences that their ideas are already being used successfully in a range of organizations. Through this characterization the gurus enhance the credibility of their ideas with audiences of managers, because they emphasize both the practical foundations of their knowledge and the fact that they are in touch with what managers are doing.

Gurus are able to further enhance the authority of their knowledge by referring either to named managers or organizations that have supported and contributed to the development of their ideas. Thus, when they describe their network, the identity of the managers and organizations with whom they have worked is rarely left anonymous. Indeed, as mentioned with respect to the conventions underpinning the presentation of their ideas in books, their book editors encouraged them to include numerous practical examples. Consequently, their books and public lectures are both replete with references to managers and organizations. Apart from providing evidence for their claims and ideas, the deliberate naming of individuals and organizations that they have come into contact with also further legitimates their message since they are:

1. known to the audience;
2. widely respected (i.e. often considered 'hero' managers); and
3. identified as successful.

In using these forms of citation the gurus are attempting to benefit from the reputation of others by:

1. demonstrating the breadth of their contacts and ready access to senior managers and organizations;
2. directly linking their ideas to people and organizations that the audience will respect; and
3. demonstrating the success of their ideas.

The implication of this is that if these people and organizations that their audience esteems are successful after doing what the guru identifies as necessary, then so should they be.

Confirming and Maintaining the Gurus' Star Status

A second important reason why gurus may deploy these descriptions of their collaborative relationships is that they enhance and affirm their star status. This is achieved in several ways. Related to the previous point, the gurus present themselves as working with managerial and organizational stars. The members of their networks of collaborative relationships are far from being ordinary. They each have one or more special qualities that elevate them to star status. Thus, gurus never admit to collaborating with managers and organizations who are failures, in traditional and declining industries, and employing antiquated management techniques. They are not interested in what they perceive to be the well-known, hackneyed, or old-world. Rather they work with managers and organizations who have star quality because they are spectacularly successful, innovative, risk-taking, leading-edge, and representative of the new world. Put differently, when describing their collaborative relationships with managers the gurus portray themselves as mingling with other stars.

However, and very importantly, within this community of stars the gurus position themselves as pre-eminent, since when employing these descriptions the gurus always situate themselves at the centre of the network. The network is presented as having been formed around them. They are the glue that binds it together. Without them the network would not exist. Furthermore, they give the impression that they did not actively construct the network. Rather the network emerged as managers, organizations, and book editors sought to collaborate with them. Hence, the network was created as these different groups recognized the importance and validity of the gurus' ideas. Linking to an earlier point, by portraying the development of the network in this way the gurus establish in the minds of other audiences that they already have a solid group of supporters who recognize the significance of and, in some cases, use their ideas.

8.5. CONCLUSION

This chapter has made two contributions to the emerging literature on management gurus. First, unlike previous studies, it is based on an empirical study of the gurus themselves. Secondly, it has focused on the back-stage processes by which gurus' ideas are created and processed. In doing so the chapter has argued that the collaborative relationships have several functions for the gurus.

First, stressing that they are part of a network of cooperating individuals is an open acknowledgement by the gurus that, without the assistance of these support personnel, they would not be where they are today (i.e. highly regarded management thinkers). From this perspective the popularity and success of a particular guru's ideas can only be understood with reference to those people whose collective actions constitute the final product. Thus, a guru is located at the centre of a web of cooperative relationships which are essential to the final outcome. A guru, from this point of view, is not a solo performer who possesses rare and special insight. Rather, this status is conferred on an individual as a result of the joint endeavours of all those people who cooperated in the creation and fashioning of his ideas. Without this network of collaborative relationships these gurus may have remained would-be gurus. This suggests that gurus' success is in part determined by the alignment of their support personnel. In other words, particular combinations of support personnel may improve an individual's chances of becoming a guru. This is suggested by a perusal of the acknowledgement sections of recent best-selling management books where the same names are referred to by different authors.

Secondly, regardless of the practical benefits of a collaborative network, reference to support personnel within their talk, particularly managers and organizations, provides the gurus with an opportunity to create impressions of their value and to enhance their star status. In other words, these collaborative relationships can be seen as having a two-fold function. At a practical level support personnel play a critical role in the creation and fashioning of their ideas. At a discursive level they provide them with a resource that can be utilized to bolster their flimsy and ephemeral status. Since most gurus, as purveyors of management fashions, have a short life-span, it may be that the judicious selection of support personnel and deployment of references to them in their public presentations enables gurus to solidify their status and thus extend their popularity. This can only be determined through a detailed comparison of gurus whose ideas have had different life-spans.

Finally, the chapter indicates that whilst the role of book editors is crucial, it has been overlooked and so is still little understood. The present study indicates the importance of these individuals both in terms of initially 'discovering' a guru and then assisting him with the writing task. In terms of the latter role, editors supported and motivated gurus who were not used to writing books. They commented on early drafts of the manuscript and helped them to alter their writing style and to frame their ideas for a particular audience. So close was the working relationship between editor and guru that several of the gurus regarded their editors almost as co-authors. Further research is needed to understand the role of editors in the creation of gurus and their ideas. Some of the key research questions would include:

1. What criteria do editors use when selecting between gurus?
2. What features of guru ideas suggest that they may become popular?
3. How do they assist gurus in the writing process?
4. What is their conception of the audience for these books?
5. How do they market books to this audience?

A further potentially fruitful area of research is into the nature of the role of other support personnel (e.g. management consultants, video production companies) in the creation and dissemination of gurus' ideas. Presently little is known about the way in which management consultancies adopt and promote gurus' ideas. Key questions include:

1. To what extent do they develop their own ideas and so are reliant on external gurus?
2. How do they develop marketable packages based on new ideas?
3. To what extent are new packages old ideas with a new name?

With respect to other collaborators, such as video production and training companies, the main issue here concerns the nature of the adaptation of gurus' ideas to other media (i.e. video and multi-media training packages, etc.). Our continuing programme of research is designed to subject the activities of gurus and those with whom they collaborate to detailed empirical scrutiny in order to illuminate the complex processes in play in this area and to answer some of these questions.

9

Consultancies as Actors in Knowledge Arenas: Evidence from Germany

MICHAEL FAUST

9.1. INTRODUCTION: MANAGEMENT KNOWLEDGE AND THE RISE OF CONSULTANTS

The creation, diffusion and consumption of management knowledge and its impact on managerial action have attracted considerable attention in organizational research (Alvarez 1998). Since the 1980s management knowledge has increasingly taken on the form of management fashions and fads that easily surmount national borders (Faust 2000: 78; Kieser 1997). Within research on management fashions special attention has been paid to the 'creators' of fashions and the 'fashion-setting community' (Abrahamson 1996; Czarniawska and Joerges 1996; Røvik 1996). The following groups are typically introduced as the major contributors to (objectified) management knowledge, as proponents of new ideas, concepts, or 'techniques' (Abrahamson 1996; Huczynski 1993a; Micklethwaite and Wooldridge 1996): consultants, academics from business schools, 'pioneer' or outstanding entrepreneurs or managers ('hero managers'), and 'management gurus'. It was not by chance that the phenomenon of management fashion emerged at the same time as commercial knowledge providers spread their activities on an almost worldwide basis (Faust 2000). The increasing significance of consultancies and gurus within the managerial discourse resulted in a growing 'commercialization' of management knowledge and a 'dramatization of newness' aided by the mass media with their general attraction to novelty (Neuburger-Brosch 1994: 4; Fincham 1995; Huczynski 1993a).

Large management consultancies act as 'producers', 'wholesalers', and 'retailers' of knowledge (Huczynski 1993a: 217); they 'practise the art of double-dealing' (Dezalay 1993: 204). The more that a consultancy develops a strong reputation as a knowledge provider, the better it can sell its services to individual firms (Kaas and Schade 1995). Demonstrable success in consulting activities is also necessary if a consultancy is to

The author gratefully acknowledges funding from the German Science Foundation (DFG) and would like to thank Christoph Deutschmann, the late Owen Gorman, Peter Jauch, Peter Kupka, Jan Lindvall, Cecilia Pahlberg, several participants at the 1999 EGOS Colloquium sub-group, and the editors of this volume for useful comments on earlier versions of the chapter. The usual disclaimer applies.

become acknowledged as a relevant contributor to management knowledge. By profiting from the aura of 'hero managers' and 'excellent' companies, consultancy firms can prove the relevance, applicability, and beneficial nature of their knowledge on a worldwide stage. Only internationally operating consultancies have a chance to become a relevant member of the 'fashion-setting community' and to launch 'discourses that anchor certain practices as rational in the public opinion' (Kieser 1998*b*: 16). Contemporary management consultancies have gained a considerable influence in most Western societies. They are acknowledged as experts on most managerial and business issues. Meanwhile they are also well-respected counsellors for many political issues (Faust 1998: 150). They can be perceived as a new 'reflection elite' (Deutschmann 1993) or as 'supra-experts' (Ernst and Kieser 2002).

Although this analysis appears to be commonly accepted in the relevant literature, there remain important questions that are not sufficiently answered or even considered. Due to the high visibility of fashion setters and popular manifestations of management knowledge, researchers direct most attention at the strategies and contributions of the 'creators' of management knowledge and its diffusion episode (Scarborough and Swan 1999), while the recipient managers are often conceived as passive adopters (Sahlin-Andersson 1996) or as 'relatively powerless victims' of management fashions (Sturdy 1997). Management knowledge has often been regarded as 'texts', while the possibility of different 'readings' of these texts has been neglected (Czarniawska and Joerges 1996: 23; Alvarez 1998: 43). Management concepts are highly ambiguous and therefore characterized by an inevitable 'interpretative viability' (Benders and van Veen 2001; Ortmann 1995: 371). The active role of recipients 'in conditioning, re-defining, and/or resisting ideas and practices' has been underplayed (Sturdy 1997: 393).

Therefore, more attention should be given to the 'interactive nature of the processes and the extent to which "popular" ideas are actually taken on and applied by managers' and how they are treated when being 'applied' (Sturdy 1997; Watson 1994; Jackall 1988). Some of the most striking fashions like 'Lean Production' or 'BPR' (Business Process Re-engineering) exist in quite different national, field, or even local versions (Benders and van Veen 2001; Benders *et al.* 1998; Lane 1997). The criticism of being inattentive to the interactive nature of the fashion-setting process not only applies to the dissemination stage but also to 'the selection stage of management fashion supply' about which, according to Abrahamson (1996: 266), 'virtually nothing' is known. Research starting from the 'diffusion' stage regularly omits even to pose the question why particular ideas or concepts are introduced into a discourse and how they are selected out of a myriad of possible ideas. The assumed autonomy of consultants in launching new ideas and concepts has been overestimated.

Taking these considerations as a starting-point, this chapter will attempt to answer the following two interrelated research questions. How do consultancies exert their influence on management knowledge? How is (simultaneously) their autonomy in the selection of ideas and concepts and their capacity to determine the outcomes restricted by the interactive nature of the process by which management knowledge emerges? With regard to both questions, the analysis concentrates on a trans-organizational level. First, the following section introduces the concept of arenas for the communicative validation of management knowledge and discusses how mass media production is related to the non-mediated discourse. The third and fourth sections will use empirical research in order to show which arenas and networks are relevant in Germany and how the different actors are involved, including the media gatekeepers. Starting with a brief summary, the fifth section discusses the empirical findings in a broader comparative and institutional perspective.

This contribution is based on a German research project titled The Growth and Changing Social Function of Management Consulting.[1] Besides a literature review, it mainly draws upon two kinds of empirical evidence. First, a quantitative analysis of media and knowledge arenas was conducted to assess the composition of participating and contributing groups of actors. The analysis comprised eight journals and magazines, two book programmes from major publishing houses, and eight regularly repeated conferences or training events. Secondly, qualitative interviews were carried out with representatives of the major groups of actors involved in management knowledge production: high-ranking managers of large and medium-sized companies; members (mostly partners) of large international consultancies, but also of medium-sized and smaller ones; professors of management science/business administration who were also editors of academic journals; and gatekeepers of media and knowledge arenas. In total some 30 interviews were conducted.[2] The research project is of an explorative nature. This, and the limited empirical basis, indicates the need to be tentative in the assertions made in this chapter.

9.2. THE COMMUNICATIVE VALIDATION OF KNOWLEDGE

Which contributions to management knowledge gain influence and which are rejected? Whether a new idea will become a fashion or will even help to create a new 'master idea' (Czarniawska and Joerges 1996: 36); what meanings are associated with de-contextualized ideas; and how the results of the enactment of new ideas are judged, are all decided within the managerial discourse. How is this discourse organized? Where does it take place? Who can gain access and who is involved, besides the most visible actors we introduced above? This section provides an analytical framework to further specify the notion of the managerial discourse for the subsequent empirical analysis.

For the purpose of this study, a distinction is made between a personal, non-mediated discourse and a mediated discourse. The first type can be identified by arenas and networks where the communicative validation of knowledge takes place. The second

---

[1] This research was funded by the DFG and carried out at the Forschungsinstitut für Arbeit, Technik und Kultur in Tübingen under the direction of Christoph Deutschmann.

[2] Ten managers, twelve representatives of consulting firms, four professors, and seven gatekeepers of media and knowledge arenas were interviewed in 1997 and 1998. The interview partners were chosen deliberately to cover different types of companies and consulting firms. The average interview lasted two hours. All interviews were tape-recorded and transcribed. For reasons of confidentiality no names or affiliations can be given in the text.

type is comprised of a variety of business-related publications and other media products. The two types of discourse are discussed separately, but their interdependencies are emphasized from the start. Personal communication is embedded in media discourse and the media discourse itself is related to the discourses going on in knowledge arenas and networks.

Knowledge Arenas and Personal Networks

The term 'knowledge arena' stresses the image of 'places' where dedicated contributors to management knowledge and other participants of a field meet personally. It is within and through these arenas that management consultancies and gurus exert their influence and it is here that the first step in the translation of any idea or concept may be found. The concept of knowledge arenas is used in order to shed more light on the trans-organizational level of analysis. It is here that the 'option-setting context' (Perrow 1986: 263) and the 'corridors' for organizational decision-making (Ortmann 1995: 40) are constructed. Processes at the trans-organizational level link local experience, along with its interpretation and assessment, to the 'general managerial discourse' (Furusten 1995) which has increasingly taken on a transnational character.

This process works in two directions. De-contextualized ideas are re-contextualized and local experiences may give rise to new de-contextualized ideas. Local actors feed their experience into the arenas and networks at a trans-organizational level. They thus deliver the 'raw material' for both the local adaptation and revision of previously proposed ideas and concepts and the production of new ones. Due to the complex causal texture of this process there is no unambiguous 'result' or 'immediate' experience available regarding the effects of previously enacted ideas. Therefore selection is necessary and inevitable both *ex ante* and *ex post*: causality is open to negotiation (Czarniawska and Joerges 1996: 47). The questions of who can take part in negotiating causality and where it takes place become crucial issues for research in the emergence and change of management knowledge. Whether consultancies can gain influence depends on their reputation as interpreters of managerial experience and as 'constructors' of cause-and-effect beliefs.

Formally institutionalized arenas and personal trans-organizational networks can be distinguished. Formally institutionalized arenas cover the whole spectrum of organized occasions where managers and other participants in the broader institutional context meet outside their organization: (trade) fairs, committees, congresses, conferences, seminars, and workshops for further training and the exchange of experiences. These arenas focus on different fields of knowledge. Some deal with general management issues, others with problems of functional management. Arenas may relate to specific organizational fields, industries, or professions. They are provided by a variety of suppliers and are formally institutionalized to quite differing degrees. Knowledge arenas are an important stage for any contributors to management knowledge, not least consultancies.

Personal networks are highly relevant for the communicative validation of knowledge, for 'localized sense-making' (Scarborough and Swan 1999: 14). Their relevance could well be underestimated because they are much less obvious and observable than knowledge arenas. A personal network may be symbolized by a couple of telephone numbers in a manager's address book. They arise from the direct personal relationships of an individual to which he or she is committed on a more or less regular basis. Again the focus is on trans-organizational personal networks in which members of boundary-spanning units, prominently managers and experts, are usually involved. The trans-organizational network is more extended and more heterogeneous but—inversely related—less dense than the intra-organizational network (Schenk 1995: 17). People can make use of 'the strength of weak ties' (Granovetter 1973) of extended networks, but also of 'stronger ties' to a smaller circle of trusted others. New ideas are mostly brought up via institutionalized arenas and mass media. The personal network operates under this 'umbrella'.

Media Production

Business-related media play an important role in the dissemination stage of management fashions (Abrahamson 1996). Their increasing significance is widely acknowledged (Mazza 1998) and coincides with the rise of consultancies and management gurus (Micklethwaite and Wooldridge 1996), who utilize the media to circulate their ideas and build up their reputations. However, too often the media have been treated as a passive container, conduit, or carrier of management knowledge. In contrast to such notions Abrahamson (1996: 268), referring to Hirsch (1972), pointed out the importance of 'the mass media in their gate-keeping role as a primary institutional regulator of innovation'. The notion of media as merely a means of 'diffusion' seems clearly inappropriate (Schenk 1995). Selectivity is the common feature of all media production (Schenk 1995; Haller 1994).

Earlier assumptions that mass media exert a formative influence on the public opinion of a given topic have been rejected by mass-media research. Rather it suggests that autonomous media influence has traditionally been overestimated. The cognitive effect of mass media is mainly their agenda-setting capacity, i.e. not the power to tell people what to think but rather what to think about. Moreover, the term 'agenda building' instead of 'agenda setting' (Rogers and Dearing 1988) better encapsulates the concept that public agendas emerge from a complex interaction within social networks in which journalists and editors are involved. In the 'cyclical process' between mass and interpersonal communication, the latter serves as a 'hinge' (Schenk 1995: 231). Therefore, attention has to be given to the interaction of mass-media producers with both management consultants as creators of new ideas and the addressed public.

9.3. CONSULTANTS IN KNOWLEDGE ARENAS AND PERSONAL NETWORKS: EMPIRICAL EVIDENCE

Starting in the 1960s, the contributions of the illustrious transnational consultancies gained an increasing influence on German managerial discourse, shaping the perceptions of the situation; the definition of problems and the choice of management techniques; business strategies; and concepts of organizing, for instance the M-Form, Overhead Value Analysis, Portfolio Analysis, Lean Production, Total Quality Management, Business Process Reengineering, and recently the Shareholder Value Concept (Faust 1998: 157–60). A more comprehensive history of this process has still to be written.[3] Nevertheless, the consultancies' contributions became widely recognized and had a considerable impact on organizational change. This can be shown in more detail by analysing the authorship of the most influential management concepts, such as Business Process Reengineering (Nippa and Picot 1995). Moreover, research on corporate restructuring and strategic change in Germany in the 1990s (Arbeitskreis Organisation 1996; Faust *et al.* 1999; Faust, Jauch, and Notz 2000; IfS *et al.* 1997) reveals that the change agents explain and justify their course of action by referring to guiding ideas introduced by management consultancies and gurus, including different 'readings' of these concepts. This view was confirmed by the German senior managers, consultants, and academics interviewed during the research project.

However, this chapter aims to direct attention to the processes by which consultancies exert their influence beyond specific consulting projects, and by which their contributions are simultaneously validated, revised, modified, and sometimes ignored or even bluntly refused. In doing so extracts from the interviews with managers may be drawn upon to explain which knowledge arenas and media they use to stay up-to-date and to make sense of new contributions to management knowledge. These results can be combined with the answers consultants gave to the questions concerning which arenas and media are relevant to them in building up their reputation, in gaining contacts and contracts, and in making sense of business problems for themselves.

Knowledge Arenas

The evaluation of these interviews and an additional exploration of the institutional structure of knowledge mediation in Germany (Faust 2000) show an impressive variety of formally institutionalized knowledge arenas. Some of these arenas have been explicitly established for management training, the transfer of the results of academic research, and the exchange of ideas and experiences between practitioners. These arenas are offered by different types of providers. Besides various commercial training institutes and conference organizers, including the leading German business newspaper *Handelsblatt*, non-profit providers play a considerable role. University chairs, universities for applied science (*Fachhochschulen*), and government-supported organizations for applied research in the field of technology and management (prominently the *Fraunhofer-Gesellschaften*) display a variety of activities besides their main functions (education and research) which are directed at knowledge transfer and a dialogue with practitioners (conferences, workshops, and training).

---

[3] With regard to some concepts and episodes we can rely on quite substantial research. For instance, the spread of the multi-divisional form in Germany (Dyas and Thanheiser 1976) can both show how US-origin consultancies could use the concept as an admission ticket to part of German top management and how the concept adopted a German hue when being introduced into the national context.

Private, state-accredited universities are generally more active in this respect than state universities, especially with regard to general management issues. The European Business School (Schloß Reichartshausen), for instance, organizes annual business symposia and is engaged in different executive training activities including a finance academy. However, the few private business schools were previously not at the heart of the institutional infrastructure of knowledge mediation in Germany and have only recently gained more significance. For the German case, the most important arenas provided by the self-organization of the business community and employers are trade and industry associations, some of which, for instance the University Seminar of Business (Universitätsseminar der Wirtschaft, USW), have been characterized as the 'hidden business schools' in Germany (Kipping 1998).

Several interview partners pointed out the relevance of the Schmalenbach-Gesellschaft (SG), an association dedicated to the dialogue between theory and practice in the field of business economics (*Betriebswirtschaft*). Personal members of the SG are academic researchers, including prestigious university professors, students, and practitioners, both experts and managers. Nearly all of the 100 largest German companies are among the corporate members. Some of their top executives are members of the board of governors. The SG organizes important annual congresses (Schmalenbach-Tagung, Deutscher Betriebswirtschaftler-Tag), miscellaneous, specialist conferences, and the 'entrepreneurs talks' (*Unternehmergespräche*) which take place at various companies. The 25 standing working groups, focusing on topics like corporate finance, R&D management, or international management, are considered to be the most important platforms for managerial discourse organized by the SG.

However, it is a specific feature of the German management tradition that it is not only business economists and their professional association that organize the managerial discourse. Due to the fact that German managers often have an educational background in engineering, the professional association of German engineers (Verein Deutscher Ingenieure, VDI) not only organizes a platform for (narrow) technological issues, but is also engaged in the general managerial discourse. The different trade and industry associations and employers' associations, in charge of collective bargaining at the industry level, are mediators and regulators of organizational fields. Alongside these functions they organize industry-related knowledge arenas with varying reference to general management issues.

Moreover, intermediary organizations that emerged from the rationalization movement of the first half of the twentieth century have to be considered, among them the National Efficiency Board (Reichskommissariat für Wirtschaftlichkeit, renamed Rationalisierungskuratorium der Deutschen Wirtschaft after the Second World War and most widely known as RKW) (Pohl 1996). The constituents, the fields of activities, and the role definition of these intermediary organizations have changed considerably since their foundation (Kipping 1997, 1998). Today, they are no longer at the heart of general managerial discourse. However, they still play a role in terms of more specific fields of expertise and in the small and medium-sized enterprises sector. Therefore, the arenas provided by these organizations are not of particular interest to the large, transnational consultancies but are highly relevant for the mass of smaller and more specialized consultancies, especially because the RKW is officially assigned to allocate Federal and *Länder* government funds to support the use of consultancies by small and medium-sized companies. RKW representatives are authorized to select and to supervise these consultancies in the case of publicly sponsored consulting services. For this purpose the RKW manages a pool of recognized consultancies.

Besides the arenas explicitly dedicated to knowledge exchange, several other types of arenas emerge from organized meeting-places, the establishment of which has not been primarily for this purpose. Nevertheless, these meeting-places are perceived and used as arenas for knowledge exchange by the participants. For instance, advisory boards, institutionalized as a means of corporate governance, take on the character of a knowledge arena in the view of their members. Industry or trade fairs fulfil similar functions and are quite often combined with conferences for the exchange of knowledge within a trade or industry. Several government programmes initiated to foster technological innovation or workplace reform offer arenas which were mainly established to coordinate joint activities by companies receiving public funds. Although not originally intended for such purposes, these organized meetings are nevertheless interpreted as opportunities to learn from managers of other companies and industries and from universities and research institutes involved in management discourse.

Consultants and Other Participants in Knowledge Arenas

Consultants are engaged in a variety of formally institutionalized arenas. Which arenas will be chosen depends on the specialization and size of the consultancy. The general capacity to invest in these activities is based upon their size and the probability of their gaining access depends on reputation. The large transnational consultancies are especially eager to gain contact with the arenas where top-ranking managers meet and where general management issues are on the agenda. For instance, in 1998 about 8 per cent of the SG members were consultancies, including most of the large, transnational firms. Consultants appreciate taking part in its standing working groups and being invited as speakers on its management training seminars. The top consultancies also sponsor the USW and private business universities. In several cases they are elected as members of the board of trustees of these institutions. Representatives of McKinsey, Roland Berger and Partners, Arthur D. Little, Booz, Allen & Hamilton, and others are often invited as guest speakers or lecturers by these institutions.

Although an obvious marketing attitude would displease the organizers of arenas, consultants try to use such occasions to promote their views and to build up their reputation. Attending conferences and workshops has the valued side-effect of consultants being able to detect both arising problems and promising new ideas and concepts. This is of particular importance for smaller consultancies who have to position their offers within the emerging trends and fashions, but members of the most influential consultancies are also aware of the fact that new ideas and concepts emerge from a complex interaction between a variety of actors. Listening to the views, experiences, and recommendations of competing consultants, academic researchers or commentators, and prominent managers is also important to consultancy firms in developing their intuition and in either confirming, revising, or modifying their own views and concepts. For instance, many large, transnational consultancies are also customers of the USW and send their consultants there for training.

Although consultants are inclined to participate as speakers in promising events, their appearance depends on the decisions of gatekeepers to grant access. Therefore, data which show the participation of consultants as speakers in arenas always reflect the acknowledgment of their status as relevant contributors to management knowledge by representatives of academia, the business community, or other commercial suppliers.

Examining the composition of contributors to the managerial discourse in different arenas reveals two major features. First, the main contributing groups identified as speakers at events are representatives of academia, some of them consultants themselves, practitioners (managers and experts from companies), and professional consultants. Secondly, the composition of contributors differs from arena to arena. Arenas organized by academic professions are dominated by their own members. Gatekeepers of these arenas express their benevolent attitude towards management practice mostly by inviting practitioners as contributors and commentators and are selective in their invitation of consultants. Arenas dedicated to the dialogue between academic knowledge and management practice, the exchange of knowledge between practitioners, and training events are each dominated by speakers from management practice. Although academics are still the second largest group in these arenas, consultants have a significant share, compared with their overall share as members of the business community.

Most practitioners taking part in the managerial discourse are not creators of new ideas. Nevertheless, managers play a considerable role in the process of fashion building and dissolution. They contribute to the ongoing debate by writing articles for books and journals, as speakers at conferences, and as teachers at training events. They confirm and sometimes—as down-to-earth practitioners—repudiate or refute a new idea. They criticize an outmoded traditional management or organizational practice, using evidence from their company and, similarly, demonstrate how a new idea can be introduced with positive effects on competitiveness, or has to be modified with reference to the specific context. Ideas that cannot find articulated support by practitioners in official and unofficial communication are not likely to become fashionable or be enacted at all, whatever their original promise.

The Personal Networks of Managers and Consultants

As has been noted above, personal networks are highly relevant for managers' individual sense-making and hence for the communicative validation of management knowledge. As our interviews with managers suggest, the main effect of a personal network for the individual is not to enable him or her to know of new ideas first, but rather to hear which ideas are noteworthy, seem plausible, or are likely to become a fashion and as such cannot be neglected. The individual seeks to develop a better understanding of the various meanings which may be associated with new ideas, how these ideas could be put into action, and what has been the experience of others when introducing a new concept. Thus, explicitly, people from other contexts are of interest. The actors in personal networks are chosen voluntarily. The relationships require a certain level of trust in order for them to be maintained.

Personal networks may arise from attending arenas, especially those providing opportunities for an immediate exchange of ideas and experiences between practitioners of a trade or profession. Informal communications and 'hidden agendas' are a crucial feature of formally institutionalized arenas. They are appreciated as places to meet members in a network who are already acquainted and to further develop one's personal network. For instance, a manager may get to know a colleague on an SG working group whom he might appreciate as a partner for further individual exchange of ideas and experiences.

Personal networks in general emerge from quite different occasions. Many of them are generated by everyday organizational activities. Personal networks arise from repeated interaction with people from customers, suppliers, or even competitors. Personal relations may emerge among the members of a supervisory board or between individual members of the board and the supervised managers. Moreover, personal contacts are maintained with former colleagues who have moved to other companies. Personal relations stem from education, as people keep in touch with colleagues in other companies with whom they shared campus life. Although these relations often require a cautious attitude, they can become detached from the type of interaction originally defined by the organizational context or contract relation. They may take on the feature of a more general knowledge exchange over the course of the interaction; sometimes this remains a casual but useful side-effect of interactions originally driven by other needs. The more the relationships with customers, suppliers, and investors are of a long-term nature, the more likely it is that personal relations between members of these organizations will emerge.

Managers and academic teachers time and again interact in the matter of traineeships and practice-oriented student research for final exams in which both sides are interested. For instance, a professor of business economy may repeatedly meet a regional entrepreneur. The professor appreciates these meetings because he can keep in contact with practical business. The entrepreneur likes to discuss his company's current problems and new concepts with an independent person without any contractual obligations. The professor describes his personal role in this relationship as an 'interpreter' of new ideas.

Top-ranking managers who are responsible for decisions on consulting activities are in frequent contact with a variety of representatives of top management consultancies because such institutions are constantly seeking opportunities to sell their services and often have continuous business relations with large firms. Managers use these contacts to sound out emerging new concepts. The CEOs of large corporations maintain a more personal relationship with selected partners of the leading consultancies, detached from any specific consulting project. The German business press reports on the high-ranking personal networks of illustrious consultants like Herbert Hentzler, the (former) managing director of McKinsey Germany. Top executives from corporations and consultancies frequently meet at a variety of occasions, for example as members of committees or speakers at major business events, which foster the emergence of personal networks. Moreover, the mutual relations between consultancies and their former members who have moved into a management position elsewhere give rise to a special form of personal networks. The managing directors of McKinsey, Arthur D. Little, or Roland Berger have become a natural part of the German business elite. Partners from large consultancies emphasize that sustainable success in the consulting business requires personal relationships with top decision-makers (see also Kipping 1999*a*).

From time to time a top executive has dinner with a consultant whom he learnt to admire during a consulting project. Sometimes the consultant takes the initiative; sometimes it is he himself who does. Without aiming at advice on a contractual basis, the manager expects the consultant to tell him about evolving problems in the chemical industry, their common field of practice, and about promising new concepts. Despite the consultant's ulterior motive to gain a new contract, the relation can take on a different character from his side, as well. Consultants regard some of these more frequent contacts with top executives as a personal 'coaching' relationship partly due to the 'loneliness' of top decision-makers within their organizations. However, as other managers reported, the suspicion that consultants are always keen to exploit relationships for contracts, or that they may face loyalty conflicts between competing clients within an industry, may well prove to be a barrier to a trusting relationship. Nevertheless, the manager can also make some use of a more reserved relationship and consultants themselves are well advised to foster long-term relationships with top executives because their value clearly goes beyond signing a single consulting contract. Top executives are the most relevant potential sponsors and supporters of new concepts and sometimes useful partners due to their ability to develop a sense for arising problems and marketable ideas within the 'insecure (consulting) business' (Sturdy 1997).

Although relationships with consultants are a relevant part of managerial networks, the immediate exchange of ideas and experiences between managers from different companies still has an important impact on the communicative validation of management knowledge. Whatever 'passes' as (management) knowledge (Berger and Luckmann 1966: 3) emerges from overlapping networks of consultants, managers, management trainers, academics, and representatives of diverse intermediary organizations.

The Increasing Internationalization of Knowledge Arenas and Personal Networks

Although German companies have been integrated into the world economy for a long time, and hence German managers have been long-term participants in transnational networks, our interviews suggest that transnational arenas and networks have significantly gained in importance, particularly during the last decade. We lack comprehensive research on this issue, but tentatively suggest that globalization goes hand in hand with the emergence of transnational arenas and more extended networks in most industries and for a greater number of managers.

Large German corporations increasingly cooperate with US and other international business schools regarding management training and even consulting projects. The highly reputed European business schools (like Insead) are gaining importance and create transnational arenas by organizing conferences and seminars. The need for an internationalization of German management has been broadly acknowledged in the last decade, strongly supported by the wave of mergers and acquisitions and by corporate restructuring that has created an increasing number of business units with worldwide responsibility (Faust, Jauch, and Notz 2000: 43–76). Participation in international arenas is highly attractive to career-oriented managers. It is not only a welcome incentive, but managers can use the input from the cutting-edge of business knowledge and receive the aura of an 'anointed' person that can enable them to attain a better position in the competition for concepts and careers within organizations. Access to these international arenas will be more restrictive than to the traditional, mostly nationally based ones. 'High potentials' and the higher ranks of management will be favoured.

Furthermore, the personal networks do not stay unaffected by the internationalization of economic activities, management education, and institutionalized arenas from which personal networks emerge (Marceau 1989): their centre of gravity changes, at least for an elite of managers. New ideas, and the advantages or disadvantages of established structures, strategies, and routines, are assessed in communication with members of an international management elite and within the type of discourse appropriate to this level. To a considerable degree this is due to the internationalization of corporate finance and the growing need to legitimate corporate strategy *vis-à-vis* the international investor community. The internationalization of arenas favours large, internationally operating contributors to management knowledge, who are held in repute: the double-dealing consultancies.

We, as a global enterprise, appreciate knowing people who can imagine how to do business in Asia and America as well. Our solutions are mostly not local, nor should they be local. If we were to suggest a solution which people in the USA would consider weird, then this will be no solution for a company as we are.... A world company has to be faced with a partner in the consulting business which is global as well (A manager from the headquarters of a transnational German corporation).

The ongoing trend towards concentration in the consulting sector (Sperling and Ittermann 1998: 22) is reinforced by the globalization of organizational fields (Arias and Guillén 1998) and its corresponding knowledge arenas.

9.4. MEDIA PRODUCTION: EMPIRICAL EVIDENCE

Consultancies have a pronounced and articulated interest in being present in a variety of business-related media, either by writing books and articles themselves or by being cited as experts in the business press. The analysis of the major contributing groups to various media products, that we undertook within the research project, shows a consistent pattern which it is possible to briefly summarize here. The more practice-oriented the media product (book or journal), the larger is the share of consultants as authors. For instance, in the book programme of one of the most significant German publishers of management literature, Campus, the proportion of authors from consulting increased to over 50 per cent between 1983 and 1997.

Not surprisingly, in contrast, academic journals are clearly less relevant for consultants as a means of diffusion for their ideas. Moreover, meeting the standards of academic discourse is an obstacle to the average consultant. Therefore, consultants are clearly less represented in academic journals. However, as will be shown below, consultants are quite successful in their efforts to be cited as authoritative experts on diverse management issues. Yet all these figures are the result of decisions made by media gatekeepers. How do media gatekeepers distinguish between relevant and irrelevant issues and individuals? By what criteria do they select relevant authors or ascribe expertise and authority to persons to whom they refer in order to legitimize a judgement?

The Case of Manager magazin

Manager magazin is one of the major German periodicals addressed to managers. It sells about 120,000 copies monthly. According to an independent media analysis almost 60 per cent of the readers come from the two upper ranks of management and 27 per cent are self-employed business people. The analysis of 'cited experts' from 1980 to 1996 follows the trends illustrated in Figure 9.1.[4] Managers are still the major group to whom the journalists refer as experts of management and business issues, but they have become significantly less appreciated as experts of their own environment. The share of other, non-managerial practitioners fluctuates with no obvious trend. Since the mid-1980s consultants have been increasingly acknowledged as experts, accounting for about 20 per cent of references. For most of the period consultants are considered more frequently than academics. Yet the increasing share of consultants has not been at the expense of academics, whose share fluctuates around a slightly increasing trend line.

The inevitable selectivity of the media gatekeepers is rooted in an intuition of the needs of their potential readers. Meeting these needs is a prerequisite for commercial success. This intuition is derived from participating in the arenas and networks for the communicative validation of knowledge. The journalist interviewed for this study attends a variety of knowledge arenas—congresses and conferences—especially those where issues from his field of specialization are on the agenda. He follows the publications of business schools like Harvard, St. Gallen, and IMD (International Institute for Management Development). He regularly takes note of the relevant national and international newspapers, magazines, and journals. Additionally, consultancies, international business schools, and German university chairs provide him with newsletters and press releases. Leading publishing houses in the field of management literature send him advance copies of new books. As the journalist is well acknowledged, all kinds of actors supply him with information, stories, and new concepts which they wish to

[4] Within each year the same four monthly issues were selected. From these we chose the 'title story' and the main topic of each number, which consisted of several articles. The articles were written by journalists, not by external authors. The text analysis counted 'cited experts', i.e. any person to whom the authors refer as a source of information, expertise, or assessment. We distinguished between 12 categories and a further category of non-attributable persons. The four groups—academics (80), consultants (144), managers (387), and non-managerial practitioners from companies (121)—account for 85 per cent of all 952 identified references. Figure 9.1 shows the time series for these four groups.

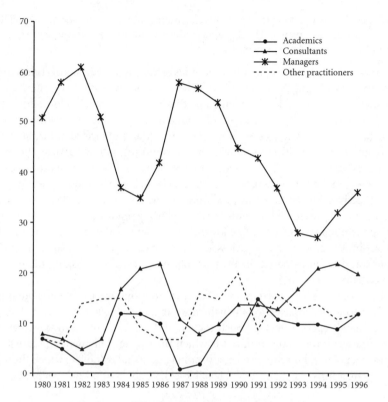

Figure 9.1. 'Cited experts' in *manager magazin*

bring to attention. Thus, he is like a spider in the web of circulating ideas and stories. However, this implies a particular selectivity. Only a few university chairs actively relate to the business press, mostly those particularly dedicated to management practice or who themselves act as consultants.

'Consultancies very actively and professionally' seek to make contact with the journal, he observes, both personally and by sending newsletters, booklets, and books. Out of this extended network emerges a smaller circle of people from academia, top management, and consultancies whom he regularly and actively contacts in investigating particular issues. In the gatekeeper's view, academics have become more attractive as a source of validation in recent years because an increasing number of them have developed closer relations to business practice. However, selected representatives of the Boston Consulting Group, McKinsey, or similar consulting firms are of particular importance because 'they deliver a different view, a global, international, or at least European view. Each of us [journalists] is in permanent contact with one of these'. The network partners serve as:

advisors to develop a thesis which is still quite vague. From time to time I visit them or ring them up, to tell them that I am considering producing a story. Is this a relevant topic, or not? Have I grasped the relevant aspects of it? Do you have consulting projects in this field? Is it still highly relevant or already outmoded? These people are important for the emergence of stories and topics, for trying to develop a judgement.

He regards management fashions as sometimes being 'mere creations of consultancies, but on the other hand these people are constantly on the spot. Very often they are sensors, seismographs of developments, and they themselves react to something which begins to emerge actually in business.' Although he emphasizes the relationships with knowledge intermediaries, he is provided with an abundance of information and assessments from practitioners. During background research for articles, he obtains much occasional information, random observations, and assessments about current events or what is about to occur in companies. He is able to hear quite different views and perspectives. Moreover, many practitioners (originating from all ranks) take their own initiative in providing him with stories, including reports about failures in implementing fashionable concepts. The journalist is aware of the fact that the magazine helps fashions to emerge. Nevertheless, he claims to contribute to a critical assessment of trends and fashions based on his personal network, always asking the question: 'What is really new about it?'

Media producers have to be aware of 'leading' opinions and the 'agenda building' in their field to arrive at selections which make their products a commercial success. Although gatekeepers select rigorously (Schenk 1995), their 'autonomy' to do so is tied to the communication community for which they write. The media discourse is an 'integral part of a wider economic, institutional and social context in which the uptake of an organization concept occurs' (Heusinkveld, Benders, and Koch 2000: 15).

9.5. CONCLUSION: KNOWLEDGE ARENAS, GLOBALIZATION, AND INSTITUTIONAL CHANGE

Management consultancies achieve their status as a 'reflection elite' by efforts to present their views and solutions in the relevant arenas and media for the communicative validation of management knowledge and by fostering personal networks within the managerial community, including gatekeepers of media and knowledge arenas. Our findings could be complemented by research dealing with the communication strategies and the rhetoric by which consultants and management gurus try to persuade their public (Clark 1995; Huczynski 1993a; Kieser 1997). However, a mere 'point-of-sale' study misses the interactive nature of both the selection and dissemination stages of the fashion-setting process (Abrahamson 1996; Clark and Greatbatch in Chapter 8, above).

Which products are offered at the point-of-sale and how the products are changed or adapted during consumption is shaped within the trans-organizational discourse. Again, other research approaches could complement these findings, including studies which examine the intra-organizational translation of popular concepts and its interdependence with the construction of trans-organizational 'option-setting contexts' (Perrow 1986: 263).

Furthermore, case-studies which examine the translation of particular 'global' con-cepts, suggesting the emergence of 'sectoral and or national patterns in the reception of fashions' (Benders, van den Berg, and van Bijsterveld 1998: 214), could enhance our understanding. Such case-studies could benefit from a focus on knowledge arenas as suggested here. Within these arenas and networks 'globally disseminated ideas' and national and local forces cross each other (Heusinkveld, Benders, and Koch 2000: 15). The question of which arenas are relevant in a given national context, and who are credible and authoritative knowledge providers within these arenas, are therefore of particular importance. The empirical evidence from Germany has given some hints at national peculiarities regarding the institutional facets of knowledge arenas and of globalizing forces undermining these arrangements. Therefore, it appears fruitful to re-examine the national findings from a broader comparative point of view in which history and culture matter.

The knowledge arenas, identified above as relevant for the German case, are mostly rooted in national institutions. The variety and density of arenas seems to be typical for the German institutional arrangement of a coordinated or cooperative capitalism. In comparison with Anglo-Saxon 'liberal capitalism' it can be characterized as a capitalist market economy 'that was and remains richly organized and densely regulated by a vast variety of institutions that have sprung from sometimes incompatible sources, from *Mittelstand* traditionalism to various stripes of organized labour' (Streeck 1997: 35–6). The core features of this peculiar institutional arrangement are:

1. an active, 'enabling state' (Streeck 1997: 38; Hollingsworth 1997*a*, 1997*b*);
2. the relevance of 'quasi-public or associationally constructed' networks (Hollingsworth 1997*a*: 143; Lane 1997: 72, 80);
3. the significance of professions (*Berufe*) in general, and 'functional management' in particular (Stewart *et al.* 1994; Faust, Jauch, and Notz 2000), defined by educa-tional background, recruitment patterns, role definition, and authority (Byrkjeflot 1998); and
4. a 'cooperative' corporate governance system with its corresponding personal link-ages (Windolf and Beyer 1996).

Such institutional arrangements coordinate and regulate economic transactions, but they are also characterized by distinct modes of knowledge production and exchange. Institutions define arenas and networking opportunities in which know-ledge is produced, exchanged, validated, and modified. They also define the actors to whom reputation is ascribed, the criteria for the legitimacy of organizations, and the authority of decision-makers.

The US consultancies which stepped onto the German stage from the 1960s onwards tried to gain access to these arenas and networks. They could only expand and stabilize their influence in so far as they succeeded in this task. Gradually, and with increasing success since the 1980s, they could establish themselves as a new, com-mercial type of intermediary organization in Germany (Kipping 1999*a*: 214–19). Management consultancies had achieved such a status much earlier in the USA due to the country's formative 'market mentality' (Hollingsworth 1997*a*: 134), corresponding neglect of associative coordination (Kipping 1997, 1999*a*), and 'enabling' state activities (Streeck 1997).[5]

The rise of transnational management consultancies in Germany can thus be described as a twofold process. On the one hand they had to adapt to the prevailing institutional infrastructure.[6] On the other hand they acted as a permanent challenge both to prevailing knowledge and the knowledge-producing and transmitting institutional infrastructure and its natural 'embedded' experts. The new actors offered new opportunities and acted as a 'ferment' of change. This can be best illustrated by the fact that German managers increasingly perceive and acknowledge transnational consultancies as natural partners in the evaluation and dissemination of foreign experiences, nowadays labelled as 'best practice' and 'benchmarking', whereas this very task, for decades, used to be fulfilled within the associative infrastructure, supported by non-commercial intermediary organizations.[7]

Transnational arenas and networks have been gaining importance. This is due to the ongoing internationalization of business organizations, and hence management, and the growing importance of the supranational level (especially the European level) in the coordination and regulation of economic affairs. Although the effects of globalization on national economies are still highly controversial, it is safe to say that a set of decisions usually associated with the process of globalization gave rise to a crisis of 'organized modernity' in Europe, a societal configuration which was bound to a set of societal conventions within the boundaries of the nation-state (Wagner 1994: 123–40). This period of crisis started in the second half of the 1970s and fully unfolded its effects in Germany during the 1990s (Faust 2000: 76; Streeck 1997). A core feature of this process can be seen in the diminishing capacity, sometimes also inclination, of nationally bound actors (predominantly the state but also trade associations and unions) to coordinate and regulate the economy. This corresponds with an increase of new opportunities for mobile actors (transnational companies, the financial sector, and consultancies).

Following Streeck (1997: 53), it could be argued that 'globalization discriminates against modes of economic governance that require public intervention' and that rely on nationally rooted associative coordination (cf. Hollingsworth 1997*a*: 143), while it 'favours national systems like those of the USA and Britain that have historically relied less on public-political and more on private-contractual economic governance' (Streeck 1997: 53). The same process which undermines modes of economic governance, rooted in national institutions, erodes the corresponding modes of knowledge construction and exchange. Similarly, the 'effect of globalization' has been interpreted by Arias and Guillén (1998: 129) 'in neo-institutional terms as the creation of both

---

[5] For a more extended version of these arguments see Faust (2000).

[6] It is still a research desideratum to find out whether and how far the German subsidiaries of the US-origin management consultancies will follow a specific German approach, and how far different national approaches may have an impact on the overall alignment of these transnationalizing firms (see Chapter 6, above).

[7] The RKW, for instance, used to be described as a 'mediator between the parts and protector of the entirety of the German rationalization movement' (Pohl 1996: 98).

transnational organizations and transnational fields of organizations that tend to facilitate transfers'.

This development is accomplished by the emergence of transnational arenas and networks for the communicative validation of management knowledge. How far this process has developed is far from evident and there are forces operating in the opposite direction, but whatever the outcome, it will be more strongly influenced by the communicative validation in globalizing arenas and networks in which a different set of actors will have the chance to raise their voices than it used to be in the nationally restricted institutional environment. This goes back to changes in power relations which include 'differentials with regard to access to valid knowledge about the effect of rules and access to the media of communication about rule-setting' (Wagner 1994: 25). The need to gain deeper insights into these processes in a comparative perspective should be on the research agenda.

PART III

RELATIONSHIP PERSPECTIVES ON THE CONSULTANCY PROJECT

10

Managers as Marionettes? Using Fashion Theories to Explain the Success of Consultancies

ALFRED KIESER

10.1. INTRODUCTION

The consulting market is exploding (Ernst and Kieser 2002). In industrialized countries the revenues of consultancies grow yearly by 10 to 30 per cent (BDU 1998; Hasek 1997; Rassam and Oates 1991). The market for management books, seminars, conferences, magazines, etc.—the market of management fashions—is also exploding. It is a central hypothesis of this chapter that the correlation between the two markets is not coincidental. It is shown that by producing management concepts, some of which succeed in becoming management fashions, consultancies are able to create a demand for their services. First, an attempt is made to clarify what a management fashion is. Then some sociological theories of fashion are discussed. On the basis of these concepts the question is raised why managers are attracted by management fashions. This leads to the discussion of the features which management consultants may use to furnish their management concepts in order to make them successful, i.e. to make them management fashions.

10.2. WHAT IS A MANAGEMENT FASHION?

A management fashion is a management concept that has become fashionable. A management concept, in turn, is a discourse that evolves around a buzzword like Scientific Management, Fordism, Lean Production, or Re-engineering. Texts—management books, articles in management magazines, presentations by consultants, etc.—are linked to a management concept that is identified by a buzzword. These texts contain some goals and a number of principles or rules of design. Take, for example, the following text from an advertisement for the conference How to Measure and Improve Internal Customer Satisfaction, organized in 1993 by the International Quality and Productivity Centre: 'Start thinking of our company as a lot of little companies. Each work area is a "mini-company" that produces a product or service for other mini-companies. This concept makes each of us both a supplier and a customer' (quoted after Wasson 1998: 5).

Since the principles and goals of a management concept are rather vague, they are likely to trigger discussions: What is meant by 'empowerment'? To what extent does the individual employee as an 'internal customer' have to behave differently from the 'traditional' employee? What has to be done to set up an internal 'mini-company'? It is predominantly from this kind of vagueness that management concepts derive their strength. Vagueness causes the people who are interested in a management concept to engage in a discussion between the text and themselves. For example, the reader or listener tries to relate the text to problems of the company they are working in, or they draw on their experience to make sense of passages that they cannot understand right away. Since this discussion is unlikely to lead to a satisfactory clarification, they are, if the initial confrontation with the concept has aroused enough interest, motivated to extend the discussion. They will perhaps read additional texts about this management concept, attend a seminar or a conference, and confer with colleagues. If, over time, they and their colleagues become more and more convinced that the concept should be implemented in their organization, they may start an initiative to do so. This initiative will lead to numerous additional discussions within this organization in the form of kick-off meetings, project meetings, presentations, etc., some of which may take the form of more informal encounters between the organization's members. Perhaps a consultant is hired who will then become a hub for the internal discourse. These discussions will eventually lead to a partial social reconstruction of the organizational reality (Wasson 1998; Zbaracki 1998). The organization's members gradually acquire new action principles, new subjective theories about how the organization should function, new cognitive schemes, and new scripts (Argyris and Schön 1978; Downey and Brief 1986; Greenwood and Hinings 1988; Porac, Thomas, and Baden-Fuller 1989). Perhaps also new technologies (e.g. new computer programs) and new management techniques (e.g. a new personnel evaluation system) are implemented. However, it sometimes occurs that predominantly the talk within the organization changes while the routines, strategies, and activities of its members stay roughly the same (Brunsson and Olsen 1993).

At a given point in time, many management concepts propagated by consultancies simultaneously compete for the attention of managers. Management concepts that relatively speedily gain large shares in the public management discourse are called management fashions. Consultancies are the main producers of management concepts, striving to 'commodify' them. Concepts that are commodified have a better chance of attracting clients. Commodification means that consultants transform unstructured problems and problem solutions into standardized problems and solutions (Elkjær *et al.* 1991; Fincham 1995; Werr, Stjernberg, and Docherty 1997; Fincham and Evans 1999). Commodified concepts facilitate marketing—Prêt-à-Porter sells better than Haute Couture—therefore they are more likely to become management fashions. Clients favour 'package solutions' as these create the impression that the methods of the respective management concept have been tested in many companies. For consultancies it is easier to convince clients of the value of specific products than just of their competence as such. Commodified concepts also allow for the rationalization of the consulting work (Ernst and Kieser 2002).

The discussion that develops around a management fashion can be conceptualized as forming an arena—a concept inspired by Crozier and Friedberg (1980)—in which different groups of participants bustle about: first of all consultants, but also professors of business schools, managers, editors of management magazines, publishers, commercial seminar organizers, organizers of internet forums, etc. The participants can achieve whatever goals they pursue—profit, public image, power, or career advancement—by widening the arena, which is brought about by luring additional participants into it. For this purpose the actors play principally cooperative games. Rhetoric is a crucial input currency in this game. Competition occurs only in some instances, for example when several consultants are competing for a contract, once they have collectively convinced the client that a fundamental restructuring of his organization is unavoidable, mainly through advertisements, public relations, and publications. The rules of the game can be further developed during the game. Moves that turn out to be ineffective—that do not increase attractiveness—are not likely to be repeated by a player or copied by others. The speed at which the arena grows depends entirely on the attractiveness of the game that the players are able to produce (Figure 10.1.).

To turn into a management fashion a management concept must become an object of public discourse. Usually, this public discourse is initiated by an article, a presentation, a management book, or a combination of events of this sort. The discourse gains momentum when widely read management magazines pick up the basic ideas of a management concept. Professors of business schools are welcomed into the arena because they provide scientific legitimacy for the fashion.

Although the actors in the fashion arena play predominantly cooperative games, since they are jointly attempting to widen the arena, each actor also strives to increase control over the arena. Publishing companies not only publish management books, management magazines, and daily newspapers with business sections, they also organize

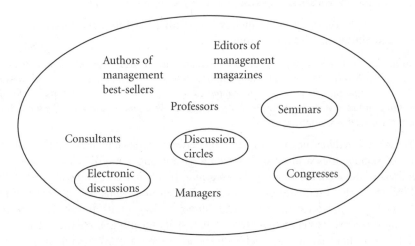

Figure 10.1. *The arena of a management fashion*

or co-organize management seminars and congresses. In this way, through orchestrated advertisements and reports, publishers simultaneously promote the circulation
of their publications and the demand for their seminars and congresses. Consulting
firms also organize seminars, which they regard as a superb marketing instrument for
a highly complex service. Consultancies also cooperate with business schools in the
setting up of executive training (Kipping and Amorim 1999/2000). And they establish
and cultivate 'old-boys' networks with their former consultants who have moved into
management (Byrne and Williams 1993).

10.3. GENERAL THEORIES OF FASHION

Management fashions are a specific kind of fashion. In this section a number of sociological theories of fashion are discussed. The purpose of this discussion is to derive
hypotheses that can be applied to explanations regarding the rise and fall of management fashions and the role consultants play in these processes.

General theories may be classified into four major paradigms (Davis 1989, 1992;
Schnierer 1995): trickle-down theories, collective selection theories, marionette theories,
and ambivalence theories. Trickle-down theories rest on a simple hypothesis: the
lower social classes imitate the styles of the higher classes and, thereby, force the higher
classes to change their styles in order to re-establish old differences. The first rudimen-
tary versions of trickle-down theory were advanced by Kant (1980; first published in
1798) and Spencer (1888). Simmel (1957; first published in 1904), however, was
the first to base the explanation of the oscillations of fashion on the motives of the
individual. He claimed:

Just as soon as the lower classes begin to copy their [the upper classes'] style, thereby crossing the
line of demarcation the upper classes have drawn and destroying the uniformity of their coher-
ence, the upper classes turn away from this style and adopt a new one, which in its turn differen-
tiates them from the masses; and thus the game goes merrily on (Simmel 1957: 545).

The individual, according to Simmel, is constantly forced to make choices between
keeping to himself or herself or joining others:

From the fact that fashion as such can never be generally in vogue, *the individual derives the
satisfaction of knowing that as adopted by him it still represents something special and striking,
while at the same time he feels inwardly supported by a set of persons who are striving for the
same thing*, not as in the case of other social satisfactions, by a set actually doing the same thing
(Simmel 1957: 547–8, emphasis added).

These fashion dynamics not only develop between classes positioned at the extreme
poles of society, they also occur between adjacent upper middle classes. Since the
members of these classes perceive their status as highly insecure and endangered, the
fashion chase there tends to be especially wild (Simmel 1957: 555; 1986: 184; first
published 1911). Nowadays, the trickle-down theory in its purest form is out
of fashion. Its critics claim that status has lost its meaning altogether in modern
societies, and that fashions can trickle up and across any groups, forcing the group of
the first adopters to invent new forms of distinction with regard to the imitators

(Blumberg 1974; King and Ring 1980). In a similar vein Bourdieu (1994) conceptualizes a competitive—'an unbroken, unending'—struggle among the classes in which aesthetic products and style are used as weapons. In contrast to Simmel, he defines a social class by the structure of relationships between all relevant characteristics of a group such as income, gender, age, profession, etc. The 'upper' classes 'defend their rarity by defending the rarity of the products they consume or the way in which they consume them. In fact, the most elementary, the simplest strategy, consists in shunning works that have become popularized, devalued and disqualified' (Bourdieu 1993*b*: 115).

In the collective selection theories that go back to Blumer (1969), fashion performs a number of functions. First, it 'introduces order in a potentially anarchic and moving present', through collectively narrowing choice. In this respect 'fashion performs in a moving society a function which custom performs in a settled society'. Second, it 'serves to detach the grip of the past in a moving world'—a world that needs individuals who are prepared to move in new directions. 'Third, fashion operates as an orderly preparation for the immediate future. By allowing the presentation of new models but by forcing them through the gauntlet of competition and collective selection the fashion mechanism offers a continuous means of adjusting to what is on the horizon' (Blumer 1969: 289–90). Thus, being fashionable appears to offer the individual some control over his or her environmental conditions. This is why most consumers of fashion experience it as something that promises orientation and stability—at least for some time.

In marionette theories fashion is conceptualized as the 'natural' outcome of the capitalist economy. Producers invent a fashion 'because through it a fictitious advantage can be achieved where a real one is not possible'. The producers increase the customers' 'propensity to buy' by adding 'small modifications' to a product. The customer replaces the old product 'because it is no longer modern, though it is by no means worn out' (Sombart 1902: 101). The most important factor, however, that is responsible for the dynamics of fashion has to do with the tendency of lower classes to imitate the upper ones. The entrepreneurs give their products 'the appearance of greater elegance and higher prestige of objects that usually serve the consumption of a socially higher class'. Thereby they appeal to 'the pride of the common man to wear the same shirts as the rich bon-vivant, of the maid to put on the same dress as her mistress . . . etc.' (Sombart 1902: 102). Sombart's line of argument is not so different from that of trickle-down theory. This becomes even more obvious when he points out that a fashion

loses its value as soon as it is imitated in an inferior quality; thus this incessant generalization of an iteration forces those classes of the population that consider good taste important to think constantly about changes in their mix of consumer goods. The result is a wild hunting for ever newer forms whose speed increases to the extent to which the techniques of production and trade are advancing. (Sombart 1902: 103)

Sombart (1902) supplements Simmel's trickle-down theory with the concept of a competition between producers of fashionable goods, the agents of fashion, who, by increasingly making use of modern technology, generalize fashion—i.e. spread it to all groups of the population—and, thereby, intensify its dynamics. The consumer is manipulated by the producers, by advertising agencies, and by the mass media. In this way, consumers are made marionettes of the industry. This is why 'fashion is capitalism's favourite child' (Sombart 1902: 104).

The representatives of the ambivalence theories who draw on Baudrillard (1981), point out that present times are characterized by 'a climate of cultural ambivalence in the sense of mixed emotions as well as mixed expressions' (Kaiser, Nagasawa, and Hutton 1991: 169). This postmodern increase in cultural ambivalence 'results in the emergence of a broad variety of clothing styles in the free market system. The clothing styles emerge to clarify and lend expression to the cultural ambivalence' (Kaiser, Nagasawa, and Hutton 1991: 180). Fashion is no longer a phenomenon of society as a whole. In the postmodern context there are only 'subgroups or subcultures' that pick up a fashion so that, simultaneously, several fashions coexist (Kaiser, Nagasawa, and Hutton 1991: 171). Another representative of the ambivalence theories, Davis (1988: 24), maintains that fashion is driven 'by what I term identity ambivalences or, as I phrase it in some other contexts, identity polarities'. These identity ambivalences are mainly caused by the loss of clearly distinct social classes. The agents who design fashions try to respond to individuals' need for a reduction of these identity ambivalences. They 'seek through the artful manipulation of the conventional visual and tactile symbols of clothing presentation to lend expression to them or, alternatively, to contain, deflect, or sublimate them' (Davis 1985: 24).

The different fashion theories complement each other (Schnierer 1995). According to trickle-down theories, individuals permanently need new fashions, since the old ones are constantly in danger of no longer providing distinction. Marionette theory adds the producers—the agents of fashion—who stimulate the fashion race in order to increase their profits. Newer trickle-down theories no longer refer to social classes but postulate that any group can challenge any other group on the basis of fashion. Fashion not only trickles down, it can also trickle up from and across the most diverse social groups. In ambivalence theories it is stressed that, in the long run, because fashions come and go quickly, they not only do not reduce, they may even aggravate identity problems that are caused by the loss of clearly distinct social classes. Most theories of fashion treat fashion as a ubiquitous phenomenon that is not restricted to clothes. And in those theories that concentrate on fashions in clothes, it is pointed out that the developed concepts should also be useful for the explanation of fashion in other forms.

What can be learned from this discussion of general theories of fashion that is useful for the analysis of management fashions? One can assume that managers also have a desire to distinguish themselves in the eyes of relevant observers (top management, investors, or other managers who compete for careers) from other managers. If they manage to appear as highly innovative and active they raise their chances of promotion. In this situation the adoption of management fashions is a very effective strategy: it is less risky than inventing completely new solutions. In Simmel's (1957: 548) words, the management fashion 'still represents something special and striking, while at the same time he [the individual, in this case the individual manager] feels inwardly supported by a set of persons who are striving for the same thing, not as in the case of other social satisfactions, by a set actually doing the same thing'. The consultancies that constantly strive to increase their growth, market share, and profit can be characterized as producers in Sombart's sense who increase the appeal of their products by adding modifications. One of their favourite sales arguments is to categorize their concepts as 'best practices', i.e. as the practices of most prestigious companies like General Electric (Hegele and Kieser 2001) or Microsoft.

10.4. A FRAMEWORK FOR ANALYSIS

In a model with which they try to explain the extraordinary growth of the consulting market, Ernst and Kieser (2002) claim that consultants boost their sales predominantly by promising managers the transfer of powerful knowledge with the help of which they can increase control over their companies, while, at the same time, also increasing their fear of control loss (see Figure 10.2.). To achieve control over events that impinge on the realization of one's plans can be regarded as one of the strongest human motives (Adler 1929; deCharms 1968; Malinowski 1955; Nietzsche 1912; White 1959). As a consequence, the perception of a loss of control is experienced as severe distress and leads to intensive efforts to escape this situation (Thompson 1981). This should especially hold for managers, since to 'have things under control' is what everybody expects from them. The successes and failures of organizations are generally attributed to the managers at the top. However, this need for control is confronted with the perception of an increasingly complex and dynamic inner and outer organizational environment and with daily experiences of control loss.

The continual production of new management concepts contributes to the managers' perception of environmental complexity. Each new management concept promises a simplification of the managers' task and more effective management solutions. However, because there is an abundance of management concepts that all promise simplification it is the unintended effect that complexity and uncertainty for the managers is increased. Those who have not yet implemented the recent management concepts wonder whether competitors who already have done so might perhaps achieve advantages. The more managers read and hear about other managers from other companies telling stories (that are often launched by the consultancies) of how they have

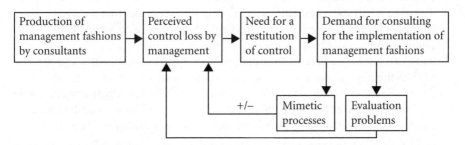

Figure 10.2. *A model for the explanation of the extraordinary growth of the consulting market* (*Source*: Ernst and Kieser 2002)

successfully implemented the new concept, the more insecure they feel. And the more inclined they become to join the bandwagon. Consultants and other participants in the arena skilfully feed the fears of those who have not yet adopted the new idea. They practise what Hammer recommends as a tactic to break resistance against organizational change: 'You must play on the two basic emotions: fear and greed'. Fear is aroused, for example, by statements of this sort: '[The] choice is survival, it's between redundancies of 50 percent or 100 percent' (quoted after Jackson 1996: 577).

However, in their presentations of management concepts, consultants not only provoke fear, they also raise hopes. They assure managers that the actual management concepts will, if implemented with their help, certainly reinstall the managers' control over their companies. This impression is created in a variety of ways:

1. By offering instruments, like the Boston Consulting Group (BCG) 'growth-share matrix', that most effectively simplify complex management problems and thereby make them controllable;
2. By providing new frames of reference and a new language that conveys an illusion of control. As a manager comments: 'Sometimes you need a new set of terms, a new framework—something you can get hold of' (cited after Watson 1994: 903);
3. By convincing managers that they will profit from the consultants' ability to foresee the threats of the future (the lively description of the apocalypse that will inevitably set in if the new fashion is not implemented is an essential element of the fashion) and to work out solutions to these threats;
4. By basing their concepts on descriptions of typical management problems. Adverse situations in the past which managers had difficulty explaining to themselves and others are now made sense of as a clear relation between cause and effect that is established by consultants through the management fashion. Also, managers often learn that the problems they were facing did not represent anything unusual and need not be attributed to personal failure.

These four ways in which management fashions create the perception of enhanced control correspond to the four generic strategies with which, according to Thompson (1981), individuals can reduce the perception of control loss:

1. They can identify new control options, i.e. courses of action that appear suitable to re-establish or increase control (behavioural control).
2. They can resort to re-evaluations, i.e. to cognitive strategies that reduce the aversiveness of control loss (cognitive control). Strategies of this kind help one to ignore, deny, disassociate, or distract oneself from control loss.
3. They can try to get hold of information that signals control losses and thereby enables them to prepare for their occurrence (preventive control).
4. They can reduce the adversity of events involving control loss by finding plausible explanations retrospectively (retrospective control). Individuals usually find control loss which they can explain less menacing than unexplainable control loss.

In the rhetoric of management concepts consultants not only promise an increase in the managers' control over their companies but also 'quantum leaps' in performance as, allegedly, early adopters have already achieved. These prospects activate greed in the potential customers. And it is also made clear that the managers who buy management concepts as commodified packages can achieve quantum leaps without running a high risk of failure. (The high percentages of failed projects that are reported are said to be due to insufficient support by or sheer incompetence of the management of these companies; however these results are reported by consultants and nobody knows exactly how a failure is defined.)

The consultancies' strategy of, simultaneously, arousing fear, making the managers believe that they can regain control, and activating greed proves highly successful. Michael Hammer refers to a market research organization that estimated that the world market for re-engineering projects could reach a volume of seven billion dollars. The consultancy business of his co-author, James Champy, CSC Index, has increased its turnover from 30 million dollars in 1988, that is before *Reengineering the Corporation* appeared, to 150 million dollars in 1993 (Jackson 1996: 576). However, the creator of a fashion does not receive all the demand he produces. After some time, all the major consultancies, for example, sold re-engineering packages as well.

In a world of uncertainty, catching up with competitors is a safe strategy. If competitors implement a fashion, one is on the safe side if one does the same and catches up, and letting consultants do the job makes it even safer. One spends about the same amount of money for consulting and has about the same chance of taking advantage of the benefits of this fashion. And if the fashion does not produce any benefits, one is no worse off than one's competitors. The point is not to come into this game too late, for the pioneers can nourish the hope that they have established an advantage they can enjoy at least for some time. However, the perceived reduction of uncertainty or control loss that is brought about by hiring a consultancy to implement a management concept does not last long. Consulting always plants the seed for new, deeper-reaching uncertainties. New management concepts and fashions are sure to come. Consultancies take care that there is a constant flow of new concepts. And managers who were not able to deal with the last fashions without the help of consultants are highly likely to call on consultants again. Consulting is addictive.[1]

Innovation through the implementation of a new management concept under the guidance of consultants is the ideal strategy for risk-averse managers. They innovate, which is a very important thing for a manager to do. However, the kind of innovation they aim at is one that has already found broad approval within the actual management discourse. As pointed out by trickle-down theory, managers who innovate along the lines that are prescribed by the current management fashion early enough can distinguish themselves from the crowd; they belong to a respectable group of pioneers. Their risks as pioneers are, however, greatly reduced because they let experienced consultancies do the major part of the job and thereby lower the risk that the innovation project is rated a failure.

As soon as the consultants are gone, questions come up among the managers of the client organization that are bound to bring insecurity back. Has the project with which

---

[1]However, case studies by Fincham (1999) indicate that some companies have succeeded in reducing dependence on consultants or not becoming dependent on them in the first place.

Kieser

the management concepts had been implemented led to a lasting improvement *vis-à-vis* competitors, the majority of whom have implemented similar projects? A proper evaluation of the project is not possible mainly because too many factors within the organization and its environment have changed during its course; because the implemented concept is, to a large extent, an intangible product; and because many consequences of the project will only become evident at some time in the future (Ernst and Kieser 2002). Insecurity not only has not been reduced, it has probably increased. It has risen because the wave of projects along the current fashion is likely to have intensified competition with regard to criteria that had been at the centre of this fashion. Most competitors have, for example, improved quality, reduced personnel costs, sped up processes, or increased customer orientation. What now? In this situation, receptivity towards a new management fashion tends to increase again. Such a new management fashion will certainly be launched by consultancies. And managers who needed consultants to come to grips with the last fashion will, in all probability, need consultants again in order to implement it. They have gained the impression that consultants are necessary to keep up with competitors who increasingly engage consultants. They have become dependent on consultants. Consultancies have made them marionettes on the strings of their fashions.

10.5. CONSULTANTS AND THE RHETORIC OF MANAGEMENT FASHION

The Buzzword

Whether a management concept turns into a fashion or not is, to a large extent, dependent on the rhetoric that its creator, the consultancy, applies in propagating it (see Røvik 2002). A first important ingredient of this rhetoric is the buzzword or label (Furusten 1998; Swanson and Ramiller 1997). A buzzword arouses attention. Good buzzwords are metaphors. 'Re-engineering', for example, implies more than a repair of the organization, it calls for a total redesign, while, at the same time, creating the impression that the organization can be engineered in a rational engineer-like manner. The Balanced Score Card (Kaplan and Norton 1996) triggers associations of sport events, fitness, and championships. The balanced athlete has a better chance of winning the multi-discipline event than the one-sided specialist. This label beautifully encapsulates in one expression the basic philosophy behind the concept. TQM also seems suited to trigger fantasies of a concept that accomplishes a radical overhaul of the organization in the interest of high quality. A memorable image like, for example, Peters and Waterman's 7S diamond (Peters and Waterman 1982), the Boston Consulting matrix, or the bell-shaped curve of the Hersey and Blanchard (1977) model of leadership also helps to win attention and to anchor the respective concept in the memories of managers.

Exemplification, Personification, and Dramatization

Rhetorical elements that fulfil the functions of exemplification, personification, and dramatization are also highly important. The consultant should not present a new management concept as the creation of a team of theoreticians but as the condensed master-plan of an ingenious practice that was discovered by an outstanding manager. Peters and Waterman (1982), for example, do no more than to tell *Lessons from America's Best-run Companies*, as the subtitle of their book promises. The principles of the concept or vision are supposedly deduced from a number of cases which represent the most successful management practices. The examples, which are generally highly stylized, are presented from the perspectives of their creators—Lean Production, for example, as being the masterful discovery of the 'young Japanese engineer' Eiji Toyoda and his 'production genius' Taichi Ohno (Womack, Jones, and Roos 1990: 53) and Lean Management as the vision of Percy Barnevik, 'the most insistent enemy of bureaucracy' (Peters 1992: 45). Often the stories told around the discovery of best practices are dramatized to make reading them or listening to them more exciting (Røvik 2002). Stories are easier to remember and to communicate than abstract principles or numerical data (Martin and Powers 1983).

The core of a management concept is a vision or *Leitbild* that consists of a number of goals and principles. Swanson and Ramiller (1997) point out that visions in management concepts fulfil three basic functions: interpretation, legitimization, and mobilization. The vision provides a focus for interpretation efforts. With the help of the schemas provided by the management concept, managers can reinterpret their problems and initiate a discourse within their own companies that attracts the attention of their colleagues and subordinates. Legitimization can be derived from the cases of best practice that 'prove' the validity and power of the concept. The degree of legitimization is correlated with the reputation of the companies in which, according to the consultants, these practices were first developed.

The consultant who advertises a management concept can also increase its legitimization by linking it to general aspects of business functioning and to generally accepted societal values. For example, the concept of 'client-server' has been linked to the issues of empowerment, team-based work processes, and self-management, while 'out-sourcing' has been linked to corporate downsizing, the 'electronic marketplace', and lean management (Swanson and Ramiller 1997: 461). Usually, management concepts are not only extolled as profit-increasing but also as job-enriching, increasing the competitiveness of the whole economy, re-establishing full employment, increasing customer satisfaction, etc. (Huczynski 1993*a*).

A Refined Balance Between Simplicity and Vagueness

To a large extent consultants increase the attractiveness of a new management concept by yielding a refined balance between simplicity and vagueness in their presentations (Clark and Salaman 1996*a*). To begin with, management concepts appear attractive if they reduce the perceived complexity of management and thereby contribute to the restoration of control. Consultants achieve simplification in several ways. First, by concentrating on only one factor, such as organizational culture (Peters and Waterman 1982), quality, leanness (Womack, Jones, and Roos 1990), intrapreneurship (Pinchot 1985), or virtuality (Chesbrough and Teece 1996; Davidow and Malone 1992). This key factor is identified as the most crucial one for success. Until now it has been, according to the consultant, gravely neglected. Therefore its discovery can be described (which as a rule the consultant does repetitively and persistently) as a revolutionary and radical departure from the management concepts that were valid up to this point.

Consultants also achieve simplification through an extensive use of metaphors. On the basis of metaphors, the superiority of the new principles appears clear and convincing: internal entrepreneurship is clearly superior to bureaucratic behaviour (Pinchot 1985), tent organizations are more flexible than palace organizations, network organizations more adaptable than centralized corporations with huge central staffs (Peters 1992), and virtual organizations are the most flexible of all. This is immediately evident to any reasonable person. 'If a new idea can be shown to be a version of common sense, its threat to the potential adopter is reduced' (Huczynski 1993a: 108). Managers find the simplicity of management concepts attractive because, in combination with the cases of successful implementations, it furnishes them with a powerful line of argumentation. The new concept most certainly appears to them as simpler and more convincing than the present organizational structure of their own company, which many of them generally experience as chaotic (Brunsson and Olsen 1993). Simplicity enhances perceived control. However, this simplicity rests on the simplicity of the metaphors, and the principles. What the tent, network, or virtual organizations look like in reality remains unclear in spite of the numerous examples that are presented.

The consultant who presents a concept can further simplify it by offering stylized examples and by the intensive use of figures which, for example, reduce complex problems to a few arrows between a few boxes. The most efficient way of achieving simplification, however, is the provision of methods which structure complex decision problems in such a way that decision-makers get a handle on them. A most striking example for such an approach is the BCG matrix. Soon after its introduction it became a splendid success: 'With its catchy labels and visual simplicity, the matrix gave corporate headquarters a tool that any dumb cluck could understand' (O'Shea and Madigan 1997: 157). In presentations of a management concept the consultants usually declare the principles of their concept as universally valid which adds to simplicity because, if this assertion holds, it is unnecessary to take differences between cultures or organizations into consideration (Røvik 2002).

However, the concept should not appear too simple. The consultant who presents a concept has to maintain a certain degree of vagueness—of mystification—so that getting his help seems advisable. Ambiguity creeps in when the reader or listener reflects on what it really means to implement something like a tent or a network organization in her own company. It is also typical that next to many common-sense statements, such as 'Complacency leads to mediocrity, which leads to failure' or 'Enlightened personnel development benefits both the employee and the company' (from Champy 1995: 42, 184), one finds sentences like the following: 'Character is required, and the best sign of it—the reengineering character anyway—is not only to hold two good, contradictory ideas, but to act on them' (Champy 1995: 38). Ambiguity is further increased by the lack of a precise description of the implementation process. Thus the manager who wants to implement a new management concept 'joins a journey whose duration no one really knows and for which there are no maps', as Champy (1994*a*: 99) describes re-engineering, with startling openness.

Ambiguity offers scope for interpretation (Astley and Zammuto 1992). The reader or listener can project the problems she presently encounters in her organization onto the concept that is presented by the consultant and can thus interpret it as the solution to these pressing problems. The expertise of the presenting consultant is also under-lined—if the concepts were easy to understand, then one would not need a consultant. It is typical that the language of experts erects communication barriers (Kieser 2002). At the same time, however, the experts offer their clients help in overcoming these barriers (Luhmann and Fuchs 1989). Often the author quite openly makes it clear that intuition such as only an expert can have is indispensable. For example, Champy (1994*b*) believes that re-engineering is dependent on intuition 'because rational analysis fails in the face of paradoxes and contradictions'. In the end, it becomes clear that one can only select an expert on the basis of an intuitive leap of faith that he or she has the best intuition or the highest reputation.

Consultants who try to make the concept of their company fashionable should not only try to establish a delicate balance between simplicity and vagueness in their pre-sentations, they should also find a convincing mixture between the familiar and the unfamiliar, it 'must strike witnesses as being somehow new, yet not so unfamiliar as to be judged unintelligible or absurd' (Swanson and Ramiller 1997: 462). A management concept is typically introduced as 'a radical divergence' from traditional management, as a 'revolution'. At the same time, however, it is signalled to the experts that they do not have to unlearn everything they know about management. On the contrary, the con-cept builds on other concepts with which the reader or listener is already familiar. Thus, TQM encompasses concepts like organizational culture, re-engineering, or customer surveys. Re-engineering, in turn, draws upon overhead value analysis (OVA), i.e. a concept in which the elimination of activities that do not contribute to value is a central point, and also upon lean management, benchmarking, out-sourcing, and empowerment (Hammer and Champy 1993). One could argue that the more a new concept is perceived as a recombination of known concepts while still maintaining the image of radical newness the higher its attractiveness for managers. Attractiveness is also a function of perceived control. Known elements increase perceived retrospective control, and the additional elements increase perceived behavioural control.

Urgent Problems in the Material World?

Whether a management concept is able to ignite a larger discourse is not only dependent on the quality of the rhetoric the propagating consultancies develop. It has been argued that only those management concepts can make it to becoming a fashion that offer a convincing solution to problems that have been plaguing organizations for some time. For example, Abrahamson (1996: 264) maintains that 'fashion setters sense incipient preferences guiding fashion demand' and that they 'during the selection stage . . . select those techniques that they believe will satiate this demand'. In other words, he assumes 'that forces external to the fashion-setting market create new demand for particular types of management techniques', and 'that there exists a reciprocal relation between what fashion setters select and fashion consumers prefer and demand' (Abrahamson 1996: 267).

Likewise, Swanson and Ramiller (1997: 466) assert that there is a consensus within business communities about which business problematics are most urgently awaiting solutions. 'The business problematic defines the organizing vision's fundamental relevance in the material economy.' A concept can only be successful to the extent that 'the business problematic is ... an important interpretation and rhetorical resource for the furtherance and ... legitimization' of a management concept.

On the other hand, consultancies who compile a new management concept also construct the business problems for which the offered solution fits; and the solution offered usually fits, as the authors point out, a wider range of problems. Was the world economy really waiting for the concept of organizational culture when *In Search of Excellence* appeared in 1982? Or was it hoping for re-engineering to emerge when *Reengineering the Corporation* hit the management book market in 1993? I think it is impossible to separate the 'reality of business companies'—the 'material economy' (Swanson and Ramiller 1997: 466)—from the rhetoric of management texts. Managers need language to socially construct their reality, and their language is heavily influenced by the rhetoric consultants produce in management books, presentations, management magazines, seminars, and newspapers. It is also impossible to separate 'normal management language' from 'rhetorical language' or 'hype language'. Thus there is no reality that can be perceived and communicated outside language.

However, there is some evidence that the attractiveness of management concepts is not independent of the beliefs of managers, some of which are more or less shared among certain business communities, and which follow a long-term pattern—long waves of management fashions—namely from 'rational' solutions like Scientific Management or System Rationalization to 'normative' solutions like human relations, welfare work, or organizational culture, and back again (Abrahamson 1997; Barley and Kunda 1992). Thus it seems that there is something like a general management discourse that influences the receptivity of managers to new concepts which come onto the market. In the upswing of a long fashion wave, those management concepts that fit into the dominant discourse receive more attention, be it rational or normative. After a while, saturation sets in, managers get the impression that additional concepts of the same kind are of limited value, and concepts of the opposite kind gain more attention. It seems, however, that the periods in which one tendency prevails are becoming shorter and shorter.

Herd Behaviour

Fashion, generally, is a phenomenon that rests on contagion processes or herd behaviour. At first, there are only a few supporters. Their example impresses others. The crowd grows bigger and bigger until a fashion no longer offers the possibility of distinction for the individual manager who initiates a project with regard to the respective fashion. This also applies to management fashions. Nothing is more convincing than cases of successful adoptions (Zbaracki 1998). Consultants are eager to spread information of this sort. Accordingly, two phases of the diffusion of a management innovation can be distinguished. The first phase, the phase before adoptions are known, is often conceptualized as being predominantly governed by external factors, i.e. by communication from sources outside the system of interconnected organizations; the second phase is considered as predominantly governed by internal factors, i.e. by communication about adoptions within the system (Loh and Venkatraman 1992). Mahajan and Peterson (1985: 18) state that the internal-influence perspective is 'most appropriate when an innovation is . . . socially visible, and not adopting it places social system members at a "disadvantage" '.

The tendency to copy practices from other organizations is especially strong when managements perceive the practices in question as complex and when rational procedures for their design are not available, i.e. when the choice is characterized by uncertainty. According to neo-institutional theory, this isomorphic behaviour is not an outflow of irrationality; rather, it can be interpreted as 'collective rationality' (DiMaggio and Powell 1983), i.e. as a rationality that is subjective, retrospective, and attributable to influence through information provided by other members of the social system. What several other organizations do cannot be wrong; if one does not achieve an advantage by also doing it, one at least does not suffer a disadvantage with regard to others, because those others are also doing it, i.e. they are also spending comparable amounts of money on the same measure.

Thus, under the condition of uncertainty, imitating complex processes from other organizations is rational. It becomes obvious that the internal-influence phase can be modelled after contagion processes (Mansfield 1961) or herd behaviour (Lux 1995). This two-phase model corresponds with an observation by Abrahamson and Fairchild (1999) that management fashions often undergo a dormancy phase before they become popular and spread rapidly. Stories about 'successful' adoptions of management concepts, as consultants like to tell them, often mean a decisive push for the distribution of these concepts (Loh and Venkatraman 1992). The dynamics of contagion are then dependent on such factors as the centrality of early adopters in the population or the frequency of contacts they maintain with other members (Pastor, Meindl, and Hunt 1998). It is a strategy used by consultancies to present early prestigious adopters of their management concepts in seminars and conferences.

10.6. CONCLUSION

As has been argued in this chapter, much of the individual manager's behaviour can be explained by Simmel's version of the trickle-down theory. Managers are in constant tough competition for careers. Being the first one who propagates a management fashion and initiates and, eventually, manages a project for its implementation, can yield important advantages in this struggle for promotion. An emerging management fashion gives the ambitious manager a chance to engage himself or herself on behalf of an organizational reform that has already acquired a high degree of acceptance in leading companies around the world and for whose implementation consultancies offer their services on the basis of standardized tools. A project based on such concepts will probably not be declared a failure after implementation.

In addition, a management fashion gives managers a chance to advance their careers with an initiative that is difficult for opponents to attack. The art is to identify and propagate a fashionable management concept before colleagues do so, but to bet on the right horse, that is, on a management concept that has the potential to become a management fashion. It is a trade-off between time and risk: if the manager waits with his initiative and tries to establish the performance of alternative management concepts, he or she increases the certainty of picking a successful—a fashionable— concept. But then he or she runs the risk of being overtaken by a colleague or of no longer receiving any special recognition. Once it becomes clear to everyone that a specific management concept has turned into a management fashion, its discoverer within a company is no longer able to claim superior management wisdom.

Without doubt, management fashion also fulfills the function collective selection theories see as central for fashions in general, namely to introduce 'order in a poten- tially anarchic and moving present' (Blumer 1969: 289). Only a limited number of management concepts develop into management fashions, thereby reducing the choices for managers who want to play it safe. However, the increasing number of management fashions that exist at a given point of time considerably curbs this function.

According to Sombart's marionette theory (1902: 101), producers invent fashions, i.e. they invent a 'fictitious advantage' for products for which 'a real one is not possible'. They also increase the propensity of potential customers to buy by furnishing 'small modifications' to their products. This is essentially what consultancies are doing: they recombine elements of management fashions in order to create new management fashions; or they add new elements to existing fashions and make them appear as new concepts. For example, re-engineering incorporates overhead value analysis, and re-engineering, in turn, is a central element of TQM. Thus, the aspiring managers dis- cover that new management fashions do not invalidate their accumulated knowledge of management techniques, that a slight change in the rhetoric and the acquisition of some new buzzwords and tools suffices for becoming an expert in the latest fashions.

Like fashion in clothes, management fashion follows a logic of planned obsolescence (Faurschou 1987: 82). Critiques of management fashions that attempt to free the manager from the dictates of the consultancies share the fate of consumer activism that tries to develop a counter-power against the producers: they become a fashion. Criticizing management fashion has become a fashion within management science.

The picture that our analysis has generated of the relations between consultants and their clients is somewhat frightening. Consultants are able to create demand for their own services by creating management fashions, by stirring up managers' fear and greed, and by making managers dependent on them (Clark 1995; Clark and Salaman 1996a; Huczynski 1993a; Sturdy 1997). While it is pretty obvious that managers are becoming increasingly receptive to management fashions and consulting—the sales of best-sellers and the turnover of consultancies support this assumption—there are, on the other hand, indications that some companies are capable of developing their own solutions, largely independent of management fashions and consultants (Starbuck 1993).

The advantage of this strategy is that these solutions tend to be much more original and difficult for competitors to copy. There are also indications that managers of some organizations have developed a critical stance towards consultants though still making use of their services. They are emancipated from management fashions and have a clear idea about what solutions to develop in cooperation with consultants (Fincham 1999).

It could be a worthwhile task for researchers to initiate a discourse with practitioners who share the aim of fostering a critical attitude towards management fashions and consultants who sell projects to implement management fashions. Enlightenment is one of the most distinguished tasks of science.

11

Promoting Demand, Gaining Legitimacy, and Broadening Expertise: The Evolution of Consultancy–Client Relationships in Australia

CHRISTOPHER WRIGHT

11.1. INTRODUCTION

In recent years a growing literature has highlighted the role of management consultancies in the diffusion of management knowledge. Consultancies have been identified as particularly adept at transforming abstract ideas into commercial products that can be sold to a wide range of clients (Fincham 1995; Wooldridge 1997). More generally, researchers have stressed the role of consultancies as 'fashion setters', which have a major impact upon the types of management knowledge that are diffused and the preferred models of organizational restructuring (DiMaggio and Powell 1983; Gill and Whittle 1992; Huczynski 1993b; Abrahamson 1996). Within much of this literature, consultants are portrayed as confident and successful, creating a demand for their services through the skilful manipulation of anxious and gullible managers (O'Shea and Madigan 1997; Ashford 1998; Pinault 2000; Kieser in Chapter 10, above).

However as Sturdy (1997) has argued, such a perspective ignores the potential for client scepticism and resistance to consultants, as well as the uncertainty and anxiety of consultants themselves. Similarly, Fincham (1999) has highlighted the way in which client–consultant relationships can take a variety of forms which include client resistance and interdependency. More generally, Kipping (2002) has observed that the history of the management consulting industry has reflected changes in management practice and ideology and that consultants have themselves been highly dependent upon the varying demands of management. From this perspective, consultancies are faced with a constantly changing and uncertain environment resulting in fluctuations in the demand for their services. In addition, management consultants lack the legitimacy of established professions and need to gain managerial acceptance for a service that is ultimately highly discretionary. This means that consultants need to convince managers that they provide a service of benefit to the client organization that cannot be performed by the organization itself. Moreover, in the process of undertaking a consulting assignment, consultants may encounter resistance from managers and employees within the client organization who view the consultants as a threat to their authority, job security or working conditions. Being able to manage such resistance and create an impression of success is therefore crucial for consultancies if client relations and the consultancy's reputation are to be maintained (Clark 1995).

This chapter examines how consultancies attempt to deal with these contingencies through a historical examination of management consulting in Australia from the 1940s through to the 1990s. Management consultancies played a central role in importing and diffusing overseas models of management knowledge in Australia (Wright 2000). However, as this chapter highlights, consultants also faced significant resistance from executives, middle managers, trade unions, and shopfloor workers both to their role as external experts, as well as the practical implications of their change agendas within client organizations.

11.2. FRAMEWORK

Three responses are identified through which Australian consultancies sought to gain legitimacy as providers of managerial expertise. First, in establishing their consulting businesses a primary concern was the creation of a core client base and the building of a reputation within the business community upon which future expansion could be based. Reputation is crucial for management consultancies in building and maintaining their businesses, given the often intangible nature of their services and the fact that clients largely rely on reputation as the principal means of selecting consultancies (Clark 1995: 17–18, 28–9). Secondly, Australian consultancies developed strategies to better manage client relations within consulting assignments and reduce organizational conflict and resistance that developed in response to their interventions. This is an issue that has received less attention within the literature on management consultancies, although Sturdy (1997: 402–5) has noted how consultancies have been well aware of a range of client criticisms levelled at their activities and have in turn developed a range of responses. Thirdly, the limited shelf-life of consulting techniques, changing client demands, and the propensity for once esoteric skills to become increasingly commonplace, also led many Australian consultancies to adapt and develop new skills over time in order to appeal to a broader business clientele. Again this is a theme that has received little attention within existing studies of consulting, although Kipping (2002) has argued that there are limits to such diversification which are shaped by the consultancy's business model and recruitment practices.

The chapter examines each of these areas in relation to the key developments within the largest Australian consulting firms. Three groups of consulting firms are examined: post-war consultancies specializing in scientific management techniques, the 'elite' American consulting firms focusing on executive-level advice, and the large accounting-based consultancies. While each of these groups demonstrates differences in the strategies used to achieve legitimacy, the chapter argues that there has also been significant continuity in these approaches over time.

11.3. THE EARLY YEARS: SCIENTIFIC MANAGEMENT AND OPERATIONAL EFFICIENCY

Despite a number of earlier short-lived examples, the first significant management consultancies operating in Australia emerged in the years immediately following the Second World War. As was the case in the United States and Britain, Australia's first management consultancies focused upon issues of shopfloor efficiency and the application of scientific management techniques. Two firms dominated the consulting market during this period—W. D. Scott & Co. and Personnel Administration (PA). W. D. Scott was formed in 1938 in Sydney by a commercial accountant, Walter Scott. After the war Scott's firm diversified into the provision of work measurement and related wage-incentive schemes and hired a number of British engineers with experience in time study. By contrast, PA was a British firm that established an Australian branch in 1948. Like the other major English management consultancies, PA had developed from the British Bedaux company of the 1930s and used time study as a way of increasing worker efficiency on the shopfloor. Both consultancies thrived during the post-war decades, as Australian manufacturers sought to maximize output as well as limit labour turnover and absenteeism within a tight labour market (Wright 2000: 87–9).

Attracting Clients and Promoting Demand

While the economic context of the post-war period proved favourable for the pioneer Australian consultants, Scotts and PA nevertheless faced the problem of building their business in an environment unaccustomed to the use of hired management expertise. Australian managers were characterized as conservative and risk averse, and the concept of paying for consulting advice was viewed by many business executives with suspicion. The early consultancies therefore faced the problem of developing legitimacy within the Australian business community and building a client base in an environment unfamiliar, and in some cases hostile, to the use of management consultants.

Two strategies were central to the early consultancies in this regard. First, Scotts and PA emphasized their links to leading overseas innovators in management practice and their ability to import international practice to local Australian clients. Secondly, both firms went to great lengths to develop relationships with key business executives who could act as core clients and provide links to other executives and businesses. In terms of the first strategy, as an English firm PA had a clear advantage in being able to import the practices and expertise of years of consulting work in the UK. More importantly the establishment of an Australian branch of PA allowed for the direct flow of consulting staff between the English and Australian branches of the company. Such an exchange relationship resulted in the training of Australian recruits in England, as well as the secondment of experienced English engineers to the Australian organization (Smith 1988: 1–4).

By contrast, W. D. Scott sought to build links with other overseas consultancies as a way of developing its international expertise. An early example of this was an alliance that developed between Walter Scott and the American industrial engineer Harold Maynard, one of the originators of a new form of work measurement called Methods–Time–Measurement (MTM). MTM was the first of a range of so-called 'predetermined motion time systems' which provided standard times for basic human motions and avoided the need for stopwatch time-studies of workers (Maynard, Stegemerten, and Schwab 1948). After meeting Maynard at the 1947 International Conference of Scientific Management in Stockholm, Scott formed an alliance with Maynard's consulting company Methods Engineering Council (MEC), and brought Maynard out to Australia to train Scott's engineers and selected clients in the MTM technique. Scott publicized Maynard's visit, highlighting his role as one of the leading American innovators of management practice, and then purchased the Australian distribution rights for MTM, marketing it as the latest advance in factory management. MTM became both a key marketing tool and a way to distinguish Scotts from its rivals, with applications across Australian manufacturing industry (Scott 1948; W. D. Scott & Co. 1947).

The second strategy used by the early consultancies to build legitimacy within the Australian business community was to develop close relationships with key business leaders who could act as referents to other executives and open the door to new work in other companies. Such a process closely mirrored the practices of management consultancies in the United States and Europe, which also used client referrals as a means of gaining acceptance amongst business elites (Kipping 1999a). The close interaction of Australian business executives, many holding seats on the board of directors of a number of companies, assisted the spread of the consultants' business. Close personal relationships also existed between the directors of the consulting companies and business executives. One example of this was Walter Scott's friendship with the Managing Director of Bradford Cotton Mills, Sir Robert Webster, with Scott later appointed to the Board of Directors of Bradford and a relationship developing in which Scott's consultants worked in the Bradford mills over the next twenty years (Wright 2000: 89). PA also developed close working relationships with client firms and used the personal recommendation of executives as a means of securing further clients and assignments (Smith 1988: 14, 24). As a former consultant noted:

A lot of it was by reference. But also we went to considerable lengths ourselves in developing what you would now call a database, where we did a lot of charting of common directorships, and we virtually looked for links and sought to exploit those links. . . . But we tended to do a lot of work in a particular industry and you tended to get handed on (former PA Director, 27 July 1988).[1]

However, not all Australian employers embraced management consulting and the new techniques. A common refrain from many pioneer consultants was the problem of

---

[1] The interviews referenced in this chapter were undertaken by the author in two phases: some in 1987–90 as part of his doctoral research and the remainder during 1997–2000 as part of a more recent study of the role and impact of management consultants in Australia. Interviewees were selected from leading consulting organizations and from a number of client companies. Interviews were conducted face-to-face based on a semi-structured interview schedule and were of an hour to an hour-and-a-half's duration. All the interviews were taped and fully transcribed. For reasons of confidentiality, interviewees' names and in some cases their organizational affiliation have been omitted.

overcoming management conservatism within Australian companies. One prominent example of corporate resistance was Australia's largest company, Broken Hill Proprietary (BHP), a large integrated steel manufacturer, which despite the best efforts of both Scotts and PA refused to engage the consultants in the implementation of their shopfloor efficiency techniques (Wright 1995: 83).

Client Management and Organizational Resistance

Over and beyond their ability to get work, the early consultancies also faced a more significant challenge once they entered their clients' workplaces. Resistance to the introduction of scientific management was a widespread phenomenon within industrialized economies (Littler 1982: 123–45), and this process was mirrored in Australian enterprises.

A key element of these early consultancy projects involved the training of selected client managers in work measurement techniques, prior to the establishment of an internal methods engineering or work study function within the client firm. One advantage of such an approach was that it created allegiance within the organization amongst key middle managers, who could act as intermediaries, smoothing the way for the consultants' activities. The emphasis on client involvement in the process also assisted the organizational legitimacy of the consultants, and meant that proposed changes, such as workforce reductions or increases in work effort, were presented by internal advocates, rather than the external consultants. For those managers chosen to be involved in the consulting project, it also presented a rare opportunity for skill enhancement and career progression. As one former methods engineer in a textile company recollected:

Looking back on it we were the elite in those days, we could do no wrong. The managing director personally attended our functions and he threw parties for us. So much so that if anybody mentioned a course for methods engineers in those days, even if it was a month long and meant living in hotels, we would all attend them. I did five one-month courses I think, run by Scotts (former Bradmill manager, 16 February 1988).

However, the involvement of selected middle managers in the consulting project and the creation of a client 'in-group' could also prompt resentment and hostility amongst other managers excluded from the consulting process. As one manager recalled of one such incident:

I remember one installation where we had all the operations together and management was standing around me as the installing engineer . . . and things weren't going too well, because the operators were obviously not paying much attention. So I said to one of my colleagues 'whip in with the operators, I want to know what they're saying' . . . My assistant came back and he said 'it's that bloody manager' . . . the manager was priming them with questions to throw us off. He was the plant manager—English, one of the old school (former Bradmill manager, 30 November 1987).

Beyond the need to win middle-management support, the consultants also faced significant worker resistance. Workers were both suspicious and resentful of strangers observing and timing them whilst at work. In many instances, they would refuse to work at the appearance of a stopwatch, downing their tools and refusing to start work again until the time-study man left. Indeed the strength of worker opposition surprised some English consultants. As one former consultant stated: 'The Australian workforce was a more independent workforce than the UK, perhaps even a more suspicious workforce. I think we had more selling and convincing to do here than in the UK. Work measurement was certainly more accepted in the UK' (former PA consultant, 20 March 1988).

Trade unions also opposed the introduction of scientific management. Work measurement and time study were seen as simply an attempt to speed up and intensify the work process. Unions also foresaw the potential for bonus schemes to divide the workforce, pitting one worker against another, each seeking to increase their output and earnings. In the heavy engineering industry and metal trades, left-wing unions proved particularly hostile to the consultants and their efficiency techniques. As a former consultant recalled, shopfloor resistance in some cases degenerated into farce:

I remember we competed for a job at Commonwealth Engineering many years ago, in the making of railway carriages. We wanted to use MTM and the local management at that time thought we were a bit soft, too gentle, and they wanted to bully the unions, they employed PA. But PA only lasted about three weeks, and in the end no one got the job. The fellows would get into the railway carriages to watch what was going on, and the union blokes would take the ladders away, so they'd have to jump down and clamber down from the carriages—all sorts of silly things like that (former W. D. Scott Director, 24 November 1987).

One response was for the consultants to seek to 'sell' their reforms to trade unions and employees. This approach was influenced by overseas trends within the broader scientific management movement, which had sought to build links with organized labour following a number of significant strikes and public criticism (Nadworny 1955: 109–21). As a first step, this usually involved consultation with the relevant trade union officials. Both Scotts and PA developed close relations with a number of senior officials in moderate trade unions such as the Textile Workers, Rubber Workers, Federated Ironworkers, and Electrical Trades Union. These union officials proved to be important allies in convincing employees to accept the presence of the consultants and their shopfloor reforms (Wright 1995: 87–8).

On the shopfloor, the consultants' approach to individual workers was also vital. In order to establish trust, consultants often sought to develop a dialogue with an individual employee prior to the appearance of a stopwatch. As one former methods engineer noted:

What we did on purpose was we always moved into the department and got to know the people in the department first. No sign of watches or slide rules or anything else . . . And then after we'd got their confidence that we were human beings and not bad blokes to talk to, then we'd turn up with a watch, and they'd still slow down the first day, and you'd just discard that totally and just stand there. And after a while they'd go back to their natural rhythm of doing it, and you'd start to get somewhere with the study (former Bradmill methods engineer, 30 November 1987).

While the emphasis upon training managers and consulting unionists and workers in many cases successfully defused conflict, industrial disputation over the introduction of scientific management was a widespread phenomenon (Wright 1995: 86–8). In industries such as the metal trades, the strength of collective worker resistance forced the consultants to adapt their approach, using work sampling techniques as an alternative to the more industrially provocative time study. As is highlighted later in this chapter, management consultants have continued to stress consultation and incorporation in order to gain client acceptance of workplace change.

Broadening Expertise

Beyond the need to manage internal client resistance, the early consultants also faced the problem of the limited life-span of specific management practices. For instance, by the later 1960s increasing mechanization of manufacturing industry shifted the focus away from a detailed analysis of individual worker performance and limited the applicability of the early scientific management techniques (Wright 1995: 154–9). Moreover, the consultants also began to experience increasing competition in the provision of basic industrial engineering services both from other external providers such as educational institutions, as well as from client managers they had trained. As one former consultant noted:

One of the contributions of consultants is to be at the leading edge and bring in new managerial techniques. As these techniques become more widely known and you get technical schools and advanced colleges turning out individuals skilled in these techniques, a lot more of these things are done in-house. So the consultants have to move on to something different and develop new products (former PA Director, 27 July 1988).

Such a strategy of diversifying their expertise and importing new forms of management practice also fitted with the need to maintain an image as experts able to link with leading-edge international management developments.

An early example of this broadening of the consultancies' product offerings was the importation of overseas techniques of clerical work measurement and work simplification practices aimed at the rationalization of managerial and administrative processes. Both Scotts and PA also developed skills in the provision of more general management services in areas such as production and financial control, quality management, and marketing (Anon 1969). Such a broadening of services allowed the early consultancies not only to appeal to a wider business audience, but also to reduce the danger of being typecast as providers of a singular form of management expertise. During the 1960s such diversification of service offerings also allowed the early Australian consultancies to expand their businesses into new markets in Africa and Asia (Wright 2000: 94–6). While such diversification allowed both firms to continue as the dominant management consultancies within Australia, by the 1970s new competitors had entered the market, offering fundamentally different models of consulting expertise.

11.4. THE EMERGENCE OF 'MODERN' MANAGEMENT CONSULTING: THE 'STRATEGY' FIRMS

During the 1970s and 1980s the Australian management consulting industry diversified both in terms of the number of providers and the range of consulting services offered.

This period was also marked by the emergence of large, international consultancies which, in establishing Australian operations, imported overseas models of operation (Wright 2000: 96–101). However, despite differences in their consulting approaches, these firms also encountered the problems of developing legitimacy within the business community, building a client base, and managing internal client resistance.

Attracting Clients and Promoting Demand

The earliest of the new breed of management consultancies to begin operations in Australia was the prestigious American firm McKinsey & Company. Established in Chicago in 1926, McKinsey had developed a reputation as the consultancy of choice for the world's largest corporations, specializing in business surveys and organizational studies for senior executives. Unlike earlier generations of consultants, who stressed an expertise in shopfloor efficiency, McKinsey emphasized its ability to provide advice on the general business direction of corporations: mergers and acquisitions, diversification, industry and market changes, and sources of competitive advantage (McKenna 1995). During the post-war decades, McKinsey was credited with diffusing the multi-divisional firm structure amongst Europe's largest corporations (McKenna 1997; Kipping 1999*a*: 210–12).

Roderick Carnegie, a young Australian McKinsey consultant working in New York, returned to Melbourne in 1962 to establish McKinsey's second international office after London. Like the parent company, the Australian branch of McKinsey positioned itself as a 'provider of unique and special-value services to chief executives', presenting an up-market image with salubrious offices decorated with Australian art, recruiting talented business graduates, and paying salaries far higher than its competitors (Carnegie 2000: 35). In contrast to earlier generations of consultants, McKinsey also rejected the need for industry expertise in favour of a broad analytical approach to questions of general business direction. This led the firm to consciously recruit young business graduates rather than experienced managers. As a former McKinsey consultant stated:

We didn't value experience. We didn't care about experience. We just wanted bright people. I mean we hired, in my time, engineers, biologists, lawyers, doctors, it didn't matter. We wanted people who were bright and curious. And the client would say 'you don't know anything about my industry' and I'd say 'that's right but because we have people who are very inquisitive and disciplined, in the process of us learning about your industry we think we'll find things out about it that you wouldn't have thought about' (former McKinsey partner, 8 April 1998).

However, despite McKinsey's overseas reputation, Australian executives were slow to accept the need for such high-level consulting. Consultants complained that many Australian managers were overly conservative and resistant to new ideas and practices (Denton 1986: 54). While the firm opened a Sydney office in 1971, until the mid-1970s the Australian practice remained small and worked mostly for the local subsidiaries of global McKinsey clients.

Like the earlier pioneering consultancies, McKinsey sought to build legitimacy within the Australian market by stressing its links to leading-edge overseas management

192   *Wright*

expertise. During the mid-1970s a number of senior American McKinsey consultants worked within the Australian practice, providing a source of internal expertise for the consultancy, as well as a powerful marketing tool for access to Australian business executives. One example was Bob Waterman, a senior McKinsey consultant from the San Francisco office (and later co-author of the management best-seller *In Search of Excellence*), who spent several years working in the Australian practice.

Relationship-building also formed a key part of McKinsey's attempts to gain acceptance within the business community. Mirroring the practice of the parent organization, McKinsey's Australian operations developed a pervasive network of business contacts and developed long-term relationships with a range of senior executives. In particular, the firm's practice of recruiting young business graduates who later went on to senior positions in the country's major corporations, provided invaluable contacts for future consulting assignments. Examples here included McKinsey's Australian founder Rod Carnegie, who left the consultancy to become Managing Director of the mining giant CRA in 1971, and John Elliott, who became Managing Director of resource company Elders IXL (Denton 1986).

By the later 1970s McKinsey's Australian business was growing as large companies embraced high-level business consulting. Long-term client relationships developed with a range of prominent Australian corporations including BHP (Australia's largest company, involved in steel, mining, and resources), mining companies CRA and MIM, resource conglomerate Elders, retail firm Myers, and the National Australia Bank. In these companies McKinsey consultants provided advice on general business strategy and corporate restructuring, particularly decentralization and the development of business units (Robinson 1980; Mallick 1984; Hewett 1988; Carnegie 2000).

The legitimacy of the McKinsey brand name and its reputation within the Australian context were enhanced during the 1980s through the consultancy's involvement in a number of major public policy debates. These included the production of influential publications on topics such as industrial relations reform, manufacturing competitiveness, regional economic development, and innovation (Hilmer 1985; McKinsey & Co. 1994; McKinsey/AMC 1993, 1994; O'Brien 1994). The use of publications has become an increasingly common means for management consultancies to heighten their profile, as well as indirectly influencing government or industry practice (Korporaal 1994).

McKinsey's success in the development of what they termed 'top management consulting' also encouraged the emergence of a number of competitors. During the early to mid-1970s, the New York-based consultancy Cresap McCormick & Paget flew in teams of consultants to Australia for projects with companies such as Qantas, Ampol, Telecom, and a number of electric utilities (Alexander 1983: 46; Anon 1990). Another competitor was the local firm Pappas, Carter, Evans and Koop (PCEK) established in 1979 by George Pappas, an Australian who had worked for US strategy firm Boston Consulting Group and three former McKinsey consultants (Alexander 1983). By the later 1980s, other overseas consultancies opened Australian offices, including the LEK Partnership in 1986, Booz Allen & Hamilton in 1989, and the Boston Consulting Group, which merged with PCEK in 1990 (Hewett 1988; McBeth 1989). More recent entrants to the Australian strategy consulting market included Bain & Company in 1992 and A.T. Kearney in 1995. Like McKinsey, these firms stressed their global consulting resources and enjoyed significant growth throughout the 1990s (McGee 1991; Lawson 1998).

However, increasing competition within the lucrative strategy market also led to failures. Examples included LEK losing consultants to new rival Bain, and Cresap, Mitchell Madison and Arthur D. Little closing down their Australian offices after belated starts (Anon 1990; Lawson 1995). While the Australian market for top-level consulting had grown significantly since the 1970s, it was still a small market in relation to North America and Europe, and one in which consultancies with a recognized 'brand name', such as McKinsey and Boston Consulting, appeared to enjoy an advantage over their competitors.

Client Management and Organizational Resistance

Like their predecessors the new global consultancies also faced the problem of managing client relations within consulting projects. A defining characteristic of the strategy consultancies was the focus upon senior management as the key contact point within the client organization. Having the imprimatur of the CEO or managing director ensured the consultants often had a free rein in diagnosing organizational 'problems'. As one former McKinsey consultant stated in a media interview:

We worked with big corporations on their most important problems, things like organization, strategy, the role of the board, a lot of work on cost reductions and improving efficiency. But it generally would not work unless we worked with the chief executive of the company. McKinsey people weren't going to waste their time unless they knew they would be working at a level where something would be done (Denton 1986: 54).

Such an elite vision of consulting, however, also prompted management criticism that the new breed of young consultants were brash and arrogant (Denton 1986). Well-publicized examples of the involvement of strategy consultancies in corporate restructuring exercises also contributed to employee and trade-union hostility. Invariably the announcement of the engagement of a prominent firm of consultants generated suspicion and fear amongst client managers and employees (Jameson 1987: 102). Such sentiments were often fuelled by a consulting process in which a small, secretive project team of consultants set up camp within a client organization for a number of months, gathering data and diagnosing the 'problem' before presenting senior management with a report setting out their recommendations (Dixon and Domberger 1995). While this model appealed to some executives, who viewed the use of consultants as a tool to shake up the management ranks, it also limited the effectiveness of consultants in working with client personnel and transferring expertise to the client organization.

By the later 1980s the traditional model of expert consulting was subject to increasing criticism within business organizations. As one observer wryly noted, the global strategy consultants were like 'seagulls', who would fly into a client organization, briefly hover around, before dropping a large report and flying home (Pratt 1994: 95). Managers were increasingly sceptical of the ability of outsiders to understand their business and provide relevant and practical advice. Critics also stressed the need for consultancies to provide more than a glossy report, arguing that consultancies should get more actively involved in the implementation of their recommendations, transfer expertise and knowledge to the client organization, and demonstrate more explicitly the value of their interventions (Morris 2000: 126–8).

In response many of the strategy firms began to emphasize a more participatory approach to their clients. Consultancies such as Bain & Company provided one example of this trend by developing an approach to organizational improvement that was closely linked to shareholder returns and close, long-term relationships with a single client in each industry (Perry 1987; Lawson 1995: 14). Increasingly, strategy consultancies moved away from a report-writing model and sought to demonstrate the financial impact of their involvement. While the high fees charged by such consultancies meant that long-term involvement in client firms was limited, these firms moved away from an explicit expert model of consulting, towards more of a partnering role with senior client managers and joint problem-solving. As one consultant stated, 'We are two things. We're facilitators of a process and we're problem solvers . . . So our job is to work with, not only these guys that we're training in the process, but to get everybody in the [client firm] involved in telling us what needs to happen. Because the knowledge is resident in the organization, not in us as consultants' (Consultant, strategy firm, 17 March 2000).

However it remains unclear to what extent such a participatory approach reduced employee suspicion and resistance. As one manager in a client company related, the pretence of joint problem-solving generated further hostility:

So you had to go round the table and say who you are, and then you had to list all the ways that they could help you. So it was just insulting in terms of pretending that they were there to help you. It was just bullshit. Like are we supposed to put up with this? We're the senior managers of the place and you've got these outside guys coming in, just giving us sort of kindergarten crap (Senior manager, client company, 21 July 1999).

Broadening Expertise

While the new breed of strategy consultancies distinguished themselves from earlier generations of consultants by their focus upon issues of concern to senior executives, changing economic conditions and shifts in client demand also meant these firms had to be flexible in the range of work they undertook.

One example of this was the significant consulting revenues generated in advising clients on ways to restructure their businesses and reduce operating costs. Throughout the 1980s and 1990s industry deregulation, increasing competitive pressures, and rapid technological change fostered a growing demand within the Australian business community for assistance in improving productivity and cutting costs. Consulting in operational efficiency once again became a growing market made up of older consultancies such as PA, as well as new entrants including the 'Big Eight' accounting firms, and specialist cost-cutting consultancies (McGee 1991: 10, 12). Within such a context, the strategy consultancies increasingly focused on cost reduction and efficiency improvement projects. For instance, a review of the business press suggests that these consultancies had a major impact on the structure and operations of many of Australia's largest financial institutions during the early 1990s, one outcome of which was significant job-shedding and downsizing (Littler *et al.* 1997). Examples included major projects undertaken by McKinsey for leading insurer AMP and the Westpac bank (Boyd 1991; Furness 1992), as well as Boston Consulting and Booz Allen's work for the Commonwealth Bank in the restructuring of its management and branch structures (Lewis 1993; Korporaal 1994).

As noted below, the importance of changing client demand was also demonstrated by the explosive growth in information technology consulting during the 1990s. While the strategy firms did not seek to compete directly with the large accounting-based consultancies which specialized in information technology implementation, they did develop internal competencies in the strategy implications of new technologies. During the e-commerce boom, this involved developing e-commerce strategies for established corporates, as well as work for small dot-com start-ups (Boyd 2000). However, the recent contraction within the so-called 'new economy' has also prompted a return to restructuring and cost reduction work. As a result, whilst the strategy firms have sought to maintain a popular image as top-level business advisers, changes in the broader context of Australian business have forced these firms to diversify their consulting services.

11.5. THE ENTRY OF THE ACCOUNTANTS AND INFORMATION TECHNOLOGY CONSULTING

While Australian business acceptance of elite strategy consulting took time to develop, a more favourable corporate reaction greeted the emergence of the other major segment in the Australian consulting market: the Big Eight accounting firms. During the late 1970s accounting majors such as Price Waterhouse, Coopers & Lybrand, and Arthur Andersen diversified into management consulting given declining returns from traditional tax and audit services (Braggs 1978; Ham 1983). Much of the work of these consulting divisions focused on the design of electronic data-processing and computer systems linked to issues of financial control and operational efficiency.

Attracting Clients and Promoting Demand

One indicator of the rapid business acceptance of consulting services offered by the Big Eight accountancies was the dramatic growth in revenues generated by the consulting divisions of these firms, amounting to an increase of between 15 and 20 per cent per annum for much of the 1980s (McGee 1991: 10). Several issues underpinned this. First, the timing of their entry into the consulting market proved fortuitous. Rapid technological change and computerization during the 1980s fuelled client demand for consulting assistance in the design and implementation of mainframe and later networked information systems. Secondly, the accounting firms had the advantage of pre-existing client relationships built upon years of tax and audit work. All of the Big Eight (which, following a series of mergers during the later 1980s, became the Big Six) were well known to large Australian corporations and already had a well-developed market presence. Despite the potential conflict of interest between audit and consulting work, these firms proved extremely successful in 'on-selling' consulting services through existing client relationships.

A third factor behind the rapid acceptance of the Big Six consultancies appears to have been growing client demand for consultants to assist in the implementation of organizational change, as well as providing advice. While the distinction between 'expert' and 'implementation'-based models of consulting was neither novel nor clear-cut, it was a point of differentiation which the accounting firms emphasized in their marketing and public relations. Rather than offering a client with a report, these firms promoted their ability to provide significant numbers of consultants to help clients design and implement complex information technologies. In a break with consulting tradition, the accounting consultancies also invested large sums in advertising campaigns and sponsored sporting events and arts festivals as a way of heightening their brand recognition. Such marketing campaigns portrayed an image of large, global organizations with extensive international experience, and tried and proven methodologies (Fox 1998; Wooldridge 1997).

The major innovator in this area was Arthur Andersen. As early as the 1950s, Arthur Andersen in the United States had begun to focus upon the impact of computers on business operations and developed a specialist consulting practice focused on information technology in addition to traditional audit work (Rassam and Oates 1991: 73–83). By the early 1970s information technology consulting had begun within the Australian branch of the partnership and grew rapidly, as a result of the demand amongst large private- and public-sector organizations for assistance in the implementation of complex mainframe computer systems. Continued growth in the consulting side of the business during the 1980s led to the formation of Andersen Consulting in 1989 as a separate business unit from the accounting practice. During the early 1990s the Australian practice grew dramatically, with annual revenue growth in excess of 30 per cent, based upon large systems-integration projects for clients such as the New Zealand Inland Revenue Department, Telecom, Commonwealth Bank, Unilever, AMP, and Standard Chartered Bank (Thomas 1992; Tabakoff 1993). Andersen Consulting promoted an image in the market of being able to rapidly deploy armies of consultants to assist clients in the implementation and project management of large information technology projects. As a former consultant recollected:

Looking back on it, it was actually obscene what we were doing, we had such a dominant position in the marketplace. We commanded whatever fees we wanted . . . But it was a great strategy. It was a strategy that said: information technology for the next 30 to 40 years, and that was a view we took in, probably, the early 1980s, that was going to define the industry . . . Andersen's strategy was to be the dominant number one in the world as a management consulting firm, on the basis of information technology (former Andersen Consulting Partner, 16 October 1998).

Andersen's dramatic growth was paralleled by the other Big Six firms (Allen 1990). As is highlighted in Table 11.1, by the 1990s these firms dwarfed the smaller strategy consultancies in terms of number of consultants and overall revenues.

Table 11.1. *Top ten consultancies operating in Australia, 1985 and 1997*

1985			1997		
Consultancy	Revenues (Aus. $m)	No. of consultants	Consultancy	Revenues (Aus. $m)	No. of consultants
PA Australia	21	165	Andersen Consulting	313.6	1,301
Coopers & Lybrand/ W.D. Scott	19	165	Price Waterhouse Urwick	129	814
Price Waterhouse Urwick	15	140	Ernst & Young	112	430
Arthur Andersen	12	120	Coopers & Lybrand	105	550
Peat, Marwick & Mitchell Services	12	80	Deloitte & Touche	82.3	410[a]
Touche Ross Services	8	80	KPMG	58	374
IBIS/ Deloitte, Haskins & Sells	6	65	Boston Consulting Group	n/a	100[a]
McKinsey & Co.	5	25	McKinsey & Co.	n/a	80
Arthur Young Services	4	40	PA Consulting	29.5	100
Pappas, Carter, Evans & Koop	2	16	Booz-Allen & Hamilton	26	75

[a] Includes New Zealand.

Source: Mallick 1984: 18; Payne 1985: 18; Lawson 1998: 12; own calculations.

Client Management and Organizational Resistance

The Big Six consultancies emphasized a higher proportion of junior to senior consultants, with much larger project teams working within client firms for significant periods of time (in some cases, years). Projects often followed a clearly defined process which the consultancy had streamlined over time, and which required minimal customization. As one consultant related:

Well how do they organize on large projects, particularly large-system implementation projects? The difference is on those projects you create a factory model. It becomes the electronic sweat-shop in some cases. One of the projects I worked on, we had about 300 people on it and probably two-thirds of those were consultants. You create this enormous machine, layer upon layer (Big Six consultant, 11 February 1999).

Given the scale and scope of such projects, the preferred approach was the formation of joint consultant–client project teams operating throughout the client organization. While the consultants emphasized the advantages of this approach in transferring knowledge and expertise to client personnel, the inclusion of client staff within project teams also ensured a greater likelihood of client commitment to the project, as well as a feeling of involvement rather than exclusion. Consulting language reflected this thinking: the aim was to 'work with the client' rather than 'do it to the client'.

Indeed the fact that the Big Six firms were involved in consulting projects with such a strong implementation focus increased the need for more formalized systems of client management and methods of diffusing resistance and conflict. As noted below, diversification into related consulting services such as business process re-engineering further re-emphasized the need to better manage client relations, particularly employee and middle management fear of job loss and resistance to restructuring. One development in this respect was the emergence of 'change management' skills aimed at better managing the organizational dynamics associated with large-scale changes in technology. In practice this entailed a more conscious consideration of the likely reactions of client staff to major organizational change, as well as the development of strategies to minimize conflict and resistance to such change. As one consultant noted:

Well in fact one of the tools we use a lot is doing good old-fashioned impact analysis about what's the change? Actually getting down to the nitty gritty detail about really understanding what groups is it going to affect? What is their likely reaction to change going to be? How do we want them to react? What can we do to minimize that? And you never get rid of it, but you try and minimize it. So really detailed stakeholder analysis. Really detailed communication planning. Lots of talking to people (Big Six consultant, 9 June 1999).

Such an approach paralleled both earlier consulting traditions of client involvement, as well as more recent organizational development literature (Kotter and Schlesinger 1979). However, change management techniques did not negate conflict, and in a number of cases the strength of employee resistance forced consultants to adopt more minimal forms of organizational rationalization. For example in the public sector, trade-union and employee resistance to proposed re-engineering forced consultants to provide alternatives to simple 'headcount' reductions (Big Six consultant, 22 June 1999).

Broadening Expertise

The rapid growth of consulting divisions within the Big Six accounting firms was also based upon a diversification of services, particularly aligning their information technology expertise with other organizational improvement strategies such as cost reduction and organizational redesign. One example of this was the extensive consulting revenue generated in the mid-1990s by business process re-engineering, a methodology originated by US consultancy CSC Index, but which Andersen Consulting and the other large consultancies adapted and applied on a much wider scale (Wooldridge 1997). Marketed as the ultimate solution to improved business efficiency, re-engineering was often seen as an essential part of the introduction of new information systems and involved radical organizational restructuring and significant job shedding. As was the case in other countries, re-engineering was widely adopted by large corporations in Australia, becoming the leading fashion in Australian organizational restructuring during the 1990s. Indeed, one study found that over 60 per cent of large Australian businesses had implemented a re-engineering programme, most often in concert with a Big Six firm (O'Neill and Sohal 1998; Bagwell 1993).

The rise in popularity of re-engineering during the 1990s highlighted a broader trend in which the Big Six firms stressed their ability to bring 'international best practice' to Australian business. Consultancy-led innovation was reinforced by a prevailing rhetoric of the need for Australian enterprises to become more internationally competitive (BCA 1989). In this respect, the promotion and propagation of new business fashions such as re-engineering, appears to have been a key strategy of the larger consultancies, aimed at increasing client demand for their services. As one senior consultant acknowledged:

We create an uncertainty in the minds of senior managers because someone is doing something and they're not, so we bring it in. As soon as we hear something is happening in Europe or North America that's innovative, we bring it out and we talk about it . . . Gets them all nervous and then they say 'well can you tell us how we can get down to that'. And we're masters at doing that . . . So, now the benefit of that is that something that's a good idea as a management practice, basically anywhere in the world, the consulting firms globalize that very, very quickly (Partner, Big Six consultancy, 3 April 2000).

Beyond re-engineering, examples of other management fashions promoted and sold by the large consultancies included the implementation of enterprise resource planning software such as SAP and Peoplesoft, Y2K compliance work, and more recently the development of e-commerce and supply-chain solutions (Lawson 1993; Bagwell 1993; Kennedy Information 1998). For the Big Six firms this has involved moves towards a 'one-stop shop' approach to consulting services, integrating information systems work with organizational restructuring, change management, and strategy work. Such an approach aimed to generate a greater flow of business from the existing client base through the ability to 'on-sell' related consulting services. However while the Big Six consultancies have focused on the propagation of codified methodologies, business resistance to consultancy-led management fashions has also become increasingly prevalent (Shapiro 1996; Micklethwaite and Wooldridge 1996). While an increasingly well-educated business community and the growing intermingling of management and consulting careers promoted greater demand for consultancy services, these trends also produced clients who were not only better informed but also more critical and demanding of consultancies.

11.6. CONCLUSION

While much discussion of the increasing role of management consultants in contemporary business has focused on their power and influence in diffusing management practices and ideas, far less attention has been paid to the constraints and resistance that consultants face. While consultants appear to be perfect agents for the diffusion of common models of organizational practice and broader isomorphic tendencies, this chapter argues that greater attention needs to be directed towards the resistance to consultants that can be exhibited by senior and middle managers, employees, and trade unions. As this review of Australian management consulting has highlighted, these sources of resistance differ according to the constituency concerned, from scepticism and rejection at a senior management level to more covert forms of resistance amongst middle management and employees. In some cases, trade unions also exhibited strong hostility to management consultants. In response, consultancies developed a range of strategies in order to overcome client scepticism and defuse organizational resistance. While there have been differences in the approaches different consultancies have adopted over time, there have also been significant continuities in approach.

At an initial level, consultancies needed to promote a demand for their services, attract clients, and gain legitimacy as reputable providers of management expertise. Unlike the established professions, they could not rely on a pre-existing professional mystique and often faced significant scepticism from within the business community. Australian management consultancies sought to overcome such resistance through an explicit emphasis on their ability to import leading-edge overseas management practice. This international focus proved important in the Australian context, particularly given the continent's geographical distance from the core economies of North America and Europe, and the perception (promoted by consultancies themselves amongst others) that Australian management was underdeveloped in relation to overseas standards. In the implementation of such a strategy, Australian consultancies forged alliances with overseas consultancies and imported foreign staff and techniques. Such a pattern was expanded by the establishment of Australian branch offices of larger British and American consultancies. As highlighted by firms such as PA, McKinsey, Arthur Andersen, and more recently a range of other US consultancies, this resulted in a direct importation of overseas staff and consulting methodologies. The ability of such global consultancies to provide 'international best practice' appears to have appealed to senior management anxieties, particularly in recent years when the rhetoric (if not the reality) of international competitiveness has forced Australian managers to greater levels of organizational change.

Like their overseas counterparts (Kipping 1999a), Australian consultancies also wooed senior executives and attempted to develop long-term relationships and referrals on the basis of such core clients. In the early years such relationships were built upon personal friendships and word-of-mouth referrals amongst senior business executives. More recently, as consultancies such as McKinsey have demonstrated, the process of relationship-building has become more systematic, through the practice of establishing an 'alumni' network of former consulting staff within the senior management ranks of the Australian business community. Building a consultancy's brand name has in some cases also involved contributions to major public policy debates, as well as a more recent emphasis on advertising and direct marketing techniques.

Beyond their external market relations with clients, management consultancies also faced the problem of better managing internal client resistance within specific consulting projects. Consultants have for the most part been clearly aware of the potential resistance, hostility, and fear towards outside experts that exist within client organizations. While some consultancies happily traded upon a reputation for engendering fear and anxiety amongst client staff, the broader trend has been to try to counter such resistance through a participatory approach to client relations. For instance, the poor public image of the earlier generation of scientific management exponents led the early Australian consultancies to emphasize an explicitly participatory approach to workers and managers in client organizations. Similar approaches have been adopted more recently by the large strategy consultancies, which have sought to respond to criticism, through the use of joint consultant–client project teams and a greater focus upon implementation as opposed to merely report-writing. These trends have been developed further by the large information technology consultancies which have emphasized joint teams within system implementation and re-engineering projects, and have also developed specific change management skills in an attempt to defuse organizational conflict.

Finally, management consultancies have had to remain flexible in the services they provide and have broadened their expertise over time. Such a process has been driven not only by economic and technological change, but also by the propensity for once esoteric skills to become increasingly commonplace. As was demonstrated in the case of the early scientific management consultancies, the diffusion of industrial engineering (itself an outcome of consulting activity) resulted in increasing competition amongst a broad range of providers, as well as the internalization of these skills within organizations generally. While some types of management consulting may be less affected by such pressures (for example business strategy), large consultancies have generally moved towards a more diversified model of consulting, given the dangers of a specialist focus in an era of rapidly changing client demand. However as Kipping (2002) has argued, such a strategy is itself problematic given the potential for consultancies to become 'trapped' within a specific business model of consulting which limits diversification. The Australian evidence is ambiguous on this point. While consultancies such as Scotts and PA did successfully diversify their services beyond the early scientific management focus, they were eventually overtaken by the Big Eight and strategy firms. By contrast, during the 1990s firms such as McKinsey and Andersen appear to have been relatively successful in diversifying their services.

While the consultant–client relationship is a market relationship which can take on a variety of forms (Fincham 1999), this chapter suggests that the historical development of management consultancies as businesses has been dominated by the need to gain client acceptance and better manage client relationships. Despite the development over time of more sophisticated strategies to achieve these goals, management consultancies appear likely to continue to face the problem of creating and maintaining legitimacy given a changing business context, as well as intra-organizational resistance to their role as external change agents.

INTERVIEWS

The following is a list of all those interviewed for the research presented in this chapter. Sufficient details are given to suggest the perspective of the interviewee, although their actual identities are not revealed to preserve anonymity.

Former Director, W. D. Scott & Co., interview conducted 24 November 1987.
Former Head Methods Engineer, Bradmill Ltd., interview conducted 30 November 1987.

Former Methods Engineer, Bradmill Ltd., interview conducted 16 February 1988.
Former Consultant, PA Consulting, interview conducted 20 March 1988.
Former Director, PA Consulting, interview conducted 27 July 1988.
Former Partner, McKinsey & Co., interview conducted 8 April 1998.
Former Partner, Andersen Consulting, interview conducted 16 October 1998.
Consultant, 'Big Six' firm, interview conducted 11 February 1999.
Consultant, 'Big Six' firm, interview conducted 9 June 1999.
Senior Manager, client company, interview conducted 21 July 1999.
Consultant, strategy firm, interview conducted 17 March 2000.
Partner, 'Big Six' firm, interview conducted 3 April 2000.

12

The Burden of Otherness: Limits of Consultancy Interventions in Historical Case Studies

MATTHIAS KIPPING AND THOMAS ARMBRÜSTER

12.1. INTRODUCTION

The literature on management consulting has recently put the focus on difficulties between consultants and their clients (e.g. Shapiro *et al.* 1993; Bloomfield and Danieli 1995; O'Shea and Madigan 1997; HBR 1997; Fincham 1999; Kieser 2001). Two recent empirical studies also present a rather ambiguous picture of the benefits client organizations can derive from consulting advice. In a survey among alumni of the London Business School, 68 per cent of those who had used external advice believed that consultancy projects made a valuable contribution to their business, but less than 30 per cent of them thought that consultants provided good value for money (Ashford 1998: 267, 270). And in interviews with the CEOs of the ten largest Swedish companies, Engwall and Eriksson (1999) obtained highly critical responses about consultants, although all of the companies actually employed at least one, usually several consultancies at the time of the interviews.

Historical case-studies confirm this ambiguous impression. One example is the introduction of scientific management during the first decades of the twentieth century, which was often conducted with the help of consultants. Several authors examining these cases have stressed the resistance of workers, and occasionally foremen, to the implementation of these methods (e.g. Littler 1982; Egolf 1985; Downs 1990). Similarly, company histories that contain descriptions of consulting projects concerned with changes in strategy and structure also highlight the ambiguous reaction of the client organization towards external advice (e.g. Church 1969; Pasold 1997; Holmes and Green 1986; Pugh 1988; Public Histoire 1991; Cailluet 1995). These studies point out that middle or even senior management often considered the recommendations as too radical and opposed their implementation. Frequently, therefore, companies introduced consultancy suggestions only partially or gradually.

This chapter argues that the ambiguous reaction to consultancy interventions is related to their otherness, i.e. to the fact that the consultants are outsiders to the client organization and that their knowledge differs from the client's. In general, this otherness is seen as a major functional feature of consultants, since it allows consultants to perform actions that clients cannot carry out on their own. This chapter will try to show that otherness is indeed helpful—up to a certain point, when it becomes the source of problems—as consultants may lack tacit knowledge and since their contested position within the client organization does not allow them to provide solutions acceptable to all involved.

Section 12.2 sketches the potential advantages clients derive from the otherness of consultants and then contrasts these with the extent to which consultants' otherness might disable the potential benefits by causing resistance to change and ambiguous implementation. Section 12.3 describes several historical cases of consulting interventions, which illustrate what could be labelled the 'natural limits' of what consultants can achieve in terms of implementation. On this basis, the analysis suggests that in order for advice to be fruitful and sustainable, external input must not only be accompanied by internal support in the initial phase, but also be discontinued in time and followed by internal succession and progression.

12.2. BENEFITS AND BURDENS OF OTHERNESS

A number of authors have pointed out that consulting services are intangible and produced at the same time as they are consumed, and that consequently their quality cannot be assessed before the service is delivered (Sauviat 1994; Clark 1995; Schade 1997; Kieser 1998a; Kipping 1999a; Glückler and Armbrüster 2001). Even after the service has been delivered, its economic impact is difficult to isolate and assess, since consulting interventions are only one of many factors influencing companies and their behaviour. In addition, the changes resulting from an implementation of their suggestions prevent comparisons with the way the organization would have evolved and performed otherwise. Thus, an assessment of consultancy advice can often only rely on subjective measures, whereby those interviewed often have an interest in stressing the success of the consulting project.

In the literature, the otherness of management consultants and the different type of knowledge they offer have been suggested as their major raisons d'être and main drivers of their success (e.g. Havelock 1969; Meyer 1996). Externality alone allows for a view on an organization that cannot be formed from the inside. It is not biased by the blindness that client employees and managers potentially develop through their daily routine and by being accustomed to the way things are done. Put provocatively, it does not even take an experienced consultant to see what client members cannot see: any external observer with common sense is potentially able to provide advice that adds value. However, as the above-mentioned ambiguity about consulting success shows, the process of 'implementing' consulting suggestions is certainly not easy. If otherness involved only benefits, these ambiguities would certainly not occur.

Based on the existing literature, this section will summarize the potential benefits clients can derive from consultants' otherness. The origins of these benefits can be found in the public reputation and image of consultants, the role of consultants in knowledge transfer and transformation, as well as their intervention in the clients' activity system. For each of these advantages the section then highlights a potential burden, also derived from the consultants' otherness—burdens that will be illustrated and explored in some detail in the subsequent, empirical section, based on historical case-studies.

Public Reputation and Image: The Issue of Legitimacy

According to neo-institutional arguments, the otherness of consultants offers an important benefit to those who hire them in terms of reputation. The public image of consultants is that of carriers of ideas and of an institution that supplies knowledge to a receiving client. This reputation, especially of large consulting firms, provides their advice with a high degree of legitimacy, and with the image of being up-to-date and at the cutting edge of business solutions. Based on a distinction between otherhood and actorhood (Meyer 1996), the otherness of consultants and their reputation as carriers of ideas provides actors, that is, organizational decision-makers who turn to consultants, with legitimacy, because the work of the consultants certifies the rationality of an approach or a decision. As Meyer (1996: 244) put it: 'Others ... do not take action responsibility for organizational behavior and outcomes. They discuss, interpret, advise, suggest, codify, and sometimes pronounce and legislate. They develop, promulgate, and certify some ideas as proper reforms, and ignore or stigmatize other ideas.'

From this point of view, the impact of consultancy advice is related to legitimizing the action of decision-makers towards internal interests and external stakeholders and thus potentially decoupled from factual changes or 'implementation'. This legitimization is based on the values of rationality and scientificity that consultants are associated with, and organizational decision-makers can refer to 'scientifically valid' standards and progressiveness if they employ them. Otherness, in this sense, provides consultants with the benefit of not being measured and controlled by quantifiable results, not even by the costs they generate. The demand for their advice may thus be decoupled from 'measurable' impact.

The possible downside of this public image of consultants is that client employees might see consultants as emissaries of undesired management concepts or, more politically, as carriers of the managerial discourse or the hired hand of top management, rather than as carriers of ideas to their benefit. With an image as representing the leading edge of management practices, consultants are constantly in danger of being perceived as arrogant, know-it-all, and on the side of the powerful. As a result, resistance to change might not or not only reflect genuine concerns about actual practices brought in by consultants. It may also be based on the very fact of the public image of consultants, decoupled from the question of whether the consultancy advice provides benefits to most or all concerned.

Hence the major burden of this type of otherness—the public image of consultants as donors of management knowledge as opposed to the client's image as receivers—is that it makes it difficult for consultants to access information within the client organization. They must constantly make an effort to establish a partnership with client employees in order to access the information they need to add value—a partnership that is structurally instable due to the potential divergence of interests and attitudes between consultants and client employees.

Knowledge Transfer and Transformation: The Issue of Implementation

Another potential benefit for clients from the otherness of consultants derives from their role in the transfer and transformation of different types of knowledge. Drawing on an earlier distinction by Polanyi (1962 and 1967), Nonaka and his colleagues (Nonaka 1994; Nonaka and Takeuchi 1995; Nonaka and Konno 1998) distinguish between, on the one hand, explicit knowledge as codified and structured knowledge the individual is aware of and can communicate, and, on the other hand, tacit knowledge that is associated with experience, is not codified, and cannot be transferred to others. Nonaka and his colleagues argue that organizational knowledge is created through a continuous dialogue between tacit and explicit knowledge.[1] Management consultants are widely seen to play a crucial role in this process: they not only transfer explicit knowledge (data, information, 'best practices') to the client, but also help explicate the tacit knowledge of client employees.

The explication of tacit knowledge within a client organization is supported by the methods and tools consultants have developed and use in their project work. Werr, Stjernberg, and Docherty (1997) argue that methods and tools translate individual experience and hence leverage tacit to articulate knowledge. These instruments provide a language to articulate the experience and function-oriented knowledge of client employees. They seem central to the consulting business in that they provide knowledge that clients generally do not have, and hence form part of the unique selling-point of the consulting business in general.

However, the process of explicating tacit knowledge has its limits. It is based on the cooperation and goodwill of the members of the client organization. The consultants' lack of knowledge about the details of the client's operations must be overcome, and the application of methods and tools may raise concerns about the consultants' intention to become involved in these details as client employees may expect. The consultants' methods and tools may then seem imposed and superficial, and the support of client employees might not be forthcoming. Therefore, though it may sound paradoxical, the methods and tools may prevent consultants from becoming involved in the intricacies of the client's business and thus engender an insufficient comprehension of the operations, for the understanding of which the tools have actually been conceived. In addition, the process of explicating knowledge from client employees may raise concerns about the stability of their knowledge base and thus about their status. They may feel that the methods consultants apply may render them exchangeable and superfluous. Hence they may openly or latently refuse the partnership with the consultants, which will render it

---

[1] There is an obvious disagreement between Polanyi and Nonaka about the transferability of tacit knowledge. For the purposes of this chapter it suffices to say that there is a type of knowledge that is experience-related and often function-specific and thus much more difficult to capture and transfer than explicit knowledge, and for our purposes it does not matter whether we label it implicit or tacit knowledge.

very difficult for the latter to obtain the necessary information. Especially the 'implementation' of their advice may become difficult if the methods and tools by which it has been generated have previously only signalled their otherness from client employees.

Hence, while the otherness of consultants potentially enables them to assist clients in the transfer of external knowledge and the transformation (explication) of internal knowledge, this otherness might become a burden when it hampers or even blocks the necessary cooperation of the client employees. However, without this cooperation the implementation of the consulting advice will be rendered difficult if not impossible.

The Client Activity System: The Issue of Change

Another dimension where the otherness of consultants might prove beneficial to clients is related to the differences in their respective activity systems: mainly regulation-driven for clients and mainly change-driven for consultants. These activity systems are connected to the interest and intention through which knowledge is generated. For example, Spender (1996) argues that knowledge is not only thinking-based, but also activity-based. Similarly, Blackler (1993) claims that research needs to move away from theories of knowledge towards theories of activity-based knowing. Organizations, therefore, must be conceived as activity systems, whereby knowledge is shaped around the main activities and interests.

The activities within the client organization are centred on running the system as it is. Knowledge within the client organization is characterized by familiarity with the tasks and issues of the value chain; it is acquired through routines and has assumed a subconscious form, since its carriers cannot freely express parts of their knowledge without an external stimulus. Grant (1996) outlines the role routines play in organizational knowledge as able 'to support complex patterns of interaction between individuals in the absence of rules, directives, or even significant verbal communication' (1996: 115). This parallels Pentland and Rueter's (1994) insight that routines are the 'grammar of action' of organizations and should hence not be dismissed as encrusted, bureaucratic behaviour.[2] The interest with which this knowledge has been gained is driven by the day-to-day tasks of running the operations. The activities in the client system are thus primarily regulation-driven. The inherent logic is to maintain the business with its current operations, and piecemeal modifications rather than fundamental change are supposed to guarantee the firm's sustainability.

This is where management consultants and their otherness come into play. Their activities are predominantly driven by triggering change in client organizations; their inherent logic and commercial objective are to change the clients' activity systems. Management consulting as a service is economically based on the need for clients to change. If there were no pressure for organizations to change, management consulting would probably not have the same function or business opportunities. Triggering

---

[2] These descriptions are based on sociological approaches to management knowledge, but they obviously resemble the arguments of evolutionary economists (e.g. Nelson and Winter 1982). Cf. also a special issue of *Industrial and Corporate Change*, 9/2 (2000), on this topic.

change in client organizations is thus one of the main capabilities of consultants and one of the main potential benefits of their otherness for the clients.

As ironic as this may sound, the change-oriented activities also involve a burden for consultants. Change-oriented activities inherently carry the danger of neglecting important details of current operations, which can be aggravated by the consultants' lack of sensitivity to the client's routines and their implicit functions. The introduction of new procedures is often based on an insufficient familiarity with the client's life-world and operations. Initiating change-driven activities without properly understanding the client system may thus increase rather than overcome the reluctance of clients to change. Internal support is not only required in order to conduct a consulting project, but even more so for making the altered tasks and processes part of the client's routine operations.

Thus while the consultants' otherness helps to promote changes in a mainly regulation-oriented client activity system, some sweeping, change-oriented activities might also stand in the way of the subsequent routinization of these changes.

12.3. OTHERNESS AND THE LIMITS OF CONSULTANCY INTERVENTIONS: HISTORICAL CASES

Overall, therefore, the otherness of the consultants is a condition for their possible contribution to client organizations, but at the same time the source of problems, which might in certain cases cancel the potential benefits of external advice. The following historical case-studies illustrate these possible burdens of otherness and delineate the limitations of external advice in the process of developing and 'implementing' solutions. They also give some indications as to how consultancies have attempted to overcome these problems and limitations.

The focus on historical cases is advantageous for the purpose of this chapter because it allows us to examine the intervention process and its outcome as a whole and from a distance. The obvious disadvantage is that the picture of the consulting process and the course of events must be reconstructed from limited sources of information. Evidence cannot be gained through more direct exposure, such as interviews or participant observation, but only through the analysis of archival documents and/or interviews with individuals who were involved in the client–consultancy interaction at the time.[3] This section focuses on two consultancy 'products' that used to be widely disseminated at different times in the twentieth century: the Bedaux system of scientific management and the introduction of the decentralized, multi-divisional organization structure (or M-form) by McKinsey & Co. The descriptions are based on existing historical studies, original archival and interview material, or both. The first part of the section provides a brief overview of the consultancies, the products they disseminated, and the companies that are the focus of the subsequent analysis.

---

[3] The time distance and the fact that they reflect on their own actions obviously distorts the views of these individuals; wherever possible their reflections are therefore combined and contrasted with the available documentary evidence.

Background: An Overview of the Consultants and Clients Studied

The first important development of the consultancy business is related to scientific management or, as it was widely known, Taylorism (Kipping 1997 and 2002). From the beginning of the twentieth century onwards, its proponents not only disseminated scientific-management concepts through publications or presentations, but also advised companies on the creation of so-called wage-and-bonus or payment-by-results schemes, which were intended to systematize and speed up the efforts of workers. These early consultants were widely known as efficiency experts or industrial engineers. One of the early movers was the consulting firm set up by the Taylor rival Harrington Emerson, which already had offices in several US cities by 1917 (Kipping 1999*a*).

The most prominent and, according to the available evidence, widespread method of measuring and rewarding worker performance was the so-called Bedaux system (cf. NICB 1930). Charles Bedaux, a Frenchman who emigrated to the United States in 1906 without much formal education, had developed it. He became acquainted with scientific management as a labourer in some of the physically demanding jobs he held during his early years in the USA, and as an interpreter for an Italian engineer who had come to the United States to study scientific-management methods. From 1916 onwards Bedaux began to offer his own system of work measurement, which standardized human efforts according to a single unit of measurement, the so-called 'B', defined as a fraction of a minute of activity plus a fraction of a minute of rest, always aggregating to unity (Laloux 1950).

Workers were expected to achieve a minimum of 60B per hour and received a bonus for higher B-values. Consultants put the different workshops in all the plants of a client company 'on Bedaux', i.e. calculated the actual and ideal B-values for all jobs carried out in the factory—a process that could take months or even years. At some point, however, they had to leave the system's maintenance to the company itself, a task usually carried out by an internal work-study department whose members had been trained by consultants. In order to provide additional incentives for workers, many companies posted the daily B-values in the factory. In addition, supervisors or a time-study department usually received 25 per cent of the bonus as a reward for their role in organizing the work and stimulating the workers to achieve higher output (Laloux 1950). Bedaux and a growing number of collaborators soon extended their activities throughout the United States, counting a large number of well-known firms among their clients, including DuPont, Eastman Kodak, and General Electric. From the mid-1920s onwards, the Bedaux consultancy also expanded very rapidly to Western Europe and other parts of the world (Kipping 1999*a*).

During the second half of the twentieth century, the first wave of consultancies was gradually overtaken by firms focusing on issues of corporate structure and strategy (Kipping 2002), which had taken off in the United States during the 1930s (McKenna 1995). From the late 1950s onwards, these American management consultants also expanded into Western Europe. One of the most successful firms in this second wave was McKinsey & Company. The consultancy opened its first European office in London in 1959, following a call from the Anglo-Dutch oil company Shell, for which it had already worked in the Americas (Kipping 1999*a*). Much of McKinsey's success during the 1960s and 1970s was based on disseminating the decentralized, multi-divisional organization, or M-form, which had been developed and implemented during the 1920s by companies in the United States such as DuPont and General Motors (Chandler 1962). Before expanding to Europe, McKinsey & Company had already divisionalized several American companies, including Ford and Chrysler (McKenna 1997). In the UK, 32 of the country's 100 largest industrial companies asked consultants to help overhaul their organization during the 1960s; 22 of these hired McKinsey (Channon 1973). The consultancy is also known to have introduced the decentralized M-form in several large French and German companies (Dyas and Thanheiser 1976; cf. Whittington and Mayer 2000).

The following part of this section will examine five cases in which companies introduced either the Bedaux system of scientific management or a decentralized organization structure with the help of McKinsey. These companies are the US meat-packer Swift, the US medium-sized steel producer Lukens, the British automotive supplier Lucas, the French oil producer Total, and the German armaments and mechanical-engineering company Krauss Maffei. The cases thus cover different countries, a wide range of industries, and companies of different sizes. They also concern different forms of ownership and control, ranging from a purely family-owned company (Lukens), through companies with external ownership combined with a certain family influence (Swift and Lucas), to companies with managerial control, but strong external ownership (Krauss Maffei as part of a holding, and Total with a significant, but minority state share). Without claiming to be representative, these cases provide some empirical illustrations of the potential burdens of otherness and the limitations of consultancy interventions.

Since the focus is on highlighting these burdens and the ways in which they might be overcome, the cases are structured not according to the different consultancy products, but according to the reactions from the client organizations prompted by the consultants' otherness. In the first two cases the otherness ultimately led to a failure of the consultancy intervention. In the following three examples, by contrast, these burdens were overcome successfully.

Indifferent Foremen: The Case of Lukens

The first case is the medium-sized, family-owned American steel producer Lukens.[4] The company started introducing the Bedaux system during the Great Depression. According to the minutes of a meeting of an executive committee meeting on 24 February 1930 (quoted in Kipping 2000: 15), the company president Robert Wolcott 'had gone into the Bedaux [*sic*] System and felt we would be benefited very materially by it'. This assessment was apparently based on his study of 'a wide range of large

---

[4] The following description is based on the historical study by Kipping (2000), which in turn relies on the Lukens company archives held at the Hagley Museum and Library in Wilmington Delaware under Accession No. 50.

companies', which in his view used the system 'successfully'. The company's executive committee authorized him to try out the Bedaux system in one department as of March 1930. This decision was apparently based on efforts to cut costs. In November 1930 the company actually ordered a 20 per cent wage cut for all managers and employees (cf. Kipping 2000: 15).

At the same time, the decision has also to be seen in conjunction with the efforts of Wolcott to assert his own authority. He had become company president in 1925, succeeding his father-in-law and the latter's brother—a decision apparently contested by the latter who unsuccessfully tried to impose his own, outside candidate. With little or no experience in manufacturing—Wolcott had been in charge of a regional sales office until then—he relied to a considerable extent on consultants (cf. Kipping 2000: 14). He was attempting to benefit from the consultants' knowledge and the legitimacy they derived from their public reputation and image in the industry, in order to compensate for his own lack of experience.

These attempts appeared successful at first: the archival documents reveal no resistance from the workers to the system. On the contrary, in a note of 30 August 1930 Wolcott reported that 'the fact that we have actually paid them more than what they received before has been a tremendous incentive, and we are now having demands from all over the plant to install this system' (quoted in Kipping 2000: 15). This made it easy for Wolcott to convince the executive committee, in its meeting on 20 October 1930, to hire an additional Bedaux consultant. But despite this lack of resistance and the apparent 'enthusiasm' of the workers for the Bedaux system, it was actually never fully implemented at Lukens.

This is documented in the report of another consultancy, which management commissioned a few years later. In a memorandum dated 17 July 1936 (quoted in Kipping 2000: 16), the consultant examining the company's machine shop identified considerable problems with the application of the Bedaux system there. He related these to the fact that 'plans or systems, whether they be Accounting, Wage Incentive, Planning, Inventory or what not, never maintain a status quo. They either improve or deteriorate with use'. Stressing that the Bedaux system was fundamentally 'a good wage incentive plan to use at Lukens Steel', he concluded 'that the loss of confidence is due to the way the plan has been operated' and blamed it on a lack of interest and enthusiasm for the system among supervisors.

Hence, there seems to be some evidence that the system never became embedded in the operating routines of Lukens Steel. According to the investigation of this consultant, low-level management played the crucial role in this respect. The lack of support by supervisors resulted in the system being abandoned rather than rejected. The consultancy intervention led at least initially to some changes, but the indifference of lower-level managers meant that they remained superficial and never really took hold.

What this case shows is that potential benefits from otherness are not 'automatic', but require internal support at the operational level—something that was lacking in the case of Lukens. The available evidence is not sufficient to say that in this case the otherness actually became a real burden. By contrast, the actual drawbacks of otherness are quite evident in the following case.

Opposing Middle Managers: The Case of Total

In the case of the French oil producer Total, the otherness of the consultants did indeed become a burden for the organizational reform on which the company had embarked at the beginning of the 1970s with the help of McKinsey.[5] As the following detailed description shows, the negative reaction of the middle managers, ranging from a lack of interest to passive resistance, was prompted by the otherness of the consultants and resulted in the failure to implement most of the changes suggested by McKinsey.

The organizational problems that the company tried to address with the help of the consultants go back to its origins. Total had been established in 1924 as Compagnie française des pétroles (CFP). In 1929 CFP created a majority-owned subsidiary, the Compagnie française de raffinage (CFR), which built a number of refineries in France. The CFR became partially quoted on the Paris stock exchange in 1961, which made the relationship between these companies and their organizational structure very complex and was one of the reasons for the decision to hire an outside consultant (cf. Cailluet 2000: 27–9). The choice of McKinsey seemed obvious. The consultancy had become an important reference in the European oil industry, namely with its work for Shell and British Petroleum (including its French subsidiary). A representative of Total had visited Standard Oil of New Jersey and Shell shortly beforehand. In addition, other French companies, especially those with activities in the United States, had already employed the consultancy earlier and thus came to act as trend-setters (Cailluet 2000: 33–4; cf. Kipping 1999a).

Hence, there are some indications that Total followed the example of its foreign competitors and the leading national companies. McKinsey might have helped the top managers of Total to be perceived as up-to-date among their peers in the oil industry and among the French business elite,[6] benefiting from the image and reputation of the consultancy. However, while external examples and pressures rendered it tricky for the managing director of Total to choose any other service provider, his choice did not automatically guarantee the acceptance of the consultancy's recommendations inside the company.

McKinsey made considerable efforts to integrate the company's middle managers in the reorganization process and find out about their concerns. As Cailluet (2000: 40) highlights, however, middle managers do not seem to have taken these efforts very seriously. He quotes the following example from internal company correspondence: 'Coming out of lunch with the Indians, I am herewith submitting my thoughts on the future organisation of the DCEP...'. DCEP was the French abbreviation for the Central Exploration and Production Department, which was actually the main focus

---

[5] The following is based on the historical case-study by Cailluet (2000), which in turn relies on documents in the archives of the company, which after a series of mergers is now called TotalFinaElf. Translations of the French originals are by Matthias Kipping.

[6] This mimetic effect may have been reinforced by the closely knit structure of the French elite, where most top managers had been to the same elite educational institutions, the Grandes Écoles, and were sitting on each others' boards (cf. Bourdieu 1998 and Henry in Chapter 2, above).

of the consultancy's efforts to decentralize the company's organization. An internal note of 24 June 1971 suggested that many middle managers saw the McKinsey approaches as 'too theoretical', their description of the company's weaknesses as a 'caricature', and their suggestions as 'seductive, but of illusionary simplicity'. Their application in practice, so the note concluded, 'has a good chance of killing the patient or at least weakening him' (quoted in Cailluet 2000: 38–40).

Thus it is not surprising that the DCEP successfully resisted the decentralization and that many of the other recommendations of the consultancy were only implemented partially or with a significant delay (Cailluet 2000: 40–1). This was largely due to the attitude of middle managers, which remained sceptical if not hostile towards the consultants, who were seen as 'emissaries' (Cailluet 2000: 36) of top management. The difficult interaction of the consultants with middle management seems to have been the major reason for the failure to change deeply engrained structures and practices.

Thus, as in the case of Lukens, the reason why Total's top management hired consultants was related to the potential benefits of their otherness. Their decision was partially prompted by the intention to simplify the organizational structure, but it also seems at least influenced, if not triggered, by the information about other companies in the same industry making similar efforts. The attractiveness of consulting was thus based either on the image and reputation of the consultancy as the carrier of ideas, as neo-institutional theory would suggest, or on the consultancy's methods and tools for improving efficiency, following more functionalist explanations. As pointed out above, legitimacy and a methodological analysis of routines, both in conjunction with the promise to trigger changes perceived as necessary, provided the selling-point for consultancies.

But the case of Total also illustrates the limits of otherness, due to the differences in client and consultancy knowledge and activities. The consultants and their recommendations never managed to become accepted inside the organization, because they were seen as 'emissaries' of top management, and as superficial and insensitive to the company's existing routines. The failure to decentralize the company's organizational structure was largely due to the reaction from those who should have played the major role in implementing the changes: middle management. Despite the efforts made by the McKinsey consultants to involve them in the process, most middle managers remained reluctant or even hostile towards the outsiders. They perceived the consultants—maybe correctly so—as willing executors of top management decisions, derided them in internal communications, and more or less openly questioned their competence—a hostility that prevented the implementation of the consultancy's recommendations.

In this case, the consultants' otherness became a burden, which could not be overcome. But as the following cases will show, other companies found ways to overcome even stronger resistance from inside the organization and managed to implement many of the consultants' recommendations.

Supportive Foremen: The Case of Swift

One of the first large companies in the United States to install the Bedaux system of scientific management was the meat-packer Swift in 1923–4. What makes this case so interesting is the fact that the system remained in place at Swift, with some modifications, for several decades, while its main rival Armour dropped it quite quickly (Street 1997: 26). A detailed analysis of the available evidence suggests that the longevity of the system was not due to a lack of resistance to the Bedaux system, but at least partially to the ability of the company's management to overcome the potential burden of the consultants' otherness.[7]

Thus, interviews conducted with Swift workers in the 1920s and 1930s already highlighted their rather ambiguous attitude towards the Bedaux system. They appear torn between the resulting speed-up and the 'significant money dividends' it yielded to many of them (cf. Street 1997: 26–7). A study based on interviews with a large number of workers, supervisors, and some management personnel in several of these plants in the 1950s, revealed a similar ambivalence (Purcell 1954: ch. 11; Purcell 1960: ch. 8). Its author noted that most of the complaints about the system were related to the fact that workers did not understand how their bonus was calculated. Random samples of workers show significant differences between different plants, with up to 55 per cent in the Chicago plant expressing a misunderstanding of its operations and distrust of its fairness (Purcell 1960: 270). A few quotes from Chicago employees illustrate this lack of understanding (Purcell 1954: 246–51):

I makes $1.50 to $1.60 a week. How they figure that bonus? Tha's what I don't understand.
I don't figure it out. They give me what they give. Sometimes, I wonder where it comes from.
They give what they feel like giving you. I don't think they give an honest bonus.
The bonus? I don't know how to figure it.

Overall, Purcell (1960: 138) nevertheless concluded that 'only a small minority of the packinghouse workers ... had so much misunderstanding-distrust that they were against wage incentives as such, preferring straight time pay'. As a matter of fact, in his 1950 survey only 16 per cent of rank-and-file workers wanted to see the system abolished completely (Purcell 1954: 244). His research helps to identify some of the conditions necessary for workers to show a negative attitude towards the system. One of them was their type of activity. In the Chicago plant, hostility was expressed most openly and frequently by those working in mechanical and craft jobs. They argued that their tasks were too varied to be measured by a standardized system and that its application forced them to sacrifice quality for quantity (Purcell 1954: 249). Of similar importance was the fact that bonuses in some departments were not calculated individually but on a team basis, which made it difficult for workers to see a clear relationship between their efforts and the bonus they received, and also encouraged free-riders (Purcell 1960: 147). There were also some differences according to the gender and race of the worker, but these seemed rather minor and could be explained by particular local and work circumstances (Purcell 1960: 144–5). Another important factor was

---

[7] For a summary of the existing research on Swift, see Street (1997). The main focus of these studies was not the reaction of the workers and foremen to the consultancy intervention and the Bedaux system, but the working life and conditions on Chicago's 'killing floors'. However, the evidence seems sufficiently rich to use it for the purposes of this chapter.

union allegiance, which certainly had an influence on the fairly negative attitude of the workers at the Chicago plant, where union leaders were quite openly hostile towards the system (Purcell 1954: 241–2).

Overall, therefore, workers appeared at best indifferent and unions rather hostile towards the system introduced by the Bedaux consultancy. The consultants' otherness seems to have proved a burden, mainly due to a feeling among workers that the consultants' understanding of the company's operations had been rather superficial and due to the reluctance of workers and foremen to change their activities. However, the Swift management seems to have been able to overcome most of the negative consequences resulting from the consultants' otherness, thus ensuring the 'implementation' of the system, i.e. its actual incorporation into the company's routines.

Management action was partially prompted by a concern to avoid worker radicalization (cf. Street 1997). This led to a number of concessions to the United Packinghouse Workers Amalgamated (UPWA). Thus, in 1945 the company agreed to a bilateral grievance procedure regarding the standards, and in 1952 it removed one of the features most strongly resented by workers—the 75–25 split of the bonus between them and the foremen. From then on, workers received 100 per cent of the bonus (Purcell 1954: 241, 237).

According to Purcell (1960: 146), however, the most important factor for the implementation and continued operation of the system was the role of the foreman, who 'could greatly influence the understanding and trust of his employees regarding the Standards System. It is the foreman's job to explain the system to a new employee and to adjust workers' complaints about premium earnings.' In the East St. Louis plant, for example, the level of output across departments was strongly related to the foremen's attitude towards the standards. According to the correlation analysis conducted by Purcell (1960: 147), the foreman's attitude scored highest among a number of different factors influencing output levels, followed by the percentage of workers on individual rather than team bonuses. By contrast, factors such as workers' attitudes towards the standards or pay in general had less of an influence. Recognizing this, during the second half of the 1950s the company 'developed a program for getting the main points of wage-incentive theory across at least to the foremen themselves' (Purcell 1960: 152).

The Swift case suggests that the Bedaux consultants had considerable problems in implementing their system, as they were apparently unable to adjust the system to the mixed and diverse tasks of the craft jobs and to sort out the contributions of individual workers involved in teamwork. It seems that the Bedaux consultants tried to use their method without making themselves familiar with the tacit knowledge embodied in the tasks of employees. Instead of the consultants, the foremen seem to have played the crucial role in the eventual implementation and maintenance of the Bedaux system. Its longevity was ensured through the adaptation to certain worker demands and, most importantly, with the instauration of a training programme for foremen. Based on this training, the foremen could explain the details of the system to the workers and thus function as a bridging link between the consultants and the employees concerned.

Despite an ambiguous attitude towards the Bedaux system, workers at Swift never actively challenged its implementation. This made it fairly easy for management to overcome the burdens of otherness, 'pacify' the unions by making a few concessions, and embed the system in the company's routines, mainly by enlisting the support of the foremen. By contrast, the following case-study gives an example of how management dealt with strong employee resistance.

Consulting in Disguise: The Case of Lucas

The British automotive supplier Lucas employed the Bedaux consultancy during the Great Depression mainly to cut costs and improve productivity. The following description is based both on the published company history (Nockolds 1976) and on additional material from the company archives—hereafter quoted as Lucas archives.[8] It shows once again that while the company management was trying to derive benefits from the otherness of the consultants, it was soon confronted with the burden this otherness entailed. But it found a rather ingenious—some might say devious—way to overcome these problems.

Like the other companies described before, in hiring the Bedaux consultancy Lucas seems to have been influenced by the implementation of their system by its competitors in the United States, which one of the top managers had visited shortly beforehand. The system was again first tried in one department, before the decision was made to extend it to the company as a whole (cf. Nockolds 1976: 260–2). The similarities with the other cases end there, however. Unlike in the previous cases, workers at Lucas rapidly mobilized against the implementation of the system. They held several meetings at the beginning of 1932 to discuss its negative consequences and ways to prevent its implementation. For example, the report of a meeting on 20 January 1932 attended by 400 workers quoted one of them already working under the system as follows: 'Bedeau [*sic*] is Slavery; . . . you are working much harder for the same money' (Lucas archives, Folder A/289).

The efforts against the Bedaux consultants were coordinated by the minority (communist) unions at Lucas. They established an ad hoc publication for this purpose called *The Lamp*. It showed, for example, cartoons representing workers hitting or chasing the 'Bedaux time men' (the consultants) (ibid.). When the Lucas management realized that workers and the unions were about to successfully organize a mass strike against the Bedaux system, they halted its implementation and withdrew the consultants, issuing notices that included the following statement (quoted by Nockolds 1976: 263):

The Directors have always prided themselves on their good relationship with the Lucas workers. They do not desire to impose a system of payment that will not have the full co-operation of the workers. In these circumstances the Bedaux system of wages payment will be discontinued and a return will be made to the ordinary Lucas system of piecework payment.

In its edition of 29 January 1932 the communist newspaper *Daily Worker* celebrated 'Victory' with the 'Bedaux System smashed' and the 'Lucas employers completely

---

[8] The Lucas archives are held at the British Motor Industry Heritage Trust in Gaydon. The relevant material is contained in Folder A/289 in a box labelled 'Industrial Relations B (Bedaux)'.

beaten' (Lucas archives, Folder A/289). However, they rejoiced too early. Several months later the management started to introduce an identical system under a different name ('Lucas Point Plan'), and with better preparation and explanation of the advantages the workers could derive from its application. One of the general managers explained their objectives in retrospect: 'We got rid of the original Bedaux engineers', he said, 'but we got another lot from Bedaux who were not called Bedaux engineers. They were called Lucas Point Plan System engineers—and that solved all of our problems' (interviewed and quoted by Nockolds 1976: 288).

The engineers who had been brought in remained in the service of the consultancy, but they 'concealed their true identity' and 'Lucas paid a third of their salary, so that they could be said to "be on the staff"' (ibid.).[9] The disguised Bedaux engineers supervised and trained several real Lucas employees in the Lucas Point Plan System. They established an internal Time-Study Department, which not only continued the efforts after the departure of the consultants, but also became instrumental in the establishment of a Process Planning Department, which focused on the optimization of the manufacturing process as a whole, rather than on individual worker effort (cf. Nockolds 1976: 289–91, 321–3).

In the case of Lucas, the consultants' otherness immediately became a major burden for the company, because it prompted a section of the workers to resist the changes it implied for their activities. Faced with this hostility, the company's management did not remove the consultants or their approach, but their otherness, by disguising them as members of the organization. This trick worked very well.[10] Subsequently, the 'internal' consultants not only embedded the Bedaux system into the company's routines, but also continued to develop it internally beyond the original objectives and methodology. As the following case shows, this example of a company overcoming initial resistance against organizational change and further developing a new routine internally after the departure of the consultants is not unique.

Direct Negotiations: The Case of Krauss Maffei

The German company Krauss Maffei encountered similar, albeit less severe problems when trying to implement a decentralized organizational structure in the late 1960s. Originally a locomotive producer, Krauss Maffei had diversified into machinery

---

[9] It is interesting to see how these incidences give way to a political-economic view on management consulting (cf. Armbrüster 2000).

[10] Another Bedaux client, the electrical goods producer Ferranti, adopted a similar strategy and disguised the consultants. As one of the former Bedaux consultants involved in this process remembered, 'I was not allowed to mention Bedaux, I was not allowed to put Bedaux in my briefcase, I was not allowed to let the company... know where I was staying because the unions used to check up on me.... I was paid £5.00 per week by Ferranti, so that everybody who saw me going up to what was called the Hollered to get my money, thought I was an employee of Ferranti'; E.N.B. Mitton, interviewed by Matthias Kipping on 23 April 1997. This and the other interview cited in this chapter were based on open-ended questions and lasted about two hours. They were taped and transcribed and the transcriptions submitted to the interviewees for verification of factual errors.

production after the Second World War and, from 1963 onwards, also assembled the battle tank Leopard. This case description is based on documents in the still unclassified company archives (hereafter: KM archives) and on an interview with its former chief executive Dr Helmut Wolf (hereafter: Interview Wolf).[11]

The decision to introduce a decentralized system of organization and to hire McKinsey for this purpose was actually not made by the company's own management. At the time, Krauss Maffei belonged to the private Flick group, a holding of a wide range of diverse businesses.[12] The suggestion came from the chair of its supervisory board, who was also the chief executive of another Flick company that McKinsey had already decentralized. The head of the McKinsey office in Germany had been able to establish a close, personal relationship with the company's CEO, who subsequently recommended the consultants to other companies in the Flick group (Interview Wolf, cf. Kipping 1999a). At the same time, however, the minutes of a meeting in April 1968 between Krauss Maffei's executive board and consultancy representatives confirm that, not unlike the Total case, top managers were quite happy to follow the example of leading firms. Managers expressed a wish to obtain 'comparative data about the organization of first-class American and European companies' (KM archives).

McKinsey was hired and elaborated suggestions for a decentralization of the company. Not unlike in the case of Total, they apparently were not always well received: 'Some people thought that the existing structure was okay, so why change it?' (Interview Wolf). However, many of the resulting conflicts were apparently resolved in conversations between the consultants, the executive board members, and the employees concerned (ibid.). One of the difficult points concerned the allocation of production units to the new divisions, because everything was physically located in one factory. Purchasing had also been conducted centrally. McKinsey not only proposed subdividing both according to the new structure, but also giving each division the power to source and produce outside. 'That was, obviously, unacceptable. It immediately caused quite a storm' (Interview Wolf). The company decided not to go quite as far and retained production as a single cost centre, yet gradually moved its units apart into different buildings, apparently causing some disruption in the production flow—at least at the beginning.

These reactions suggest that in this case there were many obstacles due to the differences between the consultancy and the client knowledge and the reluctance of the client organization to accept far-reaching changes to the existing routines. Many of those concerned in the organization apparently felt that the consultants did not make sufficient efforts to understand the existing routines and that, as a consequence, their recommendations were not adequate. Despite the initial resistance, Krauss Maffei successfully implemented the decentralization proposed by the consultants (unlike the Total case, where it was blocked by middle managers).

---

[11] Interviewed by Matthias Kipping on 10 July 1997. While already a member of the executive board during the McKinsey intervention, Dr Wolf was made chief executive in 1968, following a recommendation from the consultancy.

[12] Later on, in 1990, Krauss Maffei was acquired by Mannesmann (Wessel 1990: 493–6).

Based on the available evidence, it seems that in this case the initial resistance could be overcome during direct negotiations with the middle managers concerned, sometimes leading to compromise solutions. It was the involvement of the company management and its strong support for the new structure that led to its eventual acceptance and routinization (cf. Interview Wolf). Once the decentralization principle was accepted, the company continued to develop its organizational structure in the same direction by decentralizing responsibility even further—long after the departure of the consultants. Thus, following further diversification, Krauss Maffei created new divisions—a task accomplished by 'internal organization people', who 'invested a lot of time in this' (Interview Wolf)—and towards the end of the 1980s, the company actually transformed the divisions into separate legal units.[13]

The last two cases seem diametrically opposed to the first (Lukens Steel). There, the otherness was never a burden. However, its benefits were not realized either, because the company's management made no efforts to implement and progress the consultancy recommendations by building the necessary internal support—which meant that the changes remained superficial and were abandoned soon after the consultants' departure. In the cases of Krauss Maffei and Lucas, management had to overcome considerable internal resistance prompted by the otherness of consultants. Once this was done however, the original consultancy recommendations were not only routinized, but also developed further long after the consultants had left.

12.4. CONCLUSIONS

The historical cases of consulting interventions examined in this chapter have been described on the basis of the limited evidence available from a variety of sources, and thus can only provide a fragmentary picture of the client–consultancy interaction and its outcome. They nevertheless suggest that the widespread notion of the potential advantages client organizations can derive from the otherness of consultants needs to be modified.

On the one hand, these cases confirm that management did indeed expect to benefit from three aspects of the otherness of consultants, namely their public reputation, their ability to transfer and transform knowledge, and their capacity to change client activities. On the other hand, however, in all of the above cases their otherness proved a burden for the consultants and the implementation of their recommendations. It appears that consultants and their methods failed to fully understand the tacit knowledge of company employees and the routines embedded in the organization and its activities, and made suggestions that were perceived as inadequate by those concerned. Not surprisingly, as a result there was often considerable resistance from those concerned within the client organization to the changes initiated by the consultants.

At the same time, the historical case-studies also suggest that in many instances, company management found ways to overcome the burdens and limitations prompted by

---

[13] Whittington and Mayer (2000) have noted similar developments in a large number of other European companies, but without examining the process or the role of consultants in each case.

the otherness of the consultants. The case of Lucas is particularly interesting in this respect. Here, the management resorted to deceiving their workers by disguising external consultants as internal employees.[14] In other cases, company management gave in to some of the demands from those concerned or negotiated compromise solutions with them. In this way, it managed to enlist their support for the implementation of the changes recommended by the consultants.

More importantly, all of the above case-studies also show that overcoming the initial hostility and resistance towards the consultants was not sufficient to ensure the long-term success of new procedures. Client organizations had to make additional efforts to embed them in their own routines after the departure of the consultants. Otherwise the implementation remained superficial and the changes were likely to fall into disuse sooner or later. In the case of Swift, this effort consisted in the training of foremen, who could then explain the system to the workers. In the case of Lucas, once the initial resistance to the consultants had been overcome through the deception of an 'internal' system, it even became a source of further innovation—through internal efforts such as continued updating of the system and training of the employees concerned. Likewise, in the case of Krauss Maffei, company personnel developed the consultancy suggestions further, long after the latter had left.

In conclusion, as all these have cases shown, management consultants provide ways of thinking and a range of competences that can be highly beneficial for clients—or rather for the client management. They help legitimize decisions, supply external information, methodologically analyse client routines, raise client knowledge from an implicit to an explicit level, trigger change, facilitate communication in times of organizational change, etc. And yet at the same time their impact can only be limited, since their otherness also involves boundaries about knowledge contained in routines, boundaries of agency contained in the very fact of being hired by management, boundaries of legitimacy contained in their reputation as carriers of external knowledge—and thus boundaries of acceptance and the possibilities of implementation. Thus, when it comes to what is generally labelled 'implementation', or what could be defined as embedding new routines in the behaviour of client organizations and ensuring the internalization of new information and methods by them, there seems to be little consultants can do. After they had introduced the wage incentive system or the new organizational structure, it was investment in internal training and other subsequent efforts by client staff that made the difference in the outcome.

For client firms this can only mean that hiring consultants must not only involve the possibility of, but rather the expectation of and preparation for, terminating the

---

[14] In Germany, the internal approach towards the implementation of scientific management was institutionalized in the so-called REFA system. While similar to the Bedaux system in its technical approach and effect (cf. Rochau 1939), the system was not installed by external consultants, but by internal engineers, who had undergone a work-study training programme organized by the REFA association. Not surprisingly, this seems to have caused less hostility or outright rejection and, as a result, by the 1950s, the REFA system was much more widespread in Germany than the Bedaux or similar systems in the United Kingdom (Kipping 1999b).

cooperation with consultants. One of the most frequently heard responses from clients is that they expect consultants not only to gather data and develop recommendations, but also to 'implement' these recommendations themselves (cf. Ashford 1998: 179). The examples above indicate, however, that 'implementation by others' may be an oxymoron. In order for advice to be fruitful and sustainable, external input must not only be accompanied by internal support in the initial phase, but also be discontinued in time and followed by internal succession and progression.

13

Managers and Consultants as Embedded Actors: Evidence from Norway

HALLGEIR GAMMELSÆTER

13.1. INTRODUCTION

The idea developed in this chapter is that consultants as carriers of management knowledge are generally embedded in contexts that are external to the organization, whereas the management they interact with is embedded in internal organization-specific contexts that circumscribe the extent to which the consultants can influence changes in organizations. The chapter proceeds with a theoretical underpinning of this line of argument, followed by the presentation of two cases that serve to illustrate the theoretical points made. The first is extracted from a historical comparative multi-case study (Gammelsæter 1991, 1994) and refers to how the multi-divisional form of organization (M-form) was introduced in an Oslo-based manufacturing company back in the 1960s. The second describes the introduction of Business Process Re-engineering (BPR) in another Norwegian manufacturing company in the middle of the 1990s (Gammelsæter 1999). Discussion of the theoretical approach followed in the two cases and conclusions are presented in a final section.

Although it is imaginable that the adoption of management knowledge carried by consultants does not always challenge the power structure of the organization, such ideas will often have quite overriding consequences for the internal context, particularly if their textbook version is only slightly adapted to the previous structure of the client organization. This complicates the application of management technologies imported by such carriers as consultants. Despite having their heyday at different times, both the M-form and BPR exemplify widely adopted ideas that have had over-riding consequences for organizations, although they are not unequivocally understood and applied (e.g. Allen 1978; Jarrar and Aspinwall 1999).

The case material presented in this chapter derives primarily from interviews with managers involved in the change processes and on written documentation. Whereas in the first case the data collection was undertaken in retrospect, in the second most interviews were made as the change process was in progress, although there were also follow-up interviews.

In the first case (Elkem), interviews were undertaken during the period 1987–1990. At least 26 managers were interviewed, some of them twice. Some of the follow-up interviews were carried out by telephone, but mostly interviews were conducted face-to-face, usually lasting between an hour-and-a-half and two-and-a-half hours. Most of the informants were division managers or functional managers, and at the time of the data collection most of these were or had been included in the executive group of managers. Three of the managers were the succeeding presidents of Elkem in the period 1971–1990. A few of the informants were retired at the time of interview, but they had maintained close contacts with the company. The group union leader was also included. Before a narrative case description was published, the interviewees were sent relevant parts of the draft in order to provoke feedback in terms of corrections or verifications.

In the second case (Glamox), the data were collected between October 1996 and June 1999. During 1996 and 1997 line and project managers at department and shop level were interviewed. In addition the president of the group, and the succeeding general directors of GF (the production unit) in the period 1996–1999, were interviewed. The general director of GI (Glamox International) was also interviewed. With the former a follow up interview was conducted in the spring of 1999. Altogether 15 top or middle managers were interviewed. In 1997 the author also participated in a weekend seminar where the change efforts of a GF were discussed among shop stewards and managers at all levels. Since the consultant involved in the project was later working abroad he was not interviewed face-to-face, but he was approached by telephone and produced a long (21 page) written account as a feedback note to the author in reply to a preliminary report analysing the project. This preliminary report was sent to the interviewees in the autumn of 1997 when the project was officially finished, and after feedback comments had been incorporated, a final report was produced.

13.2. RELATIONS BETWEEN THE CONSULTANTS AND THE RECIPIENTS OF MANAGEMENT KNOWLEDGE

The issue of how knowledge is diffused has been studied for a long time by scholars representing many social disciplines (cf. Alvarez 1998). A major contribution to this research has come from the neo-institutionalist strand within organization sociology (e.g. Meyer and Rowan 1977; Powell and DiMaggio 1991), a school whose hallmark is its espousal of an embedded depiction of economic actors (Dowd and Dobbin 1997). Embedded actors pursue strategies on the basis of widely shared and implicit assumptions rooted in socio-historical contexts, in contrast to the atomized actors of neo-classical economics who calculate the benefits of different strategies. According to neo-institutionalists, the idea of the existence of optimal means to every end permeates the modern economic worldview. Economic actors therefore seek to discover optimal means (Meyer 1994) that are recast as manifestations of natural 'law' and thereby institutionalized. Thus, in the view of the neo-institutionalists, economic actors behave according to a belief that they are operating in a world where means and ends can be optimized, whereas in reality this world is a social creation in which the relationship between means and ends is far less calculable and controllable than those actors prefer to believe.

Consultants, alongside entrepreneurs and management academics (Alvarez 1998), thrive on this situation, because, on the one hand, they make their living from (re)producing and disseminating ideas and recipes that promise goal achievement, while, on the other hand, their service is hardly ever measured because the product they present is already institutionalized; since it is already considered 'good practice' (Kieser 2002) it needs no scientific documentation (Røvik 2002). In spite of the tendency that increasing commodification and marketing of their services lead to reductions in relevance and quality (e.g. Fincham 1995), and therefore increase the chances of detriment for their clients, the consultancy industry is still growing fast (Kipping and Armbrüster 1999). This paradox is explained by the political function that consultants play in serving the dominant coalition in the client organization. The demand for consultants is explicable and rational as seen from the position of the management. However, the demand for consulting cannot be fully satisfied because the uncertainties managers face can only be reduced superficially and in the short term (Sturdy 1997). As new uncertainties pop up repeatedly, managers easily become addicted to consultants (Ernst and Kieser 2002; see also Kieser, Chapter 10, above).

Another neo-institutional explanation is based on the idea that organizations are basically identity-seeking entities that constantly make comparisons between their own structures and those of 'others' (Meyer 1994). Since identity is conceived of as relational, organizations are constantly trying to imitate their role models and to differentiate themselves from organizations they do not identify with (Røvik 1996, 1998; Sahlin-Andersson 1996). Consultancy can be viewed as one of the means by which organizations compare and refurbish themselves, and the recent success of the consultancy industry can be understood as the effect of its increased ability to commodify and market its products in the face of the more complex and dynamic environments meeting modern identity-seeking organizations.

While the neo-institutional critique of approaches advocating that economic actors are calculating when adopting organization structures has been most warranted, neo-institutionalism is itself not convincing in explaining how organizations receive management knowledge. To some extent this stems from the weak empirical basis of some of its fundamental tenets, including the thesis that organizations are so embedded in their social contexts that decision-makers take new organizational recipes for granted (Davis, Diekman, and Tinsley 1994). By taking this thesis itself for granted, the neo-institutional school has largely neglected the role of agency and interests (DiMaggio 1988; Aldrich 1992; Hirsch and Lounsbury 1997), the importance of interaction, and the role of the recipient in general in the diffusion of knowledge (Sturdy 1999). The thesis of organizations as basically identity-seeking largely runs into the same inadequacies. Furthermore, the conception of management as the primary representative of the organization tends to be that it is united and monolithic. There is no tension between managers, managerial echelons, or expert groups. They seek the same identity. The focus on the persuasive diffusers and the corresponding neglect of the receptive actors not only lead neo-institutionalism to depict the diffusion process as a linear process, but also tend to portray managers as indulgent and as 'gullible victims to clever tricks' (Sturdy 1999). Actors conform to institutional mechanisms.

However, these mechanisms should not be mistaken for the institutional mechanisms rooted in the 'old institutionalism' (Powell and DiMaggio 1991). Since neo-institutionalism focuses on institutional environments, its depiction of the diffusion of structural forms tends to disregard the endogenous countervailing forces often found in organizational values and cultures, informal actions, vested interests, coalitions, etc.—in short the mechanisms of obstruction and action treated by institutionalists à la Selznick (1949, 1957, 1996). This also means that the embedded actors of the neo-institutionalist world-view are portrayed as more embedded in institutional environments than in the contexts of the organization they represent. Thus, paradoxically, neo-institutionalism is a-contextual as seen from an old-institutional perspective. Admittedly, this assertion ignores the mechanism of de-coupling (Meyer and Rowan 1977), which promises to solve this contradiction by attributing change to the managerial structure while the operational core is unaffected. This explanation is argued to be inadequate, however, both because adopted ideas have been shown to influence core activities and because of its implicit assumption that managerial structures—in contrast to core activities—are easy to change (Gammelsæter 1991, 1994). It follows that neo-institutionalism does not explicate the interaction between consultants and the organizational actors receiving management knowledge.

Concurring with the above discussion, it is suggested that the study of the interaction between consultants and organizational actors specifically takes into account that the actors have to answer to both inner and outer contexts (Pettigrew 1985). The outer context can be conceived of as exogenous events, processes, structures, and social rules that circumscribe yet do not determine organizational action. The inner context can be understood as the values, vested interests, enacted views, and patterns of action connected to the existing organizational structure. This context also circumscribes, yet does not completely determine, action.

Carriers of knowledge, such as consultants, primarily operate in an outer context as seen from the organization level. Consultants appear as a medium through which the cognitive rules and rationalities of the outer context are (re)produced and transmitted. The raw material for their production activity will often be found in the inner organizational context, however (Dowd and Dobbin 1997), and in the face of resistance in organizations the consultant may also be tempted to accept redefinitions of the problem at issue presented by the organizational actors (Jackall 1988). Yet external counsellors cannot be completely embedded in the internal context. Even if they can be used, they cannot become real players in the organizational power game (Fincham 1999). Similarly, organizational actors can be conceived of as primarily embedded in the specific context of their organizations. Following Selznick (1957: 16–17), by taking on a distinctive set of values 'beyond the technical requirements of the task at hand'—and understanding institutionalization as a process that 'happens to the organization over time'—the organization acquires a unique identity that it strives to preserve. For management it is a vital role to define and defend this identity. After all, as Stinchcombe (1968: 107) pointed out, an institution is 'a structure in which powerful people are committed to some value or interest'. If the organization structure is in fact a neatly developed power structure defending the identity of a powerful management, it must be expected that management, rather than adopting whatever recipe is presented to them, will resist or otherwise make sure that structural changes do not threaten their own status and power (cf. Willcocks and Grint 1997; Jaffe and Scott 1998).

Rather than assuming that the management in organizations is completely united, research indicates that tensions may arise, for instance between (often) younger and lower-level managers and older and higher-level managers because the former are more liable than the latter to initiate changes that violate established strategies and structures (Kanter 1982; Burgelman 1983). This was also discovered by Chandler (1962: 303) in his seminal work on the invention of the M-form. Older and higher-level managers are probably more prone to value the privileges derived from long tenures (Stevens, Beyer, and Trice 1978); the relational context in homogenous and stable groups, isolated from their task environments (Katz 1980, 1982); and the established structure as an expression of their own creation (Gammelsæter 1991) than are lower-level managers. Accordingly, organizational openness to restructuring is more likely when organizations undergo top management succession (cf. Helmich and Brown 1972; Tushman and Romanelli 1985; Ford and Baucus 1987; Wiersma and Bantel, Wiersma 1995). New top managers are often expected to create their own management teams, new patterns of formal interaction, and new values and norms to be built on. In this vein, Wiersma (1995: 199) concludes that executive succession is an antecedent to corporate restructuring, and that 'top management teams do indeed provide a stable governance structure for the firm. When these structures are upset via non-retirement related succession events, firms experience significant corporate restructuring'.

Thus, rather than assuming that a united management is persuaded by eager consultants to adopt and implement 'new' management knowledge, it is suggested that the pattern of interaction between consultants and management, and the influence of the first on the latter, depends heavily on the stability of the inner context. A general proposition would be that the influence of consultants will be greater, and the interaction across contexts tighter in times of instability in the inner power structure. Destabilization often leads to changes in management and is itself caused by the inability of organizations to meet performance requirements or by the publicity of events that bring the standards of ethics, security, quality, environment, etc. of organizations into question. At other times, the replacement of top managers follows natural incidents such as retirement, illness, or death, or strategic actions such as the acquisitions or divestments that are so commonplace in the business world of today.

The inner context is at its most malleable when it is destabilized and new managers are taking power. In such situations the interface between the inner and the outer context is being reshaped. The new management often has no need to identify with former strategies or structures. On the contrary, with new management in office, stakeholders often expect changes. As a consequence, in periods of destabilization, institutionalized inner contexts are weakened and representatives of the outer context can be expected to have great influence on the choices of management.

Since management knowledge is often presented in guises of rationality, and as neutral devices not affecting the power structure of top management, interactions between organization management and consultants will also be commonplace in times of inner context stability. However, in these situations we would expect management to translate the suggestions of consultants in such a way that their implementation is not violating the power structure of the inner context. This means that the influence of consultants will be less immediate and more circumscribed by the values, norms, and vested interests of the institutionalized organization.

13.3. CONTEXT, ACTION, AND INTERACTION IN THE DIVISIONALIZATION OF ELKEM

Background

At the end of the Second World War Elkem was a small engineering firm employing 240 people.[1] It was selling patents and constructing smelting furnaces for the metal industry. Diversification into related businesses such as ferro-silicon, aluminium, and mining occurred as the company started to exploit its own patented know-how. By the middle of the 1960s the company employed about 3,000 people, mostly in mines and plants spread around Norway. The post-war reconstruction in Europe meant an increase in the demand for metals, and the 1950s and 1960s was a prosperous period. Elkem's turnover increased every year, its results were positive, and more than 85 per cent of its sales came from exports.

Its growth and diversification had not been accompanied by any great concern for organizational structure, however. Little had changed since the company was a medium-sized engineering firm. There was, for instance, no clear-cut divide between headquarters (HQ) and the Engineering Division (ED).[2] Until 1971 the presidents and vice-presidents were always recruited from ED and the close ties between these units were also maintained by co-localization and joint functional departments. In contrast, the acquired plants and mines very much retained their former status as running companies, with their own staffs being used to manage both daily operations and strategic matters. Many plant and mine executives enjoyed great freedom in relation to the HQ. Thus, Elkem seemed to operate a combination of a holding and functional structure not uncommon in European business at the time (cf. Scott 1973).

Elkem's success over the previous 20 years had strengthened the management structure and the position of the president. The presidency had traditionally been occupied by men spending most of their vocational career in the company. When the man who had been president in 1966, the year the M-form was formally adopted, retired in 1970, he had been with the company for 34 years. His successor retired after 41 years. The inner circle of the management consisted of the president, the vice-president, the company secretary, the executive of ED, and those of the finance and law departments. Three of the six were engineers. Two, including the company secretary, had backgrounds in business economics. These managers met regularly twice a week, but as typical were a lot of ad hoc meetings orchestrated by the president, who liked to talk things over informally with his colleagues. This also included plant and mine managers

---

[1] When nothing else is indicated all references are made to Gammelsæter (1991).
[2] Curiously, the concept of 'division' was used in 'Engineering Division' long before the management was confronted with the idea of divisionalization as a form of organization.

who from time to time visited the HQ. Since most of the managers had worked in the company for a long time, they knew each other well and there was a friendly and consultative atmosphere between them. There is little doubt that the management of Elkem constituted a very institutionalized inner context.

The Divisionalization Process

The M-form is generally presented as an alternative to functional or holding forms of organization (e.g. Whittington and Mayer 2000), and its implementation means supplanting one set of management principles with a completely new one. If realized to its full extent, this implies a change in the entire organizational structure, affecting the power structure that is built to defend the values, norms, and identity of the institution.

What concerned Elkem's management at the turn of the decade was not the need for restructuring, however. Their concern was that the post-war expansion had caused a shortage of office space at HQ. According to one key manager it was in the course of planning a new HQ building that questions of organizational structure came up: 'What caused us to start thinking about organization was the necessity to think through who worked with whom before moving into the new HQ' (quoted in Gammelsæter 1991: 152). Thus, the first meeting between management and a consultancy was spurred by the HQ expansion plan. The company secretary read an article on office planning in a business magazine and contacted the author, a consultant who subsequently offered his assistance. This included time studies of central managers, followed by an analysis of the organization at HQ. The latter deemed the organizational structure at HQ obscure and delegation was suggested. This initiated a long change process involving the organization committee and the company secretary in particular.

Over the next year the consultant worked on an expanded study of the organization with the aim of 'rationalization and adjustments to the increasing demands caused by the growth of the firm' (quoted ibid.). A diagnostic report was worked out in collaboration with the organization committee.[3] It concluded that changes ought to be initiated in systems and routines in order to facilitate delegation. The M-form was not presented either as a concept or as a full-fledged structural recipe, but principles inherent in the idea of the M-form, such as 'delegation', 'long-range strategic planning', 'performance centres', and corporate services to 'serve the divisions', were introduced (quoted ibid.: 153). Thus, four years before the M-form was formally adopted, the top management of Elkem was introduced to many of the principles associated with it, still without fully realizing the connections between them and all its implications. It was symptomatic that in the aftermath of the presentation of the report focus was directed towards procedures of delegation of rather minor decisions, and towards setting up units for personnel management, sales and marketing, and long-range planning at HQ. There was no plan for establishing divisions as an intermediate level between the HQ and the plants and mines, many of which produced for the same markets.

---

[3] During the period of study, the consultant and the committee had twelve formal meetings as well as four with top management.

It is important to note that the changes suggested at this point did not threaten to disrupt the texture of the inner context. There were no managers losing their positions or being downgraded. Although some top managers were deprived of minor parts of their spheres of authority, the time studies had showed that their workload was much too great. Moreover, rather than slimming down the HQ, it was suggested that the number of functions at HQ should be increased.

The process towards divisionalization did not lose momentum, however. In 1963 the American consultant George Kenning, who was working in Scandinavia (Kvålshaugen and Amdam 2000), was invited to meet with Elkem's top management. According to the company secretary, he fascinated the managers:

Then in came Mr. Kenning and talked to the president and travelled around Elektrokemisk [the former name of the company]. Later we had a meeting with all the managers Kenning had met. He asked us whether to tell the truth, and after receiving our permission he gave us a terrible surprise. However, he was not condescending. His criticism was fierce, but we all felt it was just (quoted in Gammelsæter 1991: 154).

The president asked Kenning to be his adviser on management matters. Kenning translated the message of decentralization already articulated by the Norwegian consultants into a matter of accountability at the operational level. Thus he pushed towards establishing accountable divisions.

The piecemeal change pattern at Elkem meant that the issue of organizational design turned on the question of adopting a completely new organizational form or making minor adjustments in the old structure. Among those sceptical about adopting divisions were the plant and mine managers and the president. After years of close relationships they felt reluctant to introduce an intermediate level between them. This particular characteristic of the inner context—the direct accessibility based on personal relationships between the president and the plant and mine managers—would be sacrificed. However, a tiny group of younger managers at HQ was particularly in favour of furthering the change process. Among these was the company secretary, who had worked with the consultants all the way along, and was now accompanied by a new personnel manager recruited from another company Kenning had been consulting. The Norwegian consultant engaged in 1961 was involved with the company until late 1966, and greatly helped by the support of Kenning, these three men were able to push the rest of top management towards accepting the change of structure. Before the final decision was taken, however, Kenning had to assemble the plant and staff management twice, in May and November 1965, to explain why further structural changes should be allowed.

The construction of the divisional structure put into function from 1966 was such that none of the plant and mine managers really lost status or position. This was partly achieved by natural retirement, but more important was the trick of upgrading plants and mines to divisional status. In the insulation and aluminium industries this was to some extent logical, since Elkem operated one plant only within each industry. However, in the mining business, where there were many mines and the establishment of an overriding divisional level would imply downgrading of several managers, the divisional structure was not adopted. All the more, similar to HQ, the plants and mines were keeping their staff resources, whereas the divisional level was very thinly equipped. Thus, the divisional structure that was adopted after five years very much preserved the needs of the inner context of management.

Explaining the Fate of the Divisionalization Process

The pattern of divisionalization in Elkem can be seen in the light of the oscillation by prominent actors between inner and outer contexts. Consideration had to be taken simultaneously of both the imported ideas and the defence of valued relationships and statuses. The observation that organizations adopt similar organizational forms may, prima facie, make one believe that the strategic actors in organizations are primarily embedded in institutionalized environments. Because they are not isolated from external institutional influences, this case clearly illustrates that managers sometimes create and re-create inner institutional contexts into which it is difficult to incorporate ideas brought in from the outside. The many years of interaction between managers and consultants at Elkem, and the actual solution arrived at, tell a lesson not primarily of the difficulties in intellectually understanding new ideas, but of the difficulties arising from the challenge of translating these new ideas in light of the possibilities and constraints inherent in the inner context. If new knowledge keeps what it promises, how can it be tested without destroying the fabric—the values, interaction patterns, statuses, norms, and the inherited experience and knowledge—of the inner context?

The case also makes us ask how new managerial knowledge can be pushed through the institutionalized power structure of organizations. While Elkem's first divisionalized structure and the development of this structure over the years to come did indeed have a unique historical imprint of previous patterns of interactions, there is no doubt that the company, which in the 1970s and 1980s experienced large growth, gradually adapted to the logic of the divisionalized form (cf. Gammelsæter 1991, 1994). Thus, the influence of rules and rationalities of the outer context was undoubted. It would be misguided, however, to suggest that the gradual absorption of the logic of the M-form took place because the president and the other well-established managers in the company were seeking a new identity or that they took the new knowledge for granted.

Rather, the explanation for the growing interaction between the company and the consultants—and the gradual accommodation to the new principles—must be directed towards the role of the much younger but still respected company secretary who was the driving-force behind the organizational renewal from the very beginning and stood for the maintenance of interaction with the consultants. Since the organizational issue was a neglected concern in the company, there is little doubt that this matter was entrusted to him by the president because he was the one who found interest in it and because its scope was not realized at the time. The company secretary, then, exploited and in the end expanded the room for innovative action in the inner context. His motivation was connected to the idea that further growth of the company necessitated more coordinated action at the business level. In this sense, it can be argued that he was seeking out a new identity for the company, and as president from 1980 (the first with a business economics background) he was in fact able to reshape Elkem along this path.

13.4. CONTEXT, ACTION, AND INTERACTION IN THE PROCESS OF ADOPTING BPR IN GLAMOX AS

Background

By 1995, when the project described in this chapter was launched, Glamox AS had witnessed half a decade of shrinking profit margins and even losses. That year the turnover of the company passed one billion NOK (approximately US $112 million) for the first time, and the corporation as a whole employed approximately 1,250 people. In 1992, following the take-over by a new president, the company was reorganized from a structure where the parent company—itself producing and selling utility lighting—was operating as the central headquarters in an expanding group of companies, to a structure in which sales and production units were separated into different companies under the ceiling of a joint corporate management, Glamox AS. This meant that the production and sales companies were now depicted as customers selling and purchasing products and services to and from each other. This was a radical break from the past, when transactions between the parent and the other companies were not systematically invoiced. Now, the previous mother organization was split into the production unit Glamox Fabrikker AS (GF), in which the BPR project was initiated, and the sales units Glamox International AS (GI) and Glamox Norway AS (GN). Consequently, GF was now dependent upon GI and GN to sell its products.

In GF there was a common understanding that one important reason for the poor results in the 1990s was the new organizational model and its assumption of an internal market. The problem was that negotiating inter-company prices (ICP) turned out to be an almost insurmountable problem. The reason was that although the companies were interdependent within the same value chain, they behaved as competitors in a market more than allies integrated within a corporation. Irrespective of the external markets, according to the new structure their results depended heavily on the prices that could be obtained between them. In GF, management and employees alike felt that their company unfairly became the loser in this competition. The terms of the competition were perceived to be biased, as was the treatment by the corporate management of the different units. For instance, they believed that their commitment to a TQM project initiated by the president in 1991 had been much higher than in the other companies. Since all the companies were part of the same value chain, collaboration between them was required to obtain coordinated gains. As this was absent, GF's efforts did not pay off sufficiently.

Needless to say, the inner context of Glamox AS was not characterized by the harmony and close friendship between managers so prominent in the Elkem case. On the contrary, as time went by different strategies emerged. For GF's management, efforts at improving production processes and productivity constituted the intelligible and manageable strategy. This marked a contrast to the diagnosis of other corporate managers, who advocated that, in order to save costs, the production of GF's tight industry (TI) lighting[4] be moved and integrated with the production of a recently acquired German subsidiary. The president, the first in the company who had been trained as a business economist rather than as an engineer, hesitated to do this, arguably because he was a local man who had been with the company for a long time and knew that the closing of a factory would be unpopular in the community. In his eyes, GF's management was too keen on running productivity projects that did not pay off. His priority was to cut down on the GF staff, as well as securing a more disciplined implementation of the corporate sales strategies. Since he had advocated that the companies in the group should be accountable for their own strategies and performance, he hesitated to force this strategy on GF, however.

The new organizational model was not the only plausible explanation for the rivalry over strategies. In addition, the background characteristics of the corporate management team diverged from that of GF's, where management had always been dominated by civil engineers and long tenures. In the corporate management team, five (excluding GF's only representative) out of seven had been trained as business economists, and on average tenures were much shorter than was the case in GF's management (15 years in 1997). In this respect the 1990s marked a distinct break with the past, a break that was also underlined by a more differentiated, growth-oriented strategy. The poor results, the quarrels over ICPs, and the diversity in strategies and backgrounds in the management team—all explain why the inner context of the company was quite unstable until the corporate management team was dissolved at the end of 1997.

The Tight Industry Project

BPR has been marketed with a language that leaves little doubt that power structures have to be changed if it is to be successfully applied and its fruits harvested (Hammer and Stanton 1999): 'Re-engineering is the fundamental rethinking and radical redesign of business processes to achieve dramatic improvements in critical, contemporary measures of performance, such as cost, quality, service and speed. More succinctly, it's "starting over"' (Hammer and Champy 1993: 50). In short, an organization's history must be discounted to release the real power of BPR, an idea that, albeit imprecise and unanimously presented, premises rapid and radical redesign of core processes, including the functional division of labour, in order to reduce costs and improve speed, quality, service, and products.

The TI project at GF was launched in the autumn of 1995 as a pilot project limited to tight industry-lighting. The main objective of what was termed a BPR project was to create 'a critical mass' of the organization who would learn and demonstrate by example that large-scale change was possible, despite the recent setbacks. The targets of the project were to reduce the physical production costs by 30 per cent through a comprehensive revision of products, to reduce the number of activities in the value chain by 50 per cent, and to supply products to customers in the Scandinavian capitals within

---

[4] This is utility lighting that has to be tight because it is used off-shore or in buildings where there is a danger of gas leakage.

four days of the receipt of orders. The assumption was that these aims could be realized by switching from a tailor-made to a matrix approach to orders, and to redesign layout and materials flow at the production site, the V-factory.

During two study trips to Toyota USA, GF's production manager—then a quality manager—was given the opportunity to 'benchmark' production philosophies and facilities in the two companies. In the first of these trips he was part of a Norwegian delegation. The consultant who later turned out to be important in the TI-project also showed up at the Toyota presentation. He was known by the production manager, who had attended some of his courses, and had previously been in contact with him. Now the manager sensed that the consultant understood the Toyota philosophy better than most of the delegates.

For some years GF had been quite committed to both a TQM process and a national productivity programme (TOPP). This exposed its management to many ideas, and its commitment can be taken as proof that it was keen that the company should learn and develop. Combined with some negative experiences with consultants, this possibly explained their hesitation to hire consultants to help them sort out the situation. Their approach was hands-on. Even though it was disappointing to both management and employees that the former change initiatives were not paying off,[5] the managers were dedicated to understanding for themselves what could improve the level of productivity. In this sense the management was searching for knowledge and not simply agents who promised a solution. The way the assignment with the consultant was eventually designed underscores the fact that turning to consultancy was neither a desperate nor an unreflective move.

In interviews the production manager found it difficult to recall precisely how the consultant was hired. He recalls that in early 1995 the consultant was having talks with managers in the company. After a while his presence and ideas were taken more seriously and the discussions became more directed towards changes that could be made. He was now given a small fee without having put forward any request. As such the relationship was formalized without being formally contracted. By the end of the assignment, the fee had increased considerably.

The TI project was organized as a hierarchy of sub-projects and teams. A four-man steering group, led by the production manager, also included the general managers of GF and GI (which purchased most of the TI products), the V-factory manager, and the consultant. Three teams reporting to the steering group were given responsibility for product revisions, activity reductions, and production layout respectively. At the V-factory, several sub-groups of operators were formed around topics pinpointed as a result of a weekend brain-storming meeting.

The organization of the project was designed by the consultant. 'What would have been typically us', says the production manager, 'was to organize the three sub-projects in a series, not trying to do them all at the same time'. The management of the groups and the steering of the overall project was taken care of by the management itself, however. The production manager was important in securing systematic work and progress,

---

[5] The author was able to witness this himself when taking part in an internal weekend seminar in February 1997, where the experiences of the 'improvement process' and follow-up activities were discussed.

and, according to his own account, in the steering of the consultant who might stray from his own ideas. It turns out, then, that the consultant, although he was the designer of the project organization, was by no means taken to be an excellent process consultant. His communication in speech was characterized as clumsy rather than clear, and he was considered too academic and not down to earth enough. This did not exactly reduce the opposition he faced, for example following a talk about eliminating activities that implied the possible reduction of jobs. It followed that the task of the production and team managers was very much that of understanding, translating, and explaining his ideas. Since his strength was his knowledge of production technologies, and his ability to observe and find data that validated or refined his observations, very much of the interaction with management was based on lengthy and noisy discussions about the meaning and relevance of his observations in GF and the ideas he suggested.

Obviously, it was the understanding that the consultant's knowledge was superior and possibly useful to GF, that made GF's management keep hold of him. In retrospect, the production manager claims that what turned out to be a successful project in many respects would not have been implemented without the presence of the consultant, simply because 'we did not have the knowledge and the insight'. The lack of initiative to engage a consultant at the outset, however, was explained on the basis that 'We did not know what to ask for'. Besides exposing lack of knowledge and control, this answer also shows that the management was not eager to resolve its insecurity and apprehension by leaving the problems to any consultant. The production manager in particular wanted to understand for himself how the production process could be re-engineered. The consultant's main function turned out to be that of explaining to GF's management how re-engineering techniques could be adopted and adapted in the company.

Nearly two years after its introduction the TI-project was officially closed. Apart from a 14-month delay when measured against initial plans, and a couple of smaller design and implementation problems, the project was judged to have been quite successful, and in the aftermath the production philosophy pervading the project spread to other product lines. Once management judged that they had acquired the necessary know-how, the consultant was asked to terminate his assignment. Internal managers subsequently took charge of smoothing the re-engineering process.

Nevertheless, one of the main problems in the project was to include the sales and marketing functions in GI, a problem stemming from the conflicts in the inner context of the corporation. Since GI did not collaborate, the work of the project teams was hampered, and for a substantial period of time it was possible to question whether the project would be carried through. In GI, the unit that was, after all, supposed to market and sell the revised products, there was no commitment to the project. In one GI manager's view, 'There was no market demand'. In fact, GI and its representative in the executive team worked against the project, favouring instead that TI-production should be moved to Germany.

Explaining the Fate of the Tight Industry Project

Despite the economic situation of Glamox and the fact that BPR in the 1990s can be conceived as one of several popular models characterizing the institutionalized environments of business organizations, it would obviously be inaccurate to describe its introduction in Glamox as a process marked by aggressive consultants and a united management that grabbed every opportunity to adopt 'good practice' and 'start over'. On the contrary, the inner context was impeded by conflict, and GF's management was hesitant to hire consultants, although it was both outwardly focused and eager to pick up new ideas. The consultant who was eventually hired was being screened because management did not understand or trust his philosophy. When finally hired, the knowledge of the consultant was obviously important for the changes to come, although not without being translated by GF's management in the course of endless discussions. The interactive nature of the process was further underlined by the way the project was organized and managed.

Whereas, on the one hand, the widespread influence of the TI-project depended on the renewal of the corporate management team, on the other, the project would probably have been abandoned if another coalition had won the battle. Since the project itself demanded a much tighter interface between production and sales companies than had been the case for several years, its success would be much more unlikely if the power structure of the inner context was not changed. It must be added that in GF the credibility of the consultant's philosophy was probably helped by the fact that he (as does the BPR philosophy) supported the contention held by GF's management that a collaborative rather than a competitive relationship was required between production and sales companies. Since the previous corporate management had failed to realize this, the influence of the outer context, in this case materialized by the consultant, depended on the weakening of the inner context and the subsequent management changes.

13.5. CONCLUSIONS

The two cases that have been presented here do not, of course, qualify as an extensive investigation of the interface between inner and outer contexts and all the possible patterns and processes of interaction and fertilization between them. As always, case-studies have their strengths but also their limitations, particularly their lack of statistical representativeness. Studies of other types of firms and public organizations would certainly yield more and additional insights. Despite the validity of these objections, the cases show that the embeddedness of organizational actors in the outer context is facilitated by their interaction with carriers such as consultants. The scope for acting on external ideas is, however, strongly circumscribed by values, norms, and patterns of communication and interaction characterizing the inner context. These define who is influencing organizational action and which ideas and solutions are legitimate. Accordingly, an institutional theory of how carriers of management knowledge influence practice in organizations has to account for the mechanisms that facilitate reciprocal fertilization of the two contexts.

At Elkem the incremental pattern of implementing divisionalization, despite the active involvement of consultants, must be understood in the context of the stability that characterized the management structure, interaction, and succession pattern. Clearly, this was not a climate in which management as a whole took the new management knowledge for granted. On the contrary, consultants and some internal entrepreneurs

had to negotiate arrangements that not only implied gradual changes but simultaneously preserved (or smoothed the gradual change of) the distribution of power and
statuses. At GF, management hesitated to assign a consultant, despite its performance
problems, and at the end of the day the influence of the consultant also depended on
the outcome of the conflicts that ravaged the corporate management team. Since the
new corporate management had less to defend and also shared the view that re-
engineering the value chain was demanded, the inner context of the TI-project
changed from being rather hostile to becoming much more benevolent. This change
was decisive for the influence of the consultant.

Both cases support the contention that power-holders are hesitant to make radical
changes in organizational structures that bear their own imprint, especially in the face of
institutional norms. At Glamox even the effort to stick the popular BPR term on to the TI-
project failed to attract the support of the corporate management, obviously because the
philosophy of the project necessitated a different approach to the handling of relationships within the value chain. In this sense, the influence of the consultants was contingent
on the position and power of the managers they interacted with in the company.

The concern for the preservation of power relations and privileges for those actors
who benefited most from the old structure, and how this might potentially conflict
with the interests of managers lower down the hierarchy, is evident in both cases. Both
support the contention that in organizations characterized by a certain stability in the
top management team, it is among younger or lower-level managers that the receptivity to externally institutionalized knowledge and the ambition for change in organizational identity is found.[6] This means that consultants may sometimes find themselves
interacting most intensely not with the dominant coalition but with groups of managers
who patiently try to exploit the (sometimes) restricted scope for action that is to be
found in the inner context. In this sense consultants are used in a power game between
groups of managers, and their influence therefore depends not merely on the advice
they convey or their pedagogical and rhetorical qualities, but also on the outcomes of
these games in the long run.

The cases are certainly different with respect to external contexts. In contrast to
Elkem, which was primarily constrained by its growth and diversification, Glamox was
going through a sustained performance crisis. Since this included the loss of home
market share, it could not be explained away as reflecting a general downturn in its
industry. Despite this, management met the situation neither by standing united, nor
by turning to the nearest or most renowned consultancy. Its reaction reflected the qualities of the inner context, shaped to a large extent by the introduction of the organizational structure that separated the production from the sales companies. The
consultant who was eventually assigned was seriously constrained by this context, just
as the consultants working at Elkem were constrained by theirs. Whereas the former
were helped by the disbanding of the management team, an event not unrelated to the
company's economic performance, the latter had to make changes piece by piece, since
the inner context changed only slowly. Thus, their different working conditions were

---

[6] Support for this argument is also found in other cases explored in Gammelsæter (1991, 1994).

shaped by the degree of stability in the inner context, which in its turn was influenced by characteristics of the external context, pertaining to the contrast found between Elkem and Glamox concerning the existence or absence of performance pressures.

As pointed out earlier, the neo-institutionalist school tends to depict organizational actors as primarily embedded in institutional environments. Driven by gusts of uncertainty or the chase for identity such actors are easy prey for carriers of managerial fads promising a successful future. The 'old' institutionalism, in contrast, tends to focus on mechanisms that promote institutionalization at the organization level. Organizational actors are obsessed with defending—not changing—their identity and institutions, including their power relations and privileges. According to these schools, organizations apparently seem to be either open to change or immutable. The idea of de-coupling (Meyer and Rowan 1977) inadequately resolves this contradiction, since consultants at times affect core activities, as shown in the case of Glamox, and power-holders at times do resist radical changes in managerial structures, as shown in both our cases.

Accordingly, we have suggested a more fine-grained institutional approach pointing to the necessity of taking into account the changing characteristics of inner and outer contexts of organizations, and the action and interaction that takes place at the interface between them (cf. Greenwood and Hinings 1996) by actors embedded primarily in the outer and inner contexts, respectively. This approach in fact corresponds quite well with the evolution–revolution pattern in studies of organizational change (i.e. Chandler 1962; Miller and Friesen 1980; Tushman and Romanelli 1985). Further studies on the diffusion of management knowledge and on the roles played and the influence exerted by carriers such as consultants, should therefore account for the way inner and outer contexts are linked through patterns of interaction and influence, yet how they are conceptually different and at times unable to exert a decisive influence on each other.

References

Abbott, A. (1988), *The System of Professions: An Essay on the Division of Expert Labor* (Chicago, Ill.: University of Chicago Press).

Abrahamson, E. (1991), 'Managerial Fads and Fashions: The Diffusion and Rejection of Innovations', *Academy of Management Review*, 18/3: 586–612.

—— (1996), 'Management Fashion', *Academy of Management Review*, 21/1: 254–85.

—— (1997), 'The Emergence and Prevalence of Employee Management Rhetorics: The Effects of Long Waves, Labor Unions, and Turnover, 1875 to 1992', *Academy of Management Journal*, 40: 491–533.

—— and Fairchild, G. (1999), 'Management Fashion: Lifecycles, Triggers, and Collective Learning Processes', *Administrative Science Quarterly*, 44: 708–40.

Adler, A. (1929), *The Science of Living* (New York: Greenberg).

Affärsvärldens konsultguide 1992 (1992) (Stockholm: Affärsvärlden).

Agostini, A. (1999), 'Una cultura statica', from www.aidp.it.

Ainamo, A. (1996), 'Industrial Design and Business Performance: A Case Study of Design Management in a Finnish Fashion Firm', *Acta Universitatis Oecanimicae Helsingiensis, Series A-112* (Helsinki: Helsinki School of Economics and Business Administration).

Aldrich, H. E. (1992), 'Incommensurable Paradigms? Vital Signs from Three Perspectives', in M. Reed and M. Hughes (eds.), *Rethinking Organization: New Directions in Organization Theory and Analysis* (London: Sage), 17–45.

Alexander, J. (1983), 'Inside the Management Hot Shop', *Australian Business*, 19 Oct., 42–8.

Allen, R. (1990), 'Big Six Take the Lead in Billion Dollar Market', *Business Review Weekly*, 20 July, 84–6.

Allen, S. A. (1978), 'Organizational Choices and General Management Influence Networks in Divisionalized Companies', *Academy of Management Journal*, 21/3: 341–65.

Alvarez, J. L. (1998), 'The Sociological Tradition and the Spread and Institutionalization of Knowledge for Action', in J. L. Alvarez (ed.), *The Diffusion and Consumption of Business Knowledge* (London: Macmillan), 13–57.

Alvesson, M. (1992), *Ledning av kunskapsföretag*, 2nd edn. (Stockholm: Nordstedts Juridik).

Amdam, R. P. (1998), 'Productivity and Management Education: The Nordic Connections', in G. Gemelli (ed.), *The Ford Foundation and Europe (1950's–1970's): Cross-fertilization of Learning in Social Science and Management* (Brussels: European Interuniversity Press), 373–90.

—— Kvålshaugen, R. and Larsen, E. (eds.) (2002), *Inside the Business School: The Content of European Business Education* (Oslo, Abstrakt Press, forthcoming).

Amorim, C. (1999), 'Catching-up? The Evolution of Management Consultancies in Portugal and Spain', in W. Feldenkirchen and T. Gourvish (eds.), *European Yearbook of Business History*, 2 (Aldershot: Ashgate), 179–211.

—— and Kipping, M. (1999), 'Selling Consultancy Services: The Portuguese Case in Historical and Comparative Perspective', *Business and Economic History*, 28/1: 45–56.

Andersson, R., Bergkvist, T., Bruzelius, L. H., Dahlman, C., and Åkesson, G. (1982), *Krävande företagsledning: När handboken inte räcker till* (Stockholm: Liber).

Anon (1969), 'The Subtle Preachers of Change at PA', *Industrial Management*, Aug., 28–33.

Anon (1990), 'Tasmanian Devil Hits Cresap in Australia', *Management Consultant International*, Nov., 4.

Ansoff, H. I. (1965), *Corporate Strategy* (New York: McGraw-Hill).

Arbeitskreis Organisation (1996), 'Organisation im Umbruch. (Was) kann man aus den bisherigen Erfahrungen lernen?', *Zeitschrift für betriebswirtschaftliche Forschung*, 48: 621–65.

Argyris, C. (2000), *Flawed Advice and the Management Trap* (New York: Oxford University Press).

—— and Schön, D. A. (1978), *Organizational Learning: A Theory of Action Perspective* (Reading, Mass.: Addison-Wesley).

Arias, M. E. and Guillén, M. (1998), 'The Transfer of Organizational Techniques Across Borders: Combining Neo-Institutional and Comparative Perspectives', in J. L. Alvarez (ed.), *The Diffusion and Consumption of Business Knowledge* (London: Macmillan), 110–37.

Armbrüster, T. (2000), 'Towards a Political Economy of Management Consulting: The Case for a Macro Approach', paper presented at the 16th EGOS (European Group for Organizational Studies) Colloquium, Helsinki, July.

—— and Schmolze, R. (1999), 'Milk Rounds, Case Studies, and the Aftermath: Recruitment Practices in Management Consulting and their Consequences', paper presented at the 2nd International Conference on Consultancy Work, King's College London, Feb.

Arnoldus, D. (2000), 'The Role of Consultancies in the Transformation of the Dutch Banking Sector, 1950s to 1990s', *Entreprises et Histoire*, 25: 65–81.

Ashford, M. (1998), *Con Tricks: The World of Management Consultancy and How to Make It Work for You* (London: Simon & Schuster).

Astley, W. G. and Zammuto, R. F. (1992), 'Organization Science, Managers, and Language Games', *Organization Science*, 3: 443–60.

Auclair, A. (1999), *Les ingénieurs et l'équipement de la France: Eugène Flachat (1802–1873)* (Le Creusot–Montceau-les-Mines: Ecomusée de la communauté urbaine).

Baalen, P. van and Karsten, L. (2000), 'Legitimizing academic management education: Diffusion and shaping of an organization field' paper presented at the CEMP workshop on The Content of Management Education in Europe, Paris, 5–6 May.

Bagwell, S. (1993), 'World Obliteration? We Prefer A Bit Of Slash And Burn', *Australian Financial Review*, 23 Nov., 1.

Baritz, L. (1960), *Servants of Power* (Middletown, Conn.: Wesleyan University Press).

Barley, S. R. and Kunda, G. (1992), 'Design and Devotion: Surges of Rational and Normative Ideologies of Control in Managerial Discourse', *Administrative Science Quarterly*, 37: 363–99.

—— Meyer, G. W., and Gash, D. C. (1988), 'Cultures of Culture: Academics, Practitioners and the Pragmatics of Normative Control', *Administrative Science Quarterly*, 33: 24–60.

Bartlett, C. A. (1997), *McKinsey & Company: Managing Knowledge and Learning*, Harvard Business School Case Study (Boston: Harvard Business School).

Baudrillard, J. (1981), 'The Ideological Genesis of Needs', in J. Baudrillard (ed.), *For a Critique of the Political Economy of the Sign* (St. Louis: Telos), 63–87.

BCA (Business Council of Australia) (1989), *Enterprise-Based Bargaining Units: A Better Way of Working*, Report to the BCA by the Industrial Relations Study Commission (Melbourne: BCA).

BDU (Bundesverband Deutscher Unternehmensberater) (1998), *Facts and Figures zum Beratermarkt 1998* (Bonn: BDU).

Beaune, J. C. (1985), 'L'ingénieur en question', in A. Thépot (ed.), *L'ingénieur dans la société française* (Paris: Les éditions ouvrières), 231–42.

Becker, H. S. (1974), 'Art as Collective Action', *American Sociological Review*, 39: 767–76.

—— (1982), *Art Worlds* (Berkeley: University of California Press).

Benders, J. and van Veen, K. (2001), 'What is in a Fashion: Interpretative Viability and Management Fashions', *Organization*, 8/1: 33–53.

—— van den Berg, R.-J., and van Bijsterveld, M. (1998), 'Hitch-hiking on a Hype: Dutch Consultants Engineering Re-engineering', *Journal of Organizational Change Management*, 11/3: 201–15.

Bengtsson, L. and Skärvad, P.-H. (1988), *Företagsstrategiska perspektiv* (Lund: Studentlitteratur).

Berger, P. L. and Luckmann, T. (1966), *The Social Construction of Reality: A Treatise in the Sociology of Knowledge* (Garden City, NY: Doubleday).

Berglund, J. and Werr, A. (2000), 'The Invincible Character of Management Consulting Rhetorics', *Organization*, 7/4: 633–55.

Bergsma, S. (1965), *De vermaatschappelijking van de onderneming* (Deventer: Kluwer).

Bertalanffy, L. von (1955), 'General Systems Theory', *General Systems*, 1: 1–10.

Bessant, J. and Rush, H. (1995), 'Building Bridges for Innovation: The Role of Consultants in Technology Transfer', *Research Policy*, 24: 97–114.

Blackler, F. (1993), 'Knowledge and the Theory of Organizations: Organizations as Activity Systems and the Reframing of Management', *Journal of Management Studies*, 30/4: 863–83.

Bloemen, E. S. A. (1988), *Scientific Management in Nederland: 1900–1970* (Amsterdam: Netherlands Economic History Archives).

—— (1990), 'Hard Work! Ideology and Interest in Dutch Economic Policy at Home and Abroad between 1945 and 1951', in Boomgaard, P. *et al.* (eds.), *Economic and Social History in the Netherlands* (Amsterdam: Netherlands Economic History Archives), Vol. 2, 135–48.

—— (1997), 'Geestelijke Marshall-hulp: De Productiviteitskwestie', in R. T. Griffiths (ed.), *Van strohalm tot strategie: het Marshallplan in perspectief* (Assen: Van Gorcum), 69–77.

Bloomfield, B. P. and Best, A. (1992), 'Management Consultants: Systems Development, Power and the Translation of Problems', *The Sociological Review*, 40/3: 533–60.

—— and Danieli, A. (1995), 'The Role of Management Consultants in the Development of Information Technology: The Indissoluble Nature of Socio-Political and Technical Skills', *Journal of Management Studies*, 32/1: 23–46.

Blumberg, P. (1974), 'The Decline and Fall of the Status Symbol: Some Thoughts on Status in a Post-Industrialist Society', *Social Problems*, 21: 480–98.

Blumer, H. (1969), 'Fashion: From Class Differentiation to Collective Selection', *Sociological Quarterly*, 10: 275–91.

Boer, E. J. (1990), '60 jaar NIPG', in E. J. Boer (ed.), *Prioriteiten in Preventie* (Delft: TNO).

Boland, R. J. (1987), 'The In-formation of Information Systems', in R. J. Boland and R. Hirschheim (eds.), *Critical Issues in Information Systems Research* (Chichester: Wiley), 363–79.

Boltanski, L. (1987), *The Making of a Class: Cadres in French Society* (Cambridge: Cambridge University Press).

Bourdieu, P. (1987), 'Espace social et pouvoir symbolique', in P. Bourdieu, *Choses dites* (Paris: Editions de Minuit), 147–66.

—— (1993a), *The Field of Cultural Production* (Cambridge: Polity Press).

—— (1993b), 'The Metamorphosis of Tastes', in P. Bourdieu (ed.), *Sociology in Question* (London: Sage), 108–16.

—— (1994), *Distinction: A Social Critique of the Judgement of Taste* (Cambridge, Mass.: Harvard University Press).

—— (1996), 'Esprits d'Etat: Genèse et structure du champ bureaucratique', in P. Bourdieu, *Raisons pratiques, sur la théorie de l'action* (Paris: Editions du Seuil), 177–213.

—— (1998), *State Nobility: Elite Schools in the Field of Power* (Stanford, Calif.: Stanford University Press).

Bournois, F. and Livian, Y.-F. (1997), 'Managers, "Cadres", "Leitende Angestellte": Some Landmarks about Managerial Group Titles and Definitions', in Y.-F. Livian and J. G. Burgoyne (eds.), *Middle Managers in Europe* (London: Routledge), 25–38.

Boyd, A. (1991), 'McKinsey Reports on AMP This Week', *Australian Financial Review*, 20 May, 18.

Boyd, T. (2000), 'Consultants Respond to E-World', *Australian Financial Review*, 7 July, 71.

Braggs, J. (1978), 'The Development of Management Consulting Services in the Profession', *The Chartered Accountant in Australia*, Apr., pp. 4–6.

Brock, D., Powell, M. and Hinings, C. R. (1999), *Restructuring the Professional Organization: Accounting, Health Care and Law* (London: Routledge).

Broekmeyer, M. J. (1968), *De arbeidsraad in Joegoslavië* (Meppel: Boom).

Brown, J. S. and Duguid, P. (1994), 'Organizational Learning and Communities-of-Practice: Toward a Unified View of Working, Learning and Innovation', in H. Tsoukas (ed.), *New Thinking in Organizational Behaviour* (Oxford: Butterworth-Heinemann), 165–87.

Brunsson, N. and Olsen, J. P. (1993), *The Reforming Organization* (London: Routledge).

Buckley, W. and Sandkull, B. (1969), *A Systems Study in Regional Inequality: Norrbotten, a Fourth of Sweden* (Stockholm: SIAR).

Burgelman, R. A. (1983), 'Corporate Entrepreneurship and Strategic Management: Insights from a Process Study', *Management Science*, 29/12: 1349–64.

Burrage, M. and Torstendahl, R. (eds.) (1990), *Professions in Theory and History: Rethinking the Study of the Professions* (London: Sage).

Byrkjeflot, H. (1998), 'Management as a System of Knowledge and Authority', in J. L. Alvarez (ed.), *The Diffusion and Consumption of Business Knowledge* (London: Macmillan), 58–80.

Byrne, J. A. and Williams, G. (1993), 'The Alumni Club to End all Alumni Clubs', *Business Week*, 20 Sept., 41.

Cailluet, L. (1995), 'Stratégies, structures d'organisation et pratiques de gestion de Pechiney des années 1880 à 1971', PhD thesis (University of Lyon II).

—— (2000), 'McKinsey, Total-CFP et la *M-form*: Un exemple français d'adaptation d'un modèle d'organisation importé', *Entreprises et Histoire*, 25: 26–45.

Carlson, S. (1951), *Executive Behavior: A Study of the Workload and the Working Methods of Managing Directors* (Stockholm: Strömbergs).

Carlsson, R. H. (2000), *Strategier för att tjäna pengar: Om affärsidén och andra SIAR-begrepp* (Stockholm: Ekerlids).

Carnegie, R. (2000), 'The Way It Was', *Australian Financial Review (Boss Magazine)*, July, 35–7.

Carson, P. P., Lanier, P., Carson, K. D., and Guidry, B. N. (2000), 'Clearing a Path through the Management Fashion Jungle: Some Preliminary Trailblazing', *Academy of Management Journal*, 43: 1143–58.

Champy, J. (1994a), 'Jeder fünfte fliegt: Interview mit James Champy', *manager magazin*, Apr., 196–8.

—— (1994b), 'Quantensprünge sind angesagt: Interview mit James Champy', *Top Business*, Nov., 86–94.

—— (1995), *Reengineering Management: The Mandate for Leadership* (New York: Harper Business).

Chandler, A. D., Jr. (1962), *Strategy and Structure: Chapters in the History of the Industrial Enterprise* (Cambridge, Mass.: MIT Press).

—— (1977), *The Visible Hand: The Managerial Revolution in American Business* (Cambridge, Mass.: Belknap Press).

—— (1990), *Scale and Scope: The Dynamics of Industrial Capitalism* (Cambridge, Mass.: Belknap Press).

Channon, D. F. (1973), *The Strategy and Structure of British Enterprise* (London: Macmillan).

Chard, M. (1997), *Knowledge Management at Ernst and Young* (Stanford: Graduate School of Business, Stanford University).

Charle, C. (1987*a*), 'Le pantouflage en France (vers 1880-vers 1980)', *Annales*, 5 (Sept.–Oct.), 1115–37.

——— (1987*b*), *Les élites de la République, 1880–1900* (Paris: Fayard).

Chesbrough, H. W. and Teece, D. J. (1996), 'When is Virtual Virtuous?—Organizing for Innovation', *Harvard Business Review*, 74 (Jan.–Feb.), 65–73.

Chinnici, A. (1999), 'Knowledge Management?', from www.aidp.it.

Church, R. A. (1969), *Kenricks in Hardware: A Family Business: 1791–1966* (Newton Abbot: David & Charles).

Churchman, C. W. (1971), *The Design of Inquiring Systems: Basic Concepts of Systems and Organizations* (New York: Basic Books).

Clark, T. (1995), *Managing Consultants: Consultancy as the Management of Impressions* (Buckingham: Open University Press).

——— and Fincham, R. (eds.) (2002), *Critical Consulting: New Perspectives on the Management Advice Industry* (Oxford: Blackwell).

——— and Salaman, G. (1996*a*), 'Telling Tales: Management Consultancy as the Art of Story Telling', in D. Grant and C. Oswick (eds.), *Metaphor and Organizations* (London: Sage), 167–84.

——— ——— (1996*b*), 'The Management Guru as Organizational Witchdoctor', *Organization*, 3: 85–107.

——— ——— (1998), 'Telling Tales: Management Gurus' Narratives and the Construction of Managerial Identity', *Journal of Management Studies*, 35/2: 137–61.

Collins, R. (1979), *The Credential Society* (New York: Academic Press).

Couturaud, P. (1913/1914), 'Le congrès des ingénieurs-conseils à Gand', *La construction moderne*, Oct. and Nov. 1913 and Dec. 1914.

Crainer, S. (1997), *The Tom Peters Phenomenon: Corporate Man to Corporate Skunk* (Oxford: Capstone).

——— (1998), 'In Search of the Real Author', *Management Today*, May, 50–4.

——— and Dearlove, D. (1999), *Gravy Training: Inside the Business of Business Schools* (San Francisco, Calif.: Jossey-Bass).

Crozier, M. and Friedberg, E. (1980), *Actors and Systems: The Politics of Collective Action* (Chicago: University of Chicago Press).

Crucini, C. and Kipping, M. (2001), 'Management Consultancies as Global Change Agents? Evidence from Italy', *Journal of Organizational Change Management*, 14/6: 570–89.

Cyert, R. M. and March, J. G. (1963), *A Behavioral Theory of the Firm* (Englewood Cliffs, NJ: Prentice Hall).

Czarniawska, B. and Joerges, B. (1996), 'Travel of Ideas', in B. Czarniawska and G. Sevón (eds.), *Translating Organizational Change* (Berlin: de Gruyter), 13–48.

——— and Sevón, G. (eds.) (1996), *Translating Organizational Change* (Berlin: de Gruyter).

Danborg, T. *et al.* (1975), *Region i kris. Samhällsorganisatorisk diagnos av sydöstra Skånes växtproblem* (Lund: Studentlitteratur).

Daniels, M. J. M. (1958), *Onaangepastheid in de werksituatie*, Doctoral Dissertation (Nijmegen: Dekker and v.d. Vegt).

Davenport, T. H., (1994), 'Saving IT's Soul: Human-Centered Information Management', *Harvard Business Review*, Mar.–Apr., 119–31.

——— and Prusak, L. (1998), *Working Knowledge: How Organizations Manage What They Know* (Boston, Mass.: Harvard Business School Press).

Davidow, W. H. and Malone, M. S. (1992), *The Virtual Organization* (New York: Harper-Collins).

Davis, F. (1985), 'Clothing and Fashion as Communication', in M. R. Solomon (ed.), *The Psychology of Fashion* (Lexington, Mass.: Lexington Books), 15–27.

—— (1988), 'Clothing, Fashion, and the Dialectic of Identity', in D. R. Maines and C. J. Couch (eds.), *Communication and Social Structure* (Springfield, Ill.: C. C. Thomas), 23–38.

—— (1989), 'Of Maids' Uniforms and Blue Jeans: The Drama of Status Ambivalences in Clothing and Fashion', *Qualitative Sociology*, 12: 337–55.

—— (1992), *Fashion, Culture, and Identity* (Chicago: University of Chicago Press).

Davis, G. F., Diekmann, K. A., and Tinsley, C. H. (1994), 'The Decline and Fall of the Conglomerate Firm in the 1980s: The Deinstitutionalization of an Organizational Form', *American Sociological Review*, 59: 547–70.

Davis, M. S. (1986), ' "That's Classic!" The Phenomenology and Rhetoric of Successful Social Theories', *Philosophy of the Social Sciences*, 16: 285–301.

deCharms, R. (1968), *Personal Causation* (New York: Academic Press).

Denton, P. (1986), 'The Making of John Elliott', *Business Review Weekly*, 17 Oct., 54–69.

Deutschmann, C. (1993), 'Unternehmensberater—eine neue "Reflexionselite"?', in W. Müller-Jentsch (ed.), *Profitable Ethik—effiziente Kultur: neue Sinnstiftung durch das Management?* (Munich: Hampp), 57–82.

Dezalay, Y. (1993), 'Professional Competition and the Social Construction of Transnational Regulatory Expertise', in J. McCahery, S. Picciotto, and C. Scott (eds.), *Corporate Control and Accountability: Changing Structures and the Dynamics of Regulation* (Oxford: Clarendon), 203–15.

DiMaggio, P. J. (1988), 'Interest and Agency in Institutional Theory', in L. G. Zucker (ed.), *Institutional Patterns and Organizations: Culture and Environments* (Cambridge, Mass.: Ballinger).

—— (1991), 'Constructing an Organizational Field as a Professional Project: U.S. Art Museums 1920–1940', in W. W. Powell and P. J. DiMaggio (eds.), *The New Institutionalism in Organizational Analysis* (Chicago: University of Chicago Press), 267–92.

—— and Powell, W. W. (1983), 'The Iron Cage Revisited: Institutional Isomorphism and Collective Rationality in Organizational Fields', *American Sociological Review*, 48: 147–60; reprinted in W. W. Powell and P. J. DiMaggio (eds.), *The New Institutionalism in Organizational Analysis* (Chicago: University of Chicago Press), 63–82.

Dixon, R. and Domberger, S. (1995), 'The Review of Administration at the University of Sydney: A Case Study', *Journal of Tertiary Education Administration*, 17/2: 117–34.

Djelic, M.-L. (1998), *Exporting the American Model* (Oxford: Oxford University Press).

—— and Ainamo, A. (1999), 'The Coevolution of New Organization Forms in the Fashion Industry: A Historical and Comparative Study of France, Italy and the United States', *Organization Science*, 10: 622–37.

Dowd, T. J. and Dobbin F. (1997), 'The Embedded Actor and the Invention of Natural Economic Law: Policy Change and Railroader Response in Early America', *American Behavioral Scientist*, 40/4: 478–89.

Downey, H. K. and Brief, A. P. (1986), 'How Cognitive Structures Affect Organization Design', in H. P. Sims Jr., D. A. Gioia, and Associates (eds.), *The Thinking Organization: Dynamics of Organizational Social Cognition* (San Francisco: Jossey-Bass), 165–90.

Downs, L. L. (1990), 'Industrial Decline, Rationalisation and Equal Pay: The Bedaux Strike at Rover Automobile Company', *Social History*, 15/1: 45–73.

Drucker, P. F. (1959), *Käytännön liikkeenjohto* (The Practice of Management) (Helsinki: Tammi).

—— (1993), *Post-capitalist Society* (Oxford: Butterworth-Heinemann).

Dubar, C. and Tripier, P. (1998), *Sociologie des professions* (Paris: Armand Colin).

Du Gay, P. (1996), 'Making up Managers: Enterprise and Ethos and Bureaucracy', in S. Clegg and G. Palmer (eds.), *The Politics of Management Knowledge* (London: Sage), 19–35.

Dyas, G. P. and Thanheiser, H. T. (1976), *The Emerging European Enterprise: Strategy and Structure in French and German Industry* (London: Macmillan).

Dyerson, R. and Mueller, F. (1999), 'Learning, Teamwork and Appropriability: Managing Technological Change in the Department of Social Security', *Journal of Management Studies*, 36/5, 629–52.

Edgren, J., Skärrad, P.-H., and Rhenman, E. (1983), *Divisionalisering och därefter: Erfarenheter av decentralisering i sju svenska företag* (Stockholm: Management Media).

Edvinsson, L. and Malone, M. S. (1997), *Intellectual Capital: Realizing Your Company's True Value by Finding Its Hidden Brainpower* (New York: HarperCollins).

Egolf, J. R. (1985), 'The Limits of Shop Floor Struggle: Workers vs. the Bedaux System at Willapa Harbor Lumber Mills, 1933–35', *Labour History*, 2/2: 195–229.

Elkjær, B., Flensburg, P., Mouritsen, J., and Willmot, H. (1991), 'The Commodification of Expertise: The Case of System Development Consulting', *Accounting, Management and Information Technology*, 1: 139–56.

Elteren, M. Van (1992), 'Psychology and Sociology of Work within the Anglo-American Orbit', in H. Loeber (ed.), *Dutch-American Relations 1945–1969* (Assen: Van Gorcum), 153–78.

Eng, P. van der (1987), *De Marshall Hulp* (Houten: De Haan/Unieboek).

Engwall, L. (1985), *Från vag vision till komplex organisation*, Acta Universitatis Upsaliensis Studia Oeconomiae Negotiorum, 22 (Uppsala: Almqvist & Wiksell).

—— (1986), 'Newspaper Adaptation to a Changing Social Environment: A Case Study of Organizational Drift as a Response to Resource Dependence', *European Journal of Communication*, 1: 327–41.

—— (1992), *Mercury Meets Minerva* (Oxford: Pergamon).

—— (1999), *The Carriers of European Management Ideas*, The Creation of European Management Practice (CEMP) Report 7 (Uppsala: Uppsala University).

—— and Eriksson, C. (1999), 'Advising Corporate Superstars: CEOs and Consultancies in Top Swedish Corporations', paper presented at the 15th EGOS Colloquium, Warwick University, 4–6 July.

—— and Zamagni, V. (eds.) (1998), *Management Education in Historical Perspective* (Manchester: Manchester University Press).

Eriksson, C. and Lindvall, J. (1999), 'Haute Couture or Prêt-à-porter?', paper presented at the SCANCOR conference on the Carriers of Management Knowledge, Stanford University, Sept.

Ernst, B. and Kieser, A. (2002), 'In Search of Explanations for the Consulting Explosion', in K. Sahlin-Andersson and L. Engwall (eds.), *The Expansion of Management Knowledge: Carriers, Ideas, and Sources* (Stanford: Stanford University Press), forthcoming.

Faurschou, G. (1987), 'Fashion and the Cultural Logic of Postmodernity', in A. Kroker and M. Kroker (eds.), *Body Invaders: Panic Sex in America* (New York: St. Martin's Press), 78–93.

Faust, M. (1998), 'Die Selbstverständlichkeit der Unternehmensberatung', in J. Howaldt and R. Kopp (eds.), *Sozialwissenschaftliche Organisationsberatung: Auf der Suche nach einem spezifischen Beratungsverständnis* (Berlin: sigma), 147–81.

—— (2000), 'Warum boomt die Managementberatung? Und warum nicht zu allen Zeiten und überall?', *SOFI-Mitteilungen*, 28: 59–85; repr. in R. Schmidt, H. Gergs, and M. Pohlmann (eds.), *Managementsoziologie: Theorien, Forschungsperspektiven, Desiderate* (Munich: Hampp) forthcoming.

—— Jauch, P., and Notz, P. (2000), *Befreit und entwurzelt: Führungskräfte auf dem Weg zum 'internen Unternehmer'* (Munich: Hampp).

—— Jauch, P., Brünnecke, K. and Deutschmann, C. (1999), *Dezentralisierung von Unternehmen. Bürokratie- und Hierarchieabbau und die Rolle betrieblicher Arbeitspolitik,* 3rd edn. (Munich: Hampp).

Fellman, S. (2000), 'Uppkomsten av en direktörsprofession: industriledarnas utbildning och kärriär i Finland 1900–1975', PhD thesis (Helsinki: Finska vetenskaps-societeten).

Ferguson, M. (1999), The Origin, Gestation, and Evolution of Management Consultancy within Britain (1869–1965)', PhD thesis (Buckingham: Open University).

Fincham, R. (1995), 'Business Process Reengineering and the Commodification of Managerial Knowledge', *Journal of Marketing Management,* 11/7: 707–19.

—— (1999), 'The Consultant–Client Relationship: Critical Perspectives on the Management of Organizational Change', *Journal of Management Studies,* 36/3: 331–51.

—— and Clark, T. (2002), 'Introduction: The Emergence of Critical Perspectives on Consulting', in T. Clark and R. Fincham (eds.), *Critical Consulting* (Oxford: Blackwell), 1–18.

—— and Evans, M. (1999), 'The Consultants' Offensive: Reengineering—from Fad to Technique', *New Technology and Employment,* 14: 32–44.

Fitzgerald, B. (1998), 'An Empirical Investigation into the Adoption of Systems Development Methodologies', *Information and Management,* 34: 317–28.

Fligstein, N. (1990), *The Transformation of Corporate Control* (Cambridge, Mass.: Harvard University Press).

—— (1997), *Markets, Politics and Globalization* (Uppsala: Uppsala University Press).

Ford, J. D. and Baucus, D. A. (1987), 'Organizational Adaptation to Performance Downturns: An Interpretation-based Perspective', *Academy of Management Review,* 12/2: 366–80.

Fox, C. (1998), 'Deloitte Goes in Hard Against its Main Rivals', *Australian Financial Review,* 28 July, 32.

Frank, R. H. and Cook, P. J. (1995), *The Winner-Take-All Society* (New York: Free Press).

Fridenson, P. (1994), 'La circulation internationale des modes manageriales', in J.-P. Bouilloud and B.-P. Lecuyer (eds.), *L'invention de la gestion: Histoire et pratiques* (Paris: L'Harmattan), 81–9.

Fristedt, D. (1995), 'Metoder i användning: mot förbättring av systemutveckling genom situationell metodkunskap och metodanalys', Licentiate thesis (Institutionen för Datavetenskap, Linköpings University).

Furman, B. and Soylu, Ö. (1999), 'Consulting Firms: Their Role in the Production and Diffusion of Management Knowledge in Turkey', paper presented at the 15th EGOS Colloquium, Warwick University, 4–6 July.

Furness, M. (1992), 'McKinsey Threatens Westpac Workforce', *The Australian,* 23 Sept., 33.

Furnham, A. (1996), 'In Search of Suckers', *Fortune,* 14 Oct., 79–85.

Furusten, S. (1995), *The Managerial Discourse: A Study of the Creation and Diffusion of Popular Management Knowledge* (Uppsala: Uppsala University, Department of Business Studies).

—— (1998), 'The Creation of Popular Management Texts', in J. L. Alvarez (ed.), *The Diffusion and Consumption of Business Knowledge* (London: Macmillan), 141–63.

—— (1999), *Popular Management Books: How They are Made and What they Mean for Organisations* (London: Routledge).

—— and Bäcklund, J. (2000), 'Koncentration och differentiering på marknaden för managementkonsultation i Sverige', *Nordiske Organisasjonsstudier,* 2/1: 61–83.

—— and Kinch, N. (1993), 'Hur formas den skandinaviska ledarstilen?', Working Paper 1993/7 (Uppsala: Department of Business Studies, Uppsala University).

Galaskiewicz, J. (1991), 'Making Corporate Actors Accountable: Institution-Building in Minneapolis-St Paul', in W. W. Powell and P. J. DiMaggio (eds.), *The New Institutionalism in Organizational Analysis* (Chicago, Ill.: The University of Chicago Press), 293–310.

Galbraith, J. (1973), *Designing Complex Organizations* (Reading, Mass.: Addison-Wesley).

—— (1977), *Organization Design: An Information Processing View* (Reading, Mass.: Addison-Wesley).

Gammelsæter, H. (1991), 'Organisasjonsendring gjennom generasjoner av ledere: En studie av endringer i Hafslund Nycomed, Elkem og Norsk Hydro', Rapport 9114 (Molde: Møreforsking).

—— (1994), 'Divisionalization: Structure or Process?', *Scandinavian Journal of Management*, 10: 331–46.

—— (1999), 'Consulting at the Back of Beyond', paper presented at the 15th EGOS Colloquium, University of Warwick, 4–6 July.

Gerlach, N. (1996), 'The Business Restructuring Genre: Some Questions for Critical Organization Analysis', *Organization*, 3: 425–53.

Gerschenkron, A. (1962), *Economic Backwardness in Historical Perspective* (Cambridge, Mass.: Harvard University Press); repr. in M. Granovetter and R. Swedberg (eds.), *The Sociology of Economic Life* (Boulder, Colo.: Westview Press), 111–30.

Gersick C. J. G. (1991), 'Revolutionary Change Theories: A Multilevel Exploration of the Punctuated Equilibrium Paradigm', *Academy of Management Review*, 16/1: 10–36.

Gill, J. and Whittle, S. (1992), 'Management By Panacea: Accounting For Transience', *Journal of Management Studies*, 30/2: 281–95.

Ginneken, P. J. Van (1994), *Een menselijk instituut: Geschiedenis van GITP 1947–1973* (Nijmegen: GITP).

Glaser, B. and Strauss, A. (1967), *The Discovery of Grounded Theory* (Chicago: Aldine).

Glückler, J. and Armbrüster, T. (2001), 'Competing for Networked Reputation: The Mechanisms of the Management Consulting Market', paper presented at the 17th EGOS Colloquium, Lyon, 5–7 July.

Goddijn H. P. M., Thoenes, P., De Valk, J. J. M., and Verhoogt, J. P. (1977), *Geschiedenis van de sociologie* (Amsterdam: Boom).

Golembiewski, R. T. (ed.) (1993), *Handbook of Organizational Consultation* (New York: Marcel Dekker).

Göranzon, B. (1988), 'The Practice and the Use of Computers: A Paradoxical Encounter between Different Traditions of Knowledge', in B. Göranzon and I. Josefson (eds.), *Knowledge, Skill and Artificial Intelligence* (Berlin: Springer), 9–18.

Gosselink F. J. (1988), *Ontwikkelingen in de Organisatiekunde* (Rotterdam: Universiteits Drukkerij).

Granovetter, M. S. (1973), 'The Strength of Weak Ties', *American Journal of Sociology*, 78: 1360–80.

Grant, R. M. (1996), 'Toward a Knowledge-based Theory of the Firm', *Strategic Management Journal*, 17: 109–22.

Greenwood, R. and Hinings, C. R. (1988), 'Organizational Design Types, Tracks and the Dynamics of Strategic Change', *Organization Studies*, 9: 293–316.

—— —— (1996), 'Understanding Radical Organizational Change: Bringing Together the Old and the New Institutionalism', *Academy of Management Review*, 21/4: 1022–54.

Greiner, L. E. and Metzger, R. O. (1983), *Consulting to Management* (Englewood Cliffs, NJ: Prentice Hall).

Grelon, A. (1986), 'L'évolution de la profession d'ingénieur en France dans les années 1930', in A. Grelon (ed.), *Les ingénieurs de la crise: Titre et profession entre les deux guerres* (Paris: Editions de l'EHESS), 7–32.

Grint, K. (1994), 'Reengineering History: Social Resonances and Business Process Reengineering', *Organization*, 1: 179–201.

Grönroos, K. (1990), *Service Management and Marketing* (Lexington, Mass.: Lexington Books).

Guest, D. (1990), 'Human Resource Management and the American Dream', *Journal of Management Studies*, 27: 377–97.

Guillén, M. F. (1994), *Models of Management: Work, Authority, and Organization in a Comparative Perspective* (Chicago: University of Chicago Press).

Gummesson, E. (1991), *Qualitative Methods in Management Research* (London: Sage).

Haan, H. De (1992), 'The Impact of the United States on the Dutch Economy', in H. Loeber (ed.), *Dutch-American Relations 1945–1969* (Assen: Van Gorcum), 58–75.

Haas, E. (1995), *Op de juiste plaats: de opkomst van de bedrijfs- en schoolpsychologische beroep-spraktijk in Nederland* (Hilversum: Verloren).

Hagedorn, H. J. (1955), 'The Management Consultant as Transmitter of Business Techniques', *Explorations in Entrepreneurial History* (Feb.), 164–73.

Håkansson, H. (1987), *Industrial Technological Development: An Interaction Approach* (London: Croom Helm).

—— (1989), *Corporate Technological Behaviour* (London: Croom Helm).

Halal, W. E. (ed.) (1998), *The Infinite Resource: Creating and Leading the Knowledge Enterprise* (San Francisco: Jossey-Bass).

Haller, M. (1994), 'Recherche und Nachrichtenproduktion als Konstruktionsprozesse', in K. Merten, S. J. Schmidt, and S. Weischenberg (eds.), *Die Wirklichkeit der Medien* (Opladen: Westdeutscher Verlag), 277–90.

Ham, P. (1983), 'The Big Nine Muscle Their Way Into Consulting', *Rydges*, Dec., 74–6.

Hammer, M. and Champy, J. (1993), *Reengineering the Corporation: A Manifesto for Business Revolution* (New York: Harper).

—— and Stanton, S. A. (1999), 'How Process Enterprises Really Work', *Harvard Business Review*, 77/6: 108–18.

Hannan, M. T. and Carroll, G. R. (1992), *Dynamics of Organizational Populations: Density, Competition and Legitimation* (New York: Oxford University Press).

Hansen, M. T., Nohria, N., and Tierney, T. (1999), 'What's your Strategy for Managing Knowledge?', *Harvard Business Review*, Mar.–Apr., 106–16.

Hargadon, A. B. (1998), 'Firms as Knowledge Brokers: Lessons in Pursuing Continuous Innovation', *California Management Review*, 40/3: 209–27.

Hasek, G. (1997), 'The Era of Experts', *Industry Week*, 246 (Oct.), 60–7.

Havelock, R. G. (1969), *Planning for Innovation: A Comparative Study of the Literature on the Dissemination and Utilization of Scientific Knowledge* (Ann Arbor, Mich.: Center for Research on Utilization of Scientific Knowledge, University of Michigan).

HBR (1997), 'When Consultants and Clients Clash', HBR Case Study, *Harvard Business Review*, Nov.–Dec., 22–38.

Hedlund, G. (1994), 'A Model of Knowledge Management and the N-Form Corporation', *Strategic Management Journal*, 15: 73–90.

Hegele, C. and Kieser, A. (2001), 'Control the Construction of Your Legend or Someone Else Will: An Analysis of Texts on Jack Welch', *Journal of Management Inquiry*, 10: 298–309.

Hellema, P. and Marsman, J. (1997), *De organisatie-adviseur: Opkomst en groei van een nieuw vak in Nederland 1920–1960* (Amsterdam: Boom).

Helmich, D. L. and Brown W. B. (1972), 'Successor Type and Organizational Change in the Corporate Enterprise', *Administrative Science Quarterly*, 17: 371–81.

Henry, O. (1992), 'Entre savoir et pouvoir, les professionnels de l'expertise et du conseil', *Actes de la recherche en sciences sociales*, 95 (Dec.), 37–54.

—— (1993), 'Un savoir en pratique: Les professionnels de l'expertise et du conseil', PhD thesis. (Paris: EHESS).

Henry, O. (1994), 'Le conseil, un espace professionnel autonome?', *Entreprises et Histoire*, 7: 37–58.

—— (1997), 'La construction d'un monde à part: Processus de socialisation dans les grands cabinets de conseil', *Politix*, 39: 155–77.

—— (2000), 'Henry Le Chatelier et le taylorisme', *Actes de la recherche en sciences sociales*, 133 (June), 79–88.

—— and Sauviat, C. (1993), *Les cadres de l'expertise et du conseil—identités et trajectoires professionelles*, unpublished report for the French Research Ministry (Paris: Institut de Recherches Économique et Sociale).

Hentilä, S. (1998), 'Living Next Door to the Bear: How Did Finland Survive the Cold War?', *Historiallinen aikakauskirja/Historical Journal*, 96: 129–36.

Hersey, P. and Blanchard, K. H. (1977), *Management of Organizational Behavior: Utilizing Human Resources*, 3rd edn. (Englewood Cliffs, NJ: Prenctice Hall).

Heusinkveld, S., Benders, J., and Koch, C. (2000), 'Dispersed Discourse? Defining the Shape of BPR in Denmark and The Netherlands', paper presented at the 16th EGOS Colloquium, Helsinki, 2–4 July.

Hewett, J. (1988), 'The Company Doctors', *Financial Review*, 26 Aug., 2–3.

Higdon, H. (1969), *The Business Healers* (New York: Random House).

Hilger, S. (2000), 'American Consultants in the German Consumer Chemical Industry: The Stanford Research Institute at Henkel in the 1960s and 1970s', *Entreprises et Histoire*, 25: 46–64.

Hilmer, F. (1985), *When the Luck Runs Out: The Future for Australians at Work* (Sydney: Harper & Row).

Hippel, E. von (1988), *The Sources of Innovation* (New York: Oxford University Press).

Hirsch, P. M. (1972), 'Processing Fads and Fashion: An Organization-Set Analysis of Cultural Industry Systems', *American Journal of Sociology*, 77: 639–59.

—— and Lounsbury M. (1997), 'Ending the Family Quarrel: Towards a Reconciliation of "Old" and "New" Institutionalisms', *American Behavioral Scientist*, 40/4: 406–18.

Hobsbawm, E. (1994), *Age of Extremes: The Short Twentieth Century, 1914–1991* (London: Michael Joseph).

Hollingsworth, J. R. (1997a), 'The Institutional Embeddedness of American Capitalism', in C. Crouch and W. Streeck (eds.), *Political Economy of Modern Capitalism: Mapping Convergence and Diversity* (London: Sage), 133–47.

—— (1997b), 'Continuities and Changes in Social Systems of Production: The Cases of Japan, Germany, and the United States', in J. R. Hollingsworth and R. Boyer (eds.), *Contemporary Capitalism: The Embeddedness of Institutions* (Cambridge: Cambridge University Press), 263–310.

Holmes, A. R. and Green, E. (1986), *Midland: 150 Years of Banking Business* (London: Batsford).

Huczynski, A. A. (1993a), *Management Gurus: What Makes them and How to Become one* (London: Routledge).

—— (1993b), 'Explaining the Succession of Management Fads', *International Journal of Human Resource Management*, 4/2: 443–63.

Hutte, H. A. (1966), *Sociatrie van de arbeid* (Assen: Van Gorcum).

IfS, INIFES, ISF, SOFI (eds.) (1997), *Jahrbuch '96 Sozialwissenschaftliche Technikberichterstattung: Schwerpunkt Reorganisation* (Berlin: sigma).

IJzerman, T. J. (1959), 'Beroepsaanzien en arbeidsvoldoening', PhD thesis (Leiden: Stenfert Kroese).

Imai, K., Nonaka, I., and Takeuchi, H. (1985), 'Managing the New Product Development Process: How Japanese Companies Learn and Unlearn', in K. Clark, R. Hayes, and C. Lorenz (eds.),

The Uneasy Alliance: Managing the Productivity-Technology Dilemma (Boston, Mass.: Harvard Business School Press), 337–76.

Inklaar, F. (1997), *Van Amerika geleerd* (The Hague: SDU Uitgevers).

Iterson, A. van and Olie, R. (1992), 'European Business Systems: The Dutch case', in R. Whitley (ed.), *European Business Systems* (London: Sage), 98–116.

Jackall, R. (1988), *Moral Mazes: The World of Corporate Managers* (New York: Oxford University Press).

Jackson, B. G. (1996), 'Re-engineering the Sense of Self: The Manager and the Management Guru', *Journal of Management Studies*, 33/5: 571–90.

—— (1999), 'The Goose that Laid the Golden Egg?: A Rhetorical Critique of Stephen Covey and the Effectiveness Movement', *Journal of Management Studies*, 36: 354–77.

Jacques, E. (1951), *The Changing Culture of the Factory* (London: Routledge and Kegan Paul).

Jaffe, D. T. and Scott, C. D. (1998), 'Reengineering in Practice: Where are the People? Where is the Learning?', *Applied Journal of Behavioral Science*, 34/3: 250–67.

Jameson, J. (1987), 'The Value of An Outside Opinion', *Rydges*, July, 99–102.

Jarrar, Y. F. and Aspinwall, E. M. (1999), 'Business Process Re-engineering: Learning from Organizational Experiences', *Total Quality Management*, 10/2: 173–86.

Josefson, I. (1988), 'The Nurse as Engineer: The Theory of Knowledge in Research in the Care Sector', in B. Göranzon and I. Josefson (eds.), *Knowledge, Skill and Artificial Intelligence* (Berlin: Springer), 19–30.

Kaas, K.-P. and Schade, C. (1995), 'Unternehmensberater im Wettbewerb: Eine empirische Untersuchung aus der Perspektive der Neuen Institutionslehre', *Zeitschrift für Betriebswirtschaft*, 65: 1067–89.

Kaiser, S. B., Nagasawa, R. H., and Hutton, S. S. (1991), 'Fashion, Postmodernity and Personal Appearance: A Symbolic Interactionist Formulation', *Symbolic Interaction*, 14/2: 165–85.

Kant, I. (1980), *Anthropologie in pragmatischer Hinsicht*, 7th edn.; first published in 1798. (Hamburg: Meiner).

Kanter, R. M. (1982), 'The Middle Manager as Innovator', *Harvard Business Review*, July–Aug., 95–105.

—— (1984), *The Change Masters: Innovation and Entrepreneurship in the American Corporation* (New York: Simon & Schuster).

Kaplan, R. and Norton, D. P. (1996), *The Balanced Scorecard: Translating Strategy into Action* (Boston, Mass.: Harvard Business School Press).

Karsten, L. (2000), 'De Nederlandse Organisatieadviesbranche in Internationaal Perspectief', *M&O*, 5–6 (Sept.–Dec.), 130–59.

—— and van Veen, K. (1998), *Managementconcepten in beweging: tussen feit en vluchtigheid* (Assen: Van Gorcum).

—— and van Veen, K. (2000), 'De rol van de Nederlandse overheid bij de verspreiding van managementkennis; van voortrekker naar afnemer', *NEHA Jaarboek voor economische bedrijfs- en techniekgeschiedenis*, 63: 365–96.

Katz, R. (1980), 'Time and Work', *Research in Organizational Behavior*, 2: 81–127.

—— (1982), 'The Effects of Group Longevity on Project Communication and Performance', *Administrative Science Quarterly*, 27: 81–104.

Kennedy Information (1998), 'IT Consulting Busts Out (Again!) With Record '97 Revenues', *Consultants News*, 28/8: 4–5.

Kettunen, P. (1994), *Suojelu, suoritus, subjekti: työsuojelu teollistuvan Suomen yhteiskunnallisissa ajattelu- ja toimintatavoissa* (Safety, Performance and the Subject: Occupational Safety in the

Societal Thought and Action Patterns of Industrializing Finland) (Helsinki: Suomen histori-allinen seura).

Kieser, A. (1997), 'Rhetoric and Myth in Management Fashion', *Organization*, 4: 49–74.

—— (1998a), 'Unternehmensberater—Händler in Problemen, Praktiken und Sinn', in H. Glaser, E. F. Schröder, and A. von Werder (eds.), *Organisation im Wandel der Märkte* (Wiesbaden: Gabler), 191–226.

—— (1998b), 'How Management Science, Consultancies and Business Companies (Do Not) Learn from Each Other: Applying Concepts of Learning to Different Types of Organizations and Interorganizational Learning', paper no. 98-20, *Sonderforschungsbereich*, 504: *Rationalitätskonzepte, Entscheidungsverhalten und Ökonomische Modellierung* (Mannheim: Mannheim University).

—— (2002), 'On Communication Barriers between Management Science, Consultancies and Business Organizations', in T. Clark and R. Fincham (eds.), *Critical Consulting* (Oxford: Blackwell), 206–27.

Kijne, H. J. (1986), 'Het omgekeerde Taylorisme', *Tijdschrift voor Arbeidsvraagstukken*, 2/2: 60–9.

—— (1990), *Het gemeten tarief: Taylorisme en de Nederlandse Metaal industrie, 1945–1963* (Delft: Delftse Universitaire Pers).

Kim, D. H. (1993), 'The Link between Individual and Organizational Learning', *Sloan Management Review*, 35/1: 37–50.

King, C. W. and Ring, L. J. (1980), 'Fashion Theory: The Dynamics of Style and Taste, Adoption and Diffusion', *Advances in Consumer Research*, 7: 13–16.

Kipping, M. (1996), 'The U.S. Influence on the Evolution of Management Consultancies in Britain, France and Germany Since 1945', *Business and Economic History*, 25/1: 112–23.

—— (1997), 'Consultancies, Institutions and the Diffusion of Taylorism in Britain, Germany and France, 1920s to 1950s', *Business History*, 39/4: 67–83.

—— (1997/98), 'Bridging the Gap? Management Consultants and their Role in France', University of Reading Discussion Papers in Economics and Management, Series A, Vol. X, No. 375.

—— (1998), 'The Hidden Business Schools: Management Training in Germany since 1945', in L. Engwall and V. Zamagni (eds.), *Management Education in Historical Perspective* (Manchester: Manchester University Press), 95–110.

—— (1999a), 'American Management Consulting Companies in Western Europe, 1920 to 1990: Products, Reputation and Relationships', *Business History Review*, 73/2: 193–222.

—— (1999b), 'British Economic Decline: Blame It on the Consultants?', *Contemporary British History*, 13/3: 23–38.

—— (2000), 'Consultancy and Conflicts: Bedaux at Lukens Steel and the Anglo-Iranian Oil Company', *Entreprises et Histoire*, 25: 9–25.

—— (2002), 'Trapped in their Wave: The Evolution of Management Consultancies', in T. Clark and R. Fincham (eds.), *Critical Consulting* (Oxford: Blackwell), 28–49.

—— and Amorim, C. (1999/2000), 'Consultancies as Management Schools', University of Reading Discussion Papers in Economics and Management, Series A, Vol. XII, No. 409.

—— and Armbrüster, T. (1998), 'Management Consultants and Management Knowledge: A Literature Review', The Creation of European Management Practice (CEMP) Report No. 2, University of Reading.

—— and Armbrüster, T. (eds.) (1999), 'The Consultancy Field in Western Europe', The Creation of European Management Practice (CEMP) Report No. 6, University of Reading.

—— and Bjarnar, O. (1998), *The Americanisation of European Business* (London: Routledge).

—— and Scheybani, A. (1994), 'From Scope to Scale: Tendances récentes du marché allemand du conseil en management', *Revue de l'IRES*, 14: 173–99.

——, Furusten, S., and Gammelsæter, H. (1998/99), 'Converging Towards American Dominance? Developments and Structures of the Consultancy Fields in Europe', University of Reading Discussion Papers in Economics and Management, Series A, Vol. XI, No. 398.

Kogut, B. and Parkinson, D. (1993), 'The Diffusion of American Organizing Principles to Europe', in B. Kogut (ed.), *Country Competitiveness* (Oxford: Oxford University Press), 179–202.

Kolboom, I. (1986), *La revanche des patrons: Le patronat français face au Front populaire* (Paris: Flammarion).

Korporaal, G. (1994), 'The Change Consultants', *Australian Financial Review*, 6 (Oct.): 17.

Kostera, M. (1995), 'The Modern Crusade: The Missionaries of Management Come to Eastern Europe', *Management Learning*, 26: 331–53.

Kostova, T. (1999), 'Transnational Transfer of Strategic Organizational Practices: A Contextual Perspective', *Academy of Management Review*, 24/2: 1–22.

Kotter, J. and Schlesinger, L. (1979), 'Choosing Strategies for Change', *Harvard Business Review*, 57 (Mar.–Apr.): 106–14.

Kuhn, T. S. (1962), *The Structure of Scientific Revolutions* (Chicago: University of Chicago Press).

Kuisma, M. (1992), 'Suomi taloutena: ajopuu vai älykäs perässäkulkija', *Historiallinen aikakauskirja / Historical Journal*, 90: 215–33.

—— (1998*a*), 'Cooperation in Competition: Finland, An Example of Successful Development, 1918–1938', in J. Batou and T. David (eds.), *Uneven Development in Europe 1918–1939: The Obstructed Growth of Agricultural Countries.* (Geneva: Droz), 409–45.

—— (1998*b*), 'A Child of the Cold War: Soviet Crude Oil, American Technology and National Interests in the Making of Finnish Oil Refining', *Historiallinen aikakauskirja/Historical Journal*, 96: 136–49.

Kvålshaugen, R. and Amdam, R. P. (2000), 'Etablering og utvikling av ledelseskulturer: Norsk kenningisme', *Nordiske organisasjonsstudier*, 2/1: 84–106.

Kyrö, P. (1995), *The Management Consulting Industry Described by Using the Concept of 'Profession'*, University of Helsinki Research Bulletin 87, Helsinki.

Läckgren, C., Westerling, J., and Öberg, M. (1989), 'Managementkonsultbranschen: en snårskog av herrar och slavar', term paper, Department of Business Studies, Uppsala University (mimeo).

Laloux, P. (1950), *Le système Bedaux de calcul des salaries* (Paris: Editions Hommes et Techniques).

Lam, A. (2000), 'Tacit Knowledge, Organizational Learning and Societal Institutions: An Integrated Framework', *Organization Studies*, 21/3: 487–513.

Lane, C. (1997), 'The Governance of Interfirm Relations in Britain and Germany: Societal or Dominance Effects', in R. Whitley and P. H. Kristensen (eds.), *Governance at Work: The Social Regulation of Economic Relations* (Oxford: Oxford University Press), 62–85.

Larson, M. S. (1977), *The Rise of Professionalism* (Berkeley, Calif.: University of California Press).

Lawson, M. (1993), 'Blood On The Floor Before Gains From New Technique', *Australian Financial Review*, 23 Nov., p. 49.

—— (1995), 'Australians Make Hay While Sun Shines', *Management Consultant International*, Mar., 13–15.

—— (1998), 'Upgrading for Growth', *Management Consultant International*, June, 11–14.

Le Chatelier, F. (1969), *Henry Le Chatelier, un grand savant d'hier, un précurseur* (Paris: Editions S. Le Chatelier).

Lette, M. (1998), 'Henry Le Chatelier (1850–1936) et la constitution d'une science industrielle: Un modèle pour l'organisation rationnelle des relations entre la science et l'industrie au tournant des XIXe et XXe siècles, 1880–1914', PhD thesis (Paris: EHESS).

Levinthal, D. and March, J. G. (1993), 'The Myopia of Learning', *Strategic Management Journal*, 14: 95–112.

Lewin, K. (1951), *Field Theory in Social Science* (New York: Harper).

Lewis, S. (1993), 'CBA Plans A Drastic Structural Revamp', *Australian Financial Review*, 21 Jan., 1.

Likert, R. (1961), *New Patterns of Management* (New York: McGraw-Hill).

Lilja, K. and Tainio, R. (1996), 'The Nature of the Typical Finnish Firm', in R. Whitley and P. H. Kristensen (eds.), *The Changing European Firm: Limits to Convergence* (London: Routledge), 159–91.

Lilja, K., Räsänen, K., and Tainio, R. (1992), 'The Forest Sector in Finland', in R. Whitley (ed.), *European Business Systems* (London: Sage), 137–54.

Lillrank, P. (1995), 'The Transfer of Management Innovations from Japan', *Organization Studies*, 16/6: 971–89.

Lind, J.-I. and Rhenman, E. (1989), 'The SIAR School of Strategic Management', *Scandinavian Journal of Management*, 5: 167–76.

Littler, C. R. (1982), *The Development of the Labor Process in Capitalist Societies: A Comparative Study of the Transformation of Work Organization in Britain, Japan and the USA* (London: Heinemann).

—— Dunford, R., Bramble, T., and Hede, A. (1997), 'The Dynamics of Downsizing in Australia and New Zealand', *Asia Pacific Journal of Human Resources*, 35/1: 65–79.

Lodahl, T. M. and Mitchell, S. M. (1980), 'Drift in the Development of Innovative Organizations', in J. R. Kimberly, R. H. Miles and Associates (eds.), *The Organizational Life Cycle* (San Fransisco, Calif.: Jossey-Bass), 184–207.

Loh, L. and Venkatraman, N. (1992), 'Diffusion of Information Technology Outsourcing: Influence Sources and the Kodak Effect', *Information Systems Research*, 3: 334–58.

Loudal, M. L. (1973), *Berenschot Case*, HBR Case Study (Boston, Mass.: Harvard Business School).

Luhmann, N. and Fuchs, P. (1989), *Reden und Schweigen* (Frankfurt-am-Main: Suhrkamp).

Lundahl, U. and Skärvad, P.-H. (1982), 'Intressentmodellen i teori och praktik', in *Företagens intressenter och kontrakt: Nya synpunkter på intressentteorin* (Stockholm: SAF), 9–55.

Lundvall, B.-A. (ed.) (1992), *National Systems of Innovation: Towards a Theory of Innovation and Interactive Learning* (London: Pinter).

Lux, T. (1995), 'Herd Behaviour, Bubbles and Crashes', *Economic Journal*, 105: 881–96.

McBeth, J. (1989), 'Challengers Emerge To Vie For McKinsey's Crown', *Business Review Weekly*, 17 Mar., 86.

McCracken, G. (1985), 'The Trickle-Down Theory Rehabilitated', in M. R. Solomon (ed.), *The Psychology of Fashion* (Lexington, Mass.: Lexington Books), 39–54.

McGee, R. (1991), 'Things Are Looking Up Down Under', *Management Consultant International*, June, 10–14.

McGlade, J. (1995), 'The Illusion of Consensus: American Business, Cold War Aid and the Reconstruction of Western Europe 1948–1958', PhD thesis (Washington, DC: George Washington University).

McKenna, C. D. (1995), 'The Origins of Modern Management Consulting', *Business and Economic History*, 24/1: 51–8.

—— (1997), ' "The American Challenge": McKinsey & Company's Role in the Transfer of Decentralization to Europe, 1957–1975', *Academy of Management Best Paper Proceedings*, 226–31.

—— (2000), 'The World's Newest Profession: Management Consulting in the Twentieth Century', PhD thesis (Baltimore, Md: Johns Hopkins University).

——Djelic, M.-L., and Ainamo, A. (2000), 'Message and Medium: The Role of Consulting Firms in the Process of Globalization and its Local Interpretation', paper presented at the 16th EGOS Colloquium, Helsinki, July.

McKinsey & Co. (1994), *Lead Local Compete Global: Unlocking the Growth Potential of Australia's Regions* (Sydney: McKinsey & Co.).

——and AMC (Australian Manufacturing Council) (1993), *Emerging Exporters: Australia's High Value-Added Manufacturing Exporters* (Melbourne: AMC).

————(1994), *The Wealth of Ideas: How Linkages Help Sustain Innovation And Growth* (Melbourne: AMC).

Mahajan, V. and Peterson, R. (1985), *Models for Innovation Diffusion* (London: Sage).

Maister, D. (1993), *Managing the Professional Service Firm* (New York: Free Press).

Malhorta, Y. (2000), 'From Information Management to Knowledge Management: Beyond the "Hi-Tech Hidebound" System', in K. Srikantaiah and M. E. D. Koenig (eds.), *Knowledge Management for the Information Professional* (Medford, NJ: Information Today Inc.), 37–61.

Malinowski, B. (1955), *Magic, Science, and Religion* (New York: Anchor Books).

Mallick, M. (1984), 'Lending a Helping Hand—At a Price', *Australian Business*, 12 Sept., 110–13.

Man, H. De (1988), *Organisational Change in its Context* (Delft: Eburon).

——and Karsten, L. (1994), 'Academic Management Education in the Netherlands', in L. Engwall and E. Gunnarsson (eds.), *Management Studies in an Academic Context* (Uppsala: Uppsala University Press), 84–116.

Mansfield, E. (1961), 'Technical Change and the Rate of Imitation', *Econometrica*, 29: 741–66.

Manville, B. and Foote, B. (1996), 'Harvest your Workers' Knowledge', *Datamation*, 42/13: 78–80.

Marceau, J. (1989), *A Family Business? The Making of an International Business Elite* (Cambridge: Cambridge University Press).

March, A. (1997), 'A Note on Knowledge Management' (Boston, Mass.: Harvard Business School).

March, J. G. and Simon, H. A. (1958), *Organizations* (New York: Wiley).

Martignago, E. (1998), 'L'Ossimoro del Knowledge Management', from www.apogeoonline.com.

Martin, J. and Powers, M. (1983), 'Truth or Corporate Propaganda: The Value of a Good War Story', in L. R. Pondy and T. C. Dandridge (eds.), *Organizational Symbolism* (Greenwich, Conn.: JAI Press), 93–107.

Martiny, M. (1998), 'Knowledge Management at HP Consulting', *Organizational Dynamics*, 27/2: 71–7.

Maynard, H., Stegemerten, G., and Schwab, J. (1948), *Methods Time Measurement* (New York: McGraw-Hill).

Mazza, C. (1998), 'The Popularization of Business Knowledge Diffusion: From Academic Knowledge to Popular Culture?', in J. L. Alvarez (ed.), *The Diffusion and Consumption of Business Knowledge* (London: Macmillan), 164–81.

Memmi, D. (1996), *Les gardiens du corps: Dix ans de magistère bioéthique* (Paris: Editions de l'EHESS).

Metze, M. (1994), *Mensen op maat: vijftig jaar recrutering en selectie door Berenschot* (Utrecht: Berenschot).

Meyer, J. W. (1994), 'Rationalized Environments', in W. R. Scott and J. W. Meyer (eds.), *Institutional Environments and Organizations: Structural Complexity and Individualism* (London: Sage).

——(1996), 'Otherhood: The Promulgation and Transmission of Ideas in the Modern Organizational Environment', in B. Czarniawska and G. Sevón (eds.), *Translating Organizational Change* (Berlin: de Gruyter), 241–52.

Meyer, J. W. and Rowan, B. (1977), 'Institutional Organizations: Formal Structure as Myth and Ceremony', *American Journal of Sociology*, 83: 340–63.

—— and Scott, W. R. (1992), *Organizational Environments: Ritual and Rationality*, 2nd edn. (London: Sage).

Micklethwaite, J. and Wooldridge, A. (1996), *The Witch Doctors: What the Management Gurus Are Saying, Why It Matters and How to Make Sense of It* (London: Heinemann).

Miller, D. and Friesen, P. H. (1980), 'Momentum and Revolution in Organizational Adaptation', *Academy of Management Journal*, 23/4: 591–614.

Mintzberg, H. (1990), 'Strategy Formation: Schools of Thought', in J. W. Fredrickson (ed.), *Perspectives on Strategic Management* (New York: Harper & Row), 105–235.

Mitchell, V.-W. (1994), 'Problems and Risks in the Purchasing of Consultancy Services', *The Service Industries Journal*, 14: 315–39.

—— (1996), 'Musings on Management', *Harvard Business Review*, 74 (July–Aug.), 61–7.

Monroy, T. E. (1970), *De geschiedenis van Berenschot* (Utrecht: Berenschot).

Montgomery, D. (1987), *The Fall of the House of Labor: The Workplace, the State, and American Labor Activism, 1865–1925* (Cambridge: Cambridge University Press).

Morris, T. (2000), 'From Key Advice to Execution? Consulting Firms and the Implementation of Strategic Decisions', in P. Flood, A. Dromgoole, S. Carroll, and L. Gorman (eds.), *Managing Strategic Implementation* (Oxford: Blackwell), 125–37.

—— (2001), 'Asserting Property Rights: Knowledge Codification in the Professional Service Firm', *Human Relations*, 54/7: 819–38.

—— and Empson, L. (1998), 'Organisation and Expertise: An Exploration of Knowledge Bases and the Management of Accounting and Consulting Firms', *Accounting, Organizations and Society*, 23/5–6: 609–24.

Moutet, A. (1975), 'Les origines du système de Taylor en France: Le point de vue patronal (1907–1914)', *Le mouvement social*, 93 (Oct.–Dec.), 15–49.

—— (1985), 'Ingénieurs et rationalisation en France de la guerre à la crise (1914–1929)', in A. Thépot (ed.), *L'ingénieur dans la société française* (Paris: Les Editions ouvrières), 71–108.

—— (1997), *Les logiques de l'entreprise: L'effort de rationalisation dans l'industrie française de 1919 à 1939* (Paris: Editions de l'EHESS).

Mulder, M. (1958), 'Groepsstructuur, motivatie en prestatie', PhD thesis (University of Amsterdam) (revised in 1963 as 'Group Structure, Motivation and Group Performance').

Nadworny, M. (1955), *Scientific Management and the Unions: A Historical Analysis* (Cambridge, Mass.: Harvard University Press).

Nelson, R. R. and Winter, S. G. (1982), *An Evolutionary Theory of Economic Change* (Cambridge, Mass.: Belknap Press).

Neuburger-Brosch, M. (1994) 'Die soziale Konstruktion des "neuen Managers": Eine wissenssoziologische Untersuchung zur Managementdebatte in den achtziger Jahren', PhD thesis (Tübingen: Fakultät für Sozial- und Verhaltenswissenschaften).

NICB (1930), *Systems of Wage Payment* (New York: National Industrial Conference Board).

Nietzsche, F. (1912), *Der Wille zur Macht* (Leipzig: Kröner).

Nippa, M. and Picot, A. (1995), *Prozeßmanagement und Reengineering: Die Praxis im deutschsprachigen Raum* (Frankfurt-am-Main: Campus).

Nockolds, H. (1976), *Lucas: The First Hundred Years*, Vol. I: *The King of the Road* (Newton Abbot: David & Charles).

Nonaka, I. (1994), 'A Dynamic Theory of Organizational Knowledge Creation', *Organization Science*, 5/1: 14–37.

—— and Konno, N. (1998), 'The Concept of "Ba": Building a Foundation for Knowledge Creation', *California Management Review*, 40/3: 40–54.

—— and Takeuchi, H. (1995), *The Knowledge Creating Company* (New York: Oxford University Press).

Normann, R. (1969), 'Variation och omorientering: En studie av innovationsförmåga', Licentiate thesis (Stockholm: SIAR).

—— (1970), *A Personal Quest for Methodology*, publication no. 19 (Stockholm: SIAR).

—— (1975), *Skapande företagsledning* (Lund: Aldus).

—— (1977), *Management for Growth* (Chichester: Wiley).

—— (1984), *Service Management* (Chichester: Wiley).

O'Brien, J. (1994), 'McKinsey, Hilmer and the BCA: The "New Management" Model of Labour Market Reform', *Journal of Industrial Relations*, 36/4: 468–90.

O'Neill, P. and Sohal, A. (1998), 'Business Process Reengineering: Application and Success—An Australian Study', *International Journal of Operations and Production Management*, 18/9: 832–64.

O'Shea, J. and Madigan, C. (1997), *Dangerous Company: The Consulting Powerhouses and the Businesses they Save and Ruin* (London: Nicholas Brealey).

Olofsson, C. (1969), *Produktutveckling—Miljöförankring*, SIAR Nr S22 (Stockholm: SIAR).

Orlikowski, W. J. (1988), Information Technology in Post-industrial Organizations', PhD thesis (New York: Leonard Stern School of Business).

Ortmann, G. (1995), *Formen der Produktion: Organisation und Rekursivität* (Opladen: Westdeutscher Verlag).

Pasold, E. W. (1997), *Ladybird, Ladybird: A Story of Private Enterprise* (Manchester: Manchester University Press).

Pastor, J. C., Meindl, J., and Hunt, R. (1998), 'The Quality Virus: Inter-Organizational Contagion in the Adoption of Total Quality Management', in J. L. Alvarez (ed.), *The Diffusion and Consumption of Business Knowledge* (London: Macmillan), 201–18.

Payne, A. (1985), 'Australia's Own Brand of Consulting', *Journal of Management Consulting*, 2/4: 16–24.

Penders, J. J. M. (1962), *Kadervorming in de industrie* (Utrecht: Spectrum).

Pentland, B. T. and Rueter, H. (1994), 'Organizational Routines as Grammars of Action', *Administrative Science Quarterly*, 37: 484–510.

Perrow, C. (1986), *Complex Organizations: A Critical Essay*, 3rd edn. (New York: Random House).

Perry, N. (1987), 'A Consulting Firm Too Hot To Handle?', *Fortune*, 27 Apr., 91–8.

Peters, T. J. (1992), *Liberation Management: Necessary Disorganization for the Nanosecond Nineties* (London: Macmillan).

—— and Waterman, R. H., Jr. (1982), *In Search of Excellence: Lessons from American Best-Run Companies* (New York: Harper & Row).

Peterson, R. A. (1976), 'The Production of Culture: A Prolegomenon', *American Behavioral Scientist*, 19: 669–83.

—— (1979), 'Revitalizing the Culture Concept', *Annual Review of Sociology*, 5: 137–66.

Pettigrew, A. (1985), *The Awakening Giant: Continuity and Change in ICI* (Oxford: Basil Blackwell).

Picon, A. (1992), *L'invention de l'ingénieur moderne: L'école des Ponts et Chaussées, 1747–1851* (Paris: Presses de l'École nationale des Ponts et Chaussées).

Pinault, L. (2000), *Consulting Demons: Inside the Unscrupulous World of Global Corporate Consulting* (New York: Harper Business).

Pinchot, G. (1985), *Intrapreneuring* (New York: Harper & Row).

Pohl, M. (1996), 'Die Geschichte der Rationalisierung—RKW 1921 bis 1996', in RKW (ed.), *Rationalisierung sichert Zukunft: 75 Jahre RKW* (Eschborn: RKW), 85–116.

Polanyi, M. (1962), *Personal Knowledge: Towards a Post-critical Philosophy* (London: Routledge and Kegan Paul).

—— (1967), *The Tacit Dimension* (London: Routledge and Kegan Paul).

Porac, J. F., Thomas, H., and Baden-Fuller, C. (1989), 'Competitive Groups as Cognitive Communities: The Case of Scottish Knitwear Manufacturers', *Journal of Management Studies*, 26: 397–416.

Porter, M. E. (1980), *Competitive Strategy* (New York: Free Press).

Poulfelt, F. and Payne, A. (1994), 'Management Consultants: Client and Consultant Perspectives', *Scandinavian Journal of Management*, 10/4: 421–36.

Powell, W. W. and DiMaggio P. J. (1991), *The New Institutionalism in Organizational Analysis* (Chicago: University of Chicago Press).

Pratt, D. (1994), *Aspiring to Greatness: Above and Beyond Total Quality Management* (Sydney: Business & Professional Publishing).

Public Histoire (1991), *L'identité d'un groupe: Lafarge-Coppée 1947–1989* (Paris: Lafarge).

Pugh, P. (1988), *The History of Blue Circle* (Cambridge: Cambridge Business Press).

Purcell, T. V. (1954), *The Worker Speaks his Mind on Company and Union* (Cambridge, Mass.: Harvard University Press).

—— (1960), *Blue Collar Man: Patterns of Dual Allegiance in Industry* (Cambridge, Mass.: Harvard University Press).

Rassam, C. and Oates, D. (1991), *Management Consultancy: The Inside Story* (London: Mercury).

Rhenman, E. (1961), 'The Role of Management Games in Education and Research', Licentiate thesis (Stockholm School of Economics).

—— (1968a), *Industrial Democracy and Industrial Management* (Assen: Van Gorcum).

—— (1968b), *Organisationsplanering: En studie av organisationskonsulter* (Stockholm: Läromedelsförlagen).

—— (1969a), *Centrallasarettet* (Lund: Studentlitteratur).

—— (1969b), *Företaget och dess omvärld: Organisationsteori för långsiktsplanering* (Stockholm: Bonniers).

—— (1973a), *Managing the Community Hospital: A Systems Analysis* (London: Saxon House).

—— (1973b), *Organization Theory for Long-range Planning* (London: Wiley).

—— (1975), *Systemsamhället: Om organisationsproblem i samhället* (Stockholm: Aldus).

—— and Skärvad, P.-H. (1977), 'Svåra beslut, makt och medbestämmande', in C. J. Westholm (ed.), *Besluten i företagen* (Stockholm: SAF), 17–74.

—— Strömberg, L., and Westerlund, G. (1963), *Om linje och stab: En studie av konflikt och samverkan i företagets organisation* (Stockholm: Norstedts).

—— —— —— (1970), *Conflict and Co-operation in Business Organizations* (New York: Wiley).

Ribeill, G. (1985), 'Profils des ingénieurs civils au XIXième siècle: Le cas de centraux', in A. Thépot (ed.), *L'ingénieur dans la société française* (Paris: Les éditions ouvrières), 111–25.

Robertson, M. and Swan, J. (1998), 'Modes of Organizing in an Expert Consultancy: A Case Study of Knowledge, Power and Egos', *Organization*, 5/4: 543–64.

Robinson, P. (1980), 'CRA Calls in McKinseys', *Financial Review*, 5 Dec., 32.

Rochau, E. (1939), *Das Bedaux-System, seine praktische Anwendung und kritischer Vergleichzwischen Refa- und Bedaux-System*, 2nd edn. (Würzburg: Konrad Triltsch).

Rogberg, M. and Werr, A. (2000), 'Om acceptansen av populära managementmodeller—en studie av införandet av BPR', *Nordiska Organisationsstudier*, 2/1: 107–28.

Rogers, E. M. (1962), *Diffusion of innovations* (New York: Free Press).

—— and Dearing, J. W. (1988), 'Agenda-Setting Research: Where has it Been, Where is it Going?', *Communication Yearbook*, 11: 555–94.

Roholl, M. (1992), 'Uncle Sam: An Example For All?', in H. Loeber (ed.), *Dutch–American Relations 1945–1969* (Assen: Van Gorcum), 105–52.

Røvik, K.-A. (1996), 'Deinstitutionalization and the Logic of Fashion', in B. Czarniawska and G. Sevón (eds.), *Translating Organizational Change* (Berlin: de Gruyter), 139–72.

—— (1998), *Moderne organisasjoner: Trender i organisasjonstenkningen mot tusenårsskiftet* (Bergen: Fagbokforlaget).

—— (2002), 'The Secrets of the Winners: Management Ideas that Flow', in K. Sahlin-Andersson and L. Engwall (eds.), *The Expansion of Management Knowledge: Carriers, Ideas, and Sources* (Stanford, Calif.: Stanford University Press), forthcoming.

Sahlin-Andersson, K. (1996), 'Imitating by Editing Success: The Construction of Organizational Fields', in B. Czarniawska and G. Sevón (eds.), *Translating Organizational Change* (Berlin: de Gruyter), 69–92.

Saint-Martin, D. (2000), *Building the New Managerialist State: Consultants and Public Management Reform in Britain, Canada, and France* (Oxford: Oxford University Press).

Sandkull, B. (1970), 'Innovative Behavior of Organizations: The Case of New Products', PhD thesis (Lund).

Sargant, W. (1997), *Battle for the Mind*, 2nd edn. (Cambridge: Malor).

Sarvary, M. (1999), 'Knowledge Management and Competition in the Consulting Industry', *California Management Review*, 41/2: 95–107.

Sauviat, C. (1994), 'Le conseil: un marché-réseau singulier', in J. de Brandt and Jean Gadrey (eds.), *Relations de service, marchés de service* (Paris: CNRS Editions), 241–62.

Scarborough, H. and Swan, J. (1999), 'Knowledge Management and the Management Fashion Perspective', paper presented at the British Academy of Management Conference, Manchester, 1–3 Sept.

Schade, C. (1997), *Marketing für Unternehmensberatung: Ein institutionenökonomischer Ansatz* (Wiesbaden: Gabler/DUV).

Schein, E. H. (1988), *Process Consultation*, i. *Its Role in Organization Development* (Reading, Mass.: Addison Wesley).

Schenk, M. (1995), *Soziale Netzwerke und Massenmedien: Untersuchungen zum Einfluß der persönlichen Kommunikation* (Tübingen: Mohr).

Scherer, F. M. (1970), *Industrial Market Structure and Economic Performance* (Chicago: Rand McNally).

Schnierer, T. (1995), *Modewandel und Gesellschaft: Die Dynamik von 'in' und 'out'* (Opladen: Leske + Budrich).

Scott, B. R. (1973), 'The Industrial State: Old Myths and New Realities', *Harvard Business Review*, Mar.–Apr., 133–48.

Scott, W. (1948), 'Management Practices Overseas', *Manufacturing and Management*, Apr., 344–5.

Selznick, P. (1949), *TVA and the Grass Roots* (Berkeley, Calif.: University of California Press).

—— (1957), *Leadership in Administration* (New York: Harper & Row).

—— (1996), 'Institutionalism "Old" and "New"', *Administrative Science Quarterly*, 41: 270–7.

Shapiro, E. C. (1996), *Fad Surfing in the Boardroom: Managing in the Age of Instant Answers* (Reading, Mass.: Addison-Wesley).

—— Eccles, R. G., and Soske, T. L. (1993), 'Consulting: Has the Solution Become Part of the Problem?', *Sloan Management Review*, summer, 89–95.

Shinn, T. (1978), 'Des corps de l'Etat au secteur industriel: genèse de la profession d'ingénieur, 1750–1920', *Revue française de sociologie*, 19/1: 39–71.

—— (1980), *Savoir scientifique et pouvoir social, l'Ecole polytechnique (1794–1914)* (Paris: Presses de la Fondation nationale des sciences politiques).

SIAR (1975), *Management Survey of UNICEF* (Stockholm: SIAR).

SIAR (various dates), *SIAR alumni register* (Stockholm: SIAR).

Sillén, O. (1912), *Genvägar och kontrollmetoder vid räkning* (Stockholm: P. A. Norstedt & Söner).

—— (1913a), *Grunddragen av industriell självkostnadsberäkning*. Swedish Federation of Industry, Publications, Organisation Department, No. 5 (Stockholm: Swedish Federation of Industry).

—— (1913b), 'Kortsystem eller lösbladsböcker i bokföringen', *Sveriges allmänna handelsförenings månadsskrift*, 19/8: 182–90.

—— (1915), *Moderna bokföringsmetoder med särskild hänsyn till fabriks- och varuhandelsföretag* (Stockholm: P. A. Norstedt & Söner).

—— (1931), *Nyare balansvärderingsprinciper* (Stockholm: P. A. Norstedt & Söner).

Simmel, G. (1957), 'Fashion', *American Journal of Sociology*, 62: 541–58.

—— (1986), 'Die Mode', in S. Bovenschen (ed.), *Die Listen der Mode* (Frankfurt-am-Main: Suhrkamp), 179–207.

Smith, J. (1988), *Managers of Change: The First 25 Years of PA in Australia* (Melbourne: PA Consulting).

Söderlund, M. (1989), 'EFI 60 år: Historien om ett forskningsinstitut', in *EFIs årsbok 1989* (Stockholm: EFI), 29–84.

Sombart, W. (1902), *Wirtschaft und Mode* (Wiesbaden: Bergmann).

Spell, C. S. (2000), 'Where do Management Fashions Come from, and How Long do they Last?', *Journal of Management History*, 5: 334–48.

Spencer, H. (1888), *The Principles of Sociology*, ii. (New York: D. Appleton).

Spender, J.-C. (1996), 'Making Knowledge the Basis of a Dynamic Theory of the Firm', *Strategic Management Journal*, 17: 45–62.

Sperling, H. J. and Ittermann, P. (1998), *Unternehmensberatung: eine Dienstleistungsbranche im Aufwind* (Munich: Hampp).

Starbuck, W. H. (1992), 'Learning by Knowledge-Intensive Firms', *Journal of Management Studies*, 29/6: 713–40.

—— (1993), 'Keeping a Butterfly and an Elephant in a House of Cards: The Elements of Exceptional Success', *Journal of Management Studies*, 30: 885–921.

Stehr, N. (1994), *Knowledge Societies* (London: Sage).

Stevens, J. M., Beyer J. M., and Trice H. M. (1978), 'Assessing Personal, Role, and Organizational Predictors of Managerial Commitment', *Academy of Management Journal*, 21: 380–96.

Stewart, R., Barsoux, J.-L., Kieser, A., Ganter, H.-D., and Walgenbach, P. (1994), *Managing in Britain and Germany* (New York: St. Martin's Press).

Stinchcombe, A. L. (1968), *Constructing Social Theories* (Chicago: University of Chicago Press).

Stolterman, E. (1991), *Designarbetets dolda rationalitet: En studie av metodik och praktik inom systemutveckling* (Umeå: Umeå University).

Streeck, W. (1997), 'German Capitalism: Does it Exist? Can it Survive?', in C. Crouch and W. Streeck (eds.), *Political Economy of Modern Capitalism: Mapping Convergence and Diversity* (London: Sage), 33–54.

Street, P. (1997), 'The Swift Difference: Workers, Managers, Militants, and Welfare Capitalism in Chicago's Stockyards, 1917–1942', in S. Stromquist and M. Bergman (eds.), *Unionizing the Jungles: Labour and Community in the Twentieth-Century Meatpacking Industry* (Iowa City: University of Iowa Press), 16–50.

Sturdy, A. (1997), 'The Consultancy Process: An Insecure Business?', *Journal of Management Studies*, 34/3: 389–413.

—— (1999), 'Front-line Diffusion: The Production and Negotiation of Knowledge Through Training Interactions', paper presented to the 15th EGOS Colloquium, University of Warwick, 4–6 July.

Stymne, B. (1970), 'Values and Processes. A Systems Study of Effectiveness in Three Organizations', PhD thesis (Lund).

—— (1995), 'Eric Rhenman: nydanare inom svensk företagsekonomi', in L. Engwall (ed.), *Föregångare inom företagsekonomin* (Stockholm: SNS), 369–94.

Sveiby, K. E. (1996), 'What is Knowledge Management?', from www.sveiby.com.au/Knowledge Management.html.

Swanson, B. E. and Ramiller, N. C. (1997), 'The Organizing Vision in Information Systems Innovation', *Organization Science*, 8: 458–74.

Tabakoff, N. (1993), 'The Triumph of Arthur Andersen', *Australian Financial Review*, 30 (Nov.), 15.

Tainio, R., Lilja, K., and Santalainen, T. (1997), 'Changing Managerial Competitive Practices in the Context of Growth and Decline in the Finnish Banking Sector', in G. Morgan and D. Knights (eds.), *Deregulation and European Financial Services* (London: Macmillan), 201–15.

—— Pohjola, M., and Lilja, K. (2000), 'Economic Performance of Finland after the Second World War: From Success to Failure', in S. Quack, G. Morgan, and R. Whitley (eds.), *National Capitalisms, Global Competition and Economic Performance* (Berlin: de Gruyter), 277–89.

Thépot, A. (1979), 'Les ingénieurs du corps des Mines', in M. Levy-Leboyer (ed.), *Le patronat de la seconde industrialisation* (Paris: Les éditions ouvrières), 237–46.

—— (1986), 'Images et réalités de l'ingénieur entre les deux guerres', in A. Grelon (ed.), *Les ingénieurs de la crise: Titre et profession entre les deux guerres* (Paris: Éditions de l'EHESS), 39–47.

—— (1998), *Les ingénieurs des mines du XIXe siècle, histoire d'un corps technique d'Etat*, i. *1810–1914* (Paris: ESKA).

Therborn, G. (1966), 'Herr Eric Rhenman's omvälvning av vetenskapen', in G. Therborn (ed.), *En ny vänster* (Stockholm: Rabén & Sjögren), 169–79.

—— (1971), *Klasser och ekonomiska system* (Kristianstad: Cavefors).

Thomas, T. (1992), 'Fitness Trainer to the Service Industry: Andersen Consulting Making Organisations Leaner and More Effective', *Business Review Weekly*, 6 Nov., 70–2, 75.

Thompson, S. C. (1981), 'Will it Hurt Less if I Can Control it? A Complex Answer to a Simple Question', *Psychological Bulletin*, 90: 89–101.

Tienari, J. (1999), *Sotakorvaustyön tehostamisesta sähköisen liiketoiminnan kehittämiseen: liikkeenjohdon konsultoinnin lyhyt historia Suomessa*, Studies in Business Administration 1 (Lappeenranta: University of Technology).

—— and Tainio, R. (1999), 'The Myth of Flexibility in Organizational Change', *Scandinavian Journal of Management*, 15: 351–84.

Tisdall, P. (1982), *Agents of Change: The Development and Practice of Management Consultancy* (London: Heinemann).

Torstendahl, R. and Burrage, M. (eds.) (1990), *The Formation of Professions: Knowledge, State and Strategy* (London: Sage).

Toutain, J. C. (1963), 'La population en France de 1700 à 1959', *Cahiers de l'Institut de science économique appliquée*, supplement, 133 (Jan.): 3–249.

Tushman, M. L. and Romanelli, E. (1985), 'Organizational Evolution: A Metamorphosis Model of Convergence and Reorientation', *Research in Organizational Behavior*, 7: 171–222.

Veldkamp, T. A. and Drumen, P. van (1988), *Psychologie als professie* (Assen: Van Gorcum).

Vem är det 1993 (*Who's Who in Sweden 1993*) (Stockholm: Norstedts).

Visser, J. (1993), 'Work Councils and Unions in the Netherlands: Rivals or Allies', *Netherlands Journal of Social Science*, 29/1: 64–92.

—— and Hemerijck, A. (1997), *A Dutch Miracle* (Amsterdam: Amsterdam University Press).

Volz, R.F. and Maarschalk, J. (1955), *MTM in Nederland* (The Hague: NIVE).

Vries, T. De (1997), 'Een brede verspreiding van de berichtgeving is wenselijk', in R. T. Griffith (ed.), *Van strohalm tot strategie: het Marshallplan in perspectief* (Assen: Van Gorcum), 38–48.

W. D. Scott & Co. (1947), *Manufacturing Methods: Application of the Methods–Time–Measurement Procedure* (Sydney: W. D. Scott & Co).

Wagner, P. (1994), *A Sociology of Modernity: Liberty and Discipline* (London: Routledge).

Wallerstedt, E. (1988), *Oskar Sillén—Professor och praktiker: Några drag i företagsekonomiämnets tidiga utveckling vid Handelshögskolan i Stockholm*, Studia Oeconomiae Negotiorum 30 (Stockholm: Almqvist & Wiksell International).

Wallroth, C. (1968), 'Experiences in Organizational Change: Long-Range Planning in a Government Office', Licentiate thesis, publication no. 13 (Stockholm: SIAR).

Wasson, C. (1998), 'Employees as "Entrepreneurs": The Discursive Legitimation of Changing Workplace Relationships', paper presented at the Academy of Management Meeting, San Diego, Aug.

Watson, T. J. (1994), 'Management "Flavours of the Month": Their Role in Managers' Lives', *International Journal of Human Resource Management*, 5/4: 893–909.

Weexsteen A. (1999), 'Le conseil aux entreprises et à l'Etat en France: Le rôle de Jean Milhaud (1898–1991) dans la C.E.G.O.S. et l'I.T.A.P.', PhD thesis (Paris: École des hautes études en sciences sociales).

Werr, A. (1998), 'Managing Knowledge in Management Consulting', paper presented at the Academy of Management Meeting, San Diego, Aug.

—— (1999), *The Language of Change: The Roles of Methods in the Work of Management Consultants* (Stockholm: Stockholm School of Economics).

—— Stjernberg, T., and Docherty, P. (1997), 'The Functions of Methods of Change in the Work of Management Consultants', *Journal of Organizational Change Management*, 10: 288–307.

Wessel, H. A. (1990), *Kontinuität im Wandel: 100 Jahre Mannesmann, 1890–1990* (Düsseldorf: Mannesmann).

White, R. W. (1959), 'Motivation Reconsidered: The Concept of Competence', *Psychological Review*, 66: 297–333.

Whitley, R. (1997), 'The Social Regulation of Work Systems', in R. Whitley and P. H. Kristensen (eds.), *Governance at Work: The Social Regulation of Economic Relations* (Oxford: Oxford University Press), 227–60.

—— (2000), *The Intellectual and Social Organization of the Sciences*, 2nd edn. (Oxford: Oxford University Press).

Whittington, R. and Mayer, M. (2000), *The European Corporation: Strategy, Structure, and Social Science* (Oxford: Oxford University Press).

Wiersma, M. F. (1995), 'Executive Succession as an Antecedent to Corporate Restructuring', *Human Resource Management*, 34/1: 185–202.

—— and Bantel, K. A. (1993), 'Top Management Team Turnover as an Adaptation Mechanism: The Role of the Environment', *Strategic Management Journal*, 14: 485–504.

Willcocks, L. and Grint, K. (1997), 'Re-inventing the Organization? Towards a Critique of Business Process Reengineering', in I. McLoughlin and M. Harris (eds.), *Innovation, Organizational Change and Technology* (London: International Thompson Business Press).

Windolf, P. and Beyer, J. (1996), 'Co-operative Capitalism: Corporate Networks in Germany and Britain', *British Journal of Sociology*, 47: 205–31.

Womack, J. P., Jones, D. T., and Roos, D. (1990), *The Machine that Changed the World* (New York: Rawson Associates).

Woodward, J. (1965), *Industrial Organization: Theory and Practice* (Oxford: Oxford University Press).

Wooldridge, A. (1997), 'Trimming the Fat: A Survey of Management Consultancy', *The Economist*, 22 Mar., 1–22.

Wright, C. (1995), *The Management of Labour: A History of Australian Employers* (Melbourne: Oxford University Press).

—— (2000), 'From Shop Floor to Boardroom: The Historical Evolution of Australian Management Consulting, 1940s to 1980s', *Business History*, 42/1: 85–106.

Zbaracki, M. J. (1998), 'The Rhetoric and Reality of Total Quality Management', *Administrative Science Quarterly*, 43: 602–36.

Name Index

A. T. Kearney 50, 193
Sveriges Litografiska Tryckerier 40
Accenture (formerly Andersen Consulting) 37, 50
Alexander Proudfoot 49
AMP 195–6
Ampol 192
Andersen Consulting (now Accenture) 37, 50, 196–8, 201
Ansoff, Igor 56, 64
Argyris, Chris 56
Armour 214
Arthur Andersen (now Andersen) 195–7, 200
Arthur D. Little 50, 193
Associated Industrial Consultants (AIC) 65
Association Française des Conseillers en Organisation Scientifique (AFCOS) 29
Association Française des Organisateurs Permanents d'Entreprise (AFOPE) 31–3
Authorized Public Accountants' Association 40, 50

Bain & Company 193–4
Bardet, Gérard 193–4
Barnevik, Percy 30
Bedaux, Charles E. 186, 209–10, 213–16, 216–17
Berenschot (Consulting firm) 54, 56–7, 64
Berenschot, Berend Willem 56
BICRA 24
Booz Allen & Hamilton 192, 195, 197
Bosboom & Hegener 57
Bossard Consultants 47
Bossard, Yves 30–1, 47
Boston Consulting Group (BCG) 50, 192–3, 195, 197
BP 212
Bradford Cotton Mills 187
Broken Hill Proprietary (BHP) 188, 192
Bundesverband Deutscher Unternehmensberater (BDU) 167, 239
Bunt, H. van der 57
Bureau Univers 57

Cap Gemini (see also Gemini Consulting) 10, 47, 82, 84
Carnegie, Roderick 191–2
Chambre des Ingénieurs Conseils de France (CICF) 28–9

Champy, James 175, 178–9, 232
Chrysler 210
Clarke, Wallace C. 24
Comité National de l'Organisation Française (CNOF) 26
Commission Générale de l'Organisation Scientifique du Travail (CGOST became Cégos) 29–30, 32
Commonwealth Bank 195–6
Conservatoire National des Arts et Métiers (CNAM) 27, 31
Coopers & Lybrand 195, 197
Contactgroep Opvoering Productiviteit (COP) 54–5, 60
Corps des Mines (see also École des Mines) 20–6, 29, 34
Coutrot, Jean 24, 28, 30
Cresap McCormick & Paget 192–3
CSC Index 198

Danty-Lafrance, Louis 31
Deloitte & Touche 197
Diebold, John 65
Drucker, Peter F. 2, 77, 111
DuPont 209–10

Eastman Kodak 209
École Centrale 20, 21, 23–4, 27, 31, 34
École des Mines 25
École Polytechnique 20–1, 25
EK Konsulterna 78, 80
Elkem 222–3, 227–31, 235–7
Emerson, Harrington 209
Ernst & Young 197
European Business School 152, 157
European Productivity Agency (EPA) 63, 67

Fayol, Henri 29
FEACO 78
Federation of Swedish Industries 39–41, 49
Ford 210
Fraunhofer-Gesellschaft 151
Fundatie Werkelijk Dienen 59

Garcin-Guynet, Sabine 24, 25
Gélinier, Octave 32

Gemini Consulting 50
General Electric 209
General Motors 210
Gemeenschappelijk Instituut voor Toegepaste
    Psychologie (GITP) 61, 63
Glamox 223, 231, 234–7
Gogh, V. W. van 54
Guillet, Léon 27

H. B. Maynard (consulting firm, *see also* MEC) 11,
    78–9, 81–2
Habberstad 78
Hammer, Michael 174–5, 179, 232
Handelsblatt 151
Harvard Business School 46
Harvard University 40
Helsinki School of Economics and Business
    Administration (HSE) xi, 75–6
Herold, Josef Lodewijk Maria 56
Hijmans, Ernst 54
Hugoniot, Charles Emile 27

Ingenjörsvetenskapsakademien (IVA) 43
Initiating Committee on Labour Productivity
    (*see also* COP) 54, 60

Juran, J. 56

Kallio, Antero 73–82, 85
Kenning, George 229
Kerkhoven 57
KPMG 197
Krauss Maffei 210, 217–19, 220

Le Chatelier, Henry 25–6, 32
LEK Partnership 49, 192–3
Lesourne, Jacques 32
Liaison Committee 55, 62, 66
Loucheur, Louis 24
Lucas 210, 216–17, 219–20
Lukens Steel 210–11
Lund University 42–5, 48

Mallet, Robert 31
Manager magazin ix, 13, 158–9
Mannio, Pekka 73, 74, 76, 77
Maynard, Harold B. 187
McKinsey & Company 37, 45, 49, 65, 191–3, 195,
    197, 200–1, 208–10, 212–13, 217–19
Mec–Rastor 79–83
Methods Engineering Council (MEC, *see also*
    H. B. Maynard) 49, 57, 187

Milhaud, Jean 28
Mitchell Madison 193

National Australia Bank 192
Nederlands Instituut voor Preventieve
    Geneeskunde (NIPG) 54, 60, 63
Nederlands Instituut voor Personeelsleiding
    (NIPL) 59, 60
Nederlands Instituut voor Efficiency (NIVE)
    54–5, 63
Northwestern University 40
Nederlandse Stichting voor Psychotechniek (NSP)
    54
National Training Laboratory (NTL) 63

Ohno, Taichi 177
OOA 66

Pappas Carter Evans Koop (PCEK) 192,
    197
Peoplesoft 199
Personnel Administration (PA Management
    Consultants) 65, 186–90, 194, 197,
    200–1
Peters, Tom 5, 50, 99, 131, 176–8
Planus, Paul 24, 28–30, 32
Porter, Michael E. 3, 51, 111, 168
Price Waterhouse 50, 195, 197
PriceWaterhouseCoopers (PWC) 84

Qantas 192

Rastor 11, 73–9
RKW (Rationalisierungskuratorium der
    Deutschen Wirtschaft) 152–3, 162
RBO 24
Révész, Géza 56
Rhenman, Eric 42–51
Roland Berger & Partner 49
Royal Institute of Technology 42

SAP 199
Schmalenbach-Gesellschaft (SG) 152
Scott, Walter 186–7
Scriven, L. Edward 76–7
SER 64
Service Management Group 47
Seurat, Sylvère 30
Shell 209, 212
SIAR 42–7, 49–50
Silén, Markku 83–4
Sillén, Oscar 38–42, 48–51

Stichting Interacademiale Opleiding
   Organisatiekunde (SIOO) 58
Städtische Handelshochschule in Cologne
   39–41
Standard Chartered Bank 196
Standard Oil (Esso) 212
Stanford Research Institute 78
Stockholm School of Economics (SSE) 38–44,
   48–9
Stockholm University 44
Suurla, Leo 11, 74–82, 85
Svenska Handelsbanken 40–1, 43
Swedish Council for Personnel Administration
   (PA-Rådet) 43
Swedish Match 41
Swift 210, 213–16, 220

Tavistock Institute 60, 67
Taylor, Frederick W. 25
Telecom 192, 196
Thomas, Albert 24, 27
Thomson, C. B. 25

Nederlandse Organisatie voor toegepast-
   natuurwetenschappelijk onderzoek (TNO) 63

Total 210, 212–13, 218
Toyoda, Eiji 177

Unilever 196
Universitätsseminar der Wirtschaft (USW) 152–4
Urwick International 65

Verein Deutscher Ingenieure (VDI) 152
Vidal, André 30, 32

W. D. Scott & Co. 186–90, 197, 201
Waterman, Robert 192
Webster, Sir Robert 187
Welch, Jack 247
Westpac 195
Wolcott, Robert 210–11
Wolf, Helmut 218–19

Ydo 57–8

Subject Index

Academic Generalist 37–8
Academic research 36–9, 41–2, 47–8, 50
Academic Specialist 37–8
Accountancy firms 195–9
Accountants 40
Action research 43
Activity system 205, 207–8
Advertising 196
Alliances 186–7
Americanization 72, 80
Art world 130, 134
Auditing 38, 40–2

Balanced Score Card 176
Bedaux system of work measurement 209–11,
    213–17, 220
Best-selling books 129
Big Eight/Six/Five 194–9, 201
BKT (*see also* TWI) 56, 59
Book editors 7, 13, 130, 133–136, 139, 142–4
Business administration 38–43, 45, 48–9
Business elite 212
Business Process Re-engineering (BPR)
    198–9

Cases (*see also* Consultancy project) 102–3
Change and change management 207–8
Clinical research 42–3, 46
Closure mechanism 37–8, 42, 47, 50
Cold War 62, 71
Commercialization of management knowledge
    146
Commodification of management knowledge
    13
Communicative validation of management
    knowledge 160, 163
Consultancy organization 6–7, 11–13, 38–9, 42,
    45, 47
Consultancy project (includes assignment,
    engagement) 7–8, 13–16
Consultant training 186
Consultant-client interaction 184, 186–7, 193–6,
    198, 200–1
Consulting experience 98–101
Contract research 43
Corporate restructuring 193–5, 198–9

Cost-cutting (*see also* Downsizing, Overhead Value
    Analysis) 194–5
Critical perspectives on consulting 93–5,
    193–4
Customer Relationship Management (CRM) 116

Databases 99–103, 107
Decentralization (*see also* Divisionalization)
    217–19
De-coupling 225, 237
Dissemination of management fashions 14, 167
Diversification 185, 190, 195, 198, 201
Divisionalization (*see also* Multi-divisional from)
    xiii, 44, 227–30, 235
Downsizing 81, 92, 177, 195
Dramatization of newness 146

e-commerce 195
Engineering education 9, 20, 31
Explicit knowledge 206, 220

Fordism 167
Functional perspectives on consulting 93

Globalization 156–7, 160, 162
Great Depression 210

Herd behaviour 180–1
Human Relations 63

Identity 20, 25, 29, 33–4, 45, 72–3, 94, 111, 117,
    122, 125, 127, 134, 142, 172, 217, 224–5, 228,
    230, 236–7
Implementation 194, 196, 198, 201, 203–4, 206–7,
    215, 220–1
Impression management 94
Industrial disputes (*see also* Strikes) 189
Information technology 195–6
Institutional theory
    Neo-institutionalism 224–5
    'Old' institutionalism 15, 237
Intangibility 204
International linkages/alliances 186–7, 190, 192–3,
    200
Intrapreneurship 177, 261
IT-consulting 14

Journalists 1, 7, 13, 20, 35, 131, 141–2, 150, 158–9

Knowledge arena(s) 146–63
Knowledge codification 101–4
Knowledge Management Systems (KMS) 7, 111–13
Knowledge management 92, 96, 104
Knowledge related economies of scale 107–8
Knowledge sharing and storing 100, 107
Knowledge transfer 204, 206–7
Knowledge translation/transformation/adaptation 104–5, 206–7

Lean Production 147, 151, 167, 177
Legitimacy/Legitimization 184–5, 186, 191–2, 200, 205–6, 220

Management education 6, 77, 81, 157
Management fashion 184, 199
Management graduate 36
Management guru(s) xi, 13, 16, 111, 129–33, 139, 141, 146, 150, 160
Management practice 37, 39, 41–2, 44, 47
Management publications v
Management research 36, 48, 51
Managers
    top/senior 63, 74, 76–7, 80, 212, 216, 218, 226, 229
    middle 203, 212–13, 218
Managing clients 185, 188–9, 193–4
Marketing 196
Marshall Plan 55, 59, 63
Mass media 129, 146, 148, 150, 172
Media gatekeeper 148, 158
Media production 148, 150, 157
Methods and tools 101–2, 206
Methods-Time-Measurement (MTM) 57, 187
Moral Rearmament Movement 62
Multi-divisional form (M-form) 208, 210, 217–19

Neo-institutionalism (*see* Institutional theories)

Operational efficiency (*see* Scientific Management)
Organization studies 37
Organizational consulting 39
Organizational culture 12, 96, 177, 179–80
Organizational design 37
Organizational drift 45, 50
Organizational field 50, 53, 149, 152, 157

Organizational memory 102
Outsourcing 252
Overhead Value Analysis (OVA) 151, 179

Performance evaluation/standards 117
Personal networks 149–50, 154–7, 160
Planned obsolescence 182
Power structure 15, 16, 222, 225–6, 228, 231, 235
Practical Generalist 37–8
Practical Specialist 37–8
Professionalization 37, 40, 51
Public image of consultants 205
Public policy 192, 200
Publications (of consultants) 192

Rationality 205
Recruitment 190
Re-engineering (*see* Business Process Re-engineering)
Regulation of professions (*see also* Professionalization) 207
Reputation of consultants 185, 200–1, 204–5, 220
Resistance 203, 211, 213–20
Resistance, employee 188–9, 198, 200–1
Resistance, managerial 187–8, 191, 194, 198–201
Routines, Routinization 207, 219–20

Scientific field 37
Scientific management (*see also* Taylorism) 186–90, 203, 209–10
Service management 47
Specialization 36–8, 41, 47–8
Strategy consulting 190–5
Strikes (*see also* Industrial disputes) 216
Supply-chain management 199
Systemic context 53

Tacit knowledge 204–6, 220
Taylorism (*see also* Scientific Management) 209
Technical Assistance Programme (*see also* Marshall Plan) 55, 59
Technology 37
Theories of fashion 14, 167, 170, 172
Time and motion studies (*see also* Work measurement) 187, 189
Total Quality Management (TQM) 93
Trade unions 189, 200, 215
Training of consultants 220
Training within Industry (TWI) 56

Trust 3, 4, 8, 19, 29, 73, 78, 114, 117, 155, 189, 215–16, 235

Uncertainty 37

Wage-incentive systems (*see also* Work measurement, Bedaux system, MTM) 209–11, 213–17, 220

Work measurement, Work study 190

Work organization (*see also* Scientific Management) 9, 24–5, 28–9, 48, 75, 77

Work simplification 190

Workers 2, 8, 15, 56, 64, 66–7, 111, 185, 187–9, 201, 203, 209, 214–16